GW01271911

# Beyond Deviant Damsels

# Beyond Deviant Damsels

*Re-evaluating Female Criminality in the Nineteenth Century*

ANNE-MARIE KILDAY AND DAVID NASH

OXFORD
UNIVERSITY PRESS

Great Clarendon Street, Oxford, OX2 6DP,
United Kingdom

Oxford University Press is a department of the University of Oxford.
It furthers the University's objective of excellence in research, scholarship,
and education by publishing worldwide. Oxford is a registered trade mark of
Oxford University Press in the UK and in certain other countries



First Edition published in 2023



Published in the United States of America by Oxford University Press
198 Madison Avenue, New York, NY 10016, United States of America

British Library Cataloguing in Publication Data
Data available

Library of Congress Control Number: 2022945554

ISBN 978–0–19–883073–3

DOI: 10.1093/oso/9780198830733.001.0001

Printed and bound by
CPI Group (UK) Ltd, Croydon, CR0 4YY

*For Eliza and Grace, damsels who fill our lives with joy, love, and laughter*

# Contents

# List of Figures

# Acknowledgements

The authors would like to thank the numerous people who have helped in the writing of this book. First, we would like to express our thanks to staff at the National Archives at Kew, the British Library, the National Archives of Scotland, the National Library of Scotland, the National Library of Wales, the Higgins Art Gallery and Museum, Bedfordshire, and the Bodleian Library, Oxford, for their patience and helpful advice.

Special and grateful thanks also go to our research assistant Fiona Mann for her hard work and perseverance and to Pam Fortescue for all her administrative support and expertise with the preparation of this volume.

We would also like to thank those involved at Oxford University Press in the production of this book from embryonic idea to published work. Thanks go to our commissioning editor Cathryn Steele and to our various editorial contacts including John Smallman. We would also like to thank our anonymous reviewers for their helpful and important contributions.

# Notes on the Authors

**Anne-Marie Kilday** is the Vice-Chancellor of the University of Northampton and a Professor of Criminal History. She has published widely on the history of violence and the history of female criminality in Britain, Europe, and North America from 1600 to the present. Her most recent volume is *Crime in Scotland 1660–1960: The Violent North* (2019). She is currently completing a substantive monograph project on the history of homicide in Britain.

**David Nash** is Professor of History at Oxford Brookes University. He has published widely on the history of atheism, secularism, the history of blasphemy, and the history of shame. He has also advised NGOs, international organizations, and governments about the issue of blasphemy law repeal. He is currently working on two edited books and a monograph project on the history of atheist narratives in Britain.

# 1
# A Mistold Story?
## The Flawed History of 'Deviant' Women in Nineteenth-Century British Society—Introduction

### Setting the Scene

This book is primarily about how respective societies within mainland Britain (England, Wales, and Scotland) viewed women and how far women aligned themselves with behavioural stereotypes. It also asks how far women embraced apparent norms, or dissented from them, in the specific chronological period of the nineteenth century. From this starting point, the book analyses the potential for women to choose their own autonomous routes through the often darker reaches of these same societies. However, we hope that it will become obvious to readers early on that the implications of this subject matter and the analysis it offers is rather more ambitious and extensive.

Our book aims to offer a significant new approach to the consideration of women and their behaviour in the nineteenth century, one which offers some challenges to the existing historiography. However, it also intends to speak to the wider historical community about how attempts to categorize women in oversimplified ways persists, even in the supposedly enlightened corridors of modern gender historiography. It would be overstating the case to say that the status of women has been historically and historiographically polarized into 'roles', 'discourses', and 'gendered identities'. Yet it remains the fact that men are far more readily seen as autonomous agents who carve and create independent, empowering, and consciously fluid identities for themselves through their own agency. This same agency is also seen as instrumental in the creation of situations that have further enclosed women within patriarchal ideas which themselves have inspired and enforced relationships.[1]

In the eyes of some historians, an aspiration to autonomy has been a great deal tougher for women to achieve and, instead, they are too easily considered to succumb or subscribe to identities created by others around crime and criminality. Sometimes women's association with violence is easily labelled as somehow a result of gendered evolution and psychological makeup, to be substantially beyond their contemplation and action.[2] This conception is especially surprising since empirical evidence readily tells us that women in the latter half of the

*Beyond Deviant Damsels: Re-evaluating Female Criminality in the Nineteenth Century.* Anne-Marie Kilday and David Nash, Oxford University Press. © Anne-Marie Kilday and David Nash 2023. DOI: 10.1093/oso/9780198830733.003.0001

nineteenth century made up nearly six times more of the prison population than was recorded in the early 1990s. Women similarly more readily appeared in court in the nineteenth century and made up a remarkable 40 per cent of those tried for murder (25 per cent of those with victims aged over one year and almost all infanticides).[3]

The character of nineteenth-century society and its self-consciously public and private worlds were often deemed to be important factors restricting women's lives. But this restriction was not simply confined to the historical period investigated by historians. The historiography created by a range of historians also has the capacity to provide enduring limitations of its own. These analyses are in danger of homogenizing and generalizing experiences to an unhelpful and potentially damaging degree. This historiography sometimes produces models of explanation that shape how women find themselves confined to 'spheres', cast as protagonists into 'stereotyped narratives', or are made 'exemplars' of model cultures or paradigms.[4] Sometimes women become the object of reforming impulses aimed at restraining male behaviour, or as victims of this behaviour. Court procedures and proceedings, even when reformed to address perceived gender inequalities, sometimes have the effect of silencing or disadvantaging women still further.[5]

The prevailing historiography of female criminality in Britain is currently still too ready to accept uncritically a range of stereotypes, alongside scholarship that seems intent upon extending this narrative. Such research often falls into the trap of assigning stark predetermined roles and patterns of behaviour to men and women, ones that impact upon many other areas of cultural and social history.[6] Even some works which otherwise sought to redress the balance sometimes made the trap merely look more nuanced and sophisticated. In many ways, Mary S. Hartman's excellent study of thirteen French and English women who murdered is a case in point. Her investigation, with a sustained use of detail, instantly gave women more autonomy, motive, and agency in the conduct of their lives and choices. However, the pursuit of too many of these choices was hastily traced back to established stereotypes. These stereotypes emerged from literary constructs, plotlines compared with popular novels (notable Georges Sand), techniques of presentation, 'lying' perfected at school, and what Hartman called 'scripts' and 'novels' penned for their imagination by the women themselves. These sources of explanation appear in the analysis alongside behaviour shaped to elicit sympathy and archetypal reactions from observers.[7] Whilst this may contain some grain of truth, we would submit that these types of explanation have been too readily reached for and accepted. Surely, we would argue, women's accounts of their behaviour in their own defence deserve wider consideration, beyond the suggestion that the narratives of popular culture or societal expectation solely proscribe the imagination of women.

We might here go further and argue that the investigation of the female heroine in the Victorian novel has also had its part to play in this characterization of women's behaviour and especially around interpersonal violence. Studies of fictional female personalities, as well as their association with violence, have a history which encompasses them both as a genre and as a cultural artefact available for consumption. Some have brought this twin existence together (such as Rachel Brownstein) in the assertion that Victorian women were motivated to murder by 'life's failure to live up to romantic fictions'.[8]

Fiction as a cultural resource more generally has also been noted to have produced a reliance upon some stock female characters, such as Clytemnestra and Lady Macbeth who were referenced to personify female evil—perhaps without analysis necessarily going much further than their invocation.[9] Virginia Moore has also noted that the fictional treatment of the violent murderous female could be sympathetic, although this world was a thoroughly unforgiving moral universe which allowed women no escape from their actions, however much they deserved mitigation.[10] Yet crime fiction is also useful for giving hints around the possibility of alternative scenarios where women might gain control. Emelyne Godfrey's study of Victorian crime fiction has uncovered a significant number of instances where women are told subliminal messages about how to defend themselves in perilous situations. For Godfrey these constitute 'signposts on self-defence—tips, confessions, warnings, adverts—that sometimes lurk just behind the narrative'.[11]

Given the power of stereotypes hitherto, wherever they emerge from, this book also aims to question the construction and validity of these approaches, their direction, and their conclusions in writing the wider history of crime. From this, we hope, comes a much more nuanced reading of women's criminality and experiences which does not crudely categorize, stereotype, or essentialize their behaviour. As such, it is an important intervention in the history of crime in Britain but also, by questioning many wider gender-based discourses on the subject, the work has implications for the scholarship on the history of behaviour and gender in the nineteenth century in Britain and other societies as well.

The historiography of criminal women has been overly reliant upon a range of stereotypes, universalized reactions, and emotions.[12] Women are portrayed in this analysis as naturally maternal and as having feminized approaches to piety, belief, and morality. Their supposed separate nature is invoked by describing them as compelled by instinctive impulses rather than rational judgements, and of being incapable of premeditation in the committal of crime. In other areas of criminal history women are also 'essentialized'. The ability to 'trade' on femininity sees women accused of perennially having, and using, their female status as a bargaining chip for clemency within the courtroom. 'Essentializing' women's behaviour also sees uniquely 'feminine' failings that cast them as committing the crime of theft only to satisfy feelings of greed and acquisitiveness. It also paints them as lacking a sense of self and agency when committing crime, something which renders them passengers of their stereotypical female personality, or subordinate clients of male criminality. Economic vulnerability is also responsible for women being inexorably trapped by class, and likewise trapped by the judgement of the contemporary world upon them, thus sealing their reputation, and views of their behaviour and motivation for all time.[13]

Many of these views have come down to us from the pronouncements of both moral commentators and the historiography of sixteenth-, seventeenth-, and eighteenth-century criminality. Almost all have assigned women a passive and subordinate role, as well as creating highly gendered models of how women and men behave when contemplating and executing criminal ventures. This gendered divide has also been echoed in more recent works which examine the perpetration of violence in the nineteenth century.[14] These views of specifically gendered behaviours have themselves been enhanced and reinforced by the historiography of politeness, the historiography of separate spheres, and the historiography of the development of middle-class bourgeois society from the end of the eighteenth century and into the nineteenth century.[15] These again spoke of roles for both genders and outlined codes of behaviour which it proffered to many audiences. We also find echoes of them in a range of popular media representations of deviant women in later periods, and these have also contributed to a continued assertion that women's deviant behavioural choices and motivations can be characterized as utterly distinct from those of men.[16] What contemporaries thought about the implications of women's biology in particular have also been uncritically internalized by past and subsequent commentators.[17]

The original intention of gender history was to shine a broad light on the experience of women in society, as it was believed that they had been eclipsed or hidden from history by the male experience. Previous scholarship that attempted to investigate women, in relation to the sphere of criminal history at least, has shown that women were more independent actors in criminal activity in the nineteenth century in particular than many would have previously considered.[18] This is now an accepted component of the prevailing historiography, and scholars have tended to limit their investigations not far beyond this.

This book delves still deeper into nineteenth-century women's experiences and their behaviour to expose other aspects of their hitherto hidden histories. To neglect investigation of this is to ignore important elements of the wider history of crime and the proper development of criminology. It also aims at a more realistic depiction of the lives of nineteenth-century women.[19] As such, the research here fundamentally questions and challenges the orthodoxy within crime history that the behaviour and attitudes of women who commit crime belong in subordinate and supposedly archetypal 'feminine' roles which somehow 'serve' society and cultural ends. Every chapter in this book examines one (or sometimes more) of these assumptions regarding stereotypes of how women should behave according to expected norms. Alongside these, the contemporary cultural portrayals of female motivation and behaviour (as well as their subsequent influence) are also examined.[20] These are then questioned and problematized through the examination of case studies within each chapter. In each case the woman or women concerned step greatly beyond these norms to commit what past societies have seen as 'crimes' such as murder, infanticide, robbery, blasphemy, theft, and sexual misbehaviour. Taken as an overarching thesis, this wide-ranging analysis points to women as being far more obviously autonomous individuals, whose behaviour in the area of criminality (broadly defined) is poorly served by homogeneous classification. Nor should historiography continue to offer a characterization which renders them as largely passive or semi-passive accessories to criminal action. Moreover, the suggestion that they display quintessentially 'feminine' approaches to the committal of crime, or the contemplation of bad behaviour, is shown to be overstated and questionable.

Given the Victorian obsession with order, patriarchy, and defining appropriate behaviour, how were women who stepped outside the boundaries of acceptability regarded by the authorities and by wider society? How did Victorian society react to women who broke the rules or who did not conform to an ideal type? We would expect, in the era of sensationalism, of middle-class improving sensibilities, and 'New Journalism', that non-conforming behaviour would be exposed, censured, and controlled. However, the case studies in this volume show that responses were far more nuanced and complex than this.[21] Indeed, rather than openly manage deviant women through shame or by reinforcing their subservience to men in a public way for all to see, acknowledge, and learn from, the Victorians did their best to ignore, hide, explain away, or reinterpret women's bad behaviour. Instead, this reinterpretation made it something that was unlikely to shift or threaten established patriarchal power.[22] In this way, nineteenth-century society added a further veiled layer to women's history, both hiding agency and setting it away from the public gaze, creating new causations for and categorizations of female behaviour. This discomfort with deviant women undermines many of the established historical accounts about the power of narratives of idealized femininity. This becomes important since these ideals were so easily abandoned by society when the behaviour of women went far beyond them. Transgressive incidents had durable legacies which affected both opinion about women and how they were treated and regarded, long into the modern era. This volume exposes the profound importance of the nineteenth century in terms of the shaping of modern gender norms and expectations, but also the impact that this has had on our understanding of women's history in Britain more widely. As historian Lucia Zedner notes, we urgently crave explanations that go beyond assumptions that 'the female offender is likely to be sick or inadequate'.[23]

One of the persistent problems that emerges when we try to analyse women's behavioural choices is that women's behaviour is so easily seen as constrained in relation to the behaviour of men. The nineteenth century is regularly described as the period in which British society undertook a concerted campaign to tame the poor behaviour of men. Its portrayal of women was as recipient, observer, and victim of such behaviour. If this is to be believed, women themselves became adjacent to this purpose, reconstructed as serving and exhibiting renewed ideals of femininity and domesticity. Such ideals created more obviously static situations for women where their behaviour in some manner 'served' men. This obviously established constraints and 'boundaries'—'barriers' or 'obstacles' (whatever we seek to call them)—which were erected to explain to the populace that women and their actions were to be regularly and successfully subordinated to the needs of wider society.

The evidence offered by the chapters in the book demonstrates that all the female protagonists involved pushed at the barriers that sought to constrain them. This 'pushing' occurred to various degrees and obviously with varying degrees of intent and success. A few women we encounter only nudge the barriers in acts of individual, personal, or ideological rebellion, but there are also others whose convictions and motivations are considerably more earnest. Some see such activity as either a lifestyle choice or an attempt to circumvent greatly unfavourable choices otherwise before them. Others appear to have done so out of economic or social necessity. What emerges from these numerous encounters with these barriers is that the power to constrain seems to have been considerably overestimated by contemporary society.

The formidable nature of these barriers seems also to loom unwittingly larger than it should as a result of the construction of a women's history that focuses upon patriarchy and subordination. In practice, if the experience of the women in our chapters is to be believed, these barriers are made of more flimsy material than imagined and in some cases more or less melt away when challenged. In reality, such barriers seem to be often rhetorical, sometimes emerging as surprisingly simple, customary, or based on unexplored narratives too easily presumed to have the power of taboo and sometimes law. A co-terminus explanation might instead see this escape as confirmation of women having greater capacity for agency since, through the application of will, they find such barriers to be fallible or easily scalable. Beyond such barriers it also appears that, in contrast to the nineteenth-century campaign against the male perpetrator of poor, but especially violent behaviour, the policing of the female deviant was lacklustre, disorganized, and ill-equipped. Once beyond such barriers, deviant women discovered that society had little left in the way of a policing strategy prepared to defend contemporary ideologies and doctrines with any real desire or hope of success.

The case studies in this book also move beyond a static (unrealistic) dichotomy of either conforming to (or breaking away from) established behavioural traits and expectations. By investigating the real contexts of some specific incidents, the case studies reveal the depth of choices available to women at specific moments in their story. It also reveals the false starts, problems, and mistakes made by women in thinking through this idea of moving away from behavioural norms. Moreover, some of our instances demonstrate the fact that women actively had to learn how to operate beyond behavioural expectations if they chose to. On occasion, this was not always such a complete break away from what had been prescribed behaviour, as a recourse to some norms could prove episodically useful to them at a specific moment. Sometimes opposition to such break away behaviours also came from unusual sources—radical movements could pull women back into gender stereotypes, whilst conversely being in a hostile conservative courtroom could prove a surprising route to liberation from gender norms. A focus on context also illuminates that very often it was more than one set of expectations which became overturned—not simply those concerning gender. Only through the use of microhistories, as deployed in this work, can this deep context be explored and conclusions about wider narratives be reached.

## The Structure of the Book

Beyond this first chapter, we enter a number of case studies which unpack and critique prevailing, and much described, attitudes to the place of women in Victorian society and the responses towards their behaviour. In doing this we have looked carefully to find places where this is demonstrated in a considerable variety of contexts. We hope through this process to exhibit a range of instances and occasions upon which the 'bad' behaviour of women was evaluated, catalogued, and consumed. In pursuing this variety of 'case' studies, we have done our best to widen the definition of what this means. Whilst we obviously consider the individual case histories of individual women or in one case a criminal gang, these have been broadened to encompass a much wider range of behaviour and circumstances than has hitherto been investigated by scholars. We have also endeavoured to investigate 'cases' which span the class divide within Victorian England, Scotland, and Wales. This ranges from petty thieves, murderesses of adults and children, through the wives of prosperous artisans, to culminate in a consideration of the behavioural choices of an aristocratic woman.

In search of new insights, we have further stretched our definition of 'cases' to investigate some evidence within one element of popular culture, essentially eighteenth- and early nineteenth-century ballads. We have gone further in search of ways in which the behavioural choices of women were exemplified by a highly popular genre, but also ways in which these were in turn potentially consumed by an audience and the messages they would have received from such engagement. This initial chapter poses the fundamental problem that the errant behaviour of women offered nineteenth-century society and how the imprint of this has served to shape what subsequent historians have said about this.

Beyond the statement of historiographical intention in this first chapter, the second chapter investigates the ballad form as it would have been experienced in the nineteenth century. By analysing the contents of the two most significant ballad collections (with additional comparison to some others) the chapter aims to investigate the portrayal of women's behaviour within these. The rationale for this is that regular exposure to the ballad form amongst the populace at large would very likely have influenced their perception of women, their behaviour, and the range of narrative endings that result from this across several historical periods. Although many of the ballads depict strained, melodramatic, or exceptionally unusual circumstances, they do nonetheless depict women making behavioural choices when placed into difficult positions.

Estimating this impact of this upon wider society's views is extremely difficult, but the ballad evidence does suggest that women's behaviour, in this widely circulated and consumed medium, was problematized, ambivalent, and in places simply left open for speculation. In many ballads women perform traditionally passive roles. However, in ballads where violence occurs, there are many where women's violence is explained or rationalized. Yet there is a significant proportion of ballads where motives for women's violence are either unexplained or are simply not rationalized at all. This indicates a clear proportion of this genre where the population at large were either invited to think through the issue of motive, or conceivably filled in such a gap from memory, local knowledge, or their interactions with other forms of popular culture. As such, the chapter argues that this gap might constitute a space where the bad and violent behaviour of women was potentially debated beyond the rigidity of norms set by other institutions and stakeholders. If proven, this creates a potential paradigm of ambivalent reaction enabling greater behavioural choice amongst women that is reinforced in the subsequent examples in this volume.

Chapter 3 investigates the phenomenon of 'blasphemous' women who were a part of Richard Carlile's extended agitation for freedom of expression in the 1820s and beyond. Carlile's wife Jane, his sister Mary-Ann, Susannah Wright, and a woman involved in a later agitation, Matilda Roalfe, were prepared to embrace prosecution for selling blasphemous and seditious literature. They considered this an act that was of supreme benefit to the people of Britain. Court proceedings and press reports made a point of referencing their gender and indicating these women's lapses from the decorum required by strict and safely regulated norms of female behaviour. These 'blasphemous' women were not in the same mould as the radical women uncovered by other scholars who have noted that these latter women found ways to use their femininity. Gendered interests were used to argue for specific grievances, or to argue in specifically feminine contexts or using specifically feminine discourses. What emerges is that the 'blasphemous' women investigated in the chapter saw their behaviour motivated by enlightenment ideals of freedom of expression. These they espoused as coherently and cogently as their male counterparts. Moreover, it was ironically the 'tyrannical' establishment that gave them the platform of the courtroom in which to develop and demonstrate these. As such their behaviour sidestepped gender labels and stereotyping for them to emerge as women behaving beyond the gender constraints of either the establishment norms, or the alternative gender discourses of other radical movements. 'Blasphemous women' therefore ceased being 'handmaidens' to the male Prometheus figures of freethought agitation—instead being exemplars of the rationalist martyr Hypatia. Perhaps more importantly still, they were enlightenment radicals first and women second.

Chapter 4 investigates a mid-Victorian moral panic about the rise of the 'anti-mother' who English and Scottish society created as a pariah archetype upon which to pin a number of overlapping concerns. Mothers who practised child murder were frequently cited in rhetoric which saw them as the ultimate criminal on a sliding scale of 'anti-motherhood' that also embraced and drew attention to lesser crimes. They had blatantly turned their back on maternity, one of the key idealized roles for nineteenth-century women. Working-class women who vacated the home, in search of gainful employment, were transgressing domestic norms that this narrative enthusiastically espoused. Such women were damaging almost every part of nineteenth-century society through their challenge to patriarchal authority and ideals. However, the reality of society disciplining such women was, as this chapter demonstrates, sometimes illusory. Through the detailed examination of two cases of child murder, those against Barbara Malcolm and the serial infanticidal offender Catherine Anderson, the chapter seeks to evaluate how determined society was to punish, uphold, and strengthen its narrative of the anti-mother. Although both women were punished, it thus comes as a surprise that the press and authorities stayed their hand about the narrative created around these women and their crimes. Reporting was largely factual and murderous mothers became distanced from the narrative of the anti-mother. Thus, the overwhelming effect created by the stance adopted by the authorities was not one of choreographed action and opprobrium, but instead one of seeming bewilderment.

Chapter 5 investigates the case of the 'Potten Poisoner', an individual woman whose case illuminates the folly of contemporary views which saw deviant and murderous behaviour through the prism of instinctiveness. Women were supposedly devoid of the capacity for rational planning and forethought, so their actions emerge as 'rash', 'involuntary', and products of the uncontrollable. This formulation flourished because it reinforced dichotomous gender norms. However, this paradigm had immense problems with explaining women's use of poison as a murderer's *modus operandi*. This, by its very definition, portrayed malice aforethought, calculation, and sustained malevolence. As such, this produced something of a panic within Victorian society which saw the law and other central institutions, such as the family, challenged by this crime and its destructive power. One woman caught up in this panic was Sarah Dazley who was convicted of poisoning her husband and son, but nonetheless refused to confess her guilt when faced with the sentence of execution. Throughout her trial attempts to access the alternative acceptable explanatory paths of subordination to male agency, insanity, or other uniquely female motive were redundant. This defiance of norms of behaviour (both in and out of the courtroom) led press coverage to substantially evade commenting upon her role in their reportage of the murders. Without such censure, it was possible to see a female poisoner not choosing to avoid aggression in killing, but instead utilizing refined tools and mechanisms to achieve her particular ends. Removed from the shadows of Victorian society's stereotypes of insane impulsive women and the obsession with physical weakness portrayed by later historians, women like Dazley and others displayed agency, calculation, and self-awareness, albeit turned to murderous, destructive, and nihilistic ends.

Chapter 6 investigates female thieves in nineteenth-century Wales and takes the reader away from the conventional assumption that women were cast in subordinate roles in crimes of theft, or instead apparently succumbed to their uncontrollably acquisitive nature when doing so. Such assumptions were regularly seen to supposedly influence the actions of the courts who tried these women, pressing for leniency based upon their low level of culpability, or their inherently gendered disposition. The findings from this examination of Welsh evidence indicates that both genders engaged in the same types of property crime, undermining previous conceptions of the gendered nature of their involvement in this activity. Likewise, supposed opportunism emerges as a characteristic of both genders and the nature and pattern of goods stolen similarly lacks a gendered divide. Goods were stolen as a means by which both men and women sought to survive harsh economic realities, so that the idea of women committing theft to please their own desires and acquisitiveness emerges as a construct scarcely in tune with the harsh nineteenth-century reality.

Chapter 7 investigates violent female robbers in nineteenth-century Scotland. It begins by announcing its intention to subvert many prevailing assumptions that women were generally the victims of violent crime and did not initiate or deploy violence upon their own initiative, but rather at the behest of men. The chapter follows the case against four women who engaged in what we would now describe as a joint enterprise crime of robbery which subsequently became murder. The case against them, and the reports of the subsequent execution of two of them, marginalized their behaviour as unacceptable and cruel. Yet reporting of this did not happen in the sensationalized way that might be expected and did not focus upon the gender of the accused. Instead reports sought the moral reformation of drunken indolent men who would be vulnerable to such offenders, or equally sought the moral reformation of young impressionable witnesses to the violence and debauchery that had occurred. The press also focused on how a notorious area of Glasgow (Croiley's Land) and its denizens was described as a dangerous world apart in need of isolation and eventual reformation. The chapter concludes that this whole case displays symptoms that society and the law had lost the battle to contain some women's criminality and their wider compliance. Henceforth, their poor behaviour and its consequences would provide raw material for other agendas and discourses about moral dangers and the dangerous.

Chapter 8 investigates the life and behavioural choices of the aristocrat Lady Harriett Mordaunt, a daughter of the Moncrieffe family, who became the centre of an initially unsuccessful divorce suit instigated by her husband Sir Charles Mordaunt in 1870. Lady Harriett negotiated a kind of 'pre-nuptial' agreement in which she could continue to act in the same manner as she had done before her marriage. This involved a giddy social life and deep intimacy with a number of men in her social circle, including the Prince of Wales. When she gave birth either guilt, or a species of insanity, struck her and she confessed to her husband that the child was the result of serial adultery with a number of men. Harriett then endured what all subsequent accounts label a descent into madness, one which was either real, was created by her as a bargaining chip, or was constructed by her family to defend their interests. This chapter reassesses this story, noting the range of behavioural norms and expectations that Harriett Mordaunt transgressed, indicating a series of deliberate choices which continued into her supposed insanity.

The subsequent accounts of her conduct by the contemporary press and by biographers and historians are also investigated to establish a created 'archaeology of reputation'. This investigation looks at academic assessments of the case as well as internet blogs and electronic publishing on the subject. Our interest in the latter two forms of media arises from the fact that in the twenty-first century popular history, and especially that relating to royalty and the British aristocracy, is frequently popularized in these genres. As such these often confirm ideas that a have clearly permeated through from conventional academic study, often providing a form of confirmation for these. They also communicate such ideas to a wider audience for more cursory consumption. As we shall see sometimes these internet media studies do produce interpretations of their own, yet it is also surprising how much they still ostensibly deal in stock stereotypes.

These much later judgements, both academic and popular, have relegated Harriett Mordaunt to a touchstone of aristocratic excess, of frivolity, and as an inconvenience to the otherwise more wholesome biography of great men. Yet they have also seen her as a vehicle to establish scholarship around the nature of Victorian modes of insanity and to fuel conspiracy theories. In the end, this chapter asks if Harriett's behavioural choices should be viewed as individual and much more like those made by men. As such, these choices should not be fitted into other easy paradigms of explanation that render her and her story of significantly subordinate relevance. Ultimately the chapter suggests that making such choices could create a situation where society was clearly left far behind in its attempts to categorize and control the behaviour of women at the highest level of society.

Beyond this final chapter we include an epilogue which has some brief final thoughts upon the issues uncovered by the book and how this might relate to wider speculation about the history of women and criminality in Britain. Some suggestions in here may well take exploration wider than this and we would both be delighted if this happened. To spur other scholars on their way, we include some speculation about areas we found interesting, but could not include in the central argument of this book. There are also avenues that were unexplored or only partially investigated which may well prove a fruitful starting point for others.

After this Epilogue we hope that we have inspired other scholars to investigate the deep context of how women in the nineteenth century chose their actions alongside the more nuanced, if less coherent, way that society responded to them. In this we are observing the history of nineteenth-century women caught between the barriers of society's expectations of them on one side, and society's reaction to such women when they do not conform on the other. This is an invidious place to be, but as we shall see, the women in our case studies made efforts to realize their own individual personality and lives however badly this sometimes may have ended in practice. We hope this book enables us as scholars of crime and behaviour to move forward with greater appreciation of how both genders have historically had wants, desires, individuality, and agency. Heightening this appreciation can only enhance our full understanding of criminality and its history, as well as freeing both genders from an unnecessary explanatory straight-jacket.

## Notes

1. For a veritable catalogue of these in the context of murder see M. Hartman (1977) *Victorian Murderesses: A True History of Thirteen Respectable French and English Women Accused of Unspeakable Crimes* (London: Robson Books).
2. See M. Wiener (2004) *Men of Blood: Violence, Manliness, and Criminal Justice in Victorian England* (Cambridge: Cambridge University Press), *passim*. Wiener's opening statement argues that homicide is 'a highly gendered behaviour'—see p. 2. For similar views relating to the nineteenth century as well as other historical periods see in particular C. Emsley (2005 edition) *Crime and Society in England, 1750–1900* (Harlow: Pearson), p. 152; J. M. Beattie (1975) 'The Criminality of Women in Eighteenth-Century England', *Journal of Social History*, 8, pp. 80–116 at p. 80; J. A. Sharpe (1999) *Crime in Early Modern England, 1550–1750* (Longman: Harlow), p. 154.
3. L. Zedner (1991) 'Women, Crime and Penal Responses: A Historical Account', *Crime and Justice*, 14, pp. 312 and 319. The greater involvement of women in crime during the nineteenth century is corroborated by M. Van Der Heijden (2016) 'Women and Crime, 1750–2000', in P. Knepper and A. Johansen (eds), *The Oxford Handbook of the History of Crime and Criminal Justice* (Oxford: Oxford University Press), pp. 250–67 at p. 251.
4. See Wiener, *Men of Blood*, p. 152.

5. Ibid., pp. 38 and 92.
6. Zedner, 'Women, Crime and Penal Responses', p. 315. Zedner's analysis indicates that Lombrosian positivism built upon older assumptions to produce a criminological tradition that women's moral weakness stemmed solely from their psychological and biological inferiority to men. This also echoes older stereotypes which historians are used to seeing in explanations of the gender makeup of those accused of witchcraft.
7. Hartman, *Victorian Murderesses,* pp. 1, 20, 25, 32, 46, 48, 49, 52, 58, 60–1, 63–5, 71, 74, 76, 80, 83–4, 175, 180, 198, 256 (where it is argued roleplaying 'became...a way of life' for women of this era. They had 'lines' written for them to perform but still managed 'to write some of their own'), 258.
8. See R. Brownstein (1982) *Becoming a Heroine: Reading about Women in Novels* (New York: Viking Press), p. xxiii.
9. V. Morris (1990) *Double Jeopardy: Women Who Kill in Victorian Fiction* (Lexington, KY: University Press of Kentucky), pp. 3 and 8.
10. Ibid., p. 5.
11. E. Godfrey (2012) *Femininity, Crime and Self-Defence in Victorian Literature and Society: From Dagger-Fans to Suffragettes* (Basingstoke: Palgrave Macmillan), p. 157.
12. See Wiener, *Men of Blood*, pp. 4 and 30, which invoke, respectively, portrayals of Queen Victoria and Britannia as indicative of the 'heightened moral influence of women' alongside the feminization of piety which takes on the character of a universal and homogenizing force. See also Zedner, 'Women, Crime and Penal Responses', pp. 327–8.
13. Zedner, 'Women, Crime and Penal Responses', pp. 320–1.
14. See Wiener, *Men of Blood, passim.* Wiener's excellent study of the Victorian crusade against the violently aggressive male has opened up the debate on gendering criminality in nineteenth-century England. Whilst this volume clearly demonstrates a crusade against male behaviour, its surefooted comprehensiveness ensures that the male occupies the reader's line of vision. Although this may reflect a great number of violent crimes and incidents, it has had an unwitting influence upon the image of women in this period. Through male aggressiveness we encounter female passivity; through acts of male violence we encounter female victimhood; through the taming of men and their behaviour we encounter expectations of women's civilizing influence and capacity to provide models of redemption and salvation. Weiner has done an exemplary job in analysing what society thought of men and what it did judicially to tame them. However, women have been sidelined and artificially 'tamed' as a result of this historiographical process.
15. The power of these influential narratives has been questioned by many, with the most recent being Manon Van Der Heijden who challenges the alleged disappearance of women from the public sphere and similarly notes the upholding of domestic ideals was highly conditional upon the existence of appropriate economic and cultural circumstance—see Van Der Heijden, 'Women and Crime', p. 256.
16. An example of how this persists in the literature is furnished by looking at one of the most recent surveys of female criminality provided in *The Oxford Handbook of the History of Crime and Criminal Justice.* In the section on female criminality Van Der Heijden describes the modern process of women taking a greater share of reported

crime as 'alarming'. Such language serves to suggest, perhaps unwittingly, that the increase in crime rates amongst women needs a deeper and wider explanation than that of men, and that some mechanism somewhere has somehow failed. This reaction is perhaps enhanced by the fact that men still make up a considerable majority of those indicted for reported crime. See ibid., p. 262.

17. Zedner, 'Women, Crime and Penal Responses', pp. 336–40 and 342.
18. See in particular A.-M. Kilday (2007) *Women and Violent Crime in Enlightenment Scotland* (Woodbridge: Boydell), (2013) *A History of Infanticide in Britain, 1600 to the Present* (London: Palgrave), (2016) 'Constructing the Cult of the Criminal: Kate Webster—Victorian Murderess and Media Sensation', in A.-M. Kilday and D. S. Nash (eds), *Law, Crime and Deviance since 1700: Micro-Studies in the History of Crime* (London: Bloomsbury), pp. 125–48, (2014) 'Hair-Raising and Hell-Razing: Violent Robbery in Nineteenth-Century Scotland', *Scottish Historical Review*, 92, 2, pp. 255–74, (2014) 'Angels with Dirty Faces? Violent Women in Early Modern Scotland', in P. Blanc and R. Hillman (eds), *Female Transgression in Early Modern Britain* [published in French and English] (London: Routledge), pp. 141–62, (2013) '"That Women are But Men's Shadows": Examining Gender, Violence and Criminality in Early Modern Britain', in M. G. Muravyeva and R. M. Toivo (eds), *Gender in Late Medieval and Early Modern Europe* (London: Routledge), pp. 53–72, (2013) 'Outrageous Acts and Everyday Rebellions: Criminal Women in Eighteenth Century Scotland', in K. Barclay and D. Simonton (eds), *Women in Eighteenth Century Scotland: Intimate, Intellectual and Public Lives* (London: Ashgate), pp. 253–70. For the nineteenth century in particular see for instance Hartman, *Victorian Murderesses*; J. Knelman (1998) *Twisting in the Wind: The Murderess and the English Press* (Toronto: University of Toronto) and A. R. Higginbotham (1989) '"Sin of the Age": Infanticide and Illegitimacy in Victorian London', *Victorian Studies*, 32, 3, pp. 319–37.
19. Zedner, 'Women, Crime and Penal Responses', p. 314.
20. Ibid., pp. 307–62. Here Zedner argues that female criminality was identified until at least the mid-century as 'deviance from the "norm" of femininity' before pathologizing of their behaviour occurred beyond this date. This latter tendency was something Zedner argues persisted much further into modern conceptions of female criminality, since science followed more traditional assumptions about the origins of criminal tendencies.
21. See Wiener, *Men of Blood*, p. 227, for the suggestion that official and popular reactions to women's bad behaviour could crucially diverge at certain points.
22. Ibid., pp. 123–34 and 148, suggests that a waning fear of the horrific female killer was a clear result of 'hardening attitudes towards men', even where infanticide was concerned. Wiener goes further to suggest that reports of murder as a result of being jilted by a male lover and husband murderers began to attract discourses sympathetic to the woman. This is also as the century wore on, so Wiener suggests, likely to be behind the falling conviction rates for spousal murder by women as the authorities readily dropped unwinnable cases. All such analyses serve to minimize the role and culpability of women in crimes of violence and behaviour related to this.
23. Zedner, 'Women, Crime and Penal Responses', p. 315.

# 2
# Imagining Bad Women and Fallen Angels
## The Criminal and Violent Woman Portrayed in Popular Ballads before 1900

### Introduction

Creating a penetrating and effective survey of the criminality of women in the nineteenth century requires knowledge of widespread and popular cultural perceptions, as well as persuasive narratives of how such female criminality develops over time. Amongst many of the questions this volume seeks to investigate are those that ask how norms and expectations of women's behaviour are constructed, negotiated, and reinforced. In the wider picture, how precisely were the populace at large persuaded to think of violent women, in terms of their emotional and psychological makeup and their motivations? What was said to them, or written for them, about how these women behaved? Is it possible to conceive of how women might have had an image (or images) created about them from how individuals consumed popular culture and its narratives? Might there also be some specific and important insights to be gained from viewing how women's violence was portrayed in such popular media?

This chapter attempts to use ballads as a primary source, something which may take us closer to popular perceptions of the way women were portrayed to nineteenth-century audiences. Initially it focuses upon the range of images the ballads conjured up about women's motivations and behaviour. Many of these are recognizable from the introduction alongside other chapters in this book. Such images are perhaps more varied than those associated with Victorian society as a whole, but many conform to expectations and stereotypes created by contemporaries but also some by historians (already alluded to in the introduction to this volume). Women in some ballads are passive bit-part characters, or innocents painted into bucolic landscapes and situations. Others are in receipt of both male gaze and/or sexual attention, yet manage to escape with virtue intact. Some, as we shall see, engage in violence to protect virtues or what is generally signalled as a legitimate and worthy cause. In many of these ballads there is a didactic element in which these ideal types are 'shown' to society and to women in particular. These foster and promote values which inspire conformity (in varying degrees) to acceptable images of women's motivation and behaviour. There are others where

*Beyond Deviant Damsels: Re-evaluating Female Criminality in the Nineteenth Century.* Anne-Marie Kilday and David Nash, Oxford University Press.  DOI: 10.1093/oso/9780198830733.003.0002

the message is much more questionable, such as ballads where women indulge in violence, where the motive is declared, even if it is not by any means condoned. There are also a number of ballads where women are the subordinate accomplice figures to male criminals—something which would appear to coalesce with the views of some historians of women's criminality. But this chapter seeks to focus attention on a category of ballads prevalent in nineteenth-century culture where there appears to be no apparent motive for female violence and to unpick the potentially lasting significance of this. It investigates the idea that ballads may never have contained such a motive simply because they were entertainment, or instead they were edited for brevity or for other reasons. Yet equally it is possible that the absence of motive may be evidence of society's inability to comment upon female violence and of avoiding drawing attention to it. Whatever the reason, the chapter concludes with some questions about how we should view audiences exposed to tales of female motiveless violence and what this might say to wider popular ideas about this phenomenon.

Elsewhere in this volume we have ample evidence of how constructing the image of deviant and violent women might have been possible by reading and consuming press reports of both actual and imagined crimes. However, much of this evidence comes from what we might term the 'supply side'. These are images and perceptions of women created and controlled both by, and for, specifically literate audiences. What a rounded picture of our nineteenth-century search for images of women's behaviour craves is evidence of the wider interaction between image creator and the audience for such creation. This was an audience at least partially removed from such literate audiences and readerships, so probing outside this world would interrogate some material and produce sorely needed insights from the 'demand side'. Likewise, for the cogency of such an investigation, it would be eminently desirable if we could detect the more obviously organic production and consumption of women's behaviour narratives. These could also be placed alongside the responses of their actively targeted and cultivated audiences.

This chapter concentrates upon ballads collected independently of broadside ballad material. Historians of crime have so far investigated broadsides containing a range of material besides ballads. These have been seen as evidence of attempts to steer and manipulate emotion to create a response that reflected repugnance at violence and its consequences. As Kate Bates has argued, these were much more than gruesome entertainment, but forcefully fostered compassion and empathic responses amongst audiences, actively cultivating an establishment-friendly repugnance to violence.[1] There is, as will become apparent, some considerable crossover between ballads and the broadsides which carried some of these same ballads. Broadsides were actively published and existed for many during the nineteenth century largely as the printed word.[2] Ballads on the other hand were, at our period, songs transcribed from oral or written tradition which were not produced especially with the conception of a market in mind. However, it should be stressed that ballads would not have survived or been transferred from previous generations (or into the hands of nineteenth-century collectors) if they had not been in some sense resilient and popular. Printed broadsides containing ballads were capable of going in the other direction and often found their way into the singing repertoire of ballad singers. Our way of knowing about these comes from the folksong-collecting efforts of nineteenth-century enthusiasts.[3]

Moving from individual ballads, the chapter also looks at the overall narratives achieved by specific ballad collections (which became especially popular in the mid-late nineteenth century) in relation to the selection of ballads and the placement of these within such collections. This is to see what 'picture' of women's deviance these present. The chapter then catalogues movements within these ballads to show that both the consistency and stability of popular cultural narratives of women's bad behaviour have been considerably overstated. It also becomes obvious that the success of the paradigm of active and conscious morality construction by polite and determined nineteenth-century society has been too readily accepted.

Up to now the study of violence within these ballads has been something of a poor relation; a phenomenon previously neglected by researchers. The study of sex and sexuality within them is a considerably further and more developed discipline. From this area of study we might perhaps get some analogous clues as to the treatment of violence in ballads. According to Steve Roud, the earlier nineteenth-century period was concerned by the assault upon morals that unbridled sexual content represented. This led to censorship, omission, and bowdlerization[4] in equal measure, something which would fit with the age of growing sensibility and improvement often cited by Francis Place.[5] The later century period viewed the same songs as the outpourings of simple rustics who were (to the delight of collectors) free from the shame that had colonized more delicate sensibilities. For these later collectors, this window onto a lost world and the appreciation of its authenticity outweighed the desire to censor or render their enterprise more delicate than it seemed to be.[6] Nonetheless the imperative to censor did remain and prominent collectors such as Cecil Sharp and Sabine Baring-Gould did bowdlerize texts that otherwise would have contained considerable sexual content.[7]

Roud argues, perceptively, that the modern scholar of this area really wants to know where people like Sharp and Baring-Gould 'drew the line'.[8] This scholarship, whilst obviously not transferable to the study of violence, nonetheless does pose some intriguing questions about censorship. Bowdlerization is far less likely around narratives of violent conduct or reaction, since such episodes cannot be rendered innocent for sensitive ears. Yet the capacity for omission and self-censorship does remain, potentially exerting influence upon the study of violence as a phenomenon within this genre. It is conceivable that folksong collectors could be viewed as somehow completing the ideological 'work' and agenda of nascent and rising middle-class sensibilities and tastes. If ballads, once sung or enjoyed in banqueting halls as well as taverns, had vanished, or even been driven out from the former, then the history of such actions would, at first sight appear to resemble the actions of Norbert Elias' 'Civilizing Process'.[9] The remaining uncouth and rough nature of ballads when collected in the nineteenth century may well have suffered at the hands of improvement-minded and 'civilizing' individuals anxious to mould the behavioural expectations of women.[10]

Whilst it is possible to argue that ballads represent a more closely 'authentic' voice of the people, the authorship of many ballads cannot be established and may be less 'authentic' than imagined. A case can be made for at least some of them being no different from orthodox literary productions, rather than somehow emanating organically from a perceived folk tradition. It is equally possible to be suspicious of how such ballads 'survive' into our own time, or at least into the nineteenth century when we become aware of the procedures and agendas of folksong collectors.

Many nineteenth-century attempts at collecting ballads focus rigidly upon localities and this inevitably drives what the individual collection displays. These can be restricted to specific counties and thus display some closely defined loyalties demonstrating a substantial role in the creation of county identities.[11] Others offer a more regional perspective, presenting a vastly contrasting picture to English county and national collections, some have perspectives from Scotland or even much further afield.[12] Beyond localities, there are collections which focus upon specific themes and genres within the wider canon of ballads and folksong.[13]

Using the content of all these ballads as historical evidence of genuine concepts, feelings, and perceptions is also not without its issues and problems. How 'real' for example is our depiction of the women and female behaviour in ballads? It is fanciful to imagine that they represent some sort of 'mirror' of life, actively reflecting reality. But we should perhaps be equally wary of allocating such stories to overly stylized literary genres that play with ideals or grotesques. Moreover, the ones that survive may well have 'driven out' the ones that perished or fell from view. However, it does have to be said here that the collectors of folksong in the nineteenth century were always acutely conscious of their duty to rescue whatever they found. This propensity often accounts for songs and ballads that survive in these collections merely in fragmented form.[14] Might it also be the case that such ballads record the extraordinary and noteworthy, rather than the mundane and workaday? Should we note that they constitute sensationalist entertainment every bit as much as they may bear relation to actual reality?

Despite these searching questions, the enterprise of investigating ballads remains fundamentally worthwhile. Whatever else these ballads reflect, or however much they appear filtered, they remain possibly our closest contact with the tastes and narratives of the population at large. As such they deserve serious consideration as a touchstone of what popular culture thought of women and their criminal and/or violent behaviour. Individual authorship of these ballads is less important for reinforcing the view they purvey of women's criminality and violence than the fact that they were serially consumed by the public. Again the apparent 'reality' or otherwise of the depictions contained within these ballads is less important than the fact that they were actively consumed regularly in high numbers over a considerable period of time, something that made them in many senses ubiquitous and consequently potentially influential.

Scholars of media reception studies have noted that the increased potential access to texts evident amongst the populace since the start of the nineteenth century produced audience effects which made moral panics possible. Janet Staiger suggests: 'What the meanings are for readers may be quite pertinent to their behaviours, attitudes, and beliefs. So reception studies ask, "What kind of meanings does a text have? For whom? In what circumstances? With what changes over time? And do these meanings have any effects? Cognitive, Emotional, Social? Political?"'[15] Thus, twentieth-century media scholars 'want to know about outcomes from engagements with media and television', as well as the reactions of individuals to mass media.[16] The basis of this discipline is suggestive and encouraging to historical scholars to potentially draw analogies from these forms of media and their possible effects.

## Ballads and Criminality

Whilst we must be aware of the aforementioned limitations, this chapter uses ballad evidence to investigate just how effectively stereotypes of female criminality and violence were transmitted into popular culture. Although our conclusions must be tentative, it is possible to suggest that from these ballads emerge neither a persistent view of the female as criminal, nor a sustained and conscious depiction of types of female criminal responsibility or indeed diminished responsibility., There is only ambivalent, even highly questionable, evidence of a conscious civilizing impulse within ballads, governing attempts to marshal and shape how such female behaviour was depicted. This contrasts with broadsides which frequently had just such a driving impulse.[17]

We find instead a range of portrayals of women which are surprisingly diverse. Some ballads and broadsides show the motivations and circumstances which led women into deviant behaviour. Yet, a quite surprising number of others seem to portray apparently motiveless acts of violence and cruelty. These produce a wide and conflicting array of moral positions, ranging from censure and recognizably modern moral judgements, right through to the depiction and active deeper contemplation of an amoral universe where anything can happen. In some of these scenarios, women are castigated for adopting unfeminine forms of behaviour that shade into the immoral and even the monstrous. In others, the action of such women is merely portrayed without sanction, without significant comment and sometimes with no comment at all.[18]

## The Study of Ballads: Methodology Employed

This investigation has looked at a considerable number of ballad collections and for comparison one especially significant broadside collection held in the Bodleian's John Johnson Collection. Some of the ballad collections used are well known and comparatively mainstream, and would have been reflective of the entire ballad canon and likewise would have been substantially influential. These include, amongst others, the main focus of this chapter, Francis James Child's *English and Scottish Popular Ballads* which surveys 305 ballads.[19] However, others were investigated, such as the Roud collection of 25,000 songs.[20] Still more with an obviously more local and restricted readership and circulation were consulted.[21] It is hoped that this coverage is suggestive of the wider picture and might, in the fullness of time, be completed with additional research. As far as geographical spread is concerned, it has been important to obtain a cross-section of ballad collections. This is offered to provide both a national picture (since some collections are heavily slanted towards the different constituent parts of Britain) and a local if somewhat patchy investigation of some individual areas.[22]

In many ballad collections, there are multiple examples of the same ballad. Sometimes these contain identical accounts of the narrative alongside others where the details vary slightly, or the order of the narrative varies. The analysis outlined here has opted to use each of these examples, simultaneously considering them as single ballad stories and also as additional and separate ballads. The consideration of these simply as single ballad stories allows for an analysis of the nature of female violence as a proportion of all ballad types where female violence occurs. However the assessment of all ballads where female violence occurs (including individual variations within the sample) allows for an examination of particular ballads that were widespread and popular, which spawned variations and which made a significant potential imprint on popular consciousness. This may at first sight appear to distort the conclusions one can draw from the sample. However, to counter this argument, the appearance of individual ballads that are listed with a contrastingly small number of variations may equally signal the comparative lack of popularity of these.

Plenty of the ballads have no depiction of violence at all and many include women within the whole panoply of everyday life within scenarios that relate to work, play, emotional expression, rites of passage, recreation, and other forms of human experience. Violence remains merely a part of this wider picture. Where violence can be found within these ballads it is frequently the case that these feature no women at all. These generally contain depictions of masculinity, and even hyper-masculinity, which play themselves out within a completely male sphere or context from which women are simply absent. Thus, traditional tales of knightly combat, war, chivalric enterprise, and trials of physical, diplomatic, or metaphorical strength are what characterize this group of ballads.[23] Far more common are ballads where knights and men at arms interact with women within the recognizably constrained world of courtly behaviour, according to the full definition of the genre.[24]

There are some interesting smaller and tightly focused collections that portray brutal (often murderous) male violence perpetrated against women as born of jealousy, the recklessness of youth, and the potentially dreadful consequences of promiscuity. In these collections women appear solely as innocent victims.[25] Beyond this category, there are other ballads in which women play a subordinate role within such cultures of violence. Within these they are either the inspiration for such violence, willing passive accessory to such violence, or somehow enrolled within the male-dominated culture which sustains violence within the world of the ballad. In some they do appear as the 'orthodox' silent and unremarkable accomplice to the perpetration of violence. In others they promote and encourage the violent expression, responses, and actions of men, constituting the role of passive, if willing, accomplice in violent activity. It is tempting here to suggest that this may, in part, be an important source of this cultural stereotype of women's role in violence.

Each ballad that does depict female violence can be labelled according to the apparent or explicit motives for such violence. Within our sample from Francis James Child, it is possible to see a range of recognizable human emotions that might provoke outbreaks of violence, albeit amongst a 'fictional' cohort. Most obvious is sexual and emotional jealousy which accounts for a significant number of ballads which involve violence expressed by the woman against a spouse or paramour, or indeed against a love rival. The next most obvious category is what might simply be called jealousy. This incorporates inter-familial jealousy that does not involve a sexual relationship and typically is sibling rivalry of the very highest order, or jealousy between parent and child. Beyond these two major categories are a number of more numerically minor motives for female violence. These include material greed, response to shame, the escalation of individual quarrel, the more formalized culture of the blood feud, as well as the category of more simple and straightforward retaliation. There are also a number of instances where infanticide is explicitly indicated in reaction to social or cultural opprobrium. A somewhat anomalous category relates to ballads that mention the Jewish blood libel as a motive. These belong to an altogether different tradition, with the violence within these sometimes located within a male Jewish figure and sometimes within a female.[26] It is interesting to note that the overwhelmingly anti-Semitic tone and intention of this particular sub-genre succeeded in submerging differences between the perpetration of male and female violence.

It is possible that ballads were used to 'reinforce' what was proper behaviour through contrasting this with what was not. Were the fallen angels of the chapter's title only used in ballads so that they could be contrasted with the legitimate angels thus reinforcing gender 'norms'? Or was there a genuine interest in the 'other' and how it could be explained? Lastly we should be aware of a range of different 'uses' for such ballads. There could legitimately be a voyeuristic element to these ballads whereby they offered cultivated audiences a chance to glimpse their opposite number. Such insights could then be used to further the process of 'othering' behavioural tendencies within society and identifying them with specific classes. Finally there is the most intriguing category of all—a quite extensive number of ballads where female violence is described, yet no motive for these actions is mentioned. We will hear more about this category in due course.

## Ballads and Their Narrative Content

Francis James Child's *English and Scottish Popular Ballads* was the summative achievement of the nineteenth-century ballad publishing tradition and appeared in five volumes produced gradually between 1882 and 1898. This quite comprehensive collection went through numerous editions and is considered a standard work. It remains widely available today, having made an early appearance upon the Amazon Kindle platform. This collection, whilst covering the whole of mainland Britain, contains a significant portion of Scottish ballad material. Child's scholarship was extensive and looked far and wide for an almost ethnographic comparison with narrative and song traditions for many ballads both in Britain and Europe-wide.[27] He believed that the ballad form was a pure expression of communal ideas and conceptions. Whilst later scholars might see this as perhaps fanciful, and locate Child in a communitarian moment that infected his era of scholarship, he did nonetheless produce evidence that ballads at some time in the past were the cultural currency of the whole community, even if specific tastes might subsequently part company.[28]

Most of Child's ballads were of some antiquity, with Roud stating all were at least as old as 1700,[29] Yet they were still prevalent and used during the nineteenth century. Child's was a collection which many took to be the cornerstone of comprehensive ballad collecting and possibly represents the pinnacle of nineteenth-century ballad curating achievements. Its author noted a considerable range of individual ballads but was equally scrupulous in collecting variations of ballads and fragments which potentially offered alternative readings and outcomes. This was not simply an academic curating exercise that was investigating the past. We certainly have evidence that ballad singing was commonplace in many nineteenth-century contexts, and we can also place some of the ballads that appear in Child's collection at such gatherings.[30]

We should also take note of a number of ballads where considerable levels of female agency and autonomy show women stepping out of stereotypical gender roles. For example, the central male character of the title in 'King Henry' is made to satisfy the apparently endless appetite of a grotesque and hideous woman, a plotline replicated in 'Alison Gross'.[31] In addition, 'Young Beichan' depicts a woman prepared to traverse the oceans in search of her true love.[32] In the widely known 'Tam Lin' too, the female protagonist, Janet, goes as far as to threaten the knights portrayed in the ballad, vowing to go through life bringing up her child fatherless because none of them are worthy of her.[33] Similarly, 'The Bonny Hind' has a tragedy unfold as a woman commits suicide having committed incest with her brother.[34] In 'The Laird of Logie', a woman named May Margaret empowers her lover to resist his execution by equipping him with pistols.[35] And then in 'Robin Hood and Maid Marian' a powerful Marian, disguising herself as a page in the search for an absent Robin Hood, finds and fights him before the ballad reaches a safe resolution.[36]

Perhaps the most widely known exemplar of this kind of ballad is 'The Famous Flower of Serving Men'. This portrays a woman whose husband (a knight) is killed by her mother (motive here does not seem apparent) and she then dresses as a knight and changes her name 'from Fair Elise to Sweet William'. She then goes to the court to gain renown, something which eventually wins her the admiration of the King, somewhat ironically to be described as the 'Famous Flower of Serving Men'. 'William' betrays his gender in a song to the delight of the King who promptly declares his love and weds her.[37] This is an exemplar of ballads where women left male protection to eventually end their story within it again, but in the meantime conventional orders and expectations were overturned. This genre has persuaded Dianne Dugaw that the world of the ballad actively wanted such female characters, noting 'the Female Warrior and her story assumed the status of an imaginative archetype in popular balladry, a standard motif'.[38]

Female agency specifically related to acts of violence can be seen in some ballad stories where the women act in defence of their honour, or shame, without the assistance of men. The former is on display in 'Captain Car, or Edom o Gordon'. In this ballad a woman successfully defends herself in a castle keep, killing three assailants with well-aimed arrows.[39] 'Sheath and Knife' (a close variation upon 'The Laird of Logie') displays the latter since it has a woman discovering that she is pregnant by her brother, so that their mutual torment is only ended by her begging him to end her life with a smartly dispatched arrow.[40] Self-defence is also evident in the behaviour of the heroine of 'The Outlandish Knight' who outwits his murderous intent, pushing him in the water where he has previously drowned other women.[41] Although not in Child, 'The Farmer's Daughter', named Mary, portrays a woman refusing the unwanted attention of the local squire, killing him

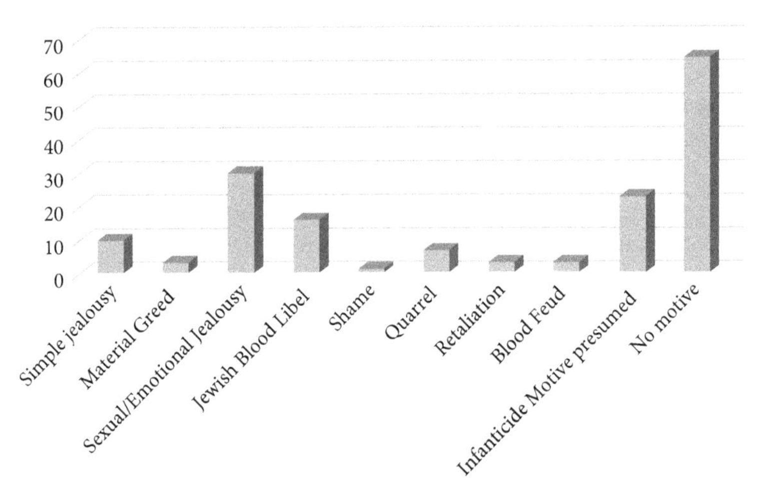


**Figure 2.1** Ballads in *Child's Popular Ballads of England and Scotland* by Motive for Women's Violence (Total Number of Ballads Listed Including Variations).

with a pistol and a sword. The reaction of her uncle puts her in peril since the death of the squire persuades him to seek the death of Mary. Before he can act, she shoots him with the remaining pistol and, in recognition of her skill and bravery, her uncle bequeaths his estate to Mary.[42] This ballad displays several elements of female initiative, agency, and the controlled use of violence turning around self-preservation and the defence of honour/chastity.

Within Child's collection, and beyond, women's violence appears with regularity. When we split these down in search of motives (see Figure 2.1), within each we can discern a figure amongst the total ballad sample (including variations) of thirty ballads with a motive of sexual/emotional jealousy and ten with motives of simple jealousy. The next most important category in this collection is the number of infanticides with explicitly stated motive. Beyond this there is a small number of ballads (all constituting single figures) that show evidence of material greed, of quarrels and retaliation (sometimes in the context of blood feuds), the motive of the Jewish blood libel, the latter's prevalence and notoriety distorting this particular sample. Of especial note here is the significantly large and notable number of ballads containing female violence which do not have a motive mentioned or even hinted at. Within Child the total number of ballads (with variations upon some ballads) that contain a female motive for violence totals thirty-nine examples. Within this same sample the total number of ballads (with variations upon some ballads) that contain no motive for violence is a quite significant sixty-five examples.

Ballads that display sexual and/or emotional jealousy are exemplified by 'Queen Eleanor's Confession' which focuses upon the apocryphal actions of Eleanor of Aquitaine, representing a dialogue between the ballad form and the historical record. Eleanor is described as having poisoned the King's mistress (Fair Rosamund) and confessing to adultery with the Earl Marshall. This circle of infamy is completed by the portrayal of her mixing poison with which to kill the King. Whilst artistic licence is taken here with history, Eleanor's motive for murdering Rosamund would have been known plainly to most if not all audiences and understood accordingly.[43]

Infanticide appears regularly in the ballad context and perhaps a typical example is 'Mary Hamilton', in which a woman convicted of this crime toasts well-wishers on her way to execution. In some versions, this occurs on top of Edinburgh Toll Booth, augmented by a coda which includes a shaming of the infanticidal mother.[44] Taken together, these two straight morality tales would appear to offer a strict line portraying a thoroughly moral universe—one in which women's behaviour is censured and brought to a secure resolution by their circumstances or conscience. Yet even this set of ballads has some wild card versions which fail to ensure this message is obvious or conveyed at all. The 'shaming' episode which occurs in Version B of the latter ballad is put into the mouth of Mary Hamilton, a woman who is described as made pregnant by the King at court. Her eventual appearance on the gallows prompts the King to save her and offer marriage; a proposition which is declined by a defiant Mary who declares that her scaffold shaming could have been prevented by him, ensuring a tragic and inevitable dénouement.[45] Version E even has a positive resolution with the father of her child (this time a noble) enticing her down from the gallows whilst offering a well-funded elopement, which it appears may well be accepted by a grateful, rescued, and rehabilitated Mary.[46] Simple jealousy is displayed by ballads such as 'Young Hunting' in which a man (Young Hunting) tells his wife or paramour that there is a another woman who he loves 'thrice better than thee'. Her reaction is to give Young Hunting a deep wound which he eventually dies from. Some versions have the woman reproached by a bird with a wholly moral comeuppance communicated at the end, whilst others merely catalogue the events leading up the murder, or dwell significantly upon the disposal of the body.[47]

The lesser category of material greed is evident in ballads such as 'Bonny Annie'. Other ballads portray less common motivations for violence including female retaliation against marital cruelty. This is exemplified by 'The Laird of Wariston' where a woman retaliates after her husband lashes out at her, except her reaction is so forceful that she kills him. This becomes the pretext for her to lament that, whilst he married her for love, she had married him for money and the ballad thus becomes a morality tale with the message 'maids take heed'.[48] Revenge appears in a small number of ballads. In 'The Fire of Frendruahgt' which appears to be a single episode in an enduring blood feud, a woman burns down a castle with a male occupant within it and the ballad has him crying to the woman 'first your husband killed my father, and now you burn his son'.[49]

In many of these ballads there is an evident comeuppance. For those women who stepped outside social or gender norms, most ballads in broadsides and many ballads have them meet a sticky end of some description and there is justice afforded to them in some way. This was a key message from broadsides in particular and aimed to reinforce gender norms. Ultimately these are female gendered, like-minded, companions of male criminal dying speeches which were imbibed with religious language, emphasizing the appropriateness of the punishment to be inflicted.[50]

Whilst much of what has been described veers between explicable motive for violence and more widely accepted performance of forms of female identity, we must now examine the category of apparently motiveless female violence in these ballads. Examples of this include 'The Twa Sisters', which is a ballad that appears widely in a number of collections in Scotland, England, and Wales and on the other side of the Atlantic.[51] Its plot portrays a series of apparently random acts of violence perpetrated upon one of the sisters mentioned in the title. The narrative commences with two 'little' sisters 'marching down the stream' when one sister pushes the other into the stream with the ambiguous words 'I'll be true to my true love because she was kind to me'.[52] The unfortunate sister proceeds to, by turns, sink and swim before sucklessly drifting downstream where she finds herself at the mercy of a malevolent miller. This man rescues her to rob her of her gold, concluding this action by pushing her back in to the stream where she drowns. Justice is served in the final verse, however, where the miller is 'hung on the gallows so high' whilst the same fate befalls the surviving sister with the same refrain uttered on pushing her sister into the stream 'I'll be kind to my true love because she was kind to me.' The actions of the male miller transparently focus upon theft and murder in pursuit of gain. Yet the motives of the malevolent sister are a mystery. The singer of the ballad as well as its audience are left to ponder her motive or potentially even to speculate that such motive might be absent.

This particular narrative was Anglicized in the 'Bonny Bows of London' which has a more elaborate plotline which suggests the two sisters were of royal blood. This involves the drowned sister's bones and entrails being made into a fiddle (in some versions this is a harp) which then plays to the King. The fiddle is only capable of playing one tune which implicates the guilty sister. Whilst she meets the same fate, once again the malevolent sister's actions appear to be without motive. In the Lucy Broadwood collection, *English Country Songs,* this plotline is in a ballad titled 'The Barkshire Tragedy' which has the miller meeting his fate as described earlier, although the guilty daughter escapes beyond the seas to eventually 'die an old maid among black savages'.[53]

The ballad 'The Cruel Mother', sometimes also known in Scotland and in other versions as 'Bonnie St Johnstone', portrays a woman's interaction with two babies. In 'The Cruel Mother' the woman travels to her father's house where she meets two babies who swiftly identify themselves as reincarnations of two children that she has previously killed. The woman herself appears to show no remorse for her actions and proceeds to ask them to tell her fortune. Justice appears in the reply that she receives from them when she is told that she shall be 'Alone, alone and lonely' for 'Seven long years... The rest of your life you'll spend in hell'.[54] 'Bonnie St Johnstone' has the same essential plotline but has earlier verses describing the former murder of the babies. In most versions of this ballad the mother routinely and clinically slits the throats of the infants. In both 'The Cruel Mother' and 'Bonnie St Johnstone', the woman is judged by her own murdered children and this invariably leads to punishment in the hereafter. Whilst a moral universe prevails in the comeuppance, in both versions of the ballad there is a total absence of female motive on display. There are no hints of poverty nor of a troubled mind, the latter only notably emerging once her fate in the life beyond is communicated.[55]

'Love Henry' (which also claims to be a variation of the earlier cited 'Young Hunting') portrays a young woman greeting her true love (Henry), asking him to stay the night. Upon his refusal, she promptly wounds him with a pen knife so grievously that he declares 'there's no physician under the sun can cure my bleeding wound'. A nearby parrot perched upon a willow tree adversely comments upon the young woman's perverse actions, and she then threatens the bird with the same fate.[56] This particular ballad has no element of retributive justice in it at all and, like other ballads mentioned here, there is no explanation for the overly extreme reaction of the woman who fatally wounded her paramour.

'Lord Thomas and Fair Annet' (sometimes 'Lord Thomas and Fair Eleanor' or simply 'Lord Thomas') portrays a love triangle between a Lord, a propertied 'brown girl', and 'Fair Ellender' who is penniless.[57] After encouragement from his mother, the Lord marries the 'brown girl' who is then publicly slighted by 'Fair Ellender' at the wedding feast. The result is the 'brown girl's' fatal stabbing of 'Fair Ellender' and retribution in the shape of summary execution for the 'brown girl' at the hands of her husband.[58] No woman emerges with moral credit from this particular ballad, but at least some motive appears to be implied even if it is not spelt out. Nonetheless, such violence bubbling so close to the surface, and the disregard for the consequences of using it, is also noteworthy. In a similar context, the ballad 'Prince Robert' portrays a man asking for his mother's blessing upon his recent wedding. This is refused and her response is instead to poison him, with no motive being stated and no comeuppance.[59] 'Lord Rendal' has the central character poisoned with a dish of eels by (according to the version concerned) his true love or his grandmother.[60] This particular ballad is conspicuous for its central preoccupation with random female violence that is foisted upon various women with different roles and status.

Nurses, supposed paragons of female nurturing, get a significantly bad press in these ballads. 'The Duke of Athole's Nurse' takes the role of hiding a fugitive man but then promptly betrays him into the hands of three pursuers, both contradictory actions apparently without motive.[61] The most widely known murder ballad from both Child and elsewhere is 'Lamkin', 'Lankin', or 'Long Lankin'. This exists in a veritable kaleidoscope of versions with a quite staggering range of motives for violent actions discussed and articulated. Several have the nurse as an accomplice to 'Long Lankin' who intends burglary and to slaughter the lady and the young child of the master of the house who has done him an unforgiveable wrong. In some versions the nurse presumes she will become mistress of the house after the current incumbent is murdered, in another she is taking revenge for her poor treatment at the mistress' hands. In one version, the nurse rudely inserts a bolt up the baby's nose! Some versions of the ballad have the two criminals meet their comeuppance, with the nurse hanged and 'Long Lankin' boiled in a cauldron, although in others the punishments are reversed. There is also a significant number of versions of this ballad in which the nurse has no motive mentioned in the text at all.[62] Of the ballads outlined, we have evidence of a number of these being sung in localities throughout England during the nineteenth century.[63] The Scottish contingent of ballads would also have been spread by the presence of Scottish, and to a lesser extent Irish, singers either living in, or passing though, English communities.[64]

Beyond the Child collection, some ballads which can be located specifically to a certain area or place also contain didactic elements and seek to describe female violence as being at the behest of men. In a privately printed collection from 1851, a ballad titled 'A Yorkshire Tragedy' constitutes a warning to female children and parents alike against being seduced from the straight and narrow by the greed and treachery of others. A suitor for a married couple's youngest daughter blackmails the daughter by demanding that the family's estate be bestowed upon him, whilst at the same time threatening to withdraw the marriage offer if this is not complied with. After stridently rejecting this the daughter 'yielded to the Devil's will' and poisoned her father and brothers. From there she contrived to implicate her own mother in the poisoning and thence the mother is prepared for execution by burning at the stake. At the very last minute, the daughter is overcome with guilt and throws herself onto the pyre as an act of atonement.[65] This ballad is noticeable as a further example of men coercing women into wrongdoing.

The significant appearance of female violence in ballads (both motivated and unmotivated) is in considerable contrast to its level of appearance in the broadsides present in the John Johnson Collection. This collection could be considered reasonably representative since, when amalgamated with the other broadsides contained in the Bodleian, it constitutes an archive of approximately 30,000 items.[66] In this large sample, there is an almost complete absence of female violence. This is also puzzling since Roud has suggested that '90 to 95 per cent of the items the Victorian and Edwardian collectors noted as "folk songs" had appeared as broadsides in the eighteenth and nineteenth century'. The only recognizable examples of female violent behaviour that match anything in the Francis James

Child collection are the five versions of 'The Outlandish Knight' and nine versions of the 'Lord Thomas and Fair Eleanor' ballads. Instead female behaviour tends to conform to the recognized series of submissive and bucolic stereotypes. This contrast with the ballad material is striking and requires explanation.

## Why did She Do That? Ballads and Motiveless Female Violence: Their Significance and Implications

So why does the representation of women and their behaviour in broadsides seem so tame, whilst the representation in ballads seems so different and ambivalent. Broadsides were popular and were an urban phenomenon that addressed markets, yet many were also officially sanctioned and may have sought to spread specific establishment-friendly messages.[67] Equally, as we have suggested, ballads themselves constituted some form of market. It may be that the two forms addressed different sectors of the market. Equally it may be that the broadside, with its obvious cost to the consumer, sought to pitch its message at a more refined and elevated level. The implications of this latter suggestion might be that this potentially embourgeoised the narrative song market and canon. If this were so, this was a process that made women into passive beings within the world it portrayed. Male violence within the John Johnson collection is commonplace and even normalized, as it is also in ballad material.[68]

If the John Johnson collection is unrepresentative of a wider canon we should remember that consumption and performance of this violent material does exist and must therefore be considered seriously. Perhaps the most likely explanation is that broadside collections somehow sought to neglect the phenomenon of female violence and its perpetration. Quite what the motive for this might be is unclear. Advocates of the 'Civilizing Process' will have three answers to this conundrum. Those who produced such broadsides may have actively eschewed female violence as subject matter, or the subsequent collection of such broadsides itself may have entailed an ideologically motivated editing process that has unfortunately left no footprint for posterity. Our third alternative, favoured by some historians, is to consider that a silence prevailed over female violence since it could not be adequately explained.[69] Alternative explanations that turn around taste may provide other avenues of enquiry, but these do not necessarily explain the phenomenon entirely.

What now should we make of the numerous ballads, and different versions of some, that portray female violence whilst stating no motive, and how should we seek to analyse them? These ballads may not have contained motive in the first place, since they were conceived of as entertainment and were less likely to do the ideologically improving work of some broadsides that contained ballads. The natural attrition of stories moving from place to place, and from individual to individual, might be another plausible explanation for this. Alternatively it may be that some regional and/or individual tastes accounted for which elements survived in a narrative and which did not. Although it is difficult to believe that motives in these ballads came to be left out as a matter of deliberate choice or policy, the vague possibility nonetheless does remain. It would also seem strange for the moral message within the ballad in question to have been precisely the phenomenon singularly removed without trace. In comparison many broadsides scrupulously maintain such moral messages within them, despite space constraints. Indeed it should be argued that species of moral warning and didactic content were a systematic staple of the genre. The John Johnson/Bodleian collections contain a significant number of these, with a category all of their own whose titles begin with the portentous words 'A Warning to....'[70]

We might first conclude that the female motives potentially contained within some of these ballads have been somehow 'lost' in their transfer from person to person, and from singer to singer. However, this scarcely explains the discovery of a substantial number of surviving collected and catalogued ballads where other versions of the same ballad equally show no motive—can it really be the case that the removal of motive was either systematic or total? Even if versions of these ballads did simply 'lose' their motive, we have to consider that these 'new' motiveless versions of such ballads survived nonetheless, to be assimilated and consumed by populations at large. Many sang, listened to, and read the texts of ballads where female cruelty and violence happened without motive, and these narratives lasted long enough to be acquired by song collectors in the second half of the nineteenth century.

If the explanation is different, however, then some other possible conclusions might be drawn. If deliberate textual intervention were involved in the construction of these ballads, or the editing of them, then our analysis of motiveless violence might now be rather different. Did authors, singers, and disseminators of such ballads actively want episodes of women's violence to appear as motiveless? If so they constructed a Manichaean universe where evil simply happened. It was not that violence was governed or dictated by gender makeup or by behavioural norms—thus all such ballads contained extraordinary actions which may simply in particular instances have been enacted by women. Perhaps the women who potentially emerge from these narratives are simply a female counterpart of the marshal, royal, and quasi-military male violence embraced by honour codes and cultures. Such violence, either at the ballad's inception or in its subsequent transfer forward in time, had thus become commonplace and either devoid of explanation, or indeed it was considered unnecessary to provide an explanation.

This possibility indicates that, if true, these ballads in contrast to the content of broadsides were still, into the nineteenth century, resisting civilising, bourgeois, and gendered approaches to the depiction of behaviour. This potentially indicates that the violent woman of the motiveless ballad is a challenge to conventional views of female behaviour generally, but especially around the committal of crime and the perpetration of violence. Even if this is a step too far, we must remind ourselves that several generations were nonetheless brought up on this picture of women and their behaviour irrespective of its intention or cause. Perhaps this latter conclusion is indeed the most significant of all, since it indicates a fundamental mismatch between gendered bourgeois civilizing values and those portrayed in the most widely consumed popular media of the nineteenth century. We can only speculate on the impact and influence of narratives of women engaged in motiveless violence upon several generations of women (and indeed men), both before and during the nineteenth century.[71]

There may also be a valid question of periodization. Certainly broadsides competed with ballads for people's attention by the nineteenth century. An interest in gender stereotypes and explanations for female violence may only have been firmly discussed in the nineteenth century when broadsides were much more popular. So it might make more sense that broadside ballads would be where explanations for female violence were found, articulated, and indeed contrasted with social norms. Yet this still leaves motiveless ballads in use and capable of collection at the end of the nineteenth century.

Certainly these women and men would have been faced with narratives where women establish and use agency in pursuit of goals that are not circumscribed by social norms, or judgements. But what of the supposedly essential moral message in such narratives? Certainly we can find ballads where motiveless acts of violence by women do attract the opprobrium of an audience, either within the ballad itself or projected to those consuming the ballad and its content. Others carry both this and a comeuppance that might detract from the female agency on view, whilst also restoring some semblance of a functioning moral universe—the apparently classic morality tale, such as 'The Bonny Hind' or 'Mary Hamilton'. Equally there are also a number of this category of motiveless ballad that have no moral resolution against the violent perpetrator. Here we are obviously tempted to think of the potentially ambivalent or nihilistic message imbibed by any audience encountering such narratives.

Media reception scholars use a variety of models to portray the impact of mass media upon the individual. These include behaviourism, psychoanalysis, cognitive psychology, functionalism, and Conflict Theory. Whilst their approaches differ, their work has shaped the debate about mass media effects, asking questions about identity, the passivity versus activity of the viewer, and the influence of text in how this might 'cause' specific reactions.[72] it is certainly possible that some of these investigations might be appropriate to the consumption of ballad material. Ultimately as historians we want to know how our audiences for these portrayals of women might have responded and acted. One path already trodden by cultural historians is to use functionalist approaches that also nod to psychoanalysis. Of particular pertinence to the subject of ballads is the approach of Robert Darnton, drawing upon insights from Bruno Bettelheim. This argues that fairy tales and fictional narratives perform psychological functions for individuals. Such individuals had their favourite tales, and these ostensibly parcelled up and mediated human concerns about rites of passage and potential psychological trauma through the repetition of narratives.[73] Whilst there is no obvious proof that ballads and their consumption can be 'read' in the same way, their status as facets of popular culture means individuals would be capable of using them in the manner described by Darnton and Bettelheim.

Beyond this, we can only speculate about the impact of messages about motiveless violence. Did ambivalence add to the entertainment value intrinsic to these ballads in performance? Did this give them self-evident shock value when presenting an audience with a malevolent and amoral universe? Was the absence of female motive a method of drawing the audience further into the world the ballad portrayed, and why is this potential experience so different from the experience of consuming broadsides? One tentative answer to this very last question might be to question precisely why there are so few of such stories and plotlines evident in the collections of broadsides that we know about. As we are aware, broadside publication was intensely market-led, so that this reflected at least urban public taste to an extremely close degree. If songs containing motiveless violence were a central part of public taste, then perhaps there might be more concerted evidence of this within broadside collections. However, we must also consider that the printed nature of broadsides created constraints that may have been addressed by ignoring motive. Nonetheless, the anomaly of the different treatment of female agency and violence within ballads and broadsides is suggestive.

If we now concentrate upon the phenomenon of motiveless female violence solely in ballads, we are still left asking other questions. Did these ballads instead invite audiences to mentally 'write in' a presumed motive for female violence? Was this something done from family history/experience or from knowledge of their own locality, or perhaps from their own reading or knowledge of other genres and depictions of women. If so such creation of a presumed motive was scarcely controlled, consistent, stable, or reliable. Most importantly of all, it would not necessarily support, condone, or indeed even preface any middle- or upper-class project of codifying, defining, and regulating the behaviour of women. If the ballads lacked motive they may have been capable of inspiring independent thought about how and why women may have perpetrated violence, drawing upon experience and reality as much as imagined knowledge or behavioural ideals.[74]

Much of this obviously poses further questions and presumption, rather than sustained evidence, and caution must be used to go any further distance. However, clues remain about how contemporary society responded to the perceived dangers offered by the ballads with no moral explanation. Some folksong collectors actively created motive where it was otherwise absent, communicating this in the anthologies they published. As such, they rationalized and brought wayward narratives into the typology of the other ballads with clear motive. John Harland's 1875 collection *Ballads and Songs of Lancashire* contained two ballads with motiveless female violence which also appeared in Child's *Popular Ballads*. The ballad listed as 'The Radcliffe Tragedy of Fair Ellen' reiterates the version present in Child. The heroine listed in the title is described by the introduction as murdered because of the 'malice and cupidity of a stepmother'.[75] Similarly this collection also contains a version of 'The Three Sisters' familiar from Child and as 'The Bonny Bows of London'. As we know, almost all versions of the ballad have the eldest sister pushing the youngest in the swirling and fast moving stream without apparent motive. Alongside this titled version is a very similar ballad titled 'The Miller and the King's Daughter', which repeats the narrative of 'The Three Sisters' (and 'The Bonny Bows of London'). In introducing the ballad, the editor included the comment that it was described as 'said by "Seleucas" to belong to South Lancashire [and] has the merit of telling consistently a tragedy of sisterly envy and jealousy'.[76] Harland had earlier produced another, even less adventurous volume of ballads that he had collected which carries little or no female agency, and indeed includes a whole extensive section which idealized ballad women solely as the love object of men.[77]

This civilizing project appears in the numerous works of the Revd Sabine Baring-Gould, whose collections often seem devoid of female violence at all, never mind apparently motiveless violence.[78] In the world of Baring-Gould there is not much beyond bucolic pastoral idyll and women are generally placed in sanitized, safe, and subordinate milkmaid/shepherdess roles. These eventually found their way into many literary forms in which the genre of folksong was repackaged for popular markets. Taking this genre into schools to make an indigenous folk culture live again was one of the missionary objectives undertaken by Baring-Gould and Cecil Sharp.[79]

After viewing the Baring-Gould packaging of folksong in the volumes intended for adults, one might expect a still more intensive drawing of the sting from the whole canon of folksong, and the passive and safe depiction of female protagonists within these songs. Strangely, the selection of the material for children emerges as a good deal more ambivalent. Amidst some of the ballads with classically passive pastoral women, there are some which display women with considerable degrees of agency, some of it clearly malevolent. 'Lord Rendal' is reproduced with its tale of a knight poisoned by eating eels fed to him by his sweetheart. 'The Outlandish Knight' also appears here, with its portrayal of a woman successfully resisting the violent intentions of a man. The collection also contains 'Lord Thomas and Fair Eleanor', with its tale of jealousy, venom, and death here presented undiluted for a young audience.[80]

With the sheer and considerably visible range of ballads that display episodes of apparently motiveless female violence, it becomes evident that these should not be considered in a cultural vacuum. The legal perspective on women's violent behaviour inevitably interrogated the concept of insanity. As many historians have noted, this concept was constantly debated and remained in a serious degree of flux throughout the nineteenth century and the wider period in question.[81] Obviously linking these two very different occurrences together may involve considerable elements of speculation and guesswork. Was it the case that this apparently blank space exists in many of these ballads because popular judgement upon women's motivations to violence and its connection to insanity was problematic for singers and audiences? Alternatively, how many of the female psychological maladies ascribed to them in the nineteenth century were presumed simply without comment, allowing audiences to draw their own conclusions? Would a much deeper analysis of the descriptive language used in these ballads supply some rather different answers? Might these ballads represent a potentially individual, and perhaps even collective, popular dialogue upon women's behaviour?

Beyond this, deeper research might reveal how contemporary beliefs became reflected in some of these ballads. Some sentiments and beliefs might equally be mapped by noting the moment of collection alongside the summative history of ideas and contemporary judgements associated with women's insanity. Such an analysis might note some differences between versions of the same ballad collected for posterity at different times. How far might these reflect new insights creeping into popular perceptions of women's violent behaviour? Alternatively, might we witness these popular ballads maintaining older perceptions, or creating a 'mixed motive economy' of older and newer conceptions of women's behaviour? Might this also possibly also comprise part of a matrix that includes (for want of a better term) 'folk discourses' in dialogue with more professional and officially gendered narratives? Could these also be filtered through other facets of popular culture such as newspapers and other popular media? A still further alternative might be to observe the maintenance of the motiveless blank space that makes the ballad a potentially discursive area for debating, eventually resolving, and assimilating the behaviour of women in and around violence.

If we were to rely upon these ballads for our picture of what eighteenth- and nineteenth-century society thought of violence, and the women who perpetrated it, without our knowledge of official sources, we would perhaps encounter a world stripped of the moral categories and certainties of official commentators. This would also be beyond the law which passes judgement upon all who act beyond social and cultural norms—whether men or women. If these ballads had influence at all, then popular reactions to the violent behaviour of women appeared to be more ambivalent, discursive, and perhaps more open-minded, or even tolerant, than official accounts and more elite sources tend to portray. Indeed, the opportunity and cultural spaces to think through what motivated women to acts of violence seem to have been in plain sight after all, manifested in popular ballad culture.

This last speculative section has emphatically posed more questions than sustained answers. Nevertheless, by doing so it has opened a window onto the possibilities that lie within these historical sources when they are used to investigate popular attitudes to extreme forms of female motivation. Hopefully, this also serves as a valuable reminder of how far popular understandings, narratives, and discourses can differ from the more readily studied and understood professional and moral discourses. In these latter framings we are obviously aware of agendas, ideal types, and deliberate constructions of gendered ideals, as well as spectacular aberrations from these. Looking at more popular forms of culture such as ballads can give us a rather different picture. These customary forms show a much wider, less constrained and less readily explicable range of behaviour around the violence perpetrated by women. These reactions may not turn to sympathy, admiration, or celebration—but they do at least indicate studied and cautious ambivalence.

The later collectors working on the cusp of modernity brought new initiatives to bear, but the supposed 'moralizers' necessary for a 'civilizing process' found themselves working alongside 'rescuers' and 'completists' whose efforts contradicted and potentially cancelled out their own. Thus, raw male violence flourished in these works, and was never purged from view by any potential 'civilizing process'. As some argue, depictions of male violence actually flourished during this period.[82] But the failure of this has equally left us with a legacy and footprint of motive-driven *and* motiveless female violence. Both of these last two phenomena also ask questions about the wider role of female violence that survived for audiences in this genre. Was it indicative of a much wider discussion of the nature of female criminality that survives now only in glimpses? Such directionless violence points to an ambivalence that appears when placing so many of these ballads alongside one another. This also makes the polarities of overarching 'civilizing projects', or forms of dogged and determined sub-cultural resistance to apparent improvement, equally difficult to either coherently explain or sustain.

## Conclusion

However desperate official discourses were to categorize and classify female behaviour and its consequences, it was popular cultural reactions that may have unwittingly propagated a narrative that such matters were unfortunately (or indeed fortunately) not nearly as simple as that. For once popular culture may have spread a more nuanced, sophisticated, and arguably more civilizing outlook than learned professional and legal cultures. The latter have often been found wanting when faced with the imperatives of regulation, control, and the upholding of morality. What now becomes clear is that the singing, hearing, and reading of ballads gave the nineteenth-century populace a rounded picture and image of women and the violence they were capable of. This leads to the inevitable conclusion that such violent behaviour and its contemplation by consumers of ballads was in some senses more evidently near the surface and ultimately normalized than we have hitherto appreciated.

The conclusion of most media reception studies of violence is that the cause/effect relationship cannot be established with anything resembling academic rigour.[83] It is also likely that establishing such a relationship in the distant past between violent content in nineteenth-century ballads and its potential inspiration of subsequent violence is a project which might founder very quickly. However, media reception theory can be more forthcoming around the issue of role models. This has inspired a disciplinary shift from examining alleged 'causes' and 'effects' of media, to instead focus upon their 'uses'.[84] Observers of modern media are relatively convincing in their conclusions that film and television media are often (though importantly not always) utilized by individuals to construct identities and moral outlooks.[85] Certainly, it was also true that consulting audiences brought forth surprising revelations about how such audiences constructed heterogeneous meanings from the same text.[86] Whilst we obviously have no proof of this happening with nineteenth-century ballads, such self and moral fashioning may nonetheless have occurred for individuals in some cases throughout the period in question. The possible consideration of this phenomenon may well alter our view of the censorious and bowdlerizing influence of folksong collectors, and their motives, in the latter half of the nineteenth century.

Indeed did some of our moralising folksong collectors (barring some exceptions already mentioned) actually exhibit some proto-media reception ideas of their own, potentially staving off some dangerous messages that the canon of folk ballads otherwise contained. We have speculated about what this canon seemed to potentially say about women, but it may be worth considering what such a canon said about the nature of the whole moral universe. Did such motive-hunting folksong collectors think beyond the portrayal of women to contemplate the potential random nature of the moral universe? How far might they have seen this as inherently unstable and dangerous for the maintenance of wider morality and the narratives that sustained this? In this we might be glancing at a fear of what the lower orders made of narratives of violence, whether remote and implausible, or credible and close at hand. Indeed, does the sometimes random universe of the ballad stimulate imagined concerns about how these ambivalent narratives are actually consumed, a 'dark moral panic' in the making?

Media reception studies' arguments about the potential function of texts emphatically tell us that no text can any longer be regarded as neutral. Thus, any investigation of ballads and their content ought to be aware of their possible effects upon consumers of the medium. That media might reinforce values, provide escape, or construct sites of cultural resistance and their appropriation to a wide variety of cultural tasks must be entertained.[87] Whatever the outcome, it must be considered that the ambivalence of the genre taken as a whole conceivably had an effect, or a series of effects, upon those audiences exposed to it.

Given all of this, scholars need to further contemplate the multifarious impacts that the portrayal of motiveless female violence in so many of these ballads may have had upon men and women of this period. At the very least, we must acknowledge that anyone who thought about the ballads they were hearing either accepted the messages within them, negotiated their meaning for their own individual context, or constructed oppositional reactions. If these ballads had any influence at all, then it is not stereotypes of women that now need to be studied, but instead our view of how stereotypes are and were constructed in the historical past. Perhaps indeed it is us who, hitherto, have been the blinkered and biased audience, one involved in the construction of less than helpful stereotypes of past historical actors and how they receive and respond to the media to which they are exposed.

## Notes

1. See K. Bates (2014) 'Empathy and Entertainment? The Form and Function of Violent Crime Narratives in Early-Nineteenth Century Broadsides', *Law Crime and* History, 4, 2, pp. 1–27.
2. For an introduction to broadsides and their song content see S. Roud (2017) *Folksong in England* (London: Faber & Faber), pp. 431–6. See also P. Fumerton (2021) *The Broadside Ballad in Early Modern England: Moving Media, Tactical Publics* (Philadelphia: University of Pennsylvania Press) and P. Fumerton and A. Guerrini (2010) (eds) *Ballads and Broadsides in Britain, 1500–1800* (Farnham: Ashgate).
3. C. J. Bearman (1997) 'Resources in the Vaughan Williams Memorial Library: The Lucy Broadwood Collection: An Interim Report', *Folk Music Journal*, 7, 3, pp. 357–65 at p. 362. See also D. Harker (1981) 'Francis James Child and the "Ballad Consensus"', *Folk Music Journal*, 4, 2, pp. 146–64 at p. 148.
4. Bowdlerization is the rewriting of texts to remove obscene, sexual, or offensive material, leaving the text effectively sanitized.
5. See F. Place (1972) *The Autobiography of Francis Place, 1771–1854,* ed. Mary Thale (Cambridge: Cambridge University Press).
6. Roud, *Folksong in England*, p. 549. Roud's is the most recent comprehensive survey of the area and does not investigate the phenomenon of violence, still less female violence in folksong.
7. Ibid., p. 550. Roud notes that Cecil Sharp saw this as exemplifying a wider tendency within the genre: 'The keynote of folk poetry…is simplicity and directness without subtlety.' This phrase is from C. Sharp (1907) *English Folk-Song: Some Conclusions* (London: Simpkin & Co.). Roud also notes that textual intervention did occur in other contexts beyond expressions of sexuality—see p. 54.
8. Roud, *Folksong in England*, pp. 550 and 97.
9. N. Elias (2000) *The Civilizing* Process, tr. E. Jephcott (Oxford: Wiley Blackwell).

10. For a discussion of ballads, class, and sensibilities see M. J. Bell (1988) '"No Borders to the Ballad Maker's Art": Francis James Child and the Politics of the People', *Western Folklore*, 47, 4, pp. 285–307 at pp. 289–90 and 294–5.
11. See e.g. (amongst many others) R. Anderson (1815) *Ballads in the Cumbrian Dialect* (Wigton: E. Rook); A. G. Gillington (1907) *Eight Hampshire Folk Songs: Taken from the Mouths of the Peasantry* (London: Curwen); J. O. Halliwell (1851) *The Yorkshire Anthology: A Collection of Ancient and Modern Ballads, Poems and Songs Relating to the County of Yorkshire*(London: n.p.); J. O. Halliwell (1852) *The Norfolk Anthology: A Collection of Poems, Ballads and Rare Tracts Relating to the County of Norfolk* (London: n.p.) and E. Waugh (1857) *Poems and Lancashire Songs* (London: Whittaker).
12. See e.g. G. Farquar-Graham (1884 edition) *The Popular Songs of Scotland* (Glasgow: J. Muir Wood) and L. Broadwood and J. A. Fuller Maitland (1892) (eds) *English County Songs* (London: Cramer). For an American collection see E. Moore and C. O. Moore (1966) *Ballads and Folk Songs of the Southwest: More than 600 Titles, Melodies, and Texts Collected in Oklahoma* (Oklahoma: University of Oklahoma Press).
13. See E. D. Gregory (2006) *Victorian Songhunters: The Recovery and Editing of English Vernacular Ballads and Folk Lyrics 1820–1883* (Oxford: Scarecrow Press), pp. 265–92. This lists themed collections dealing with localities, naval themes, specific trades, and politics broadly defined.
14. Examples of this abound in Child such as 'The Maid and the Palmer' (ballad 21), 'Long Lankin' (ballad 93), 'Sir Hugh and the Jew's Daughter (ballad 155), "Mary Hamilton" (ballad 173), 'Captain Car' (ballad 178), 'The Laird of Wariston' (ballad 196) all have preserved fragments included alongside the more or less complete and seemingly complete versions. See F. J. Child (1904) *The English and Scottish Popular Ballads* (5 vols) (London: Houghton & Mifflin).
15. J. Staiger (2005) *Media Reception Studies* (London: New York University Press), p. 2.
16. Ibid.
17. See Bates, 'Empathy and Entertainment?', *passim* and especially A. Fox (2011) 'The Emergence of the Scottish Broadside Ballad in the Late Seventeenth and Early Eighteenth Centuries', *Journal of Scottish Historical Studies*, 31, 2, pp. 169–94. This article indicates the function of ballads in broadsides as political propaganda to serve Scottish interests.
18. See examples of this in A.-M. Kilday (2007) *Women and Violent Crime in Enlightenment Scotland* (London: Boydell & Brewer); C. Conley (2020) *Debauched, Desperate, Deranged; Women Who Killed, London 1674–1913* (Oxford: Oxford University Press) and S. D'Cruze (1998) *Crimes of Outrage: Sex, Violence and Victorian Working Women* (London: Routledge).
19. Child, *English and Scottish Popular Ballads*. This is most easily approached online through the Kindle edition.
20. The Roud Index is housed in the Vaughan-Williams Memorial Library at the English Folk Song and Dance Society. <https://www.vwml.org/component/content/article/20-vwml-site/vwml-help-pages/256-roud-index-guide>.
21. See n. 41, 42, 52 53, 56, and 58 to this chapter.
22. The nineteenth century witnessed a particularly county-orientated focus upon folklore and folksong collecting.

23. See e.g. in Child's *English and Scottish Popular Ballads* 'King John and the Bishop' (Child ballad number 45, Roud number 302, Child ballad number 58, Roud number 41). Many of the ballad narratives surrounding Robin Hood also fall into this category.
24. See e.g. in Child's *English and Scottish Popular Ballads* 'Glasgerian' (Child ballad number 67), 'Clerk Sanders' (ballad number 69), 'Johnie Scott' (Child ballad number 99, Roud number 63) and 'Willie O' Couglas Dale' (Child ballad number 101, Roud number 65).
25. See the account in L. E. Broadwood and A. G. Gilchrist (1923) 'Songs of Crime and Prison Life', *Journal of the Folk Song Society*, 7, 27, pp. 41–9. Although dated to 1923, many of the items in this collection were collected in the very first years of the twentieth century and so were in circulation before this. It is also worth remembering that such themes were also commonplace in the more obviously 'one-off' single-sheet or single publication broadsides. But see also Lucy Broadwood's late nineteenth-century collection (n. 10) which has a more obviously eclectic mix and full variety of female violence mentioned within it.
26. See C. Sharp and L. Broadwood (1916) 'Narrative and Historical Ballads and Songs', *Journal of the Folk-Song Society*, 5, 20, pp. 253–67 at pp. 254–5 for their collected version of 'Sir Hugh' which has a female villain solely responsible for the innocent boy Hugh's demise. See also Broadwood and Fuller Maitland, *English County Songs*, p. 86, where the ballad is titled 'Little Sir William' and was collected from Lincolnshire.
27. Bell, 'No Borders', p. 297.
28. Ibid., pp. 286, 288, and 289.
29. Roud, *Folksong in England*, p. 114.
30. Ibid., pp. 321–40. This section describes regular pub and alehouse entertainment as well as setpiece events where singing was expected, such as sheep-shearing and harvest homes. Roud also notes the sheer ubiquity of the ballad singer who, like as not, sought to earn a living as much as entertain. Ballads and their performance were also seen by middle-class bystanders and moral improvers as an uncouth nuisance which potentially degraded the morals of the urban population—see also pp. 435 and 438.
31. Child, *English and Scottish Popular Ballads*, ballad number 32 and 35, Roud number 3967 and 3212.
32. Childballad number 53 with variations A–N (14 versions), Roud number 40.
33. Child ballad number 39 with variations A–N (15 versions—there are two variants of version 'J'), Roud number 35.
34. Child ballad number 50, this is also the plotline of 'The King's Dochter Lady Jean' at ballad number 52, Child ballad number 50, Roud number 205.
35. Child ballad number 182 with variations A–D (5 versions—there are two variants of version 'A'), Roud number 81. See also Broadwood and Fuller Maitland, *English County Songs*, pp. 60–1, for the ballad 'The Beautiful Damsel' which has the main protagonist shooting three robbers without any description of distinctive behaviour, courage, or fortitude.
36. Child, *English and Scottish Popular Ballads*, ballad number 150.
37. Child ballad number 106, Roud number 199.
38. D. Dugaw (1989) *Warrior Women and Popular Balladry, 1650–1850* (Cambridge: Cambridge University Press), p. 5.

39. Child ballad number 178 with variations A–I (9 versions), Roud number 80.
40. Child, ballad number 16 with variations A–F (6 versions), Roud number 3960.
41. Sometimes recorded as 'Lady Isabel and the Elf Knight', see Child ballad number 4 with variations A–G (7 versions), Roud number 21. See also Broadwood and Fuller Maitland, *English County Songs*, pp. 164–5.
42. Broadwood and Fuller Maitland, *English County Songs*, pp. 116–17 for 'The Farmer's Daughter', a variation on 'The Banks of the Sweet Dundee' (which also appears in the American *Songs from the South West*).
43. Child, *English and Scottish Popular Ballads* ballad number 156 with variations A–G (7 versions), Roud number 46. See also 'Binnorie or the Cruel Sister' for sisters squabbling murderously over a suitor. This appears to be a further variant upon 'The Twa Sisters' and 'Bonny Bows of London' as discussed by Gregory, *Victorian Songhunters*, pp. 371–2.
44. Child ballad number 173 with variations A–Bb (28 versions), Roud number 79.
45. Child, ballad number 173 version B.
46. Child, ballad number 173 versions E and F.
47. Child, ballad number 68 with variations A–K (11 versions), Roud number 47.
48. Child, ballad number 194 with variations A–C (3 versions), Roud number 3876.
49. Child ballad number 196 with variations A–E (5 versions).
50. See J. A. Sharpe (1985) '"Last Dying Speeches": Religion, Ideology and Public Execution in Seventeenth-Century England', *Past and Present*, 107, pp. 144–67.
51. Roud notes it in the collection from the West of England collected by Davies Gilbert (1767–1839); see Roud, *Folksong in England*, p. 67, and Child, *English and Scottish Popular Ballads*, ballad number 10, Roud number 8.
52. Moore and Moore, *Ballads and Folk Songs of the Southwest*, pp. 18–20. This American collection is included in this analysis because it reflects the wide reach of these ballads, which also appear in Child, throughout the English-speaking world. The introduction notes how the area was particularly colonized by Scottish emigrants in the nineteenth century.
53. Broadwood and Fuller Maitland, *English County Songs*, pp. 118–19.
54. Ibid., pp. 33–4. See also Child, *English and Scottish Popular Ballads*, ballad number 20, Roud number 9.
55. See also Gregory, *Victorian Songhunters*, pp. 379–80, for an Anglicized version of 'Bonnie St Johnstone' transposed to York and called 'Christ Made a Trance' and also alongside this, a version titled 'The Cruel Mother'. 'Christ Made a Trance' intriguingly uses a particular motiveless phrase in describing the murders of the children in that 'She did not care if they felt the smart'.
56. Moore and Moore, *Ballads and Folk Songs of the Southwest*, pp. 47–50.
57. Other versions of this ballad call the central female protagonist 'Eleanor'. Child, *English and Scottish Popular Ballads*, ballad number 73, Roud number 4.
58. Moore and Moore, *Ballads and Folk Songs of the Southwest*, pp. 51–3.
59. Child, *English and Scottish Popular Ballads*, ballad number 87 with variations A–D (4 versions), Roud number 55.
60. Child ballad number 12 with variations A–U (21 versions), Roud number 10.
61. Child, ballad number 212 with variations A–F (6 versions).
62. Child, ballad number 93 A–Y (25 versions), Roud number 6.

63. Roud's brief survey in chapter 9 and elsewhere in *Folksong in England* uncovered evidence of 'The Outlandish Knight', 'Lord Lovel', 'The Two Sisters', 'Lord Thomas and Fair Eleanor', and 'Lankin', see pp. 322, 333, 640, 641, and 645.
64. Ibid., pp. 327, 328–9, and 627.
65. Halliwell, *Yorkshire Anthology*, pp. 205–12.
66. Roud estimates that there may be as many as 500,000 separate versions of broadsides and that their 'golden age' was between the 1790s and the 1860s, see Roud, *Folksong in England*, pp. 433–4.
67. The John Johnson Collection of Ballads can be accessed at <http://ballads.bodleian.ox.ac.uk>.
68. See Roud, *Folksong in England*, pp. 631–3, for ballad material created in response to the infamous Maria Marten 'Red Barn' murder.
69. See n. 19.
70. The John Johnson Collection gives examples that warn (amongst others) 'young ladies', 'wicked livers', 'money hoarders', 'wicked sinners', 'disobedient children', 'all maidens', and 'all perjured young men'.
71. This is especially pertinent when we consider Carolyn Conley's assertion that popular culture genuinely could inform public reaction since 'Nineteenth-century accounts of women who killed often resorted to fictional models to describe the accused'. See C.A. Conley (2020) *Debauched, Desperate, Deranged: Women Who Killed, London 1674–1913* (Oxford: Oxford University Press), p. 203.
72. Staiger, *Media Reception Studies*, pp. 4–7.
73. R. Darnton (1999 edition) *The Great Cat Massacre* (New York: Basic Books), pp. 9–72.
74. It is pertinent to note here the apparent rarity of female violence that produced court cases as a proportion of the whole. This would potentially make female violence still more worthy of comment or of a search for motive. See Darnton, *Great Cat Massacre*, pp. 47–50.
75. J. Harland (1875) *Ballads and Songs of Lancashire*, corrected, revised, and enlarged by T. T. Wilkinson(London: George Routledge & Sons), p. 44.
76. Ibid., pp. 83–4.
77. J. Harland (1866) (ed.) *Lancashire Lyrics: Modern Songs and Ballads of the County Palatine* (London: Whittaker).
78. S. Baring-Gould (1895) *English Minstrelsie: A National Monument of English Song* (Felinfach: Llanerch); S. Baring-Gould and H. Fleetwood Sheppard (1895) *A Garland of Country Song: English Folk Songs with their Traditional Melodies* (London: Methuen) and S. Baring-Gould and H. Fleetwood Sheppard (1892) *Songs of the West: Traditional Ballads and Songs of the West of England: A Collection Made from the Mouths of the People* (London: Methuen). For a brief biography of Baring-Gould see Roud, *Folksong in England*, pp. 77 and 92–9.
79. See M. Hughes and R. Stradling (2001 edition) *The English Musical Renaissance 1840–1940: Constructing a National Music* (Manchester: Manchester University Press).
80. S. Baring-Gould and C. Sharp (1910) *English Folk-Songs for Schools* (London: Curwen & Sons), pp. 1–5 and 15–20. See also Roud, *Folksong in England*, pp. 128–31.
81. See e.g. H. Marland (2007) *Dangerous Motherhood: Insanity and Childbirth in Victorian Britain* (London: Palgrave); J. Eigen (2004) *Unconscious Crime: Mental*

*Absence and Criminal Responsibility in Victorian London* (Baltimore: Johns Hopkins University Press) and N. Walker and S. McCabe (1984) *The Historical Perspective; Crime and Insanity in England* (Edinburgh: Edinburgh University Press).

82. See e.g. J. Carter Wood (2004) *Violence and Crime in Nineteenth Century England: The Shadow of our Refinement* (London: Routledge).
83. Staiger, *Media Reception Studies*, pp. 166–9 and 173.
84. Ibid., p. 53.
85. Ibid., p. 34. Staiger notes a number of studies of content analysis seeking to deny or reinforce a range of stereotypes. Interestingly for our purposes one of these is a study by Martha Wolfstein and Nathan Leites who considered the construction of the 'good-bad girl' in Hollywood cinema of the 1940s. See M. Wolfstein and N. Leites (1977 edition) *Movies: A Psychological Study* (New York: Atheneum Press).
86. Staiger, *Media Reception Studies*, p. 54.
87. Ibid., p. 170.

# 3
# From the Handmaidens of Prometheus to the Heirs of Hypatia
## Women, Blasphemous Sedition, and Fashioning Ideological Agency

### Introduction

In Georgian society women of all classes were expected to accept and assume subordinate roles, and likewise to display deferential forms of respect to all forms of authority. This was mirrored through many social relationships with men, but also with institutions that maintained hierarchies of authority such as the law. The role of women within radicalism involved challenging some positions of subordination both within society and within the radical movements themselves. Women were considered to be auxiliaries, helpmeets, and allies to causes where men took the lead and also often took upon themselves the mantle of radical martyrdom. The women were intended to stay behind, maintaining a respectful distance from legal proceedings, and instead were often cast as the silent deferential martyr. They became individuals enduring privation alongside caring responsibilities for a family often suffering destitution caused by a man's absence.

Recently our understanding of Georgian marriage, domesticity, and the idealized role of women has become more nuanced. Amanda Vickery stated a patriarchal ideal in arguing: The married housewife was a pillar of wisdom and worth, with a prominent position in the hierarchical institution that society recognized as both normal and fundamental to social order, the male-headed conjugal unit.[1]

Only to qualify this a page later by suggesting:

> Married women were at once deferential wives and powerful mistresses, a conceptual inconsistency that women often manipulated to their advantage and a contradiction from which men often profited...a sexy battleaxe was what many busy men liked in practice—nimble, capable and commanding—to free them to pursue their own affairs without distraction.[2]

This latter quote indicates that women had more discursive power within Georgian marriage than has often been recognized. Elsewhere Vickery has noted

*Beyond Deviant Damsels: Re-evaluating Female Criminality in the Nineteenth Century.* Anne-Marie Kilday and David Nash, Oxford University Press.  DOI: 10.1093/oso/9780198830733.003.0003

the waning explanatory power of the concept of 'separate spheres'.[3] However the final epithet in the quote above indicates the apparent separateness of men and women's lives which would eventually give the appearance of them living in separate spheres. Moreover, it does reinforce the notion that the wives of artisans were expecting to organize the necessaries of life, however innovatively, to enable the household's men to pursue skilled or professional activity.[4] Likewise, the wives of middling and genteel men were expected to be skilled household managers, whilst skilled working men left a woman at home 'on garrison duty'.[5] Vickery also notes that the eighteenth-century ideal appointed women as potential arbiters of taste, taming the excesses of men. This was also believed to have a pan-class/status appeal which was augmented by the demonstration of domestic handicraft skill.[6]

Stepping back this appears to be combination of an organized domestic and familial contract where women were an enabling entity. They had freedom within roles that the social and economic system carved out for them, or on occasion it also allowed the colonization of less familiar roles, stepping into the breach to address the system's episodic failings. It was evident that artisans viewed their wives as providing external assistance to enable the success of male income-generating and even cultural pursuits. This point made by Anna Clark served to reconstruct the concept of separate spheres as a reactive male response to early nineteenth-century pressure on the artisan trades. This was a component paving the way for sharpened male and female perspectives upon the political radicalism Clark went on to describe, and the activism that resulted.[7]

This chapter suggests that this particular picture is somewhat overdrawn, especially if we go beyond consideration of some of the more obvious radical movements of the nineteenth century. By investigating the campaigns against the blasphemy laws, commenced in the early 1820s, we start to get a different picture of how some women chose to involve themselves in a radical movement and how, in doing so, they were making some fundamentally different choices.

The chapter investigates the phenomenon of female blasphemers in nineteenth-century Britain and their cultivated, active participation in this form of criminality of the mind. Before this period, the typical offender indicted for this crime was male.[8] In the period before the early eighteenth century, these offenders had been a considerable mix of the male population. Many historians associated this identity-gendered criminality with artisans, soldiers, and sailors, providing evidence for a blasphemous subculture related to masculine occupations.[9] Others have seen the spaces of the alehouse and the gambling house as places from which blasphemous activity and speech emanated as a form of consequence and overspill.[10] These latter incidents were involved in the opaque worlds of drunkenness and/or reckless gambling, and thus were instrumental in making blasphemy a gendered male offence, although the limited presence of some women here can be detected.[11] More obvious direct manifestations of female blasphemy before 1800 were associated with insanity or the 'inner light' subculture that clustered around antinomian or other deliberately dissolute religious groups.[12]

Previously, the very isolated appearances of these women as defendants in blasphemy prosecutions are as the manifestly insane (such as unfortunately deluded Susannah Fowles explored by David Lawton) or the charismatic Ranter prosecuted at the Old Bailey in 1676, who claimed variously to be God and the Holy Ghost![13] However, the late eighteenth century saw an important change whereby ideologically motivated offenders challenged the power and claims of established religion. These individuals, actively inspired by their engagement with radical texts, found the courtroom to be a profitable platform for publicizing and disseminating their views. In facing authority with studiously and carefully prepared defences, they acquired both considerable autonomy and also had access to a vast range of rhetorical and dramatic devices. Contemplating the press and published reporting of their case, whole episodes contain the flavour of a concerted and premeditated radical enterprise. Moreover, such enterprises seemed a worthy gamble since the workings and process of blasphemy cases in particular were quite unpredictable. Both the government and the private agencies that effectively sponsored such prosecutions could scarcely count on their unqualified success. Thus, both male and, as we shall discover, female freethinkers were able to use the uncertainty of proceedings to their advantage in creating an authentic oppositional voice that would be heard beyond the courtroom.

The case against Thomas Williams in 1797, for example, had provoked sympathy on the grounds of the destitution that had led him into selling blasphemous publications. This resulted in a highly publicized and quite embarrassing rebuke concerning the sustained cruelty of the prosecution directed at both the court and the Society for the Suppression of Vice. This came from none other than the prosecuting council Thomas Erskine.[14] The case against the renowned and skilful satirist William Hone in 1817 had proved still more instructive for the would-be radical defendant. Hone had parodied religious texts to take aim at other forms of the political and social establishment. The government decision to prosecute Hone was greatly ill judged and he was acquitted after running proverbial rings around the prosecution case. This did not happen before he had used a range of specific voices and precedents to argue his own case, becoming a revered radical hero in the process. Hone had produced a stylized defence which drew obviously upon enlightenment ideals of discovery and liberation, as well as mercilessly lampooning the pretensions of the morally righteous. He drew self-consciously upon leveller pamphleteers such as John Lillburne, whilst also portraying himself as a plain-speaking individual, benevolently bringing ideas into the light—an action juxtaposed with the dark and indistinct operation of the laws used against him.[15]

Appreciating and further developing such tools and opportunities gave the articulate and motivated considerable power and freedom of thought, strategy, and action. This freedom has left a considerable body of underexplored evidence, and for our purposes, its exploitation by a number of female radicals gives us the opportunity to consider in depth how they presented themselves and their arguments in these circumstances. What emerges from the study of the 1820s is that this confrontational situation meant that women radicals were able to escape from the gendered constraints imposed upon them by cultures of protest and radicalism which dealt in female radical stereotypes.

The evidence speaks of considerable female agency, energy, and verve. In places this is augmented by episodes of active and individual leadership. What is of considerable interest is the comparative absence of references to uniquely female or feminine stereotypes or related and specific modes of female expression. The radicalism of the women discussed emerges as identical to the same enlightenment ideals expressed by men. This at least qualifies the conclusion that women's performance of public speaking and expression was either separate, or different, or somehow uniquely female. Indeed, their appearance in the dock as thought criminals in some respects actively freed them from the chains of expectation and preassigned gender roles.

## Women and Radicalism in the Nineteenth Century

In the first half of nineteenth century, we can see the progressive acquisition of effective voice and autonomy amongst women radicals. These women and their actions represented a considerable departure from the world of masculine subculture or the misbehaviour of previous female defendants. We can readily identify a number of women with an enlightenment worldview which produced the roots of early nineteenth-century radicalism. Past historiography has noted the involvement of women in radical movements as often having a strictly separate identification, which resulted in a stratification of gender roles and discourses, whether desired by the women involved or not. Helen Rogers, for instance, has painstakingly uncovered these and has noted the trajectory of many women involved in nineteenth-century radical movements before Chartism. Her discoveries highlight how these women found themselves either forced into compliance with the gender role ascribed to them by the actions and rhetoric of men; or instead defined by their stance in a species of opposition to such forms of assignment.[16] In creating an obviously female-defined radicalism, gender roles around support and auxiliary background work were either adhered to, subverted to produce meaningful alternatives, or cast aside in the face of newly forged identities and radical personas.

When confronted by the urge to conform, many female radicals described the hierarchy within the radical cause itself as an unfortunate mirror of wider society's unequal and damaging gendered power structures. Such criticisms frequently emerged when they found themselves described and portrayed with specific and pointed reference to their feminine qualities, both as individuals and a part of a range of stereotypical ideals as suggested above. Helen Rogers has also noted the range of obstacles that prevented radically inspired women from entering the nineteenth century's militant public world. These meant women were not so much driven into a 'separate spheres' approach to creating a specifically feminine radicalism, but rather they actively and positively embraced this for themselves. As such, in many movements, the persona and arguments of radical women turned upon a unique and specific series of definitions, both around the 'radical woman' and about her precise relationship with the other radical concept of 'the people'.[17] A similar story emerges from Jutta Schwartzkopf's study of the female presence and activities within the much later Chartist movement. In many cases women's involvement was blocked, or their presence short-lived, as disillusionment inspired retreat from the public sphere. This drove them instead into reforming such aspects of 'domestic life' as they could attempt to wrest control over, through causes such as the Co-operative movement.[18]

In other ways, what radical women perceived as their subordination irritatingly relegated them too often to 'auxiliary' roles or indeed effectively silenced radical women altogether. This subordination, perhaps even soft oppression, has rightly occupied the work of a number of historians of feminism, gender relationships, and radical politics.[19] Their investigations have been motivated by the search for women's own unique voice and contribution which, for obvious reasons, focuses upon the redefinition of their contribution as uniquely shaped by their experiences as women. These are often expressed in forms which deliberately defined themselves in opposition to many of the prevailing male idioms and biases evident in many nineteenth-century radical movements. Attention has so far sought to examine women within these movements and has charted the numerous strategies they employed to be heard above male radicals, or occasionally instead of them.[20] These were often expressed through a distinctively feminine and feminist reading of oppression and its causes. Such historical accounts have thus seen such women as too often embattled and struggling to be heard amongst the biases and prejudicial practices of the movements of which they sought membership.

In the examination of spaces where women were comparatively free from such manacles, this chapter considers the act of offering a courtroom defence as a specific space where women initially tentatively, but eventually wholeheartedly, left behind the constraints that many aspects of radical culture either wittingly or unwittingly imposed upon them. Paradoxically, whilst made captive by the authorities, some women were arguably freer to speak and outline their views without constraints from their own side or society at large. Moreover the courtroom's language and attitude that characterized the person before them as a legal entity, a defendant, rather than a gendered individual and all that this entailed, formed a more neutral space in which these women could create more independent and frequently ungendered narratives of oppression and resistance. Given this fairly unique situation where such constraints on women's speech and ideas were—if only temporarily—removed, we are offered an opportunity to view women's own initiative and radical agency in how they constructed arguments. From this point, they were able to offer these freely, safe from forms of potential influence which would shape the otherwise gendered discourses.

This chapter considers the indictments, court appearances, and defence testimonies of four women prosecuted for blasphemy between 1821 and 1844. These were respectively Jane Carlile, Mary-Ann Carlile, Susannah Wright, and Matilda Roalfe. The first of these, Jane Carlile, was prosecuted in January 1821 and again the following month for (respectively) continuing to sell printed material that advocated the killing of tyrants—something released in the aftermath of the Cato Street conspiracy plot to murder the cabinet and then for publishing an illegal libel. The second case study, Mary Anne-Carlile, was the sister of Richard Carlile. When her brother was imprisoned, she intervened to keep his bookshop open and was indicted in 1821 for selling Thomas Paine's theological works. Our third example is Susannah Wright, who was prosecuted before the Court of King's Bench on 14 November 1822 for writing and publishing a blasphemy which called the Thirty Nine Articles of the Church of England into question. Then our last and later individual Matilda Roalfe was prosecuted in Edinburgh on 23 January 1844 for her involvement in running the so-called 'Atheistical Depot' in Nicolson Street and for publishing a manifesto and other books such as the *Oracle of Reason*, *A Home Thrust at the Trinity*, and *The Bible an Improper Book for Youth and Dangerous to the Excited Brain*. All of these works allegedly brought 'the Holy scriptures and Christian Religion into contempt'.[21]

When the defences, performances, and attitudes of these women are considered both separately and together, there are some intriguing insights that emerge. The courtroom, and indeed specifically the dock, served as a discursive place where discourses and arguments could be produced to serve the defendants' own purposes and powerfully reflect their own agendas. It is the story of intelligent individual women spotting the cracks and fissures in the edifice of church/state and law acting as one. It shows individuals exploiting these cracks and fissures to demonstrate how the apparently strong eighteenth-century order (or at least that which survived into the early nineteenth century) was fragile and flimsy. They also show how this apparent strength could be used against the established order itself, and how the act of doing so demonstrated its very fragility and flimsiness to a range of different audiences. What emerges is that by publicizing the courtroom as a kind of canvas on which to paint the fundamentals of their radicalism, these women could use aspects of what happened in court as demonstrations of society's wider ills and inequities. Their denial of the truth of Christianity and their seditious blasphemy struck at the whole legitimacy of the criminal justice system in a very obvious way. Yet ironically, it was also precisely this criminal justice system which plucked these women out of their radical milieu—one which historians have demonstrated to us was actively riddled with social, cultural, and economic constraints that might otherwise have prevented them from finding a voice.[22] Ironically, draconian authority placed them in a situation where their own voice might be heard speaking outwards to society as a whole and not necessarily to audiences within their own radical cultures.

One major reason for this was the precedent of the Hale judgment in the case against Taylor in 1678. The presiding judge Sir Matthew Hale had argued that religion was 'part and parcel of the laws of the land' and thus, anyone who sought to criticize religion was seeking to dissolve the ties that bind society together.[23] In any case, such an assault upon religion constituted an assault upon the law—the law was clear on this as well. For conservatives, the sight of rationalist defendants questioning the law's legitimacy in the cases that came before courts also constituted a questioning of that same religion's legitimacy. Because these were fused together in the legal area of blasphemy, it meant the stakes were considerably higher for the prosecuting authorities. Such interests went into these cases believing they were protecting religion, but because of the Hale judgment they were surprised, disconcerted even, to discover that they had to protect the law and its legitimacy as well. In some cases this last aspect only dawned on the surprised authorities when it was arguably too late to prevent embarrassment and the appearance of tyranny.

Quite obviously for radicals and committed freethinkers, the courtroom was the perfect place to accomplish the questioning of both religion and the law. As we shall hear, this questioning of legitimacy included these motivated women offering defences which included the verbatim reading of anti-religious works: giving them press coverage and newspaper space. It also involved questioning the religious knowledge and standing of witnesses, as well as offering strongly and carefully worded rebukes to members of the judiciary who were deemed to 'interfere' with the proclamation of their defences against free speech. A cornerstone of this approach was also questioning the legitimacy of the jury system which these women argued was manipulated by dark forces and malignant interest groups. If they could prove this, or even intimate that it was likely to be true, then this was an incendiary idea to pass on to other radicals, and in dangerous times, these were radical and transgressive ideas to be circulating in the public domain. Lastly these women used the suppression of their views as a further source of radical argument and means for their wider publicity.

## Jane Carlile

After Richard Carlile had been imprisoned, his wife Jane took over the day-to-day business of Carlile's publishing and bookselling enterprise. Since many of the works still published were seen by the authorities as inflammatory, seditious, and blasphemous, it was little surprise when she was arrested for publishing editions of *The Republican* and *The Life of Thomas Paine*. This point was made quite early on in the trial by the prosecution who stated that 'she could not complain, after continuing to give to the world the mischievous work in question, after the warnings which she had received from former prosecutions'.[24] Jane Carlile must have been cognizant of the opinions contained within the works she was selling, and in some manner was willing to be involved in this radical and dangerous enterprise. However, from the outset, her attitude was to declare that she had 'neither the power nor the ability to undertake any alteration in the manuscript transmitted for the press and I have never read it until printed'.[25] From this she intimated that the court and the Attorney General would be far better examining the views of her husband, rather than relentlessly pursuing a subordinate who only acted 'out of conjugal duty'. With this in mind, Jane Carlile had in front of her a letter for the Attorney General which would prove the culpability of her husband Richard Carlile rather than herself. This was a tactic intended to alleviate her situation and had been designed to test the previous indications that both the Attorney General and the Solicitor General were merely interested in prosecuting the author and originator of such works. This subtly directed the prosecution case along the pathway of assuming ordered and established gender norms within the Carlile household.

When the Attorney General failed to appear, Jane Carlile was left in 'an awkward predicament' and was faced by the Solicitor General who was now eager for a prosecution.[26] From this point, Jane Carlile indicated how disadvantaged she was by this unexpected turn of events and fell back upon gendered excuses, suggesting that the Solicitor General's decision to be combative with a woman was unbecoming and his choice of an easy target really did him no credit. Nonetheless Jane Carlile still had enough manoeuvrability to try and create discomfort about this supposedly cheap tactic amongst those present when she said:

> Had the defence of this extract devolved to upon the proper person, my husband, he would have loaded this table with volumes from the best authorities, and from such authorities as no man in this Court would rise to decry,...I consider a defence to be scarcely necessary, as it is impossible to distort the meaning of the words, unless that distortion be made wilfully: there is nothing vague, there is nothing obscure but the language is honest and manly, and as plain and intelligible as the letters of the alphabet.[27]

Faced with having to defend the act of slaying a tyrant, she declared 'as a female, I would not shrink form defending this doctrine before any company of females in this country'. After this, her lengthy defence cited Hugo Grotius, Tertullian, St Augustine, Sophocles, Aristotle, and numerous biblical precedents. For a woman who emphasized her humble origins and detachment from the views contained in the works she had sold, this remained a considerable performance. Especially so since Jane Carlile did not expect to have to present this verbally in court and would manifestly have preferred for the written version to have formed her defence. Moreover, she also had to take note of the young child which she had carried in her arms into court.[28] Whilst the text of her argument was almost certainly prepared by her husband (a view also taken by the Solicitor General), her performance thus far would have impressed some.

At certain points of the defence we can perhaps hear her authentic words when she emphasized quite strongly that her own moral character was scarcely infringed by the prosecution and any consequences that it might have, declaring 'it may punish but it cannot disgrace'.[29] The Judge, Chief Justice Abbot, noted that the jury clearly had to decide 'whether the share which the Defendant has taken in this publication be sufficient, to establish the charge of the record against her'.[30] After a fifteen-minute recess, the jury returned a verdict of guilty. When Jane Carlile later returned to receive her sentence she had obviously decided, at least in part, to throw herself in some manner upon the mercy of the court. She emphasized again her humble social origins and this time added an indication of her comparative lack of education, an assertion which the Solicitor General summarily rejected. Interestingly, Jane Carlile's recent protestations of ignorance constituting innocence had been aggravated by her proceeding with her earlier defence, and her absence of regret was not accepted as placing herself at the mercy of the court. She was thus sentenced to be imprisoned for two years and to find two sureties each of £100.[31]

At first sight, her tactic of denial of responsibility alongside her episodic emphasis upon her female vulnerability appeared to be back-pedalling, moreover the reliance upon the words of her husband appears to make Jane Carlile appear simply as a compliant wife drawn into a situation of which she had only a tenuous grasp. However, her decision to proceed with presenting the defence verbally, and her protestations of her ongoing morality and failure to be contrite, demonstrate some level of distinct agency. Her protestation of ignorance concerning the contents of the works she had sold was an attempt to evade the *Mens Rea* implications of the charges against her. Despite these caveats, the spectacle of an enlightened woman doing herself less than justice in the courtroom was probably in the final analysis slightly unedifying, and as we shall discover, one woman present was watching closely and was to take these lessons deeply to heart.

## Mary-Ann Carlile

Jane Carlile's place in Richard Carlile's bookshop was thereafter taken up by his sister Mary-Ann. Very soon afterwards, she too found herself in court but was initially acquitted of a first charge of blasphemy laid against her when the jury could not agree upon a verdict despite an eighteen-hour sojourn in the jury room. Her demeanour and the outcome of the case severely irritated the publishers of the periodical *John Bull*, who launched something of a journalistic tirade against her, one that interestingly forgot gender-related or derived insults, as it railed against her 'pert grovelling and absurd insolence'.[32] However, the determination to call her to account persisted and she was indicted a second time, on this occasion for selling the *An Appendix to the Theological Works of Thomas Paine*. In offering her defence she declared 'I am not backward to put my moral character in competition with any of my secret prosecutors or any female which might belong to their families.'[33] Her defence rested on a number of issues, some stable and effective arguments and some less so, but she was only able to proceed on the basis of one of these. Not unreasonably, Mary-Ann Carlile asked why the charge on which she was held was based on common law and not statute, implying that the common law was 'a common abuse'.[34] This last phrase infuriated the judge who declared he was unwilling to enable the law to 'be reviled' in his presence (*John Bull* reported this as blasphemous) and instead brought her appearance in court to an end in somewhat ignominious circumstances.[35] Justice Best demanded such phrases be expunged from the trial proceedings, but Mary-Ann Carlile refused to comply with this request and, even after a recess, returned to the court with further resolution, stating 'if the court means to decide that an Englishwoman is not to state that which she thinks necessary for her defence, she must abide the consequence of such a decision'.[36] Thereafter the court moved swiftly to a verdict of guilty, with the jury not even bothering to deliberate. Mary-Ann Carlile was sentenced to a year's imprisonment and a £500 fine which she was unable to pay. When her year's sentence expired she remained in gaol as an alternative method of paying the fine. She eventually petitioned Parliament for remission of the remaining fine and found she had some support. The radical MPs Sir Francis Burdett (1770–1844) and Joseph Hume (1777–1855) were prepared to speak up, criticizing the level of the fine as against good principles of law and the case itself reminiscent of the dark ages of religious oppression.[37]

The outcome of the trial was a considerable disappointment once again for the radical cause. Mary-Ann Carlile had been thwarted from offering a defence, once again most likely created by Richard Carlile as the ideological mentor behind the whole campaign. This would have potentially ranged over such territory as the legitimacy of England's common law alongside its association with Christianity—given it had usurped Druidism and subsequently been interrupted by Saxon and Viking rule and similarly its inheritance from Catholic Christendom was less than certain. As judge-made law, it was also painted as capricious and anathema to reason and representative government. The argument it was 'part and parcel' of the law of the land was made to seem spurious and the concept of blasphemy incapable of meaningful and widely understood definition. The defence also pointed out that those without conception of a deity could not blaspheme against it, nor could simple religious texts be the subject of such prosecutions, especially since they could now be shown to be fallible, even in the eyes of the religious.[38]

As we know, none of this was ever heard in court since the judge curtailed proceedings before this point. These arguments were instead subsequently circulated in the pamphlet which offered the arguments from Mary-Ann Carlile's suppressed defence.[39] Although Richard Carlile's campaign could make some political capital about the oppressive nature of courts that would silence a woman with legitimate arguments that ranged reason against tyranny, this was only a response after the fact. The actual impact of both prosecutions was unedifying to women who might have been willing to involve themselves in Carlile's cause. Whilst Carlile himself had created arguments for them to use, there was little he or anyone could do if these ran aground against spiky legal procedures or the opinion of the presiding judge. Nonetheless, there were glimpses of the impact of enlightenment selfhood and independence exhibited by both Carlile women. Jane Carlile's dogged determination to present her defence when she had merely hoped to present a written defence was venturesome, and her insistence upon the preservation of her own virtuous image meant she eventually received a ruling from the judge that she clearly did know her own mind. Her dogged persistence was similarly poorly received and read as the antithesis of a plea for mercy. Mary-Ann Carlile's foray into the publishing and bookselling enterprises of her brother also foundered in court. Yet within this process she had exhibited stubbornness that refused to alter the defence that she was intent upon expounding, even refusing the offered assistance of male legal minds made available to her on the day.

Although women who were at least in part inspired by radical and enlightenment ideals were having their day in court, they found themselves thwarted by its procedures and had to bow to the authority it used against them—a seemingly obvious attempt to label these women's forays into court as misadventure. The outcomes from these cases were thus rather minimal triumphs that showed some limited potential, rather than a full and successful flowering of women's involvement in the radical freethought cause. Moreover, the rhetoric they chose to offer had rather boxed them in and limited their ability to respond effectively. It could even be argued that the choice of argument created for them had not always been effective. The 'ignorance as innocence' strategy, that was part of Jane Carlile's defence against what was primarily a sedition accusation, might have been far better deployed against the prosecution for blasphemy aimed at Mary-Ann Carlile.

Yet watching these cases and their outcome was a woman who was taking extensive note of all that transpired, as well as what had been effective and what had not. Whether what had happened to her female fellow travellers actively inspired her actions is certainly not clearly known. Whatever the truth of this speculation it seems abundantly clear that obvious lessons were learned by

Susannah Wright from observing the prosecution of the two Carlile women and other male defendants.

## Susannah Wright

Susannah Wright, our third female defendant in the series of trials surrounding the Carlile agitation, has already partly been given greater autonomy and agency by other scholars.[40] Between her first committal and the eventual trial, she had over six months to consider how best to approach her defence, and within this period had resolved to take the lead.[41] When she was eventually brought for trial on 8 July 1822, she was immediately de-gendered by the indictment's description of her as 'an evil and wicked person' whose sole intent was 'to bring the Christian Religion into disbelief and contempt among the people of this kingdom'.[42] The indictment reflected the fact that she had sold the works of Richard Carlile which had argued that priests were either 'imposters' or 'idolaters' (in that they denied the revelation of the natural world); that Christianity was a mythology; that Religion was the 'chief source of war', and that the 'Representative System of Government' advocated would usher in the abolition of religion.[43]

Whilst it was reiterated that these opinions emanated from the writings of Richard Carlile, and it is known he helped with the construction of her defence, Susannah Wright maintained vigorously that she was considerably more than an accomplice in promoting them and she would speak on her own account.[44] The courtroom de-gendering of Susannah Wright continued since the Society for the Suppression of Vice indicated that it had hesitated to bring her to trial, not because she was a woman, nor because she had an infant child, but instead because they were frightened that the trial would 'excite the public mind'.[45] Susannah Wright had sold and was prepared to defend the words of Carlile, but the prosecuting counsel hesitated and fought shy of mentioning them for the uncontrollable uproar they would cause. When the essence of the prosecution case was completed, this gave Susannah Wright the opportunity to undermine the prosecuting counsel's status in the court, by likening him to 'a parrot' who endlessly repeated jargon egged on by the lure of a golden reward.[46]

There followed some interesting exchanges about the apparent 'status' of Susannah Wright. The prosecuting counsel made a note of the fact that she was 'the wife of a person engaged in trade, which enabled him to support his family in comfort'.[47] The interjection of this fact was to establish that Wright's actions in selling the works was actually wilful, since she could scarcely claim, as others had, that she had been driven to selling Carlile's works through poverty. If it was not poverty that drove her, it was apparently instead more insidious and base motives of basic profit and gain. When the chance arose for Susannah Wright to reply, she scotched this particular accusation and in doing so, turned her apparently secure domestic position into an advantage in her wider argument. This was about establishing the uncompromised nature of her own expression of free will and opinion. In doing this she also had remedied and addressed one of the principal bars preventing other radical women from entering and fully participating in active radical politics. Not only could she rely on the wholehearted support of her husband, but she exhibited an artisanal pride in the fact that she had 'been bred to a genteel employ, as a lace-mender, and an embroiderer, at which I could earn double the wages that I have received from Mr Carlile'.[48] With the security of her economic status established, she was effectively undermining the supposed baseness of her motives.

This was not solely about establishing Susannah Wright's independence, the ability to make up her own mind, and take action to condone it with the support of her husband. It went much further, to be an integral part of her demonstration of freedom—now encompassing both mind and physical body. Unlike the line taken by other female radicals, this argument was not about the wrongs and evils perpetrated against woman and the evils of patriarchal systems. It was much more squarely aimed at perceiving religion to be injurious to the totality of humankind. Thus, Wright's arguments owed almost nothing to embryonic feminism and instead owed almost everything to enlightenment enthusiasm for natural philosophy and its accompanying disdain for religion's apparently inflated and arrogant claims.

Wright greatly wanted her day in court to demand that religion 'be brought to the touchstone of free discussion, and that there shall be no persecution for matters of opinion'.[49] In true enlightenment style, Susannah Wright wanted free discussion to be enabled so that she (and others) might be empowered to investigate religion and is potential to convey and reveal its own capacity for truth, should this be actively forthcoming. The fact that she was hampered from this course of action tipped her into what had become a standard Paineite critique. It was entrenched, yet fearful, vested interests which had occasioned her arrest and appearance in court. Hireling priests who grew rich off the protection of religion's monopoly over belief clearly had the intention of preventing further free discussion. In this, 'priest craft' was aided and abetted by 'Lord craft' which kept the productive classes away from accessing such enlightening material.[50]

She argued she had undertaken what seemed the only just and sound form of action in the circumstances. Continuing to offer Carlile's writings for sale was enhancing the spread of reason and the chance of free expression. Saying this also became an important part of her defence, as she aimed to argue strongly an apparent purity of motive. This was intended to access one of the most important defences potentially available to the blasphemy defendant. Susannah Wright's establishment of enlightenment rights and duties, alongside her independence and free choice of gainful employment, were component parts of a deeper argument about motive. As her lengthy defence pointed out, she had endlessly declared her intention to enable free inquiry and free discussion. This was in some contrast to the spirit of the charges which forcefully indicated she was engaged upon the moral ruination of the country. Her accusers persistently claimed that the honesty of her motives was a ploy to problematize the enduring legal conundrum of establishing to any degree of comfort the *Mens Rea* of the offence of blasphemy. This meant for almost all blasphemy cases that the intention of the offender was scarcely established unequivocally. This has always made the law of blasphemy and its implementation somewhat difficult for those charged with its prosecution. The safest course of action, and one instinctively resorted to by the authorities, was to continually suggest that such opinions themselves self-evidently led to the ruin of morals and the hope of salvation which the community clung to. Their very nature was conducive to ruin and this circular argument overtook consideration of the defendant and the context that they had created within individual cases.[51]

Nonetheless by the 1820s such court proceedings still contained an element of risk, which at least partly explained the desire of government to have private prosecutions brought. These came under the auspices of moral prosecution societies such as the Society for the Suppression of Vice employed in this case, which itself had swiftly become a bête noire for Richard Carlile. Early in the proceedings, Susannah Wright very effectively used her own appeal to enlightenment discussion and reason as a clear motivation for her action, thereby seeking to short-circuit the argument around the words and sentiments themselves constituting the offence in its entirety. The authorities believed this latter argument would resolve such cases. However, the actions of determined defendants actually spun them out, giving them the opportunity to display sustained proof of the purity of their motives. For our purposes, we should particularly note that mounting defences against blasphemy allegations functioned as both invitation and sustained encouragement for female defendants to press forward. This demonstrated the acquisition of enlightened learning and the development of skills which they could use effectively in the courtroom. The action of the courtroom also allowed them to display their grasp of scholarship and the creation of rhetoric.

Honesty was the fundamental point at issue when Susannah Wright also confronted and questioned a witness at her trial. James Rignal had proved that he purchased two pamphlets cited in the indictment for 2d. each, at No. 55 Fleet-Street, and that they were delivered to him by the hand of the defendant. He was then cross-examined by Susannah Wright who sought to expose him as a disreputable and malicious hired mercenary.

SW: How do you get your living?

JR: I have a pension from the Government, and am agent to the Society for the Suppression of Vice.

SW: How have you obtained a pension from the Government?

JR: I was thirty years in the service of the Customs.
SW: But you were dismissed without a pension?
JR: I was dismissed with several others, but afterwards received a pension.
SW: Were you not discharged for giving false evidence?
JR: No, I was not.
SW: Why were you discharged?
JR: I cannot very well tell; seventeen/or eighteen of us were discharged at once; but since that time the Lords of the Treasury have taken our case into consideration, and have allowed me a pension of seventy pounds a year.
SW: When you were in the Customs what religion did you profess?
JR: No answer.
SW: What is the ninth commandment?[52]

The Chief Justice presiding over the case was infuriated and intervened to say such questions were improper. In response, Susannah Wright turned from her questioning of the witness to instruct the judge and question the direction in which proceedings were headed: 'I do not think this man is to be believed upon his oath; if I had a little more time I could prove it.' The Chief Justice, undeterred by this, replied: 'You have had abundance of time to prepare your defence. It is for the Jury to say whether he is to be believed on his oath.'[53]

This series of actions by Susannah Wright called into question the functioning of oaths in the court in a fairly spectacular way and invited ridicule about the legitimacy of court proceedings. But it also went further and was a calculated attack upon the basis of the law. If religion was the fundamental basis of the law—as the Hale judgment and its precedent argued—then the law was here aided illegitimately by witnesses and accomplices who were astonishingly ignorant of the religious beliefs they were supposedly defending—and doing so in a manner that wholly contrasted with that of the defendant.

Susanna Wright was determined to make the Society for the Suppression of Vice regret its high-handed action. Having vehemently expressed the purity of her motives, she then moved on to criticizing the indictment for its wording which declared that she had spread a libel about the Christian religion. However, as Wright pointed out, at no point did the indictment declare that she had falsely libelled it. This was an argument which aimed at proving her tormentors were themselves uncertain how far the statements within blasphemous publications could be shown to be true. Again opening up such a loophole was inviting defendants to indulge in lengthy expositions of their motives and the claims within their publications—all of which was irksome to the authorities whilst at the same time enabling these ideas to be exposed to wider publicity.

The court hastily closed this loophole down. Yet Susannah Wright was still not to be deterred. She pressed on with a defence which amounted to a total of fifty of fifty-nine pamphlet pages, all filled with arguments intended to refute accusations of bad faith displayed by her actions. She instead turned the accusation upon her accusers who were, throughout the harangue, accused of blasphemy, ignorance of natural religion, and the failure to preach the Christian virtues of tolerance and dialogue with non-Christian thinkers.[54] This was clearly an elaborately constructed and determined defence which Susannah Wright emphatically played to the gallery—her audience was obviously intended to reach beyond the court to consumers of the court reports and pamphlet literature. In connection with the arguments around toleration, she commenced reading in its entirety the contents of a pamphlet sermon delivered by the Unitarian W. J. Fox who strenuously argued that the recent prosecution of Richard Carlile had been unwarranted and counterproductive. She got some ten pages into the sermon before the prosecuting counsel attempted to intervene by requesting the judge to call a halt because the reading of the pamphlet was 'a ruse to get all this published'.[55] However Wright's recitation of the work of a Unitarian clergyman had been shrewd, since the presiding judge had no grounds for finding the sentiments contained within it offensive, even though it argued the case for toleration and condemned proceedings such as those under which she had been indicted.[56] This seemed a clear lesson learned from the events of the Mary-Ann Carlile court case and the sustained ripples from her 'suppressed defence'. In sum this was a bravura display of overturning and subverting many of the conventional assumptions about the behaviour of women. Forsaking the role of supporting her husband and of playing a subordinate role in radical activity, this performance plunged Susannah Wright into transgressing other behavioural norms expected of women. Respect for patriarchy and time-honoured hierarchies of social, cultural, and religious kinds were all under attack from activities and outspoken opinions. She also showed scant respect for the law, its officers, and its mechanisms. This further undermined the expected deference for society's existing arrangements that women were supposed to demonstrate.

During Susannah Wright's defence there were a total of six interventions from the presiding judge. Such interventions were also potentially counterproductive and were made the most of in the pamphlet report of the case. On four of these occasions, Susannah Wright refused to yield and employed a variety of tactics, from failing to notice the judge, to yielding temporarily and simply resuming the defence she had been criticized for offering. The wisdom of such interventions and their sustained effects must have been difficult for the judge to calculate, since Susannah Wright's defiance of authority resonated through the court with 'merriment' and 'amusement'.[57] Of course the discomfort of authority also resonated throughout the radical England that consumed the pamphlet reports of these events after the fact.

Wright returned to conclude her case, advising the jury to ensure that they were prepared to think for themselves and not be swayed by partial or incomplete arguments.[58] The jury obliged, swiftly returning a guilty verdict. It would be four months before Wright again returned to court for sentencing. This time, her notoriety attracted more of the public gaze in both crowd numbers and press interest. When offered the opportunity to address the court in a 'plea of mitigation of punishment', Wright defiantly refused to comply, again perhaps in response to the outcome of the Jane Carlile prosecution. Instead she challenged the validity of her guilty verdict, arguing that Christianity had no legitimate function within the law. The Chief Justice warned her to desist from profaning the Law and the Church in his court. To the amusement of the crowded courtroom she retorted, 'You, Sir, are paid to hear me'.[59] Infuriated by her obstinacy, the Judge sentenced Wright (and by default her infant) to be confined for ten weeks in the detested Newgate prison to deliberate on her plea. Susannah Wright carried her agitation on into the prison and her incarceration proved something of a headache for the prison authorities.[60]

On the surface Susannah Wright's performance in July 1822 was a great deal of effort beyond that offered by Jane and Mary-Ann Carlile, but arguably for the same result. Yet the court had visibly lost control of the concept of justice being seen to be done in a crowded and hostile courtroom. The closed down logic of the law's assumption that blasphemous words contained their own justification had been subverted by a skilled defendant.

In her defence she had offered the opinions of respected Christian authors who denounced persecution as unworthy of religion and saw in it the dangers of counterproductive actions which encouraged and sustained the spread of deist and atheist principles. Pointedly, Susannah Wright had not sought on this occasion to utilize her gender in any specific manner and her actions indicated that she took her place as an enlightened reader and proponent of truth alongside Carlile and the other male defendants who continued to sell his works. Ironically, though its verdict and reaction to her was draconian and intolerant, the very act of being indicted and made to appear in court had created a moment and space for her own ungendered liberty of thought and expression. Unencumbered by the assumptions of female radicals who had to care about radical narratives of decorum and appropriate female behaviour, Susannah Wright had taken her lead from classless and genderless rhetoric associated with enlightenment enquiry. Although the court had de-gendered her, it was interesting that the hostile sections of the press deliberately used her gender as a means to discredit her amongst the conservative public. This was intended to highlight her flouting of patriarchal norms and indicated she should step back and assume the deferential role that nature had assigned to her. The *New Times* likened her behaviour to that of a prostitute which was calculated to attract shame in some considerable measure. Those women who had accompanied Susannah Wright to court also attracted sustained bile from the same source.[61] Nonetheless, with views about women's role in public and in radicalism polarized, such written attacks were obviously to be expected.[62]

When Susannah Wright's gender was linked to her crime this seemed especially shocking to conservative England. But there was no sense of her establishing a counter-cultural virtuous womanhood. Likewise, she was not offering a gendered radical reading of the texts in question, nor a specifically gendered dimension to her defence. Court proceedings served to de-gender her, although the all too human judge would regularly offer pained observations regretting that he had a woman before him on such heinous a charge. Many male radical supporters saw no need to distinguish between the radical efforts of the male compatriots of Richard Carlile and the two Carlile women alongside Susannah Wright and they were lauded equally.[63] Their collective efforts seemed to have had an effect in galvanizing female support of various kinds into the agitation and indeed wider radicalism.[64]

## Matilda Roalfe

Matilda Roalfe was not unlike Susannah Wright in that answering the call of a radical agitation which had inspired her was the essence of why she found herself in court charged with blasphemy. This was a part of the agitation in Edinburgh in the first years of the 1840s that offered the city's inhabitants a secular and atheist alternative during the years of the Disruption. Roalfe's involvement was testimony to the growing power of radical periodical reporting. She had been preceded in the Edinburgh 'blasphemy depot' by Thomas Paterson whose trial and imprisonment for selling a translation of *Ecce Homo*, as well as *The Life of David* and Thomas Paine's *Aphorisms*, all of which were publications that conveyed waspish and rationalist criticism of biblical stories and highlighted what they regarded as biblical absurdities.[65] Paterson was followed into the dock by Thomas Finlay who had published *The God of the Jews or Jehovah Unveiled* and finally by Henry Robinson who had also published *The Protestant's Progress from Church-of-Englandism to Infidelity*. These prosecutions had been painstakingly reported in the pages of George Jacob Holyoake's *The Reasoner*.[66] This was the organ of Holyoake's Anti-Persecution Union which had been convened to protect both the religious and unbelievers alike against the predations of autocratic and arbitrary justice.

Matilda Roalfe left London to join the agitation in Edinburgh with what the trial account labelled 'more than woman's usual courage'.[67] Upon arriving at the Nicolson Street 'Blasphemy Depot', Roalfe immediately publicized her own manifesto which made it evident that she had a 'determination to sell such books as contained sentiments she deemed useful to be known'.[68] Very soon her premises were turned over by agents of the Procurator Fiscal and she was arrested and thrown into prison where she endured a most uncomfortable night with a bed alive with vermin.[69] When released on bail, she then had to endure the nightly attentions of a 'riotous mob' whose threatening manner degenerated into acts of violence against her fellow shop workers, actions she suspected had been incited by a neighbouring Methodist Minister.[70]

Eventually she came for trial at a crowded Sherriff's Court on 23 January 1844 where she pleaded not guilty to a charge of blasphemy. Cleverly, she was able to manipulate the precise wording of the charge by pleading guilty to some elements of it, whilst putting to valuable use the enlightenment urge to publicize opinions considered valuable, no matter what prohibitions existed against them. After it had been proved that Roalfe had sold the books listed in the charge, she denied the subsection of the charge which declared this had been done 'wickedly and feloniously'. This distinction was of sufficient note to resonate in the local press's otherwise brief reporting of the case. This highlighted Roalfe's desire to provide distinct and separate answers to the entire wording of the charge and noted that she had built on this to demonstrate that 'so little did she consider her conduct criminal, that, so soon should she be at liberty, she intended to resume the same practice'.[71]

At the outset, Roalfe was quite forthright about knowing the contents of the works in question. Her denial of 'wicked and felonious intent' once again was also attempting to use *Mens Rea* issues as a problematic in blasphemy prosecutions. Roalfe also exposed that a number of witnesses called by the prosecution had been deliberately sent by the Procurator Fiscal to purchase these—this was not an issue in itself for the prosecution, but some other matters that subsequently emerged were problematic. Witnesses denied all knowledge of the contents of the book that they had purchased, but Roalfe wanted to question them further. When asked if the book's contents had exerted any sort of effect upon them, the witnesses indignantly replied that the sentiments contained in the works had exerted no effect upon them and that their moral condition remained unaltered.[72] This potentially demonstrated the fortitude of the witnesses, but by definition also exposed the potential over-reaction of the authorities and their high-handed presumption that such material was by its very nature actively dangerous.

The considerable support that had turned out to inspire Matilda Roalfe were all heartened by this and the prosecution embarrassed. The prosecution then swiftly moved to return focus to proving the purchase of the books from Matilda Roalfe, which it argued was the central and indeed sole matter for discussion. In reply, Roalfe went back to the *Mens Rea* defence of denying an intention to corrupt the readership of these works and instead propounding a motive of social utility. Her belief in this was cemented by her offer to cease publication if it could be proved such works did demoralize within the strict meaning intended in the wording of the indictment. This was also an inversion of the central argument contained in *The Bible an Improper Book* which had pointedly noted that the Bible contained obscenities which unguided youth would likely find inappropriate and indeed gloat over. Moreover, this work further argued that the Bible had also supposedly given birth to the science of profaning and swearing and constituted a contradictory 'bone of contention, hatred and bloodshed to the inhabitants of this world'.[73] In stating these arguments Matilda Roalfe again stepped away from deferring to existing legal and religious hierarchies that presumed to impose morality upon the whole society. As such she was adopting the role of judge and jury on existing moral codes, leaving deferential acceptance of them very far behind.

From this point, Matilda Roalfe's defence narrative displayed what might be described as the 'reverse piety' of freethought. In this, she stated to the court that she had become a freethinker, or rather had actually been converted, by her sustained encounter and interaction with the Bible and its inherent immorality; this eventually persuaded her to reject Christianity as 'mere fable'.[74] Such sentiments were evident in the material that appeared in the indictments and the passages that these quoted within them.[75] Subsequently she was driven on 'To destroy the "fabulous trash" peddled by religion to the ever deceived multitude'. This had become 'the great, the sole object of my ambition'.[76] She regretted nothing and saw the case as turning around the issue of rights for atheists in the face of a Christian establishment unerringly protecting its privileged status. The result of this was that she readily confessed that she had derived more comfort and pleasure from reading science than religious works.[77]

Matilda Roalfe was found guilty and imprisoned for sixty days in Edinburgh gaol; she described the conditions there and the privations she suffered as severe. However, she noted how far this had stiffened her resolve further and had convinced her of the power of enlightened reason, saying:

> Amid all the privations I endured there was yet one glorious privilege of which they could not rob me, my thoughts were still unfettered; our persecutors have yet to learn that when they have turned the dungeon key upon us, there is still that, over which they have no control, thought free as ever, defies all their attempts to enslave it, and until they can do this their triumph is incomplete. I still feel the most thorough contempt for that law which will concede to one portion of society those rights which it withholds from another, I therefore resolved to act in defiance of such a system, and having weighed all the consequences before I did so act, I have never for one moment regretted it. Let us unite our energies, not relax our endeavours until we have obtained an abrogation of a law, which is an insult alike upon common sense and justice.[78]

## Conclusion

Whilst this chapter has so far argued that the defendants in these four trials for blasphemy/sedition managed to unhook themselves from gender stereotypes, these remained of episodic use to them as occasional rhetorical tools rather than established narratives. Certainly we can observe what we might interpret as the very fleeting and subtle 'use' of gender in some aspects of courtroom proceedings. Jane Carlile spent the first few paragraphs indicating she had neither means nor ability to offer an adequate defence of the opinions in the works in question, and her husband would make a better fist of this were he actively in court. Mary-Ann Carlile in 1822, towards the very end of her defence, most of which was suppressed by the judge Justice Best, ended her long speech appealing to the judges by describing herself as 'a forlorn female, with no other friend or relative than an imprisoned brother, to whom I can look for support or protection'.[79] This was however after an inordinately long lecture to the jury who would very likely have been weary and unsympathetic at this stage of proceedings.

Susanna Wright in 1822 took the opportunity very pointedly to use the language of being 'bold enough to display a mind of her own' and her case being dedicated 'To the Women of the Island of Great Britain; This specimen of female patriotism, love of liberty, bold and honest daring.'[80] She juxtaposed suckling her crying new-born infant with a deliberate mocking of stereotypical assumptions of assumed female piety by arguing her own sufferings as a freethinking woman were as deep and anguish-filled as the suffering of Christ. Yet she hastily switched again, snapping the court out of this image, by painting herself as an enlightenment philosophe, saying:

> I come not with a plea of feigned humility and false penitence, but with a mind elated with pride, from the assurance that the cause which has brought me here has been a common good, and not an evil to the community, nor an offence against the known laws of the country.[81]

This was followed by the attempt to make her own stand undermining the supposed masculinity of the court. She emphasized the fact that the court needed six individual men to prosecute one woman, arguing that she was a female setting them an example of 'duty, courage and honesty'.[82] A female not intimidated by the wigs and robes of a court that she subtly feminized.

Beyond that, what is striking through all these examples here is the similarity of language, approach, and argument offered by these women to their fellow male defendants. Whilst defences were prepared for the two Carlile women, which on the face of this easily explains this similarity, both Jane and Mary-Ann Carlile still chose to face the court and at least attempted to use its freedom to state their own case. They even managed some moments of rhetorical resistance in what must have been two unsatisfactory outcomes, and the court emerges as a more fluid space where stepping outside of expectations was a legitimate course of action. Jane Carlile, Mary-Anne Carlile, as well as Susannah Wright actively refused to offer affidavits as to their previous good conduct in contrast to established practice. They constantly affirmed the honourable nature of their actions, their honesty, and their sincere belief in the social utility of the free expression they played a part in. For them this trumped every other consideration, including the legal peril they potentially saw ahead of themselves. They were allies of Richard Carlile, albeit familial ones, and discharged their duties as handmaidens of Prometheus. Yet those first two trials provided a significant learning experience for Susannah Wright, who much more actively grasped and manipulated her own defence and court appearance. She confronted witnesses and demanded to be heard in a manner which shocked the judge and cheered the radical public who supported her. In concluding her defence she stated:

> I am satisfied that I stand upon the rock of truth! With all the laws of morality for my shield: my banner is the emblem of candour and simplicity, my weapons are reasonable arguments, and my enemies are tyrants, robbers and oppressors.... The balm of public approbation will be mine. The lash of public disapprobation will fall on my tyrant persecutors.[83]

This lead in proceedings, as we know, had a contemporary influence on other radical women and we can see the essence of this defence reappear in the court appearance of Matilda Roalfe. Female freethinkers had transformed from being handmaidens of Prometheus into the autonomous and more powerful heirs of Hypatia.

These women considered themselves atheists, philosophes, and radical citizens before they were uniquely, and *differently*, women. Revisiting the power of the enlightenment and in particular the reverence for reason that this unleashed became a subculture with universalist ideals that a surprising number of influential women subscribed to. We also discover from these cases that women constituted important reading publics within radical circles and were radicalized into freethought in exactly the same way that men were. Crucially, their presence as agitators alongside male radicals is unremarked upon within these movements themselves. Given this, historians may legitimately ask how far it was widely accepted that women would be part of the freethinking movement precisely as freethinkers before they were anything else; indeed how far it was actively expected of them? Women stepping out of forms of deference fitted well with freethinking critiques of society and informed work to secure greater freedoms in the fields of political reform and birth control knowledge.

As such, the presence of women in these agitations represents a valuable corrective to many pieces of historiography that have shaped the history and role of women in nineteenth-century Britain. Work on women's involvement in radicalism has discussed women negotiating gendered spaces that needed to be defined in movements themselves as well as outside. Yet there have been gaps and it has not fully discussed their empowerment in the earlier freethought movement. It is also true that women's identification as autonomous readers, thinking and arguing alongside men, especially in a freethinking context, equally provides a corrective jolt to orthodox class-based conceptions of gendered separate spheres. Philosophically empowered freethinking women constitute a challenge to the feminization thesis which argued that the nineteenth-century survival and episodic flourishing of religion in Western Europe rested on its tailoring of its appeal to a constituency of female piety which actively and enthusiastically responded to this.

To an extent some of the directions these conclusions point us to are linked to the concept of 'reverse piety' mentioned earlier. As such, they lead on to more developed critiques which offer moral revolt against Christianity later in the nineteenth century and again we can see women such as Harriet Law, Annie Besant, Hypatia Bradlaugh Bonner, and others all taking a central role in this.[84] Freethinking allowed women access to knowledge and the opportunity to be philosophes alongside men. However it was the courtroom and its potentialities, seen by the astute, that gave them episodes of autonomy and authentic opportunities to step outside the constraints that elsewhere hemmed them in.

## Notes

1. A. Vickery (2009) *Behind Closed Doors* (London: Yale University Press), p. 17.
2. Ibid., p. 18.
3. A. Vickery (1993) 'Golden Age to Separate Spheres: A Review of the Categories and Chronology of English Women's History', *Historical Journal*, 36, 2, pp. 383–414.
4. Vickery, *Behind Closed Doors*, p. 19.
5. Ibid., p. 20.
6. Ibid., pp. 24–5 and 27.
7. A. Clark (1993) *The Struggle for the Breeches* (London: University of California Press), chapters 2 and 3.
8. For an examination of the gendered nature of this crime and its cultural implications see D. S. Nash (2013) 'Blasphemy and Witchcraft: A Gendered Mirror Image?', in K. Reyes and M. Muravyeva (eds), *Why Gender? The Concept of Gender Relations in the Medieval and Early Modern World* (Abingdon: Routledge), pp. 153–71.
9. See A. Cabantous (2002) *Blasphemy: Impious Speech in the West from the Seventeenth to the Nineteenth Century* (New York: Columbia University Press); F. Loetz (2016) *Dealings with God: From Blasphemers in Early Modern Zurich to a Cultural History of Religiousness* (Abingdon: Routledge); and M. Flynn (1995) 'Blasphemy and the Play of Anger in Sixteenth Century Spain', *Past and Present*, 149, 1, pp. 29–56.
10. J. Villa-Flores (2006) *Dangerous Speech: A Social History of Blasphemy in Colonial Mexico* (Phoenix, AZ: University of Arizona Press), *passim*.
11. See Loetz, *Dealings with God*, *passim* and Villa-Flores (2006) *Dangerous Speech*, *passim*.
12. See D. S. Nash (1999) *Blasphemy in Modern Britain 1789–Present* (Aldershot: Ashgate), pp. 29 and 31, and D. S. Nash (2007) *Blasphemy in the Christian World: A History* (Oxford: Oxford University Press), pp. 118–19.

13. For Susannah Fowles see D. Lawton (1993) *Blasphemy* (London: Harvester Wheatsheaf). For the case against a woman described simply as 'The Maid' see the Old Bailey Proceedings Online <www.oldbaileyonline.org>, 14 September 2021, t16780828: 28 August 1678.
14. See Nash, *Blasphemy in Modern Britain*, pp. 77–8.
15. See M. Wood (1994) *Radical Satire and Print Culture, 1790–1822* (Oxford: Clarendon Press), pp. 98 and 100–1. See also Nash, *Blasphemy in Modern Britain*, pp. 80–4.
16. See H. Rogers (2000) *Women and the People Authority: Authorship and the Radical Tradition in Nineteenth Century England* (Aldershot: Ashgate).
17. Ibid., p. 7.
18. See J. Schwarzkopf (1991) *Women in the Chartist Movement* (Basingstoke: Macmillan), *passim* but esp. p. 287.
19. Ibid.
20. Perhaps the trailblazer for this was B. Taylor (1983) *Eve and the New Jerusalem: Socialism and Feminism in the Nineteenth Century* (London: Virago).
21. Anon. (1844) *The Trial of Thomas Paterson for Blasphemy, Before the High Court of Justiciary, Edinburgh, With the Whole of his Bold and Effective Defence. Also, The Trials of Thomas Finlay and Miss Matilda Roalfe (For Blasphemy), In the Sheriff's Court* (London: H. Hetherington), p. 75.
22. See Rogers, *Women and the People*, and Clark, *The Struggle for the Breeches*.
23. See Nash, *Blasphemy in Modern Britain*, pp. 32–7.
24. Anon. (1825) *Report of the Trial of Mrs Carlile on the Attorney General's Ex-Officio Information for the Protection of Tyrants* (London: Richard Carlile), p. 9.
25. Ibid., p. 11.
26. Ibid., pp. 11–12.
27. Ibid., p. 13.
28. *John Bull*, 21 January 1821, p. 48.
29. Anon., *Report of the Trial of Mrs Carlile*, p. 30.
30. Ibid., p. 31
31. Ibid., p. 33.
32. *John Bull*, 30 July 1821, p. 260.
33. Anon. (1821) *Suppressed Defence: The Defence of Mary Anne Carlile to the Vice Society's Indictment against the Appendix to the Theological Works of Thomas Paine* (London: Richard Carlile), p. 6.
34. Ibid., p. 10.
35. *John Bull*, 18 November 1821, p. 387.
36. Anon., *Suppressed Defence*, p. 10.
37. Hansard: House of Commons Debates, 26 March 1823, vol. 8, cols 709–34.
38. Anon., *Suppressed Defence*., pp. 4–5, 16, and 21–3.
39. Ibid.
40. See C. Parolin (2010) *Radical Spaces: Venues of Popular Politics in London, 1790–c. 1845* (Canberra: Australian National University Press), pp. 83–103, and I. McCalman (1980) 'Females, Feminism and Free Love in an Early Nineteenth Century Radical Movement', *Labour History*, 38, pp. 1–25.
41. Parolin, *Radical Spaces*, p. 86.

42. R. Carlile (1822) *Report of the Trial of Mrs Susannah Wright for Publishing, in his Shop, the Writings and Correspondence of R. Carlile; before Chief Justice Abbott, and a Special Jury in the Court of King's Bench, Guildhall, London, on Monday, July 8, 1822: Indictment at the instance of the Society for the Suppression of Vice* (London: Richard Carlile), p. 3.
43. Ibid.
44. Parolin, *Radical Spaces*, pp. 86–7.
45. Carlile, *Report of the Trial of Mrs Susannah Wright*, p. 6.
46. Ibid., p. 9.
47. Ibid., p. 10.
48. Ibid.
49. Ibid., p. 11.
50. Ibid., p. 12.
51. See D. S. Nash (2020) '"Police Fiasco", "The Black Army", "Devil Dodgers" and "Humbug": The Apparent Inevitability of Unfair Blasphemy Trials up to 1922', in D. S. Nash and A.-M. Kilday (eds), *Fair and Unfair Trials in Nineteenth Century England* (London: Bloomsbury), pp. 175–94.
52. Carlile, *Report of the Trial of Mrs Susannah Wright*, pp. 8–9.
53. Ibid., p. 9.
54. Ibid., pp. 14–25.
55. Ibid., p. 36.
56. Ibid.
57. Ibid., pp. 44 and 48.
58. Ibid., p. 55.
59. *The Times*, 22 November 1822.
60. Parolin, *Radical Spaces*, pp. 92–9. Parolin notes that Susannah's offer to desist from spreading her ideas was a powerful incentive for the authorities to extend relatively lenient treatment to her whilst incarcerated.
61. Ibid., p. 91.
62. Ibid., p. 93. Christina Parolin cites Lucia Zedner's assertion that female immorality (which blasphemy was considered to be) became a most spectacular fall from grace, which meant the language used to describe them degenerated swiftly into the realm of the monstrous.
63. Ibid., p. 98.
64. Ibid., p. 102.
65. See Anon., *The Trial of Thomas Paterson for Blasphemy*, pp. 13–59.
66. See *The Movement and Anti-Persecution Gazette*, 8 June 1844. Henry Robinson was also charged with publishing family limitation literature (some from Carlile) and *Fanny Hill*. Robinson's output included satirical assaults on the Bible written in verse.
67. Anon., *The Trial of Thomas Paterson for Blasphemy*, p. 75.
68. Ibid., p. 76.
69. Ibid.
70. Ibid.
71. *The Edinburgh Evening Courant*, 25 January 1844.
72. Anon., *The Trial of Thomas Paterson for Blasphemy*, p. 78.

73. Cosmopolite (1843) *The Bible an Improper Book for Youth and Dangerous to the Easily Excited Brain; with Immoral and Contradictory Passages from Holy Writ* (Edinburgh: Henry Robinson), pp. 3, 4, and 8.
74. Anon., *The Trial of Thomas Paterson for Blasphemy*. See within this the *Indictment against Thomas Paterson*, pp. 12–14.
75. Ibid., pp. 11–28. See also within this *Indictment against Thomas Finlay*, pp. 2–14 and the *Indictment against Henry Robinson*, pp. 9–21.
76. Ibid, p. 74.
77. Ibid.
78. Ibid., p. 80.
79. Anon., *Suppressed Defence*, p. 46.
80. R. Carlile (1822) *Speech of Mrs Susannah Wright before the Court of King's Bench on the 14th November 1822*, p. 4.
81. Ibid., p. 5.
82. Ibid., pp. 4–5.
83. Ibid., p. 23.
84. For more on this see L. Schwarz (2013) *Infidel Feminism: Secularism, Religion and Women's Emancipation, England 1830–1940* (Manchester: Manchester University Press).

# 4

# 'Angels of the House' or 'Angel-Makers'?

## Problematizing Murderous Mothers in the Nineteenth Century

### Introduction

Although motherhood had clearly been revered in early and ancient history, it was not until the early modern period that the specific traits of 'good' motherhood were properly identified and discussed.[1] According to historians such as Shari Thurer and Emma Griffin, mothers were to be sensible, patient, gentle, and kind. They were to serve as beacons of virtue for their children and were to be selfless and unfailing in the care and nurturing that they offered.[2] From the eighteenth century onwards, good motherhood was regarded as an essential component of respectability and maternity came to be admired and idealized as a result.[3]

The indisputable importance of motherhood was something nineteenth-century commentators were acutely aware of and repeatedly wrote about.[4] Consider, for instance, the views of Alice King, writing in *The Girl's Own Paper* in 1882:

> Motherhood is women's highest, fullest royalty, her season of most splendid prerogative, of her widest rule, when her influence, her broad dominion, her sovereign power, stretches far on into rising generations, sways the men and women who are to be, mould and colours the minds, and manners, and deeds of the distant future. Yes, motherhood is queenly with a supremacy of royalty that shines out in a noontide radiance to which scarcely any light on earth can compare... Motherhood is the highest crown of womanhood.[5]

A similarly reverent but exalted tone was evident in correspondence sent to *The Women's Signal* magazine just a few years later, again offering a description of motherhood:

> To be a mother is the grandest vocation in the world. No other human being has a position of such power and influence. She holds in her hands the destiny of nations, for to her is necessarily committed the making of the nation's citizens... To her is entrusted in a large measure the working out of God's ideal for

*Beyond Deviant Damsels: Re-evaluating Female Criminality in the Nineteenth Century.* Anne-Marie Kilday and David Nash, Oxford University Press. © Anne-Marie Kilday and David Nash 2023. DOI: 10.1093/oso/9780198830733.003.0004

> each child given to her care; and upon her it largely depends whether characters shall be rounded out into fulness of a noble manhood or womanhood, or dwarfed by neglect, and deformed by sin.

This time, however, in recognizing the importance of the role, the author finishes their commentary by encouraging society to continue its campaign to 'educate and cultivate *good* mothers' and 'to develop the science of *good motherhood*'.[6]

In the wake of burgeoning concerns over the levels of maternal mortality and infant mortality, nineteenth-century social commentators recognized that, although the qualities of good motherhood were largely innate and based on the manifestation of natural maternal instinct, interventions to improve mothering were still possible. Consequently, medical professionals increasingly publicized their advice and prescriptive literature on child care abounded, as scholars such as Patricia Branca and Deborah Gorham have observed.[7] Through these means, the techniques and practices of motherhood could be enhanced or even professionalized, to secure the health and moral welfare of future generations. More subliminally, of course, such mechanisms could also be used to reinforce key elements of the prevailing patriarchal order, as they encouraged motherhood to be a life-long career for women.[8]

The problem with this new 'cult of maternity' was that it was founded on middle-class ideologies which encouraged the separation of the world of work from the world of domesticity. However, the notion of separate spheres, where men went out to work and women remained the 'angels of the house', was certainly not relevant to working-class women. As historians such as Ellen Ross and Jenni Calder have shown, they could not afford to participate in such ideological ideals as they needed to earn a wage in order to survive.[9] The rejection of 'good' motherhood by working-class mothers, even if out of practical necessity, rendered them problematic to respectable Victorian society. Working women did not adhere to gender norms, they challenged patriarchal structures, they threatened to undermine the male wage, and they put the cultivation and moral development of future generations in doubt.[10] Concerns were voiced from the middle of the nineteenth century that a cult of '*bad*' motherhood was spreading across nineteenth-century society, and like a contagion, if it was not halted, it would begin to infect Victorian society more widely.[11] The crime of infanticide was considered to be one extreme manifestation of this trend towards anti-motherhood and, by the 1860s, the offence was assumed to be rampant across Victorian Britain.[12]

The killing of unwanted children by their mothers is a criminal act with a long history.[13] Typically, but not exclusively committed against new-born children and known as infanticide, this type of offence, prior to the 1900s at least, was commonly committed by young, unmarried, working-class women, often in domestic service, who had concealed their pregnancies, given birth in secret, and then killed their offspring, believing that they had little alternative than to do so.[14]

The methodologies of child murder could be both active and passive in nature and whilst the deployment of violence was not uncommon, it was typically used to expedite the death of the infant and thereby minimize the chance of it crying and alerting anyone to the clandestine event.[15] The relentless opprobrium associated with illegitimacy (for both the mother and the child), the persistent financial difficulties to be encountered, as well as the limitations unmarried motherhood posed for a woman's career ambitions. Likewise impact upon her personal development, and indeed any future marital prospects, were all deemed to be potential causal factors for historic child murder, as the work of Anne-Marie Kilday has clearly testified.[16]

In the nineteenth century, however, and as we have seen, this kind of homicidal activity increasingly came to be considered within a context where the traits of 'good' motherhood had been defined, identified, and exemplified. Thus, it became more straightforward to contrast 'good' motherhood with 'bad' motherhood or even 'anti-motherhood', of which child murder was the ultimate, extreme example. So how were women accused of this crime regarded by a nineteenth-century populace who increasingly held maternity as something sacrosanct and undefilable? Were these women more vilified by the vagaries of the Victorian press than other violent or homicidal women, as they had not only betrayed the gentility of their sex by their actions, but had also betrayed their inherent, God-given maternal instinct too?

This chapter will examine the impact of the moral panic over motherhood in the nineteenth century through the analysis of the experiences of two Scottish women accused of child murder at that time. We will determine how Scottish women accused of this crime fared within this pressurized and opinionated context. Interestingly, some newspaper reports at the peak of the moral panic argued that Scotland was immune from the types of 'anti-motherhood' that so persistently plagued its southern neighbours.[17] Does this revelation explain why the Scottish experience of child murder in the Victorian period has largely been ignored by historians? Was child murder really a rare occurrence in the Scottish context? How were women accused of this crime regarded when instances of this offence were brought under the public gaze? Were they condemned, maligned, and ostracized for their actions as we would assume from the evident strength of public and authoritative feeling on this issue?

## The Rise of the 'Anti-Mother' in Nineteenth-Century Britain

At the very start of the nineteenth century, before the concepts of 'good' and 'bad' motherhood had been fully established or articulated, the legal context for child murder changed in Britain, largely in order to put prosecutions for the offence on a surer footing. Effectively, legislation passed in England in 1803 and in Scotland in 1809 made concealment of pregnancy a separate, alternative, and lesser charge to that of child murder or infanticide, when they had formally been conjoined.[18] In addition, the punishment upon conviction for concealment was no longer to be execution, as it had been since the seventeenth century, but a maximum sentence of two years' imprisonment.

Although women could still be indicted for child murder, as the work of Kilday has shown, crimes of this nature were now to be tried as a species of homicide and subject to the same legal directives and penal sanctions as that offence.[19] As the nineteenth century wore on, concerns were voiced at how many women were being prosecuted for concealment of pregnancy rather than for child murder, even in the face of damning evidence, so that the thorny issue of the capital punishment of women could be avoided. Some Victorians argued that the judicial authorities were turning a blind eye to murderous mothers. Others went as far as to say that the legislation effectively sanctioned 'anti-motherhood'.[20]

These publicly voiced concerns undoubtedly contributed to the notion that there was a growing problem with immorality, child welfare, and indeed child homicide in nineteenth-century Britain. Indeed, it came to be suggested that, despite the best efforts of social and moral reformers, practices associated with 'bad' motherhood rather than 'good' motherhood were the ones taking hold across British society. Further evidence to substantiate these fears regularly appeared throughout the Victorian era and was eagerly promulgated by the press. In the first instance, reports circulated that illegitimacy rates were spiralling out of control, with the situation particularly acute in Scotland, where rates there regularly ran higher than in England and Wales in the nineteenth century. The fact that the infant mortality rate had commensurately risen to extraordinary levels too over the course of the period caused some commentators to link the two issues and blame immoral women and feckless mothers for both.[21]

In a similar vein, and as we have already seen, there was a belief that the rate of infanticide or child murder in Britain was ever increasing and that, by 1860, it had reached an unprecedented level. Commentators bemoaned the fact that little was being done to curb the ravages of the murderous mother.[22] Indeed, they argued that not only was the early nineteenth-century legislation too lenient and too forgiving in relation to infanticidal mothers, but that the standards of evidence required for a conviction for either concealment or child murder proper had become so exacting as to render them effectively unattainable for the discerning prosecutor.[23] Furthermore, as the work of Hilary Marland has indicated, it was increasingly evident that accused women were now able to deploy pleas of temporary insanity to explain their actions, avoid execution, and reinstate themselves at some future time as appropriate representatives of their gender within the prevailing patriarchal structure.[24]

As historians such as David Bentley and Lionel Rose have indicated, additional evidence came in the form of scandalous newspaper exposés about back-street abortions, illicit adoptions, and baby-dropping or baby-farming practices. All of these testified to the fact that people, especially women, had a considerable number of different routes open to them whereby they could rid themselves of an unwanted child with relative ease and discretion.[25] Whilst for some liberal Victorians, all of this evidence was palatable and indicative of a welcome move towards modernity, many others believed it to be collectively symptomatic of a barbaric, uncivilized, and fated society. One that had become devoid of reverence for religion, morality, or those intrinsic social values formerly deemed so essential for the nurturing, development, and survival of future generations.[26] These concerns had multiplied to such an extent by the mid-point of the century that, when fuelled by press sensationalism and other societal fears, they resulted in the creation of a moral panic and the conception of a new figure that was to take centre stage in the late Victorian consciousness: the 'anti-mother'.

Effectively, the burgeoning problems associated with Victorian motherhood had all stemmed, as we have seen, from women who worked and who had thereby rejected the tenets of 'good' motherhood propounded to them by respectable society. Such women had despised suggestions that the adoption of nurturing qualities within the domestic context would enhance the survival rates for infants. They had ignored arguments that the child was the most valuable commodity for the future prosperity and strength of the nation and thus should be their singular priority. They had spurned the notion that the adoption of maternity would result in improved social equality and enhanced familial happiness. In sum, and as scholars such as Elisabeth Badinter and Tracy Nelson have pointed out, they had discarded the gift of maternal instinct and instead were selfish, negligent, unworthy, and debased. Instead they favoured the material world of work (or education) rather than the maternal world of the home.[27]

The moral panic over motherhood that originated in the middle of the nineteenth century, principally occurred in response to fears regarding the disintegration of stable family life in the wake of industrialization. The traditional emotional, cultural, and economic functions of the family were said to be diminishing in the domestic context and were being transferred instead into the public sphere of wider society, where they were of far less importance. It was believed that this process would weaken the moral, financial, and demographic future of the British nation and its people, and would decrease national efficiency, whilst at the same time increasing its vulnerability to external threats. As historian Meg Arnot explains, the fear-mongering that escalated as a result of the widely publicized articulation of these beliefs, initiated a frantic clamour and public campaign to preserve the traditional family unit at all costs.[28]

In order to discourage this flight from the home, working mothers in particular, were vilified by the press, by social commentators, and by the government. Such women were said not to love their children. This in itself, was 'considered an unforgivable crime that no virtue can redeem. It put that mother beyond the pale of humanity, since she had lost her true female self.'[29] The mothers of *illegitimate* children, who had little choice other than to work, given that they had to support both themselves and their offspring on their own, fared even worse in the context of this moral panic. Not only did they have to endure the social opprobrium of bearing an illegitimate child, but their shame was further compounded by suggestions that they were not 'good' mothers either.[30] The temptation to avoid all of this stress, hardship, and disgrace must have been significant amongst Victorian working-class mothers. Indeed, and as we will see in our case studies below, getting rid of the burden of maternity may well have been seen by some as the *only* solution—albeit a desperate and radical one—where an individual's survival could be potentially secured within a context of relentless penury.

As we have seen, illicit abortions, baby-dropping or abandonment, baby-farming, or even killing an infant to recoup its burial insurance or to avoid the ongoing pressures of its upkeep, were all options open to, and utilized by, nineteenth-century women. Indeed, and according to the Victorian media at least, these unscrupulous, mercenary, and avaricious practices had essentially become commonplace amongst the poorest classes of Britain by the mid-point of the century.[31] The public health reformer Joseph Kay (1821–78) summed up contemporary fears in 1850, saying:

> a greater part of the poorer classes of this country are sunk into such a frightful depth of hopelessness, misery, and utter degradation, that even mothers forget their affection for their helpless little offspring and kill them, as a butcher does his lambs…and therewith lessen their pauperism and misery.[32]

Although there had been some misplaced bravado in some quarters of the Scottish press suggesting that 'anti-motherhood' was non-existent north of the Tweed in the nineteenth century, a cursory examination of newspapers in the second half of the century reveals similar concerns over maternal malpractice to be evident. There were numerous well-publicized instances of baby-farming for instance and concerns over child murder endured.[33] By 1862, for example, infanticide was said to have become 'fearfully common' in Scotland and was 'increasing at a frightful rate' to the extent that finding the dead body of a newly born infant had been rendered an 'ordinary occurrence'.[34] In the next decade, the situation had seemingly worsened as 'infanticide was becoming not the crime, but the custom of a nation that calls itself the most civilised on the face of the earth'.[35] In 1893, it was reported that child killing remained 'a fearful plague preying on the vitals of the Scottish population'.[36]

However, it would seem that perennial reports were nothing more than hyperbole on the part of the sensation-seeking Scottish press. Extensive research by Kilday has shown that the number of reported instances of child murder and concealment of pregnancy diminished over the second half of the nineteenth century.[37] Moreover, the number of indictments brought to court fell at a faster rate over this period and the number of convictions were fewer still and falling over time.[38] So did the panic over 'anti-motherhood' in the Scottish context stem from the way the crime was perpetrated and the reactions to it, rather than the incidence of the offence? An examination of the experiences of two women indicted for child murder in nineteenth-century Scotland will help us to answer this question and to learn more about prevailing attitudes to motherhood and to those women who seemingly shunned that role.

## The 'Anti-Mother' Personified? The Crime of Barbara Malcom (1808)

In December 1807, when the concept of the 'anti-mother' was not yet fully developed or exposed to the public gaze, newspapers reported that a woman called Barbara Malcolm had been committed to the Tolbooth of Edinburgh on a charge of unlawfully killing her 18-month-old daughter Margaret.[39] Despite this case occurring two years before the passing of the revised Scottish legislation on child murder discussed above, it was evident that the authorities were going to deal with this particular episode as a homicide, rather than an infanticide. At first glance, we might have assumed that this was because the age of the victim was beyond the upper limit of what might be categorized as a new-born-child murder: normally defined as the killing of an infant under the age of one. However, it is more likely that the real reason for the distinctive judicial treatment of this case at this particular point in the nineteenth century related to the specific methodology deployed by the perpetrator of the offence. For, as press reports went on to reveal, the accused had poured a quantity of oil of vitriol down her daughter's throat and that, as a result, 'the child expired in the most dreadful torments. So powerful was the poison, that in a few minutes the bottom of the new tin jug, in which it was contained, was entirely destroyed.'[40] Evidently, the unusual nature of this fatal criminal episode had necessitated an unorthodox reaction from the Scottish authorities.

The trial against Barbara Malcolm began at the High Court of Justiciary in Edinburgh on 5 January 1808.[41] The court heard that a few years before, whilst the accused had been a domestic servant in the New Town of Edinburgh, she had begun a relationship with a soldier in the Inverness-shire militia called Sutherland. The pair had a child together—the erstwhile victim in this case Margaret Sutherland—but not long after Margaret's birth, the couple's relationship broke down.[42] Initially, Barbara had tried hard to adopt the qualities of a 'good' mother, despite the illicit context within which her maternity had been conceived. For instance, she managed to support herself and to sustain her daughter's welfare after losing her job and being abandoned by Sutherland and left on her own.[43]

She put Margaret out to nurse with the Gordon family who resided in the Portsburgh area in the south-side of the city, and then offered herself as a wet-nurse to a family nearby.[44] In Scotland, even by the nineteenth century, this was a very common strategy deployed by new mothers to make the most of their post-partum condition, by providing breast milk for a child whose own mother could not or would not do so. Moreover, and as the plethora of advertisements offering this service amidst the pages of Scottish newspapers testify, it must have been a convenience which remained in high demand throughout the post-1800 period.[45]

To begin with, Barbara was just about able to make ends meet as she earned £3 per quarter in wages as a wet-nurse and had to give £2 per quarter to the nurse she herself employed. However, when her mistress's child was weaned, her wages were reduced to £1 per quarter and Barbara Malcom grew increasingly desperate and despondent due to her penury.[46] She must also have felt frustrated by the limited options she had to remedy her situation, given nineteenth-century views on working mothers and the unsympathetic attitude of parish officials and private charities towards bastardy.[47] She became determined to extract financial assistance from Mr Sutherland and repeatedly went to Musselburgh to see him and to beg that he contribute to the upkeep of their daughter. However, as the couple's relationship had evidently soured further by this point in time, Barbara's entreaties were either blatantly ignored or forcefully refused.[48]

The court heard that, after Barbara was repeatedly rebuffed in this way by her former lover, 'her temper, which was described to be very mild, underwent a material alteration... She did not appear to be the same person as formerly.'[49] This is an interesting observation and one that might go some way to explain the actions of women like Barbara Malcolm who, when seduced and abandoned in this way, became determined to take out their vengeance upon the child that had been begotten through this illicit union, which served as a pervasive and very public reminder of their personal rejection and intimate humiliation.[50]

On Sunday 6 December 1807, Barbara Malcolm decided to visit her daughter and, when she arrived, the head of the household where she was being nursed, Adam Gordon, reported to Barbara that the child (Margaret) had a sore mouth on account of having a cold.[51] Two days later, Barbara visited the Portsburgh residence again, but this time she brought the child she was nursing along with her too. She gave Mr Gordon that infant, lifted Margaret up on to her knee and sent Mrs Gordon out to get some honey for the child.[52] Whilst Adam Gordon was walking about trying to hush the child he was caring for, he heard the infant Margaret Sutherland 'scream out violently'. When he asked Barbara Malcolm what she was doing to her child, she answered 'that she was only giving it some raw sugar to settle her cold and clear her throat' and she 'put a piece of sugar into his hand'.[53]

Gordon was not persuaded by this explanation, especially when Barbara Malcolm left the premises with her mistress's child, leaving her daughter with him 'in great agony, which increased during the forenoon'.[54] Adam Gordon and his wife became increasingly concerned about the wellbeing of Margaret Sutherland as she seemed to be suffering much pain and distress. At about two o'clock in the afternoon, they sent for a 'medical gentleman' who came to their house and dispensed some linctus for the child.[55] Sadly, however, this treatment had no remedial effect and, as Adam Gordon described to the High Court, Margaret Sutherland then 'languished in excruciating torment till between five and six in the evening, when she died'.[56]

When Barbara Malcolm was arrested by the authorities in the wake of her daughter's death, she told police officers that she had given her daughter some sugar of lead.[57] Although, this elucidation differed somewhat from Barbara's previous comments to Adam Gordon, it did not necessarily implicate Barbara in the murder of her child, as lead acetate or sugar of lead was commonly used as a sweetener in the nineteenth century, long before its toxic qualities were fully appreciated. However, Barbara changed her story to the authorities once again, just a few days later, admitting, in a declaration before the Sheriff, that she had given her daughter oil of vitriol, which she had purchased at an apothecary shop, the day before visiting the Gordon household.[58] This latter, more damning testimony, was corroborated by the evidence of two surgeons who performed a post-mortem on the body of Margaret Sutherland. Based on their examinations, they concluded that it was 'clearly proven' that the child 'died of strong poison' as when its body was opened, 'the stomach was found much burnt and corroded'.[59] The clothes that Margaret Sutherland wore at the time of her death were also produced in court as evidence for the prosecution. They were burnt through in several places, where the child had vomited upon herself.[60]

Oil of vitriol was the colloquial term for sulphuric acid. It is colourless when in its purest form, is of an oily consistency, is free from smell and highly corrosive.[61] From the eighteenth century onwards, it was used in agriculture and in various manufacturing processes, particularly in the textile industry where it was commonly used for bleaching and dyeing purposes, with the largest vitriol factory in Britain established at Prestonpans near Edinburgh in 1749.[62] This facility undoubtedly aided the rapid expansion of the Scottish linen and cotton industries from the dawn of the 1800s and thus oil of vitriol had an evident part to play in the nation's industrial development. Oil of vitriol was present in the domestic context too, where it was used as a fast and efficient cleaning accelerant in diluted form. For instance, it became a popular aid in the scouring of copper pots, cooking vessels, and other kitchen utensils and, as a result, it 'became a relatively ubiquitous substance', both in Scotland and elsewhere.[63] It could be purchased cheaply, in concentrated form, from a variety of different retailers.[64] As well as these practical uses, oil of vitriol came to be associated with a new type of urban criminal activity from the first third of the nineteenth century onwards, as there were various documented reports of the acid being deliberately thrown at intended victims in order to disfigure them or burn through their clothing; either during a heated industrial dispute or in the process of an interpersonal assault of the kind we remain familiar with even today.[65] However, in 1807, when Barbara Malcolm killed her daughter, the practice of vitriol throwing was a wholly unfamiliar phenomenon.

The famous Scottish physician and toxicologist Professor Robert Christison (1797–1822) wrote about the particular deployment of oil of vitriol in the case against Barbara Malcolm in his *Treatise on Poisons* published in 1829.[66] He noted that it would be effectively impossible to kill an adult using oil of vitriol 'on account of the powerful taste and excessively acrid properties' of the poison, which would mean that no one 'in a state of consciousness' would voluntarily drink it.[67] Christison knew of only two other cases of deliberate application of oil of vitriol, besides the Malcolm case, and both of these involved infant victims. He pointed out that, in his view, oil of vitriol was 'the most violent of all irritants' and thus it rapidly proved fatal to those who consumed it.[68] Indeed, just a few years earlier, a contemporary of Christison, the surgeon and professor of medical jurisprudence, John Gordon Smith (1792–1833), had offered a detailed description of the catastrophic effects that drinking concentrated sulphuric acid had on the internal workings of the human body. He noted:

> Taken into the stomach, it produces the most dreadful sensation: excruciating pain—nausea and excessive vomiting—the black matter ejected from the stomach being often very black, from the destruction of the fibre, or red from the mixture of blood, giving extreme pain, as it passes through the mouth, from its highly styptic quality... Tenderness and pain occur in the abdomen, accompanied either with costiveness, or bloody stool: there is universal uneasiness; general restlessness; and dejection; difficulty of respiration; quick, small, and irregular pulse; convulsive startings in the countenance; and, (what is peculiarly observable in these cases) conservation of the intellectual faculties. While all this is going on, the destruction of the soft parts about the mouth, as well as the fetor emanating from them, will be palpable to the observation of the by-stander.[69]

We must remember, of course, that this graphic description from Smith pertains to the impact that the consumption of sulphuric acid would have on an adult. The proportional horrific effects on the tiny body of an 18-month-old baby can only be imagined.

Despite evidence being presented to the court of Barbara Malcolm's formerly good character and her attentiveness as a servant, the evident context of desperation and desolation within which she had committed her crime, and the initial attempts she had made to assume the traits of the 'good' mother, there were various elements in this case which counted heavily against the accused.[70] First of all, and rather surprisingly given her detailed confession to the Sheriff, Barbara

Malcolm had pled not guilty to the crimes she had been charged with. Given the number of times she had changed the story of what had happened to her daughter in the course of the investigations into this case, this must have seemed like just another volte-face to the assembled courtroom and a deliberate ploy towards self-preservation on the part of the accused. The second element of the case which Barbara Malcolm's defence team had to wrestle with is one that will be more fully explored in the next chapter of this volume. This was the premeditation evidenced by their client when she purchased the oil of vitriol before coming to see her daughter a second time in the space of just a few days. This was tricky to explain away, especially when the court heard that Barbara had always been wholly lucid and 'of sober mind'.[71] Such testimony meant that the typical defences used in child murder cases by the nineteenth century to explain irrational instantaneous acts of violence, and explored in the introductory sections of this chapter, could not be applied in this instance. Finally, there was the gruesome methodology deployed in this case which was not only unusual, as the work of Kilday and Cathy Monholland has shown, but was irrefutably cold, calculating, and cruel.[72] For a mother to end the life of her own child in this vicious way is as unfathomable to us today as it must have been in 1808. When considering all of these issues, it is unsurprising that the assize did not need long to deliberate their verdict in this case. After 'a very short time' they unanimously declared Barbara Malcolm to be guilty of murder and the presiding judge ordered her to be executed at Edinburgh on 10 February and her body thereafter to be given over for public anatomization.[73]

Before this sentence was duly carried out, Barbara Malcolm was described as being 'very penitent and resigned' on her way to the gallows, but she was also deemed to be extremely feeble and weak, so much so that 'two men were obliged to support her at the place of execution' where she met her fate in front of 'a vast concourse of spectators assembled for the occasion'.[74] In a broadside produced in the aftermath of this case, the author was evidently at pains to point out the contrast between the purity and necessity of 'good motherhood', and the malevolence and brutishness of 'anti-motherhood', which was so clearly exemplified in the actions and persona of Barbara Malcolm. The document noted that:

> The wise and benevolent author of our being hath implanted in the human breath a principle of love and affection towards their offspring; which appears not only necessary to the continuation of the species, but is also the fountain of all the other social and benevolent affections, and the grand source of human happiness. Next to that of self-preservation, no principle is more powerful, or more universally diffused throughout creation. Indeed, the females of many of those in a domesticated state, and which are remarkable for the mildness and docility of their disposition, will attack in defence of their young, with astonishing ferocity.

> What apology therefore shall we make for a being...who, in contradiction to the voice of reason and the general law of animated nature, destroys, in the most cruel manner, her own offspring? Let us consider such a one, through the image of humanity, as *a monster of the species*, rarely to be met with amongst civilised beings.[75]

## The 'Anti-Mother' Personified? The Crimes of Catherine Anderson (1883 and 1890)

At the opposite end of the Scottish nation and at the other end of the nineteenth century, when the concept of the 'anti-mother' was far more firmly entrenched, another woman stood accused of the murder of her child. By many people's standards, this Aberdeenshire woman, Catherine Anderson, might also be considered, alongside Barbara Malcolm, as 'a monster of the species', as well as a rather unique character in the annals of Scottish crime, as she was an infanticidal recidivist. The first of her two prosecutions for child murder came on 26 June 1883, when the 18-year-old bleachfield worker was indicted at the High Court in Aberdeen.[76]

The court heard a lot of detailed evidence about this case from a variety of different witnesses; most of whom were for the prosecution. One of the most crucial pieces of testimony was provided by Ann Hunter (or Anderson), the mother of the accused. She explained to the court that on 8 March 1881, when Catherine Anderson was barely 16 years of age, she gave birth to an illegitimate child—a son.[77] Ann and her husband James took the decision to support their daughter in her exigent circumstances and allowed both the new mother and her baby to remain in the family home.[78] The father of the child, who was an overseer at the bleachfield where Catherine worked, initially acknowledged his responsibilities to the baby and paid the Anderson family a small amount towards its upkeep, but not long after the child's birth he left the Hardgate area of Aberdeen and did not return.[79] Mrs Anderson went on to testify to the sound and responsible behaviour of her daughter in the wake of this episode. She also variously described how Catherine was a 'good' mother to her young son, and how she would regularly lie with him in bed to ensure his comfort and to get him to sleep.[80]

In October 1882 (approximately six months before this particular trial), Mrs Anderson began to suspect that her daughter 'had fallen with child once again'. She repeatedly 'taxed' or questioned Catherine about her condition, but 'she distinctly denied it.' Despite these protestations, and when Ann Anderson believed her daughter's confinement to be near, she talked with Catherine once more about her condition and made it plain that she 'would need to look out for somebody to take charge of her child when it should be born as I could not accommodate it in

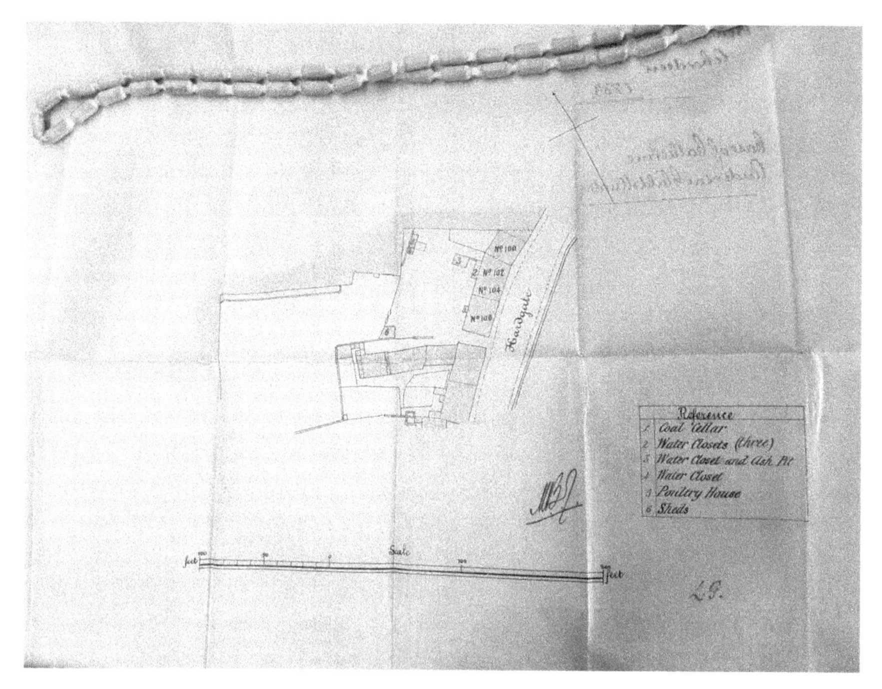


**Figure 4.1** Map of the Hardgate Vicinity as it Relates to the Prosecution Against Catherine Anderson (1883).

my house'.[81] This was probably because the 'half flat' at No. 100 Hardgate which the Anderson family occupied (see map in Figure 4.1[82]), already housed three adults and three children (two small infants and a chronically ill teenager) in just two tiny rooms.[83] Catherine Anderson told her mother she 'need not trouble herself about it as she knew who would take it'. Ann Anderson accepted her daughter's words 'as a distinct admission that she was with child'.[84]

This discussion may well have terrified, unnerved, and unsettled Catherine, as her mother had made it plain that the existing network of support which had enabled Catherine to continue working, and thereby support both herself and her first child, was about to disintegrate. She must have considered what social stigma would be heaped upon someone who had not one, but two illegitimate children in late nineteenth-century Scotland. More importantly, she must have realized that she was going to be on her own for the first time and would have to fend for not only her son and for herself, but for a new baby too, who would have to be fed, clothed, and cared for. How would she manage without her family's help? As she was able-bodied she would be ineligible for poor relief under the Scottish system put in place after 1845 and there was seemingly little prospect of any financial support coming from either of the absent fathers. But how could she manage to continue to work, if she had two young children to tend to on her own? We can only imagine the unremitting apprehension and burgeoning panic that Catherine Anderson must have felt in the latter stages of her second pregnancy.[85]

On 4 April 1883 at about 10 p.m., Mrs Anderson was returning from running an errand to a neighbouring shop when she bumped into Catherine who was hurriedly leaving their residence. Catherine had the key to the communal outdoor water closet in her hand and a candle. She asked her mother for the shawl she was wearing and went out. When Catherine did not return for some time, James Anderson, her father, went out to look for her but he could not find her anywhere and noted that the water closet was empty. At around 1 a.m. the next morning, Mrs Anderson heard her daughter return. When questioned by her mother on her whereabouts, Catherine claimed she had been visiting her good friend Maggie Gray, who also lived in the Hardgate. She then drank a considerable quantity of cold water, washed her hands and arms in a basin, took off her boots, and went to bed.[86]

Shortly after this, a 'vile moaning sound' was heard coming from the room Catherine slept in. Presently, Margaret Anderson (Catherine's teenage sister) called out 'Mother! There's something the matter with Kate tonight, she's moaning awfully!'[87] Mrs Anderson quickly got out of bed, assuming that Catherine had gone into labour. When, by chance, she looked in the basin that her daughter had washed herself in, she found 'the sparks of soap suds round about it and the piece of soap beside it tinged with the colour of blood'. Then, upon going into the other room, she discovered a chamber pot at the side of Catherine's bed 'half full of blood' and became 'convinced that a child had been born'. Ann Anderson immediately wanted to send for a doctor for Catherine, but the girl 'pleaded with her not to do so'.[88] She asked her daughter where the child was and Catherine said she had given birth at the back of the water closet door after 'such a struggle' and she had then taken the baby to the bleachfield.[89] Mrs Anderson could not understand why her daughter had left the baby at her place of work, rather than bring it into the family home. Catherine explained that she did this because the baby had been born dead after falling from her head-first on to the hard floor of the water closet. When further questioned by her parents as to who the father of the child was, Catherine said she did not know his name. She explained that she had been attending a sick child in a neighbour's house one evening, and the said man had been an acquaintance of the family and had come to visit them. He stayed the night with Catherine, left the next morning, and she never heard from him or saw him again.[90]

Ann Anderson went outside just before daybreak to inspect the truth of what her daughter had told her and she did indeed find a great deal of blood both inside the water closet and on the pavement outside. She also located a quantity of afterbirth in a nearby passageway. She gathered all of this up with a shovel and put in a dust bucket and then proceeded to wash away as much of the blood as she could. Her efforts were not wholly successful, however, as early that morning, a neighbour—Helen Henderson—came to complain to Ann Anderson about blood she had found on the floor behind the door of the water closet. Mrs Anderson suggested to Mrs Henderson 'that it might have been occasioned by dogs killing a cat'.[91] Having seemingly satisfied her neighbour's curiosity, Ann Anderson once again suggested to her daughter that she should send for medical help as she remained weak and in a stupefied state, but as before, Catherine begged both of her parents to be left unattended.[92]

Mrs Anderson was acutely aware of the potential gravity of the situation that she, her family, and especially her daughter found herself in. As she revealed in court:

> We felt sure enough that the matter would be known somehow or other, but we were at our wits end and our other daughter who had fainted repeatedly was in such a state that we thought that it need to be by us that it should be published.[93]

So they agreed between themselves to remain quiet about the whole affair and keep both the pregnancy and the baby's death a secret. A few days later, Mr Anderson read from the newspapers that the corpse of a baby had been found, but not at the bleachfield as Catherine had said, but at the seaside at Torry, approximately a mile and a half from the Anderson home at Hardgate.[94] Hearing the description provided of the articles that the body had been wrapped in, Catherine Anderson acknowledged to her parents that the gruesome find related to her own newly born child and she became determined to immediately leave the family home and go to Dundee to stay with relatives.[95]

Upon discovery of the infant's remains, a criminal investigation was launched by Aberdeen Police. Officer Alexander Smith testified to the court that the police initially believed that the hunt for the mother of the dead child might prove difficult, but their enquiries were expedited when the watch house received two anonymous letters which focused their attentions on the family residing at No. 100 Hardgate and upon Catherine Anderson in particular. Upon visiting the house, the investigating officers discovered various articles of bed linen and a green shawl 'distinctly stained and presenting the most extensive marks of blood'. In addition, they found some worsted cloth under the dresser which appeared to compare well with that found around the body of the dead child. They took away all of these items as evidence.[96] Then, when conducting house-to-house interviews with some of the Anderson's neighbours, the officers learnt that the Hardgate community believed Catherine Anderson to have been with child and to have lately been delivered of it, recounting having seen marks of blood in various places in recent days, but especially in and around the communal water closet. When they went to investigate the water closet for themselves, and after striking a match to improve their visibility, the officers did indeed find 'very distinct marks of splashes of blood on the back of the door near the flow'. They also noted that the floor of the water closet was comprised of earth, not stone.[97]

After Catherine Anderson was formally apprehended and detained by police in Dundee, she was medically examined by two doctors. From their observations, the medical men agreed that Catherine had given birth about ten days before and that the child had been delivered 'at or about the full term of pregnancy'.[98] No comments were offered about Catherine's mental state. With evidence mounting against her, Catherine eventually admitted to the authorities in a sworn declaration that she had concealed her pregnancy, not made any preparations for the birth, and had delivered her baby in secret. She explained that she had given birth standing up and that the baby came away from her entirely and she did not need to separate it from her. However, she did not know whether it had been born alive or dead as at no time, did she touch the child to check its status. She did not hear the baby cry or see it move.[99] Catherine was adamant that she had not used 'any violence to the child' and utterly refuted allegations that she had assaulted her new-born infant in the wake of its birth.[100] She did acknowledge that she had hidden the baby's body in an outside cellar for a few days until she had recovered from her parturition. Once this had been achieved, she explained that she had wrapped it all up in an apron and a piece of cloth that she had found in the cellar, carried it over to Torry, 'and flung it into the sea'.[101]

Catherine also revealed that she had not been entirely truthful to her parents with regard to the events surrounding the conception of her late child. She did, in fact, know the father of the baby and named him as Alexander Mackie, a tinsmith from Aberdeen. Catherine explained that, as he had left for America before she found out that she was pregnant, she decided not to contact him or seek his support.[102] However, the police investigation cast doubt on Catherine's claims. After checking town and transportation records, Officer Smith was satisfied that Alexander Mackie was a fiction and had never existed. Furthermore, he was also able to prove that Catherine's story of a one-night-stand when looking after a sick child was also a fabrication. Rather, it was his belief that the father of the child was the resident manager of the bleachfield where Catherine Anderson worked. This man was the successor to the previous manager and father of Catherine's first-born child: a seemingly unfortunate case of history repeating itself.

Further evidence which undermined Catherine's sworn statement came from Drs Robert John Garden and William John Ritchie Simpson who performed a post-mortem on the body of the new-born infant discovered at Torry. They jointly reported from their examinations that the body was that of a female child which had come to its maturity, had been born alive, and had breathed freely.[103] Although there were strings of fabric wound around its neck, these were loose and had not occasioned the infant's demise. They were clear that 'The child had neither been strangled nor drowned...and it had not bled to death either.'[104] Indeed, the medical men observed just two injuries upon the body of the child:

several fractures of the ribs and multiple fractures of the skull. They determined that the former of these two injuries, the rib fractures, had been deliberately inflicted, with the damage being caused through a kick to the trunk of the child or by someone treading firmly upon its torso. However, they deemed that, in their professional opinion, the receipt of this injury had not proved fatal for the baby girl.[105]

Instead, Garden and Simpson linked expiration in this case to the discernible skull fractures. From their internal and external scrutiny of the cadaver, the men were able to conclude that the baby had died suddenly 'Either by it having been struck sharply *with* some hard substance, or by its having been sharply struck *upon* some hard substance.' Both professionals were convinced that

> the fractures of the skull could not have been occasioned by any ordinary accident at the birth such as rough handling or falling a short distance. Fractures from accidental falls are generally slight, whereas these were multiple, extensive fractures.[106]

From the available forensic evidence and from their combined experience, the two medical men were unconvinced by Catherine Anderson's claims that the child had been delivered from a standing position. Instead, they believed 'the mother had been lying or kneeling on the ground' during parturition and that, post-delivery, 'one or two determined kicks with the toe of an ordinary stout women's boot might well have made the fractures.'[107] Given this suggestion, it is interesting for us to note that, upon her arrest, Catherine Anderson was wearing a pair of very distinctive yellow leather stout boots of the Victorian style.[108] Moreover, when she made her declaration to the authorities Catherine said: 'I did not put my foot upon it. I am sure enough of this.'[109] She made this part of her statement without being prompted and in ignorance of the specific injuries uncovered by the autopsy performed upon her baby daughter. In any event, Drs Garden and Simpson 'concluded with certainty that the injuries to the skull were inflicted *during life* and were the cause of death.'[110]

Despite the various revelations made to the Scottish authorities and the damning prosecution testimony offered in court that pointed to the accused as the very personification of 'bad' motherhood due to her recurrent depravity, her insolence, and her violent tendencies, Catherine Anderson pleaded not guilty to the charge against her.[111] Described by the press as having 'a prepossessing appearance,'[112] it was a surprise to many that Catherine did not deploy the typical defence tactic used to explain episodes of Victorian child murder and claim that she had suffered from temporary mental instability during parturition. Instead, she rested the entirety of her case on medical evidence provided by two Aberdeen doctors, Robert Beveridge and Forbes Maitland Moir, who testified that the infant's injuries could, after all, have been caused by a standing delivery and not necessarily by deliberate violence inflicted by the child's mother. The men further suggested that the act of hurling the child's remains off the cliff at Torry may well have inflicted additional injuries to the baby's skull and ribs post-mortem, as the area there 'is a rocky mass'. They argued that, in their considered opinion, it was utterly impossible to discern when, where, and how the various injuries observed upon the body of the baby had occurred.[113] This testimony, by two well-established and well-respected medical professionals must have been persuasive to some extent, as after a lengthy deliberation the jury in this case decided unanimously that Catherine Anderson was guilty of the lesser charge of culpable homicide, rather than of murder. The judge in the case, Lord Deas (Sir George Deas, 1804–87) believed the verdict to be 'very lenient' and sentenced Catherine to five years' penal servitude; a relatively severe punishment, especially for a woman, within the confines and traditions of Scots law in the late nineteenth century.[114] The press recorded that the convicted prisoner 'seemed initially stunned by the sentence, but her pale demeanour soon evaporated and she became flushed and indignant at the declaration of her fate'.[115]

As well as being someone who seemingly exemplified the attributes of 'anti-motherhood' to an anxious Victorian populace, Catherine Anderson was also the quintessential slow learner who repeatedly struggled to learn from her mistakes. Remarkably, just nineteen months after the end of her five-year prison sentence, Catherine Anderson appeared at the High Court in Aberdeen in January 1890, charged with child murder for a second time.[116] On this occasion, concealment of pregnancy was suggested as an alternative indictment, as per the legislation passed in Scotland in 1809 and discussed earlier in this chapter. However, this was not used as Catherine chose to plead guilty to a charge of culpable homicide and this admission was accepted by all of the legal authorities concerned.[117]

Although Catherine Anderson's guilty plea negated the need for a full trial and thus no witness testimony was formally presented, the details of what transpired in this case can nonetheless be gleaned from the precognition evidence collected by the authorities in preparation for the criminal trial that they had assumed would take place. Outdoor worker and close friend of Catherine Anderson, Margaret Barrow spoke to the authorities on 13 November 1889. In the summer of that year, when the two women spent a lot of time together, she noticed her friend's appearance altering 'and was sure she was pregnant'. Margaret Barrow did not challenge her friend about this or ask her to confirm her condition, as 'she was not a woman to take liberties with'. Seemingly Catherine's experience of imprisonment had hardened her character and sensibilities somewhat!

In any event, Margaret noted that, by the very end of October, Catherine's shape had altered once more, and she was by then 'quite flat'. She overhead her neighbour, Mary Ann Slessor, remark to Catherine Anderson at that time about how she had managed to lose so much weight and so quickly. Catherine had replied that it was all an illusion, and she only looked slimmer because she was now 'wearing stays'.[118] Margaret Barrow was not persuaded by this explanation and being suspicious of her friend, and probably not wanting to be implicated in any criminal activity, she searched Catherine Anderson's room in Aberdeen's Stevenson Street (about a mile from her previous home at Hardgate) when she was out. She 'looked in the bed and about the room but saw none of the marks of a recent confinement'.[119]

Other women were similarly suspicious of Catherine Anderson's condition, but were also concerned about her welfare too. Catherine Hussy (or Strachan) was a colleague of the accused and worked with her as an outdoor gardener at Braeside of Pitfodels. She told the police that, as early as April 1889, rumours were circulating amongst the labourers that Catherine Anderson, whom she called Kate, was with child. Nothing was said to the accused at that time, but by the very end of September, she had evidently been 'paid off for being very irregular at her work'.[120] Mrs Strachan was perturbed by this turn of events and feared for the wellbeing of her friend. She told officers that the accused

> was very badly off being out of work. She had nothing to support her, and she has often told me that she had neither fire, nor light, nor food...I myself have several times given her food.[121]

Not for the first time, Catherine Anderson found herself in a desperate situation. She was alone, impoverished, starving, unemployed, and facing an uncertain future.[122] She must have been acutely aware of her circumstances as she had already been in this situation twice before. Of course, we can only speculate as to Catherine Anderson's mind-set at this moment. Had she already determined what the outcome of her pregnancy would be, or had she decided to let fate run its course?

Mrs Strachan caught up with Catherine Anderson about a fortnight after her dismissal to check on how she was faring and learnt that she was planning to go back to her erstwhile employer and ask if she could get work 'lifting potatoes' on the estate. Mrs Strachan then recounted the detail of the conversation that followed, which started with her exclaiming:

> 'Good Gracious Kate! You needn't speak about getting work! It wilnae [won't] be long or you be cry-in (meaning that she would soon be confined).'
>
> Kate said, 'How do you think that?'
>
> I said 'Do you think we're blind? They told us when you came out in the beginning of the year, that you were in that condition.'
>
> Kate gave a laugh and replied 'Well, I won't cry this year.'[123]

Mrs Strachan said no more on the matter to her friend and colleague and last saw her on 28 October 1889, when it was evident 'that she had not yet been delivered'.[124]

Margaret Deans was also interviewed by the authorities in mid-November 1889. She explained that she had known the accused for only about a week, when Catherine Anderson asked if she could borrow her shawl. When the garment was not returned the next day, Margaret Deans went to where Catherine lived to get it back. Margaret knocked on the door but got no answer. Finding the door to the third-floor premises unlocked, she went inside and seeing a chest in the room she lifted its lid, speculating that her shawl might be located therein. Rather than finding her property, Margaret Deans discovered 'a small deal [pine] box covered with white linen. She put her hand below the linen and felt the dead body of a child. She removed the linen sufficiently to see the face of the child which was bare. A bit of old dark blanket was round the child tied with a worsted thread.' Without disturbing the body any further, Margaret Deans went back downstairs to tell the other people in the house of her discovery and to send for the police.[125]

Alan McMath and James Flaws, detectives with Aberdeen City Police, came to Catherine Anderson's room at 23 Stevenson Street and Margaret Deans showed them a chest wherein they 'found the body of a newly born female child with clotted blood in both nostrils'. They removed the box, and all of its contents from the property, and brought it to the 'Dead House' to be examined by doctors. The detectives also found a blanket with some spots of blood on it lying on Catherine Anderson's bed. They confiscated this too and labelled it as criminal evidence.[126] Detectives McMath and Flaws eventually apprehended Catherine Anderson at her mother's house. When she was told she was being arrested as a dead child had been found in her house, Catherine said 'she knew nothing about it'. At this declaration, Mrs Anderson, who had not seen her daughter for many months, said:

> 'Oh Kate! What's this you have done?! Why do you bring such a disgrace upon us again?! Do you know who's the father of it?'
>
> Catherine replied to her mother 'You have no business with that.'[127]

Catherine then undermined her original denial of knowledge and responsibility regarding the dead child by telling Officer McMath that, although she did not call for assistance in the birth of the child, she never denied her condition to anyone.[128] On her way to the police station, Catherine asked Officer McMath who it was that had found the body of the baby? When he explained that it was one of her neighbours, Catherine said: 'this will be a bad job for me, but what could I do?' 'You have charged me with murdering the child, but I only took hold of it by the head to pull it out, and it cried.'[129]

Drs Matthew Hay and Alexander McGregor performed an autopsy on the body of the dead child and their evidence contradicted Catherine Anderson's claim about how the baby had met its demise. The medical men first ascertained that the baby had been a new-born female child, that it had reached maturity by the time of parturition, and that it had breathed after birth. There were no defects evident to them in the heart, lungs, or thymus gland (which would indicate issues with poor immunity) of the child, which made them conclude that the child 'was well developed, well nourished, free from disease and viable'.[130] Hay and McGregor did notice that the child had numerous discolourations or bruises on the right side of its abdomen, the lower part of its chest and across the greater part of the right side of its scalp. Like the police officers, they observed dried blood present in the nostrils of the infant. They also noted:

> an abraded patch of skin, of the size of a penny, extending from the right angle of the mouth, downwards over the right side of the chin which was rough to the touch as if produced by pressure or friction.[131]

Similar marks, some of which were deep abrasions, as well as further bruises, were found around the neck of the child. From this evidence, the two medical professionals determined that 'the child met its death by suffocation...with the hand or some other instrument being pressed on the mouth and or the neck'. Hay and McGregor further concluded that the new-born baby had been dead about a week before it was examined by them.[132]

When 25-year-old Catherine Anderson was brought to the police station, she declined to answer any questions put to her by the authorities and she was unwilling to provide them with any sort of declaration as to her guilt or innocence of the crime of child murder. She had been given access to legal representation and her barrister had recommended that she remain silent, save for admitting that she 'was not able to write at present due to extreme agitation'.[133] The authorities reasonably assumed from this statement and from Catherine's general demeanour that she was going to defend herself robustly at the criminal trial that would follow in the new year. It came as something of a surprise to them, then, when she entered the High Court and pleaded guilty to the lesser charge of culpable homicide; the same offence she had been found guilty of just a few years before.[134] This previous verdict, and the sentence that went with it, was then read over to the court, to acknowledge the inherent recidivist in their midst.[135] Once again, Catherine Anderson saw history repeating itself. She was sentenced by the judge to exactly the same penalty in 1890 as had been meted out in 1883: another five years of penal servitude at Peterhead prison.[136]

It seems that, in the end, and after this subsequent spell of internment, Catherine Anderson did finally learn the lesson of her past misdeeds as there were no further indictments brought against her for the rest of her lifetime. We know this, as using census data, it is possible to track Catherine Anderson to various residences in Aberdeen from her the time of her release from prison in 1895, until her death from pneumonia in May of 1954 at the ripe old age of 87. Catherine Anderson never married and had no further children. It is remarkable that this determined but unfortunate woman managed to maintain herself by her own means, living for many decades trouble free, after being convicted of not one, but two, instances of new-born-child murder. The fate of Catherine's first and only surviving child, her son, remains unknown.[137]

## Infanticidal Mothers: Maternal or Infernal?

The blatant disregard for infant life demonstrated by the actions of women such as Barbara Malcolm, Catherine Anderson, and numerous others convicted of child murder in the nineteenth century, made them the epitome of the kind of 'bad' motherhood or 'anti-motherhood' that Victorian commentators had repeatedly warned contemporary society about. As the work of Kilday and Ruth Homrighaus has shown, their obvious rejection of maternity, alongside the autonomous criminal agency that they had displayed, clearly set these women apart from respectable society and challenged Victorian notions of how women were expected to behave and react.[138] Their deviation from normality was all the more evident as they did not even attempt to deploy the general tactic of a plea of temporary insanity in their defence. This route at least offered some sort of explanation for the abhorrent actions of murderous mothers. It also paved the way for reinstatement of gender norms and the assumption that women were not innately criminal, just occasionally mad and sometimes ungovernable.[139] Yet neither of the women in our case studies entertained this option.

For all of these reasons, women like Barbara Malcolm and Catherine Anderson appeared to validate the nationwide moral panic regarding Victorian motherhood. We would expect, therefore, that the press would follow these cases forensically and offer regular, detailed, and highly sensationalized accounts of what transpired in each episode, as occurred regularly in the reporting of other crimes of violence during the nineteenth century after the adoption of more investigative journalist techniques as we have discussed elsewhere.[140] This would seem even more likely, given the unusual nature of these specific cases in terms of the brutal methodology employed by Malcolm and the remarkable recidivism of Anderson. However, in fact, neither case was reported on in any depth. There were only a handful of newspaper articles on each and these contained no lurid headlines or sensational details. The reportage was factual, it was brief, and it almost rendered the assailants as anonymous actors in their own criminality, as it gave next to no details about the women involved.[141]

The unexpectedly subdued press reaction towards Barbara Malcolm and Catherine Anderson appears strange within the context of the vigorous and well-publicized moral panic over maternity that pervaded Britain during the second half of nineteenth century. Even though the prevalence of the most ultimate form of anti-motherhood—child murder—had been greatly exaggerated as we have seen,[142] it still seems peculiar that so little attention was afforded these women and indeed others like them. One explanation for the apparent popular disinterest in murderous mothers is that the wide-ranging discussions related to the prevailing moral panic had fostered the belief that inherent social problems were to blame for the advancement of 'bad' motherhood, rather than the actions and behaviours of feckless mothers alone.[143]

Poverty, overcrowding, low wages, malnourishment, poor hygiene, poor social care, and a lack of affordable, state-sanctioned childcare facilities were just some of the factors said to prevent 'good' motherhood according to Victorian commentators and historians such as Ann Higginbotham and Ginger Frost.[144] However, solutions to these particular problems were not easy to come by and there were many other competing concerns such as Home Rule, the rise of the trade union movement, and attempts to retain the nation's imperial interests which were seen as higher priorities by successive Liberal or Conservative governments.[145] In any event, by encouraging the spotlight to shine on these broader contextual issues and their potential remedies, the focus of the moral panic moved away from the specific individuals who exemplified 'bad' motherhood or 'anti-motherhood' and more towards the state and what it was doing to ensure the cultivation of 'good' motherhood. In this way, as Homrighaus has explained, the moral panic blurred the lines of responsibility for infanticidal women's actions in the social context, in much the same way that the use of the temporary insanity plea had done in the judicial sphere.[146]

Nineteenth-century murderous mothers were not met with public and authoritative vilification as we might have expected. Nor were their actions or personas sensationalized as objects of fascination for a Victorian populace interested in the unusual and the macabre. These women were not met with sympathy either, however, and their actions were neither condoned nor absolved. Opinion was somewhere in between and, in general, the only evident sentiment shown towards women indicted for killing their own children in the nineteenth century was bewilderment, coupled with a sense of moral discomfort that could only be allayed by a habitual secretiveness regarding the women and indeed the children concerned.

## Conclusion

As we have seen in the case studies of Barbara Malcolm and Catherine Anderson in this chapter, gendered capabilities held to be intrinsic, such as maternal instinct, could in reality be transient, if they occurred in a context where self-preservation had become paramount. We will never know the true reasons why these two Scottish women chose to kill their children. However, they and many other nineteenth-century women who found themselves abandoned and alone in a shameful and desperate situation, with no obvious amelioration or solution on the horizon, must have felt that they had little alternative but to commit child murder and take their chances with the prevailing judicial system.[147] Some may even have believed that what they were doing was in the best interests of their offspring and others may have been so distracted that they had become effectively indifferent to the child's fate or indeed their own.[148]

The obsession with maternity that came to dominate the second half of the nineteenth century suggested that 'bad' motherhood was taking hold in British society at the expense of 'good' motherhood. Infant mortality was certainly excessive by the mid-point of the century and the fact that so many women had entered into the world of work by that time was seen as a key causal factor in this. Yet, as we have seen, the moral panic that prevailed became less of a crusade against feckless mothers in and of themselves, and more of a campaign to ease the burden of maternity, in order to make it more palatable and to encourage it to be done well for the sake of future generations and the strength of the nation.

Murderous mothers were similarly side-stepped in this campaign, despite predominant anxieties about the rise of the 'anti-mother'. So even though women like Barbara Malcolm and Catherine Anderson had behaved just like men and committed horrific, callous, and calculated crimes likely born of selfishness and desperation, they were largely ignored by a society undecided upon where the ultimate blame for this criminality should lie. This society was ultimately unaware of how to respond to women who had so clearly and explicitly defied multiple gender norms.[149]

## Notes

1. See S. L. Thurer (1994) *The Myths of Motherhood: How Culture Reinvents the Good Mother* (London: Penguin).
2. For further discussion of the supposed traits of good motherhood see E. Griffin (2018) 'The Emotions of Motherhood: Love, Culture, and Poverty in Victorian Britain', *American Historical Review*, 123, 1, pp. 60–85 at pp. 67–8; A. Dally (1983) *Inventing Motherhood: The Consequences of an Ideal* (London: Schocken Books); C. Nelson (2007) *Family Ties in Victorian England* (Westport, CT: Praeger), pp. 50–1, and Thurer, *Myths of Motherhood*, pp. 141–2.
3. See for instance J. Rendall (1990) *Women in an Industrializing Society: England 1750–1880* (Oxford: Basil Blackwell), pp. 97–8, and E. Badinter (1981 edition) *The Myth of Motherhood: An Historical View of the Maternal Instinct* (London: Souvenir Press), pp. 161 and 189–90.
4. See for instance P. Branca (1975) *Silent Sisterhood: Middle Class Women in the Victorian Home* (London: Croom Helm), p. 74; Nelson, *Family Ties*, p. 57, and J. Calder (1977) *The Victorian Home* (London: Batsford), pp. 128–31 and 163.

5. *The Girl's Own Paper*, 8 July 1882, p. 649.
6. *The Woman's Signal*, 15 February 1894, p. 114. (Author's emphasis added in italics.)
7. See Branca, *Silent Sisterhood*, p. 76; Badinter, *Myth of Motherhood*, pp. 169–77; D. Gorham (1982) *The Victorian Girl and the Feminine Ideal* (London: Croom Helm), pp. 65–8; J. Harris (1994 edition) *Private Lives, Public Spirit: Britain 1870–1914* (London: Penguin), pp. 81–2; Calder, *The Victorian Home*, p. 163, and R. R. Pierson, A. Lévesque,and K. Arnup (1990) 'Introduction', in K. Arnup, A. Lévesque, and R. R. Pierson (eds), *Delivering Motherhood: Maternal Ideologies and Practices in the Nineteenth and Twentieth Centuries* (London: Routledge), pp. xii–xxiv at pp. xix–xx.
8. See for instance Gorham, *The Victorian Girl*, p. 108; Badinter, *Myth of Motherhood*, p. 188; and Harris, *Private Lives*, p. 80.
9. See for instance E. Ross (1993) *Love and Toil: Motherhood in Outcast London, 1870–1018* (New York and Oxford: Oxford University Press) and Calder, *The Victorian Home*, p. 131.
10. For further discussion of the problems that came to be associated with women working in the nineteenth century see Badinter, *Myth of Motherhood*, pp. 238–46, and A. Hunt (2006) 'Calculations and Concealments: Infanticide in Mid-Nineteenth Century Britain', *Victorian Literature and Culture*, 34, 1, pp. 71–94 at p. 74. The phrase 'the angel in the house' comes from a poem written by Coventry Patmore about his wife in 1854, see C. Patmore (1858 edition) *The Angel in the House* (London: J. W. Parker & Son) [British Library, 11,650.c.3].
11. See for instance A. S. Holmes and C. Nelson (1997) 'Introduction', in C. Nelson and A. S. Holmes (eds), *Maternal Instincts: Visions of Motherhood and Sexuality in Britain, 1875–1925* (Basingstoke: Palgrave), pp. 1–12 at pp. 3 and 5 and Hunt, 'Calculations and Concealments', pp. 78–9.
12. See for instance Hunt, 'Calculations and Concealments', pp. 71–94, and A. R. Higginbotham (1989) '"Sin of the Age": Infanticide and Illegitimacy in Victorian London', *Victorian Studies*, 32, 3, pp. 319–37 at p. 319.
13. For further discussion see A.-M. Kilday (2013) *A History of Infanticide in Britain, c.1660 to the Present* (Basingstoke: Palgrave).
14. Ibid., pp. 137–40. See also C. S. Monholland (1989) 'Infanticide in Victorian England, 1856–1876: Thirty Legal Cases' (MA dissertation, Rice University), pp. 64–8.
15. See Kilday, *History of Infanticide*, pp. 140–3.
16. See ibid., pp. 143–6, and chapter 6.
17. See for instance *The Dundee Courtier and Argus*, 21 June 1870, n.p.
18. *Parliamentary Papers*, 43 Geo III, c. 58 (1803) and 49 Geo III, c. 14 (1809).
19. For further discussion of this legislation and how it differed from the previous legal context for child murder see Kilday, *History of Infanticide*, pp. 113–17.
20. See for instance C. L. Krueger (1997) 'Literary Defenses and Medical Prosecutions: Representing Infanticide in Nineteenth Century Britain', *Victorian Studies*, 40, 2, pp. 271–94 at p. 274, and G. K. Behlmer (1979) 'Deadly Motherhood: Infanticide and Medical Opinion in Mid-Victorian England', *Journal of the History of* Medicine, 34, 4, pp. 403–27 at pp. 412–14.
21. For further discussion see A. Reid, R. Davies, E. Garrett, and A. Blaikie (2006) 'Vulnerability among Illegitimate Children in Nineteenth Century Scotland', *Annales*

*de Démographie Historique*, 1, 111, pp. 89–113 at pp. 91–4; L. Rose (1986) *The Massacre of the Innocents: Infanticide in Britain 1800–1939* (London: Routledge & Kegan Paul), pp. 3 and 23; G. Frost (2003) '"The Black Lamb of the Black Sheep": Illegitimacy in the English Working Class, 1850–1939', *Journal of Social History*, 37, 2, pp. 293–322 at p. 295; Higginbotham, 'Sin of the Age', pp. 320 and 336; Nelson, *Family Ties*, p. 4; F. M. L. Thompson (1988) *The Rise of Respectable Society: A Social History of Victorian Britain 1830–1900* (London: Fontana Press), p. 115, and Rendall, *Women in an Industrializing Society*, pp. 93–4.

22. See for instance the references at n. 11 as well as *The Caledonian Mercury*, 6 September 1838, n.p., for the Scottish perspective, along with Behlmer, 'Deadly Motherhood', pp. 404 and 422; T. Hager (2008) 'Compassion and Indifference: The Attitude of the English Legal System towards Ellen Harper and Selina Wadge, who Killed their Offspring in the 1870s', *Journal of Family History*, 33, 2, pp. 173–94 at p. 177, and R. E. Homrighaus (2001) 'Wolves in Women's Clothing: Baby-Farming and the *British Medical Journal*, 1860–1872', *Journal of Family History*, 26, 3, pp. 350–72 at p. 353.
23. For further discussion see Hunt, 'Calculations and Concealments', pp. 72–3; Higginbotham, 'Sin of the Age', pp. 330 and 332; Monholland, 'Infanticide in Victorian England', pp. 28 and 56; Krueger, 'Literary Defenses', pp. 271 and 274; Hager, 'Compassion and Indifference', p. 179; Rose, *Massacre of the Innocents*, p. 71; Behlmer, 'Deadly Motherhood', pp. 410–11; and Kilday, *History of Infanticide*, pp. 104–8 and 136.
24. See esp. H. Marland (2004) *Dangerous Motherhood: Insanity and Childbirth in Victorian Britain* (Basingstoke: Palgrave); J. Newton Ainsley (2000) '"Some Mysterious Agency": Women, Violent Crime, and the Insanity Acquittal in the Victorian Courtroom', *Canadian Journal of History*, 35, pp. 35–55; and Kilday, *History of Infanticide*, pp. 164–79.
25. For further discussion of some of these options see Kilday, *History of Infanticide*, chapter 4; Rose, *Massacre of the Innocents*, chapters 6, 9–11, and 15–16; D. Bentley (2005) 'She-Butchers: Baby-Droppers, Baby-Sweaters, and Baby-Farmers', in J. Rowbotham and K. Stevenson (eds), *Criminal Conversations: Victorian Crimes, Social Panic, and Moral Outrage* (Columbus, OH: Ohio State University Press), pp. 198–214; J. Pearman (2017) 'Bastards, Baby Farmers and Social Control in Victorian Britain' (PhD thesis, University of Kent); M. L. Arnot (1994) 'Infant Death, Child Care and the State: The Baby-Farming Scandal and the First Infant Life Protection Legislation of 1872', *Continuity and Change*, 9, 2, pp. 271–311; C. Smart (1993 edition) 'Disruptive Bodies and Unruly Sex: The Regulation of Reproduction and Sexuality in the Nineteenth Century', in C. Smart (ed.), *Regulating Womanhood: Historical Essays on Marriage, Motherhood and Sexuality* (London: Routledge), pp. 7–32; and Homrighaus, 'Wolves in Women's Clothing', pp. 350–72.
26. For further discussion see Hager, 'Compassion and Indifference', p. 177, and Homrighaus, 'Wolves in Women's Clothing', p. 353.
27. For further discussion see Badinter, *Myth of Motherhood*, pp. 120–50; Nelson, *Family Ties*, pp. 65–7; Hunt, 'Calculations and Concealments', p. 80; J. Manheimer (1979) 'Murderous Mothers: The Problem of Parenting in the Victorian Novel', *Feminist Studies*, 5, 3, pp. 530–46 at p. 530; Bentley, 'She-Butchers', pp. 199 and 204; Homrighaus, 'Wolves in Women's Clothing', pp. 356 and 358; Arnot, 'Infant Death',

p. 282; and A. Digby (1992) 'Victorian Values and Women in Public and Private', *Proceedings of the British* Academy, 78, pp. 195–215 at p. 197.

28. See Arnot, 'Infant Death', pp. 271–311; Harris, *Private Lives*, p. 61; and Nelson, *Family Ties*, p. 56.
29. Badinter, *Myth of Motherhood*, p. 239.
30. See Frost, 'Black Lamb', pp. 295, 304, and 309.
31. See W. Burke Ryan (1862) *Infanticide: Its Law, Prevalence, Prevention, and History* (London: T. Richards) [Bodleian Library, (OC) 151 c/345] and W. Tyler Smith (1867) 'An Address on Infanticide and Excessive Infant Mortality', *British Medical Journal*, 12 January 1867, pp. 21–5. For further discussion of the belief in an epidemic of child murder in the late Victorian era see Kilday, *History of Infanticide*, pp. 111 and 119–20; Rose, *Massacre of the Innocents*, pp. 37, 39, and chapter 5; Monholland, 'Infanticide in Victorian England', pp. 20–5 and 48; Behlmer, 'Deadly Motherhood', pp. 404–6 and 415; Arnot, 'Infant Death', pp. 278 and 280–1; Bentley, 'She-Butchers', pp. 201–2; Homrighaus, 'Wolves in Women's Clothing', pp. 352–3; and Krueger, 'Literary Defenses', pp. 285–8. For further discussion of the likely causes of this moral panic see Kilday, *History of Infanticide*, pp. 120–2.
32. J. Kay (1850) *The Social Condition and Education of the People in England and Europe—Volume I* (London: Longman, Brown & Green), p. 447. [Bodleian Library Ref. 247,126 e.207.]
33. See for instance *The Glasgow Herald*, 2 January 1868, n.p., 15 September 1874, n.p., and 13 November 1888, n.p.; *The Aberdeen Journal*, 26 July 1871, n.p.; and *The Dundee Courier and Argus*, 6 May 1872, n.p., 6 January 1873, n.p., 8 February 1878, n.p., 26 September 1879, n.p., 12 November 1880, n.p., 6 January 1890, n.p., 2 December 1892, p. 3, 7 November 1896, p. 4, and 23 September 1897, p. 7.
34. See respectively *The Caledonian Mercury*, 1 May 1862, n.p., and 20 September 1862, n.p.; and *The Glasgow Herald*, 10 September 1862, n.p.
35. *Aberdeen Weekly Journal*, 29 September 1877, n.p.
36. *The Glasgow Herald*, 20 December 1893, n.p.
37. Kilday, *History of Infanticide*, pp. 122–3.
38. Ibid. as well as A.-M. Kilday (2018) *Crime in Scotland 1660–1960: The Violent North* (London: Routledge), pp. 46–7.
39. *The Lancaster Gazette and General Advertiser*, 26 December 1807, n.p.
40. Ibid.
41. National Records of Scotland (NRS), Justiciary Court Records, Books of Adjournal, JC4/4.
42. Ibid.
43. We have already established elsewhere in this chapter how vulnerable domestic servants like Barbara Malcolm were in the eighteenth and nineteenth centuries. Their precarious status had the potential to leave them open to seduction on the promise of a more formal relationship and if such a tryst resulted in an illegitimate pregnancy, they would suffer the ignominy of being sacked without a reference. For further discussion see Behlmer, 'Deadly Motherhood', pp. 419–20; Rose, *Massacre of the Innocents*, pp. 18–19; and Monholland, 'Infanticide in Victorian England', p. 67.

44. *The Scots Magazine and Edinburgh Literary Miscellany: Being a General Repository of Literature, History and Politics for 1808—Volume LXX* (Edinburgh: Archibald Constable & Co.), p. 75.
45. A sample survey of Scottish newspapers between 1850 and 1870 revealed an enormous abundance of advertisements placed by women offering their services as wet-nurses. For examples see *The Glasgow Herald*, 11 March 1857, n.p., 4 December 1861, n.p., and 13 July 1866, n.p. For further discussion of the use of wet-nurses in the nineteenth century see V. Fildes (1988) *Wet Nursing: A History from Antiquity to the Present* (Oxford: Basil Blackwell); Bentley, 'She-Butchers', p. 199; Rose, *Massacre of the Innocents*, p. 51 and chapter 6; Thurer, *Myths of Motherhood*, p. 74; and Rendall, *Women in an Industrializing Society*, p. 95.
46. *The Caledonian Mercury*, 7 January 1808, n.p.
47. For further discussion see Reid et al., 'Vulnerability among Illegitimate Children', pp. 89–90; Rose, *Massacre of the Innocents*, pp. 21 and 31; Bentley, 'She-Butchers', p. 199.
48. NRS, Justiciary Court Records, Books of Adjournal, JC4/4.
49. *The Scots Magazine—Volume LXX*, p. 75.
50. For further discussion of the motives associated with child murder see Kilday, *History of Infanticide*, chapter 6.
51. NRS, Justiciary Court Records, Process Papers, JC26/1808/27.
52. Ibid. See also *The Aberdeen Journal*, 13 January 1808, n.p.
53. NRS, Justiciary Court Records, Process Papers, JC26/1808/27.
54. Ibid.
55. Ibid.
56. Ibid.
57. *The Scots Magazine—Volume LXX*, p. 75.
58. *The Caledonian Mercury*, 7 January 1808, n.p.
59. NRS, Justiciary Court Records, Process Papers, JC26/1808/27. See also *The Aberdeen Journal*, 13 January 1808, n.p. See also J. Burnett (1811) *Treatise on Various Branches of the Criminal Law of Scotland*(Edinburgh: George Ramsay & Co.), p. 549.
60. NRS, Justiciary Court Records, Process Papers, JC26/1808/27.
61. K. D. Watson (2009) 'Is a Burn a Wound? Vitriol-Throwing in Medico-Legal Context, 1800–1900', in I. Goold and C. Kelly (eds), *Lawyers' Medicine: The Legislature, the Courts and Medical Practice, 1760–2000* (London: Hart Publishing), pp. 61–78 at p. 63.
62. Ibid. For further discussion of the industrial use of oil of vitriol see A. Clow and N. L. Clow (1945) 'Vitriol in the Industrial Revolution', *Economic History Review*, 15, 1–2, pp. 44–55.
63. Watson, 'Is a Burn a Wound?', p. 63.
64. Ibid.
65. Ibid., pp. 61–78. See also K. D. Watson (2016) 'Love, Vengeance and Vitriol: An Edwardian True-Crime Drama', in D. S. Nash and A.-M. Kilday (eds), *Law, Crime and Deviance since 1700: Micro-Studies in the History of Crime* London: Bloomsbury), pp. 107–24 and two blog posts by K. D. Watson: (25 March 2017) 'Doom for Demembring: Assault in Scots Law' and (13 September 2017) 'Acid Attacks in Nineteenth-Century Britain', <https://legalhistorymiscellany.com> (accessed 26 December 2018). For discussion of more contemporary episodes see *The Guardian*, 11 February 2017, and *The New Statesman* (UK edition), 27 July 2017.

66. R. Christison (1829) *A Treatise on Poisons, in Relations to Medical Jurisprudence, Physiology, and the Practice of Physic* (Edinburgh: Adam Black).
67. Ibid., p. 114.
68. Ibid., pp. 114–16.
69. J. G. Smith (1824 edition) *The Principles of Forensic Medicine, Systematically Arranged, and Applied to British Practice* (London: Thomas & George Underwood), p. 139.
70. NRS, Justiciary Court Records, Process Papers, JC26/1808/27.
71. *The Caledonian Mercury*, 7 January 1808, n.p.
72. For evidence to support the contention that the methodology deployed by Barbara Malcolm was unusual in nineteenth-century episodes of infanticide see Kilday, *History of Infanticide*, pp. 96–101, and Monholland, 'Infanticide in Victorian England', p. 35.
73. NRS, Justiciary Court Records, Minute Book, JC8/5 and Process Papers, JC26/1808/27. See also (1810) *The Edinburgh Annual Register for 1808—Volume I*, Part II (Edinburgh: James Ballantyne & Co.), p. 4; *The Morning Post*, 11 January 1808, n.p.; *The Bury and Norwich Post*, 13 January 1808, n.p.; *The Ipswich Journal*, 16 January 1808, n.p.; *The Lancaster Gazette and General Advertiser*, 16 January 1808, n.p.; and *The Examiner*, 17 January 1808, n.p.
74. See *The Bury and Norwich Post*, 24 February 1808, n.p.; and *The Ipswich Journal*, 27 February 1808, n.p.
75. Anon. (1808) *An Account of the Crime, Trial and Behaviour of Barbara Malcolm Who was Executed at Edinburgh on Wednesday last, February 10, 1808* (Gateshead: Marshall Printer). [John Johnson Collection, Allegro ID 20080125/16:54$kg.] [Author's emphasis added.]
76. NRS, Justiciary Court Records, Minute Book, JC11/110/99.
77. NRS, Justiciary Court, Precognition Papers, Testimony of Ann Hunter (or Anderson), AD14/83/260/1.
78. Ibid.
79. Ibid.
80. Ibid.
81. It was evident that Mrs Anderson even went as far as to arrange the attendance of a doctor (Dr Cheyne of King Street, Aberdeen) and a midwife (Mrs Stewart in Dee Street, Aberdeen) for Catherine when her labour pains began. Not only did this evidence testify to the fact that Catherine's pregnancy had been revealed to others, but it also implies that Mrs Anderson knew that the pregnancy would likely go to term. See NRS, Justiciary Court, Process Papers, JC26/1883/25.
82. Ibid.
83. Ann Hunter explained how she, her husband, and her young child slept in one room, whilst Catherine, her son, and Ann's 'delicate' 16-year-old daughter (Margaret), slept in another. See NRS, Justiciary Court, Precognition Papers, Testimony of Ann Hunter (or Anderson), AD14/83/260/1.
84. Ibid.
85. The loss of kin support networks, the ongoing burden of social opprobrium, and the likelihood of enduring abject poverty have all been regularly cited as reasons why some women chose to dispose of unwanted and illegitimate infants in nineteenth-century Britain. See for instance Frost, 'Black Lamb', pp. 295–7; Higginbotham, 'Sin of

the Age', pp. 321–32; Rose, *Massacre of the Innocents*, p. 21; and Reid et al., 'Vulnerability among Illegitimate Children', pp. 89–90. For further discussion of the Scottish Poor Law system in the nineteenth century see R. A. Cage (1974) 'The Scottish Poor Law, 1745–1845' (PhD thesis, University of Glasgow) and Peter Higginbotham's work found at <www.workhouses.org.uk/Scotland> (accessed 5 January 2019).

86. *Aberdeen Weekly Journal*, 27 June 1883, n.p.
87. Ibid.
88. Ibid.
89. It is evident that many unmarried Victorian women chose to give birth to their infants in water closets or privies due to the privacy they offered. Concealment of the pregnancy and of the clandestine birth would be more likely to succeed if conducted in private. For further discussion see Higginbotham, 'Sin of the Age', p. 325.
90. Ibid.
91. NRS, Justiciary Court, Precognition Papers, Testimony of Helen Henderson, AD14/83/260/1.
92. *Aberdeen Weekly Journal*, 27 June 1883, n.p.
93. NRS, Justiciary Court, Precognition Papers, Testimony of Ann Hunter (or Anderson), AD14/83/260/1.
94. Ibid. See also the testimony of the 16-year-old girl who discovered the body when gathering dulce (seaweed): NRS, Justiciary Court, Precognition Papers, Testimony of Mary Walker, AD14/83/260/1 and that of the police constable who retrieved the corpse: NRS, Justiciary Court, Precognition Papers, Testimony of Constable James Gibson (Kincardineshire Police), AD14/83/260/1.
95. NRS, Justiciary Court, Precognition Papers, Testimony of Ann Hunter (or Anderson), AD14/83/260/1.
96. NRS, Justiciary Court, Precognition Papers, Testimony of Officer Alexander Smith (Aberdeen Police), AD14/83/260/1.
97. NRS, Justiciary Court, Precognition Papers, Testimonies of Inspector Lewis Gordon (Aberdeen Police) and Officer Daniel Ross (Aberdeen Police), AD14/83/260/1.
98. NRS, Justiciary Court, Precognition Papers, Testimonies of Dr Robert John Garden and Dr William John Ritchie Simpson, AD14/83/260/1. The doctors also reported to the press that the prisoner was in a weak condition upon her arrest and recommended that she not be transferred from Dundee to Aberdeen until she had regained her strength. See *Aberdeen Weekly Journal*, 12 April 1883, n.p.
99. NRS, Justiciary Court, Process Papers, JC26/1883/25.
100. Ibid.
101. Ibid.
102. Ibid.
103. NRS, Justiciary Court, Process Papers, JC26/1883/25.
104. NRS, Justiciary Court, Precognition Papers, Testimonies of Dr Robert John Garden and Dr William John Ritchie Simpson, AD14/83/260/1.
105. Ibid. See also NRS, Justiciary Court, Precognition Papers, Medical Reports, AD14/83/260/1.
106. NRS, Justiciary Court, Precognition Papers, Testimonies of Dr Robert John Garden and Dr William John Ritchie Simpson, AD14/83/260/1. For further details of the

skull fractures observed see the meticulous account provided in the *Aberdeen Weekly Journal*, 12 April 1883, n.p.

107. NRS, Justiciary Court, Precognition Papers, Testimonies of Dr Robert John Garden and Dr William John Ritchie Simpson, AD14/83/260/1. It is evident that Victorian medical men were rarely persuaded by claims that an infant had been fatally injured through the process of a standing delivery as they believed the propulsion of the baby would not be fast enough for a mortal wound to be inflicted—see Rose, *Massacre of the Innocents*, p. 73.
108. NRS, Justiciary Court, Precognition Papers, Testimony of Elizabeth Sage (or Stewart) (Matron of the Prison of Aberdeen), AD14/83/260/1.
109. NRS, Justiciary Court, Process Papers, JC26/1883/25.
110. NRS, Justiciary Court, Precognition Papers, Testimonies of Dr Robert John Garden and Dr William John Ritchie Simpson, AD14/83/260/1.
111. NRS, Justiciary Court Records, Minute Book, JC11/110/99. See also *Aberdeen Weekly Journal*, 27 June 1883, n.p.
112. See *The Dundee Courier and Argus*, 12 April 1883, n.p.
113. See the details provided in the *Aberdeen Weekly Journal*, 12 April 1883, n.p.
114. NRS, Justiciary Court Records, Minute Book, JC11/110/99. See also *Aberdeen Weekly Journal*, 27 June 1883, n.p. For further discussion of penal servitude as a punishment see Anon. (1878) *Five Years Penal Servitude: By One Who Has Endured It* (London: Richard Bentley & Son); L. Williams (2016) *Wayward Women: Female Offending in Victorian England* (Barnsley: Pen and Sword History), pp. 4–5 and 8–10; and J. Cameron (1983) *Prisons and Punishment in Scotland* (Edinburgh: Canongate).
115. *The Dundee Courier and Argus*, 27 June 1883, n.p.
116. NRS, Justiciary Court, Minute Book, JC11/113.
117. Ibid.
118. NRS, Justiciary Court, Precognition Papers, Testimony of Margaret Barrow, AD14/90/14/1.
119. Ibid.
120. NRS, Justiciary Court, Precognition Papers, Testimony of Catherine Hussy (or Strachan), AD14/90/14/1.
121. Ibid.
122. All these factors, as well as the opprobrium associated with an illegitimate pregnancy have been cited as motivating factors in the committal of new-born-child murder. See for instance Kilday, *History of Infanticide*, chapter 6; Reid et al., 'Vulnerability among Illegitimate Children', p. 102; Higginbotham, 'Sin of the Age', pp. 321–2; and Frost, 'Black Lamb', pp. 297 and 300.
123. Frost, 'Black Lamb', pp. 297 and 300.
124. Ibid.
125. NRS, Justiciary Court, Precognition Papers, Testimony of Margaret Deans, AD14/90/14/1. [Author's addition in parentheses.] See also *Aberdeen Weekly Journal*, 13 November 1889, n.p.
126. NRS, Justiciary Court, Precognition Papers, Testimonies of Detective Alan McMath (Aberdeen Police) and Deceptive James Flaws (Aberdeen Police), AD14/90/14/1. A dead house was a secure building used across nineteenth-century Scotland to house corpses for up to three months before burial. They were instigated in order to prevent

resurrectionists or grave-robbers from stealing cadavers to sell to anatomists and other interested buyers.

127. Ibid.
128. Ibid.
129. Ibid.
130. NRS, Justiciary Court, Precognition Papers, Testimonies of Dr Matthew Hay and Dr Alexander McGregor, AD14/90/14/1.
131. Ibid.
132. Ibid.
133. NRS, Justiciary Court, Process Papers, JC26/1890/222.
134. NRS, Justiciary Court, Minute Book, JC11/113.
135. The previous indictment for child murder brought against Catherine Anderson was also reported by the newspapers following this second indictment in 1890—see *The Dundee Courier and Argus*, 15 November 1889, p. 5, and 22 January 1890, n.p.
136. NRS, Justiciary Court, Minute Book, JC11/113. See also *Aberdeen Weekly Journal*, 22 January 1890, n.p., and *The Dundee Courier and Argus*, 22 January 1890, n.p. For details that Catherine Anderson was sent to serve her sentence at Peterhead prison see the *Aberdeen Weekly Journal*, 11 February 1890, n.p., and 12 February 1890, n.p. For further discussion of penal servitude in this establishment from 1897 until 1942, see C. Holligan (2018) 'Life in a Forgotten Scottish Gulag: Punishment and Social Regulation in HM Peterhead Prison', *Journal of Historical Sociology*, 31, pp. 165–81. For discussion of a woman's experience of a convict prison in the nineteenth century see H. Johnston (2018) 'Imprisoned Mothers in Victorian England, 1853–1900: Motherhood, Identity and the Convict Prison', *Criminology and Criminal Justice*, 18, 6, pp. 1–17.
137. See NRS, Census Records for 1881, 168/2/19/6, p. 6; Census Records for 1891, 387/37/9, p. 9; Census Records for 1901, 168/1/46/25, p. 25; Census Records for 1911, 168/2/57/1, p. 1; as well as NRS, Statutory Death Registers for 1934, 168/2/161, which records the death of Catherine's mother Ann Hunter (or Anderson) and Catherine's whereabouts at that time, and that for 1954, 168/1/668, which records Catherine Anderson's own death at Woodend Hospital.
138. See Kilday, *History of Infanticide*, pp. 165–6 and Homrighaus, 'Wolves in Women's Clothing', p. 357.
139. See the references at n. 24 as well as Hager, 'Compassion and Indifference', p. 180.
140. See for instance A.-M. Kilday (2016) 'Constructing the Cult of the Criminal: Kate Webster—Victorian Murderess and Media Sensation', in A.-M. Kilday and D. S. Nash (eds), *Law, Crime and Deviance since 1700: Micro-Studies in the History of Crime* (London: Bloomsbury), pp. 125–48. For more on the developments in journalism in the second half of the nineteenth century see A. J. Lee (1979) *The Origins of the Popular Press, 1855–1914* (London: Rowman & Littlefield) and J. O. Baylen (1972) 'The New Journalism in Late Victorian Britain', *Australian Journal of Politics and History*, 18, 3, pp. 367–85.
141. See for instance for Barbara Malcolm *The Morning Post*, 11 January 1808, n.p., and *The Ipswich Journal*, 16 January 1808, n.p., and for Catherine Anderson, *The Dundee Courier and Argus*, 15 November 1889, p. 5, and the *Aberdeen Weekly Journal*, 22 January 1890, n.p.

142. See the references at nn. 37 and 38 above as well as Monholland, 'Infanticide in Victorian England', p. 63.
143. Another key factor was said to be the rise of the role of the coroner whose very public pronouncements on criminal matters intensified public concerns regarding child murder in the nineteenth century. See for further discussion Behlmer, 'Deadly Motherhood', p. 407, and Krueger, 'Literary Defenses', p. 282.
144. For further discussion see Higginbotham, 'Sin of the Age', p. 337; Rose, *Massacre of the Innocents*, pp. 15–17; Frost, 'Black Lamb', p. 299; Kilday, *History of Infanticide*, pp. 144–6 and 153–64; Branca, *Silent Sisterhood*, pp. 98–9; Harris, *Private Lives*, pp. 82–4; Monholland, 'Infanticide in Victorian England', pp. 57–8; Bentley, 'She-Butchers', p. 199; and Thompson, *Rise of Respectable Society*, p. 123.
145. See Rose, *Massacre of the Innocents*, chapters 12–13 and 17; Bentley, 'She-Butchers', pp. 207–12; Higginbotham, 'Sin of the Age', p. 337; Manheimer, 'Murderous Mothers', p. 532; Hager, 'Compassion and Indifference', p. 174; and Kilday, *History of Infanticide*, pp. 146–9.
146. See Homrighaus, 'Wolves in Women's Clothing', pp. 364–5; Kilday, *History of Infanticide*, p. 423; Arnot, 'Infant Death', pp. 275 and 286; and Frost, 'Black Lamb', p. 299. For further discussion of the preoccupations of the government in the nineteenth century see D. Cannadine (2019) *Victorious Century: The United Kingdom, 1800–1906* (London: Penguin).
147. For further discussion that the judicial process facing infanticidal mothers has historically been something of a lottery see Kilday, *History of Infanticide*, pp. 124–5; Bentley, 'She-Butchers', p. 205; Higginbotham, 'Sin of the Age', p. 323; and Arnot, 'Infant Death', p. 291.
148. For tentative evidence to support this contention see Hager, 'Compassion and Indifference', pp. 178 and 184.
149. See Hager, 'Compassion and Indifference', p. 186; D. E. Roberts (1993) 'Motherhood and Crime', *Iowa Law Review*, 79, pp. 95–141 at p. 107; and A. S. Holmes (1997) '"Fallen Mothers": Maternal Adultery and Child Custody in England, 1886–1925', in Nelson and Holmes (eds), *Maternal Instincts*, pp. 37–57 at p. 54.

# 5

# 'The Life and Loves of a She Devil'

## The 'Potton Poisoner' and the Premeditation of a Serially Deviant Woman

### Introduction

It has been long accepted by scholars that, throughout history, women have rarely engaged in the perpetration of fatal violence, and when they have done, it has typically been an impulsive act committed in hot blood, rather than a premeditated or planned episode committed in cold blood. This trope implies a rather polarized view of women's innate aptitudes and suggests they have limited individual agency and autonomy.[1] To put it another way, as women could not be seen as innately bad, as this was too far removed from prescribed gender norms and accepted female character traits, it was much more convenient to associate their murderous behaviour with rash, involuntary actions based on instinctiveness. Although violent female behaviour was thus regarded as the antithesis of logic, contemplation, and reason, it could be more easily explained away as a fleeting, uncontrollable moment of madness. In this context and through these explanations, as historians Clive Emsley and Helen Johnston have explained, gender norms could be retained and reinforced rather than undermined or eroded.[2] However, there was one methodology of fatal violence which was highly problematic to this generalized overview: poisoning.

Not only was poisoning commonly regarded as a premeditated form of killing that required malice aforethought and a great deal of guile, it was also a methodology that came to be closely associated with female perpetrators, especially in the nineteenth-century period. Female poisoners were hugely problematic for Victorian society. They undermined gender norms by being criminally autonomous, enterprising, and scheming. Moreover, as Judith Knelman has suggested, they were deemed 'doubly deviant' as they also defiled gendered expectations by utilizing the domestic context and usurping women's role within it as the providers of care and nourishment, to better facilitate their homicidal intentions.[3] Concern over such women became manifest in the middle decades of the nineteenth century, and intensified greatly when several serial poisoners came to light. Where contemporaries might have been able to discount the actions of a woman delivering a single fatal dose to a husband, relative, or paramour as an accident or a solitary ill-thought-through act of treachery, it was almost impossible to explain

*Beyond Deviant Damsels: Re-evaluating Female Criminality in the Nineteenth Century.* Anne-Marie Kilday and David Nash, Oxford University Press. © Anne-Marie Kilday and David Nash 2023. DOI: 10.1093/oso/9780198830733.003.0005

away repeat offending of this nature. In the case of serial poisoners, their cunning, deviance, and plotting was perspicuous and this made their thought processes and actions a real challenge for social commentators and authority figures determined to uphold prevailing patriarchal structures and associated character traits.

This chapter will examine the life and crimes of one such 'problematic' woman, Sarah Dazley, who was suspected of killing multiple victims through the use of arsenic poisoning in both Bedfordshire and Cambridgeshire from the late 1830s until the early 1840s period. The chapter will begin by investigating attitudes to female murderesses in the Victorian era, and the emergent moral panic associated with female poisoners in particular, to determine how society regarded such individuals and how it dealt with them. We will then go on to examine the case study of Sarah Dazley and consider the extent to which her crimes were intentional, potentially excusable, or comparable with that of other Victorian killers. Finally, the chapter will then proceed to analyse the ways in which society chose to deal with female serial offenders. Were attempts made to understand them or excuse them? Were they made examples of, or were they more typically ignored as an aberration? How did Sarah Dazley fair in this respect?

## The Victorian Murderess: Mad, Bad, or Dangerous to Know?

We have already established that women rarely engaged in fatal violence throughout history. One of the implications of this, from the Victorian era onwards, was that on those occasions where female killers *did* come to the public's attention, their actions and personae were routinely sensationalized by the media.[4] This press coverage served to heighten a prevailing and historically persistent morbid curiosity with episodes of unexpected violence, committed by atypical perpetrators.[5] As historian Judith Knelman explains, the murderess attracted unfettered attention and the public followed their histories 'with a prurience fuelled by both admiration and disgust. To this audience, the murderess represented passion unleashed. She had spurned constraints imposed on civilised society and had given in to animal impulses.'[6] In the nineteenth century, the focus for this fascination with deviant criminality was on female poisoners in particular, as the work of Judith Flanders has highlighted.[7] Female poisoners were regarded as a blatant threat to society. By tending to kill male relatives and suitors, the actions of these women inverted extant patriarchal norms. Moreover, the secretive and clandestine nature of poisoning as a murderous methodology meant that their actions were regarded as wholly unpredictable and potentially indiscriminate. For these reasons, as Mary Hartman and other scholars have shown, female poisoners instilled fear amongst Victorian society.[8]

According to medical historians such as Ian Burney and Katherine Watson, public anxiety relating to poisoning reached unprecedented levels during the middle decades of the nineteenth century, despite its sporadic deployment in comparison with other homicidal methodologies and despite the rarity of proven episodes.[9] After the sensationalized coverage of a flurry of poisoning trials, the press and social commentators fuelled a 'moral panic' over what they described as the omnipresent nature of 'secret poisoning'.[10] Despite the fact that these claims proved to be ultimately unfounded or unsubstantiated in the main, the cumulative media frenzy that resulted repeatedly warned the public to be vigilant against the 'rising tide' of this 'sinister offending', conducted by harridan 'traitors' to the notions of domesticity and the characteristics of the gentler sex.[11] For these observers, female poisoners were causing marriage to be in crisis, patriarchy to be under threat, and gender norms to be in question.[12]

It was also suggested by the press at this time that the few trials that had come to the public's attention offered only a superficial exposure of what was a much more extensive problem.[13] Indeed, it was argued that numerous poisoning fatalities had been concealed from the authorities and had been treated as natural deaths. This was because of the range of hidden and devious means by which toxins could be deliberately applied to unsuspecting victims and the fact that the symptoms exhibited by poisoning victims mimicked those of contemporary illnesses such as cholera and influenza, as the work of George Robb explains.[14] The recognition that, of all murderers, the poisoner was the hardest to uncover and convict meant that the panic regarding the frequency of poisoning quickly escalated and spread.[15] Victorians came to claim that poisoning was 'The Crime of the Age' and that the 'epidemic' in evidence from the 1830s to the 1860s period, was 'far more formidable than any plague which we are likely to see imported from the East'.[16]

It was also evident from the reportage which prevailed at this time that arsenic was by far the poisoner's weapon of choice.[17] As scholars such as James Wharton have pointed out, arsenic was cheap to procure and easily available in the Victorian era, as it had a wide range of uses in medicine, trade, animal husbandry, and agriculture. In the domestic setting, arsenic was typically found on fly papers and in rodent poison. The pervasiveness of arsenic and its versatility of use, coupled with a general ignorance regarding the extent of its toxicity, meant that it was potentially responsible for a significant number of accidental deaths in the nineteenth century in particular.[18] In relation to its deliberate use by individuals with injurious or homicidal intentions, the fact that arsenic was odourless and almost tasteless meant that it was simple to administer but delivered the required effect.[19] In her description of the 'excruciating and lengthy process' involved in a victim's death, historian Katherine Watson makes a compelling case for why murder by arsenic poisoning should be considered a brutal and violent crime. As she describes, the symptoms began

> with nausea, burning in the throat, and pain in the stomach. Sufferers were known to report an almost instant feeling of pressure and swelling in the

stomach, so forceful that they feared they would burst. Uncontrollable vomiting and diarrhoea soon followed, and these were affected by the patient's intense thirst: the stools became thin and watery, and they eventually started to vomit up all the water they consumed. As a result of dehydration, painful cramps could develop in the legs. A feeling of general weakness often abated during periods of remission, but improvements were usually short-lived. The mind remained clear until close to the end, which was often preceded by delirium, convulsions or coma. The time between the onset of symptoms and death varied, depending on the size of the dose and how much of the poison was absorbed, but was usually between a few hours or two or three days.[20]

In sum, victims of arsenic poisoning suffered 'painful, dirty and undignified deaths.'[21]

In part, the recognition that arsenic poisoning was a growing and serious problem was due to an actual rise in its incidence by the middle decades of the nineteenth century, but it was also because chemical tests had been developed by this point in time to detect the presence of arsenic in the human body. As we will see in the case study below, these scientific advances facilitated the prosecution of more cases and allowed for a more accurate determination of cause of death.[22] Although, as we have seen, female poisoners were the initial preoccupation for Victorian social commentators and the press during the prevailing moral panic,[23] the advent of these tests resulted in attention moving away from perpetrator typologies and more towards efforts at controlling the sale of poisons. As it was believed that the majority of 'poisoners' inflicted a single dose of toxin on their victims, and many may have done so accidentally, the legislative changes that followed this campaign, beginning in 1851 with the Sale of Arsenic Regulation Act,[24] were attempts to spread awareness of the potential dangers associated with arsenic. It was hoped to limit fatal errors by regulating and recording the sale of arsenic to members of the general public, as research by Peter Bartrip has indicated.[25] Unsurprisingly, the portrayal of poisonings as impulsive, unintentional episodes was quickly endorsed by Victorians. This was because women were the key protagonists in these instances and the notion that female criminals were irrational and impetuous had already been widely accepted. But what was the societal reaction to a serial poisoner, where there could be no excuse made for the actions undertaken, where deliberate intent was manifest, and where premeditation was explicitly and repeatedly evident?

## Sarah Dazley: The Potton Poisoner

Born in Potton, Bedfordshire, Sarah Reynolds was baptized on 28 May 1815 by her parents Philip and Ann.[26] Sarah's father was a barber in the village, but despite his best efforts, he struggled to make ends meet and ended up being incarcerated in Bedford gaol for bad debt. Whilst imprisoned, Philip Reynold's health deteriorated, and shortly after his release he died, when Sarah was still an infant.[27] Rather than devoting her time to the care of her young daughter in the wake of this tragic episode, Ann Reynolds began living a life of promiscuity, and openly embarked on a series of dalliances with local men.[28] Evidently then, during her formative years, Sarah was heavily influenced by her mother's blithe behaviour and seemingly came to adopt similar character traits. On the 22 November 1835, at the age of 19, Sarah married Simon Mead and two years after their nuptials, they moved from Potton to Tadlow in Cambridgeshire, reportedly in order to break off an extra-marital affair that Sarah had been engaged in.[29]

In February 1840, Sarah gave birth to a son, named Jonah. However, the joy created by this new addition to the Mead family was short-lived. By June of that same year, Simon Mead had died unexpectedly and just a few months later his baby son was laid to rest beside him in the local graveyard, leaving Sarah both childless and alone.[30] This set of unfortunate circumstances did not last long, however. Just a few weeks after her husband's demise, to both the surprise and the consternation of locals, Sarah had publicly taken up with local man named William Dazley.[31] To avoid the scandal and gossip that their ill-timed relationship had generated, Sarah and William moved back to Bedfordshire and were married at Wrestlingworth on 11 October 1840.[32] However, it soon became evident that their relationship was not a harmonious one. Rumours abounded, soon after the nuptials had been concluded, of Sarah enjoying the company of innumerable lovers in the marital bed, and William resorting to bouts of heavy drinking in the village pub.[33] Furthermore, and just two years into the marriage, routine public displays of aggression between the couple had been keenly witnessed by Wrestlingworth residents.[34] The resolution to this picture of domestic strife came on 30 October 1842, when William Dazley died after a short illness. Although the doctor tending to Dazley was rather surprised by his patient's untimely demise, as he thought his illness was not of a life-threatening nature, a subsequent inquest found no suspicious circumstances surrounding the death.[35]

At the tender age of 27, then, Sarah Dazley had lost a child and been twice widowed. For many individuals, this series of catastrophic episodes would have resulted in paralysing grief and mental anguish. Yet Sarah Dazley did not succumb in this way. Instead, within just a few weeks of William's death, she had found herself a new paramour, a young man called George Waldock, and they quickly announced their intention to marry.[36] On hearing this news, the disquiet of villagers intensified. Realizing that something was amiss, they first persuaded George Waldock to break off his engagement to Sarah Dazley. One neighbour summarized their collective fears by asking Waldock: 'Surely you are not going to marry that she-devil, who has already murdered two husbands and a child?'[37] They then persuaded Francis Pym, Chairman of the local Quarter Sessions, to investigate the death of William Dazley. He acceded to their request and, as well as ordering the coroner (Mr Ezra Eagles) to exhume Dazley's body, he directed Superintendent Blunden (of the Bedfordshire Police) to find Sarah Dazley and investigate her conduct.[38]

Sarah Dazley was not too keen on helping the police with these enquiries. Upon hearing of this turn of events and the likely warrant for her arrest, she fled to London with yet another suitor, Samuel Stebbing.[39] She was soon captured there and taken into police custody, before being returned to Bedfordshire for the inquest hearing.[40] The inquest into the death of William Dazley began on 20 March 1843 at the Chequers Inn, Wrestlingworth, and a wealth of evidence was placed before the coroner, so the hearing took several days to complete.

The deceased man's mother, Elizabeth Dazley, told the coroner that her son died within a week of first exhibiting symptoms of illness. She explained that, during the time she tended William, he was 'very sick' and 'vomited frequently'. Although he also persistently complained to her of having a persistent 'great heat' in both his throat and chest, she did not think him to be in any danger, as a local surgeon, Mr Henry Sandell, had called in to see the patient, prescribed him a saline draught, and allayed her fears. Initially, William seemed to respond well to this treatment. However, a few days later his health deteriorated sharply once more, and so Elizabeth tried various remedies (such as a bran poultice, a laudanum-based tonic, and the application of leeches) to alleviate her son's suffering, but all to no avail. At this point, Sarah Dazley announced that she, personally, would visit Mr Sandell to acquire a more effective medication for her husband.[41]

Sarah Dazley was accompanied on her errand by Mary Carver, a neighbour and long-standing friend of William Dazley. Mary told the inquest that in the week before William Dazley was taken ill, his wife Sarah told her that her husband would soon have to take to his bed, as he had become very short of breath. Yet when Mary visited him, 'he was as well as usual'. Just a few days later, Mary returned to the Dazley residence and found her friend William to be 'wonderful sick all the while'. Mary and Sarah visited Mr Sandell in Potton where Mrs Dazley asked the surgeon for some pills to aid her husband as he was no longer able to take medicine in draught form. Mary Carver testified that Mr Sandell gave Sarah Dazley three white 'resting pills' to help settle the ill man's stomach. Mary recalled that, on the way home from this visit, Sarah Dazley

> threw the pills that Mr Sandell had given her into the ditch. She took a paper out of her pocket, like a piece of newspaper, and took three pills out which she put into the box which held the pills she had [from] Mr Sandell. She told me she [got] the pills from Mrs Gurry.

Mary noted that the swapped pills were darker and much larger than those prescribed by Mr Sandell.[42] By way of corroboration, Sarah Gurry then testified before the inquest jury and acknowledged that she had sold Sarah Dazley some pills during the week that William Dazley had become ill. She recounted that Sarah had come to her shop (where Sarah had occasionally worked) and said that her husband had sent her 'to have some pills or a powder, as he had had them before when he had become stout and bloated and they seemed to do him good'. Sarah Gurry subsequently sold Sarah Dazley some pills, along with a pennyworth of treacle and a pennyworth of flour of brimstone, but insisted that none of these items were 'of a poisonous nature'.[43]

Ann Mead provided additional testimony to the inquest jury. As the daughter of Simon Mead from an earlier marriage, she was thus step-daughter to Sarah Dazley and had come to live with her step-parents, to work as their domestic servant. She had been in their employment for nine months when William was taken ill. Ann recalled that, at the very start of William's biliousness, she saw Sarah Dazley 'make some pills [which] she mixed in a blue saucer. She then rolled them up with her hand and put them into a piece of newspaper and put them in her pocket.' Sarah left her husband three brown pills by his bed-side and told him to take two of them, whilst she made a visit to Eyeworth. When Sarah had gone, William told Ann that he could not take pills easily and so, by way of encouragement, Ann took one of the pills and seeing this, he managed to do the same. About two hours later, Ann was taken violently ill. As she explained: 'I became very sick and remained sick all night.' William was similarly unwell and grew very weak as a result. When Sarah returned she 'scolded' Ann several times for taking the pill, told visitors that her step-daughter was ill with a 'sick headache', and asked her to leave the Dazley residence for fear of contaminating other members of the household or making William Dazley sicker than he already was. Ann left the next morning and the next time she saw her step-father he was dead.[44]

William Dazley's brothers—John and Gilbert—were both witnesses to the care afforded their brother by his wife Sarah Dazley, particularly towards the latter stages of his illness. At the inquest hearing, Gilbert described how he saw Sarah take some white powder from a folded piece of paper and mixed it with some water in a teacup and gave it to William. He refused at first to drink the concoction, but Sarah told him that the surgeon Mr Sandell had prescribed it and had advised that if he took it, 'it would either make him better or worse in the course of a few hours'. It should be noted here that, in his own testimony, Mr Sandell did indeed admit to having given Mrs Dazley what he called 'an aperient powder' to act as a purgative and relieve the victim's symptoms when he had seen her earlier in the week.[45] About an hour after taking the medication, William Dazley began 'retching violently' and his brothers watched as he brought up 'water with a little blood'. By this time, William constantly complained of a great heat in his chest and throat and John Dazley suggested to Sarah that he should run and get Mr Sandell, but as he recounted 'she said I had better not, it was of no use'. William Dazley died just a few hours later.[46]

Isaac Hurst and George Dixon Hedley were the two surgeons asked to perform a post-mortem in Wrestlingworth Church on the exhumed remains of William Dazley. Although the surface of the body was evidently in a state of decomposition, upon opening the chest cavity, the medical men found sufficient preservation of the internal organs to enable them to offer a proper examination of the supposed victim. They initially observed that William Dazley's stomach and intestines were 'of a redder colour than is ordinarily observed'. Seeing this, they decided to remove the entirety of the alimentary canal for further inspection back at Bedford Infirmary where they both worked. When they were removing these body parts, Hurst and Hedley noticed some grains of white powder on the part of the bowel called the duodenum which aroused some suspicion. Upon examination of the specimens in more detail, numerous abrasions and ulcerations were uncovered on the lining of sections of the digestive tract, sitting alongside yellow patches of discolouration. In addition, more of the white powder was found in a variety of gastrointestinal locations, including the stomach. Particles of this powder and quantities of fluid from various parts of the extracted sections were then collected and exposed to further scrutiny and systematic scientific analysis. The combined results of the five tests painstakingly conducted by Hurst and Hedley left the two medical men in no doubt as to the cause of death of William Dazley. As George Dixon Hedley explained: 'judging from the symptoms I have heard described, from the appearances I observed in the parts I have examined, and from the tests I have applied ... the deceased died from the effect of arsenic'.[47]

Despite the abundance of the testimony before them, and the complexities associated with the scientific evidence presented, the inquest jury retired for just a few minutes before returning with their verdict. They declared 'That William Dazley died from the effects of arsenic administered to him with a guilty knowledge by Sarah Dazley his wife.' The coroner deemed that as 'the verdict was equivalent to wilful murder against the accused' several of the witnesses should be bound over and the prisoner, Sarah Dazley ought to 'be fully committed to Bedford gaol to take her trial at the next assizes'.[48] In the wake of this verdict, local suspicions regarding the general character and past behaviour of Sarah Dazley emerged, proliferated, and reached the ears of the press. Soon newspapers reported that the demise of Sarah's first husband, Simon Mead, and potentially that of their son Jonah, may not have been so innocent or so natural as had originally been assumed.[49]

The upshot of all this speculation was a request made by the Reverend Mr Twiss, rector of Wrestlingworth parish, to the aforementioned coroner Ezra Eagles, that the bodies of Simon and Jonah Mead be exhumed from Tadlow churchyard in Cambridgeshire and appropriately examined.[50] The coroner acceded to this request on 14 April 1843 and two inquests were held a week later in front of the same jury that had deliberated over the William Dazley case. The first inquest was that of Simon Mead and, to begin with, the jurors heard a lot of familiar testimony. Betty Mead, Simon's sister, explained that her brother had died swiftly; just five days after becoming ill. He had complained to her of a painful heat and pressure in his chest and a continual thirst, although he was unable to pass liquid down his throat. She recounted how his 'breath was very much affected and smelt offensively' and that she saw 'white froth running from his mouth'.[51] Another witness, Hannah Dart, had also tended to Simon Mead during his illness and saw him on the night before his death. She remembered him 'complaining of a fire in his throat and mouth'. She noted that his eyes were red and his face swollen. As she recalled, 'He attempted to swallow, but could not. He complained of great heat and thirst. He appeared to be in great pain.'[52]

The prevailing evidence clearly alluded to the potential for foul play in the demise of Simon Mead. So when the surgeons Isaac Hurst and George Dixon Headley appeared before the hearing, the individuals assembled expected that their evidence would be as damning and incriminatory as it had been a month earlier in relation to the death of William Dazley. However, Hedley reported that, when the body of Simon Mead had been exhumed, it was discovered that very little of his remains had been preserved and instead, his coffin was effectively empty, save for a quantity of soft black matter, some clothing remnants and some undistinguishable soft tissue. Crucially for Hedley and corroborated by Hurst, 'There was no trace of the stomach or bowels or any of the contents of the chest or belly.'[53] On hearing this testimony, the coroner decreed that it would be useless to carry the case further and the jury concurred.

The inquest of Jonah Mead immediately followed that of his father. Various witnesses (including Betty Mead and Sarah Hall) testified to Jonah being a sickly child at times, but from what was said, there was no evidence of any obvious chronic complaint.[54] Around the time of her son's death, Sarah Dazley (then Mead) complained to friends and locals from the village of Wrestlingworth that Jonah was 'very ill' and that she wanted to go to nearby Potton to see if the surgeon, Mr Pratt, could give her anything for the baby. Sarah left Jonah with her neighbour Mrs Morley and set off to get the doctor's help. Whilst Sarah was away, Mrs Morley observed that the child was clearly ill as he was continually restless and 'moaned a great deal', but noted that he had not been sick at all whilst in her care. When Sarah Dazley returned some two hours later, she said she had got three powders from the doctor and had been told to give the child one of these as soon as she got home. According to Mrs Morley, 'The mother took the child home with her, and came back about an hour-and-a-half after, when, on my asking how the child was, she said he was dead and laid out.'[55]

Unfortunately for Sarah Dazley, both Isaac Hurst and George Dixon Hedley had more to say at this inquest than they had in relation to the preceding case as the child's coffin was found intact. Moreover, although much of the mortal remains therein had wholly decomposed, 'the parts contained in the belly were in a tolerably good state of preservation'. Said parts were removed by the two medical men and placed in a jar for subsequent forensic examination. Upon later inspection of this material, Hurst and Hedley noticed various features that were not unlike those discovered in the intestinal parts that they had extracted from the body of William Dazley. Jonah's Mead's digestive organs and gastric system were similarly inflamed and ulcerated and there were yellow patches of discolouration in proximity, although there were no visible traces of any powder or foreign substance. The doctors excised some of the boy's intestines and carried out the same range of tests as they had done on the fluid and powder removed from various sections of William Dazley's alimentary canal. As before, Hurst and Hedley concluded that the cumulative results from their analysis showed that the child died from the effect of arsenic. Although their findings suggested that the child had only been exposed to a few grains of the poison, it was their contention that this was sufficient to kill him, upon account of his age, size, and his seemingly sickly nature.[56]

The coroner then advised the jury that, although there was a lack of evidence relating to the cause of the initial sickness in the child, 'there could be no doubt as to the presence of arsenic in the stomach of the deceased after the testimony that had been given by the medical gentlemen'. What they had to consider now was whether the arsenic had been administered to Jonah Mead deliberately or unintentionally and he ordered that they retire to consider this and their verdict. Although the jury's deliberations were much more prolonged on this occasion than they had been in relation to the William Dazley inquest, the outcome was the same. The jury agreed: 'That Jonah Mead died from the effects of arsenic, administered to him with a guilty knowledge by his mother, Sarah Dazley.'[57] Consequently, when Sarah Dazley came to be arraigned at Bedfordshire Assizes in July 1843, she was charged with not one, but two murders. When it came to the actual trial, however, the prosecution opted to proceed solely with the indictment related to the killing of William Dazley. They kept the charge relating to the murder of Jonah Mead in reserve.[58]

The likely reason for limiting the nature of the proceedings against Sarah Dazley was the nature and complexities of the evidence required to prove a case of deliberate homicidal poisoning. As Ian Burney explains:

> Poison, like the poisoner, was capable of deceitful, disguised appearances. The ideal poison was tasteless, odourless, colourless—a substance without manifest quality. As such, it could dissolve itself into the stuff of everyday life, substances that in their apparent intent were signed as benign or healthful. Its action upon the body of the victim completed the circuit of secrecy, duplicity and interiority. It was an article of faith amongst professional and lay commentators alike that the body of the victim, in contrast to the victims of cruder violence, was illegible at the surface level.[59]

In the first instance, establishing cause of death required a tranche of complicated scientific testimony which was often hard for jury members to follow or understand. Then, on top of this, there was the question of determining who precisely had administered the poison in question, how they had acquired it and whether this had been done accidentally or intentionally.[60] This aspect of culpability was notoriously difficult to substantiate, especially if it was unclear how many doses of the toxin had been administered to the victim. When faced with all of these difficulties, the prosecution probably thought it prudent to stick to just one of the murders and use the cumulative effect of all the evidence they had to make their case.[61]

In the criminal trial against Sarah Dazley, a large part of the evidence presented by the prosecution was a reiteration of the material put before the inquest jury. Aside from this, however, and in addition to a thorough explanation of the scientific methodologies that had been employed to prove the presence of arsenic in the remains of William Dazley,[62] the lawyers for the Crown also introduced some fresh evidence. This supported their contention that the accused had not only the means, but also the motive and the opportunity to murder her husband. First of all, the court heard testimony from local chemist John Burnham and his apprentice Robert Norman that Sarah Dazley had visited their shop in Potton on at least two separate occasions to purchase some arsenic, which she said was needed to eradicate rodents from her home.[63] This allowed the prosecution to establish that the accused had direct access to the kind of poison that had killed William Dazley. In addition, the reiteration of Ann Mead's testimony that she had become ill after consuming one of the tablets prepared and administered by Sarah Dazley, and testimony from a neighbour that a pig which had died soon after eating from a basin of William Dazley's vomit left outside their property, quickly eradicated any suggestion that the victim died from an undiagnosed illness.[64] Instead, the forensic testimony was corroborated, and the link between Sarah Dazley and the dispensation of arsenic to her husband was established.

The prosecution then set about establishing a potential motive for the murder of William Dazley. Neighbour John Hanley testified before the court that, just two weeks before William Dazley was taken ill, he saw the victim and his wife Sarah embroiled in a prolonged and violent physical fight in the front yard of their house. He heard Sarah Dazley say to her husband: 'I don't care a damn for such a man as you, nor never will! Blast you! I'll be a match for you some time or other!'[65] Another neighbour, Mary Ann Nibbs, recounted how she was told by Sarah Dazley 'that she would never allow any man to strike her without doing for him' and that she was 'determined to have seven husbands in ten years'.[66] Then the court heard from the two female servants that Sarah had shared lodgings with whilst in London and on the run from the authorities. Seemingly the accused had told both Fanny Simmons and Elizabeth Garnham that she was wholly unconcerned about her plight. She was confident that 'she should not be hanged, for none of her family saw her buy the arsenic or give it to her husband'.[67] The prosecution argued that, collectively, this evidence suggested that Sarah Dazley wanted to be rid of her husband, partly in vengeful response to the violence he had publicly shown towards her and partly because her amorous and marital intensions lay elsewhere.[68] Interestingly, the underlying motives ascribed to Sarah Dazley in the perpetration of William's murder were not atypical amongst female poisoners of the Victorian era.[69]

The lawyers for Sarah Dazley's defence decided to take advantage of the judicial change that permitted them to summarize their case before the jury in criminal proceedings after 1836.[70] However, their tactics in this endeavour were completely misjudged and bordered on the absurd. First, they postulated that William Dazley may have poisoned himself by accident; a claim which was wholly unsupported by any of the testimony and evidence brought before the court. Then they tried to persuade the jury that William Dazley had poisoned Simon and Jonah Mead so that he could then have Sarah all to himself, but when Sarah came to discover what he had done, she decided to get revenge for her former husband and son, by poisoning William in return. Clearly, this was not the best defence tactic to employ for someone accused of William Dazley's demise![71]

Perhaps for this reason and on account of the accumulated medical, scientific, and circumstantial evidence against the accused, the jury did not take long to reach their verdict. In less than fifteen minutes, they declared Sarah Dazley to be guilty of murder.[72] As was customary at the time, the judge in the case implored Sarah to confess her culpability in the murders of both William Dazley *and* her son Jonah Mead. Partly this was done so the criminal had the chance to attain forgiveness in the afterlife and partly it was done to confirm their guilt to any who doubted it.[73] The judge then advised Sarah Dazley that there would be no chance of a pardon and sentenced her to be hanged, directing that her body be buried within the precincts of Bedford gaol.[74] Whilst imprisoned awaiting her fateful punishment, the prison chaplain and a local judicial official who visited her both reported that Sarah Dazley was wholly resolute in denying her guilt. She refused to confess to any of the crimes she had been implicated in and protested her innocence at every opportunity. Indeed, the Justice noted that 'the strength of her nerves throughout appeared to be most extraordinary and beyond any that I could have conceived'.[75] Despite this impressive show of defiance in the weeks that followed the trial, the verdict and sentence against Sarah Dazley was never appealed against nor challenged, and so her execution was proceeded with as ordered by the assize court. Due to the extensive press coverage of both the inquests and the trial, a great deal of local, regional, and national interest had been generated in relation to this particular episode of judicial punishment.[76] Thus, on Saturday 5 August 1843, a crowd of nearly 12,000 people assembled outside Bedford gaol where they watched the so-called 'Potton Poisoner' being 'launched into eternity'.[77]

## Women and the Potential for Premeditated Murder

A female serial poisoner posed innumerable problems to Victorian society, as they defied convention in a range of different ways. Most obviously, women were meant to be the maternal nurturers of society and the moral guardians for upcoming generations, not harbingers of death and destruction who spent their time preying upon unsuspecting victims. Then, and as we saw earlier in this chapter, female criminals were abstruse as not only had they committed an offence, but they had betrayed the notional qualities of their sex in doing so and, as a result, female perpetrators were often considered more 'monstrous' than their male equivalents. In addition, and as Knelman has explained, by adopting an underhand but thoroughly calculated methodology, female poisoners, more specifically, exhibited deliberately deviant behaviour that was far removed from the irrational and impulsive traits typically associated with women criminals. These latter had been readily (and all too easily) attributed to their emotionally driven disposition.[78] In 1882, the Home Secretary, Sir William Harcourt (1827–1904) neatly summed up these arguments by saying:

> Women have as a rule less power of self control than men, and often act hastily under the influence of feelings and emotions to which men are comparatively, or perhaps altogether strangers. In cases of poisoning, especially when more than one dose has been given, there is no room for questioning the fullest premeditation.[79]

Thus, if we add in the fact that serial poisoners like Sarah Dazley exhibited all of these characteristics on separate but recurrent occasions, rather than in a one-off episode of villainy as Harcourt suggests, we can see the scale of the problem such women posed to social commentators and judicial authorities alike. How could the 'unnatural conduct' of a woman like Sarah Dazley be explained or understood, and could it ever be excused?[80]

In the first half of the nineteenth century, determining the motive for the actions of female killers was seen as the key to unlocking the mystery of their peculiar conduct. As it was thought that women could not be autonomously bad or innately evil in their own right, questions were routinely asked about the existence of (typically male) accomplices, and theories proffered to explain away evident behaviours. Increasingly, and over the second half of the century more particularly, these explanations focused upon mental incapacity and the proposition that inherent madness or temporary insanity must account for women's violent transgressions and their divergence from putative gender norms. Such considerations were not typically afforded to men similarly accused of homicide at this time, but then shows of aggression, supremacy, and physicality were accepted masculine traits and so their actions did not require justification.

In relation to the Sarah Dazley case, it was difficult to discern an obvious motive for her actions. There did not seem to be any pecuniary reason for the killings and no evidence of hardship was presented, either in the press or in the courtroom. There was no mention of mental health problems either, nor any indication that Sarah behaved unusually or abnormally at the time of the murders. Whilst there was, as we have seen, some suggestion of domestic strife in her relationship with her second husband, this was anecdotal and based on the witnessing of one heated argument, rather than a documented catalogue of quarrels. Moreover, and in any event, there was no suggestion that the accused had suffered physical abuse at the hands of any of her victims, rather the evidence said that she would not tolerate being struck by a man.[81]

Historian Richard Clark has suggested that promiscuity may have been the motive for the murders. He argues that Sarah Dazley simply eliminated anyone who got in the way of the next relationship that she wanted to move on to.[82] Indeed, a broadside written prior to Dazley's execution states that she killed 'for the sake of enjoying the pleasures of sin for a season'.[83] Katherine Watson reinforces this proposition by saying that spousal murders often 'resulted from the inability of all but the wealthy to extricate themselves legally from unhappy unions'.[84] Whilst this theory does seem plausible, and indeed an anticipated need for freedom may explain the killing of Jonas Mead, her son, it is more problematic if we consider that Sarah was evidently already openly engaged in other relationships during both her marriages and thus she had already relaxed the confines of the marital relationship to suit her own needs.

When a suspected female killer was in the dock, if a motive was not readily discernible, an accomplice was not evident, nor mental capacity in question, how did Victorians process the individual before them? Certainly such individuals were magnets for the 'morbid curiosity' of the general public, as the copious applications to visit Sarah Dazley when in gaol awaiting her trial and latterly her execution testify.[85] We might have assumed from this, from our understanding of attitudes to female criminality and from our appreciation of the treatment of other female killers from the Victorian era such as Kate Webster (1849–79), that the press would have portrayed Sarah Dazley as a monster and her actions as hideous, grotesque and unfeminine.[86] However, in reality the Dazley case was hardly sensationalized at all by the media of the 1840s period. Although jovially described as a 'female bluebeard' in one publication,[87] and despite coverage of the inquests and the subsequent criminal trial being heavily syndicated at the time, by and large the reporting of the Sarah Dazley case was factual and understated rather than hyperbolic and shocking. Variously but blandly described as 'impassive', 'indifferent', 'nonchalant', and 'unconcerned',[88] it is rather remarkable that Sarah Dazley is almost consigned to a position of insignificance in the reportage of the various murders that she is accused of perpetrating. Indeed, perhaps the lack of detailed press attention given to Sarah Dazley and her crimes explains why so many inquisitive individuals applied to see her in person whilst imprisoned.

It is interesting to note that the issue of premeditation was not raised at any point in the criminal proceedings against Sarah Dazley; neither in the testimony presented in court, the closing arguments offered by the prosecution and defence lawyers, nor in the judge's proclamation of sentence. This appears to be a rather odd omission, given the evidence that clearly pointed to the fact that Sarah Dazley was a serial killer whose *modus operandi*—poisoning—was the quintessential form of murder with evident malice aforethought.[89] However, and as we have seen, the accepted traits of female criminals did not allow for rational, planned behaviour. Poisoners in their thoughts and in their deeds blatantly challenged these traits and it would seem that rather than try to tackle this betrayal to gender head on, Victorians did their very best to ignore the actions of serially deviant and criminal women. This explains why the prosecution and the judicial authorities were silent on the evidence which clearly pointed to Sarah Dazley's determination and planning. It also elucidates why the press did not sensationalize the murders of Sarah Dazley with their customary determination for a readership which was unquestionably eager for gory details and tales of the unexpected.[90]

Serial poisoners like Dazley, Sarah Chesham (1809–51), Catherine Wilson (1822–62), Mary Ann Cotton (1832–73), and Mary Ann Britland (1847–86) were simply put to one side by society and regarded as aberrant women. They were considered too unusual for diagnoses, classification, or comment, as their characters and their actions were not easily explained within the confines of prescribed normative and gendered behaviours. Serial killers, and serial poisoners in particular, showed a myriad of traits that belied their gender and they did so on successive and multiple occasions. It was better to ignore them than bring attention to them. That way, no explanation would be required for their anomalous existence and patriarchal boundaries and gender norms could remain intact and unimpeded.

## Conclusion

The case of Sarah Dazley has revealed much about nineteenth-century attitudes to criminal women and to serial poisoners in particular. It is, of course, well known that the Victorians were fascinated by murder and those who perpetrated it, especially homicides conducted in an unusual manner or committed by atypical perpetrators such as women. However, nineteenth-century society and those who governed it were evidently unsettled by female poisoners and by those who used this methodology repeatedly in order to kill multiple victims. By patently planning their crimes and evidencing deliberate, cold-blooded intent, these women had entirely broken out of the behavioural boundaries afforded to their sex. Instead, they had behaved just like their male counterparts. They had dispatched their victims easily, often leaving no trace of their murderous actions and they had regularly done so without an obvious motive, perhaps just because they had wanted to and because they could. That made serial female poisoners not only menacing and unpredictable but, more importantly, it made them uncontrollable.

Sarah Dazley was certainly not a woman who could be easily contained. She had shamelessly and openly engaged in various extra-marital affairs, she was evidently not afraid to speak her mind on various issues in a public forum and, even when it came to murder, she made little effort to hide her culpability. For instance, she crudely replaced medications prescribed to her by medical professionals with her own concoctions in front of witnesses and she then boldly administered these 'medications' in full view of her victims' relatives. She was a woman who was doggedly determined to get her own way by effecting the result she desired, regardless of the seriousness of what she was doing, the impact of her actions, or the numerous casualties that occurred along the way. It would seem that even her own survival was a mere afterthought to the satisfaction of her homicidal intent.

For those women who brazenly used murder as a simple tool to achieve a means to an end, time and time again, killing seemingly came all too easily. For the Victorians who had to deal with these offenders, it was almost impossible to offer an explanation for the murderous behaviour as it did not fit neatly with any of the excuses typically offered to rationalize homicidal activity by female protagonists. Crucially, it was the serial poisoner's blatant engagement with malice aforethought that was central to the resultant quandary. One strategy was to ignore these women so that they would effectively be written out of history as if they had never existed. Whilst this approach was convenient and may have worked to some extent in relation to the individual murderesses concerned, it was also somewhat naïve as the threat of female deviancy remained long in the collective consciousness.[91] Sarah Dazley's crimes occurred at the initiation of a moral panic about 'secret' poisonings and, although legislation made poisons like arsenic harder to purchase later on in the century, the belief of a potential malevolence amongst Victorian women in relation to the use of toxins persisted nonetheless. This ongoing fear was undoubtedly due to the actions of Sarah Dazley and the moral panic regarding female poisoners like her.

For far too long, historians have taken women's use of poison as an indication of their criminal inferiority and a sign of their physical weakness. They have argued that women preferred to use poison as it could be administered quickly and simply and it meant they could avoid having to engage in any physical act of aggression or interpersonal violence.[92] This supposition marries well with the chauvinistic attitudes to female offending that have pervaded criminal history for too long. Women who engaged in serial poisoning to kill others did not pick an easy route to murder. Rather they picked a more sophisticated and refined option which required stealth, cunning, autonomy, nerve, and acumen.[93] Although these qualities were not ones readily associated with subordinated Victorian women, all of the attributes were categorically demonstrated by the actions of killers from that era such as Sarah Dazley. Arguably then we should not still be treating these women as aberrant mythical 'she-devils' who need to be erased from society and from memory at the earliest opportunity, due to their inability to fit in with the prescribed boundaries of a given historical context. Instead, can we consider these individuals to be intriguing prototypes for the strong, self-assured, and more modern independent women that we more readily recognize today? It is of course inescapable that these women were criminals, and deadly *femme fatales* at that. Yet, trapped in marriages they could not escape from due to the prevailing socio-legal context of the nineteenth century, these women could potentially be considered as pioneers, not only in terms of their criminal careers, but more especially in terms of their attempts at individualism and self-determination.

## Notes

1. For further discussion see A.-M. Kilday (2016) 'Constructing the Cult of the Criminal: Kate Webster—Victorian Murderess and Media Sensation', in A.-M. Kilday and D. S. Nash (eds), *Law, Crime and Deviance since 1700: Micro-Studies in the History of Crime* (London: Bloomsbury), pp. 125–48 at pp. 129–30 and the references at p. 144 nn. 29–30; M. B. W. Emmerichs (1993) 'Trials of Women for Homicide in Nineteenth-Century England', *Women and Criminal Justice*, 5, 1, pp. 99–109 at p. 99; S. D'Cruze, S. Walklate, and S. Pegg (2006) *Murder: Social and Historical Approaches to Understanding Murder and Murderers* (Cullompton: Willan), p. 46; M. Hartman (1977) *Victorian Murderesses: A True History of Thirteen Respectable French and English Women Accused of Unspeakable Crimes* (London: Robson Books), p. 5; and L. Zedner (1991) *Women, Crime and Custody in Victorian England* (Oxford: Clarendon Press), p. 29.
2. For further discussion of the construction of gendered ideologies in the Victorian era specifically see C. Emsley (2005) *Crime and Society in England, 1750–1900* (Harlow: Pearson), chapter 4; and H. Johnston (2015) *Crime in England 1815–1880: Experiencing the Criminal Justice System* (London and New York: Routledge), pp. 123–4.
3. See Johnston, *Crime in England*, pp. 124–5. See also J. Knelman (1998) *Twisting in the Wind: The Murderess and the English Press* (Toronto: University of Toronto Press), pp. 10–11 and 230; A. Ballinger (2000) *Dead Woman Walking: Executed Women in England and Wales 1900–1955* (Aldershot: Ashgate), pp. 52–3; and Zedner, *Women, Crime and Custody*, pp. 2 and 28.
4. L. Worsley (2013) *A Very British Murder: The Story of a National Obsession* (London: BBC Books), p. 139; and Knelman, *Twisting in the Wind*, pp. 3, 12, and 274.
5. J. Flanders (2011) *The Invention of Murder: How the Victorians Revelled in Death and Detection and Created Modern Crime* (London: Harper Collins), p. 413; and

C. A. Conley (2007) *Certain Other Countries: Homicide, Gender, and National Identity in Late Nineteenth-Century England, Ireland, Scotland, and Wales* (Columbus, OH: Ohio State University Press), p. 84.

6. Knelman, *Twisting in the Wind*, p. 15.
7. Flanders, *Invention of Murder*, p. 182.
8. Hartman, *Victorian Murderesses*, p. 5; Knelman, *Twisting in the Wind*, p. 10; and Flanders, *Invention of Murder*, p. 183.
9. I. A. Burney (2012 edition) *Poison, Detection and the Victorian Imagination* (Manchester: Manchester University Press), p. 20; K. Watson (2004) *Poisoned Lives: English Poisoners and their Victims* (London: Hambledon), p. 41; L. Stratmann (2016) *The Secret Poisoner: A Century of Murder* (New Haven: Yale University Press), p. 156; M. Wiener (2001) 'Alice Arden to Bill Sikes: Changing Nightmares of Intimate Violence in England, 1558–1869', *Journal of British Studies*, 40, 2, pp. 184–212 at p. 198 and Flanders, *Invention of Murder*, pp. 28 and 183.
10. S. Perrini (2012) *Women Serial Killers of the 19th Century: The Golden Age of Poisons* (London: CreateSpace Publishing), p. 1; P. Bartrip (1992) 'A "Pennurth of Arsenic for Rat Poison": The Arsenic Act, 1851 and the Prevention of Secret Poisoning', *Medical History*, 36, pp. 53–69 at p. 57; G. Robb (1997) 'Circe in Crinoline: Domestic Poisonings in Victorian England', *Journal of Family History*, 22, 2, pp. 176–90 at p. 177 and Flanders, *Invention of Murder*, p. 232.
11. K. Watson (2006) 'Criminal Poisoning in England and the Origins of the Marsh Test for Arsenic', in J. R. Bertomeu-Sánchez and A. Nieto-Galan (eds), *Chemistry, Medicine, and Crime: Mateu J. B. Orfilia (1787–1853) and his Times* (Sagamore Beach, MA: Science History Publications), pp. 183–206 at pp. 13–14; Stratmann, *The Secret Poisoner*, p. 12; Flanders, *Invention of Murder*, p. 234; and T. Ward (2005) 'A Mania for Suspicion: Poisoning, Science and the Law', in J. Rowbotham and K. Stevenson (eds), *Criminal Conversations: Victorian Crimes, Social Panic and Moral Outrage* (Columbus, OH: Ohio State University Press), pp. 140–56 at p. 140.
12. For further discussion see Robb, 'Circe in Crinoline', p. 185, and Nagy, *Nineteenth-Century Female Poisoners*, p. 27.
13. I. A. Burney (1999) 'A Poisoning of No Substance: The Trials of Medico-Legal Proof in Mid-Victorian England', *Journal of British Studies*, 38, 1, pp. 59–92 at p. 68, and Ward, 'A Mania for Suspicion', p. 144.
14. Robb, 'Circe in Crinoline', p. 186; Stratmann, *The Secret Poisoner*, p. 6; Watson, *Poisoned Lives*, pp. 8–9; V. M. Nagy (2015) *Nineteenth-Century Female Poisoners: Three English Women Who Used Arsenic to Kill* (Basingstoke: Palgrave Macmillan), pp. 60–1.
15. T. R. Forbes (1985) *Surgeons at the Bailey: English Forensic Medicine to 1878* (New Haven and London: Yale University Press), pp. 124 and 127; and Watson, *Poisoned Lives*, p. 30.
16. See respectively *The Times*, 22 September 1848, issue 20, p. 4, and 19 April 1886, issue 31,737, p. 4; C. Dickens (1851) 'Household Crime', *Household Words—Volume IV* [December] (New York: Angell, Engel & Hewitt Printers), p. 277; R. Ogden Doremus (1893) 'Can Chemical Analysis Convict Poisoners?', *The Forum*, 16, pp. 229–39 at p. 229; and also Burney, *Poison, Detection and the Victorian Imagination*, p. 5.

17. J. Parascandola (2012) *King of Poisons: A History of Arsenic* (Washington, DC: Potomac Books), pp. 2 and 7; Dickens, 'Household Crime', p. 279; Forbes, *Surgeons at the Bailey*, p. 131; B. Lane (1992) *The Encyclopaedia of Forensic Science* (London and New York: Headline Book Publishing), p. 30; and Perrini, *Women Serial Killers of the 19th Century*, p. 2.
18. For further discussion on the broad uses of arsenic see J. C. Wharton (2010) *The Arsenic Century: How Britain was Poisoned at Home, Work and Play* (Oxford: Oxford University Press); J. Emsley (2005) *Elements of Murder* (Oxford: Oxford University Press), chapters 5 and 6; Watson, *Poisoned Lives*, p. xii, pp. 32–3 and 36; Robb, 'Circe in Crinoline', p. 182; Nagy, *Nineteenth-Century Female Poisoners*, p. 18, and Perrini, *Women Serial Killers of the 19th Century*, p. 4.
19. Parascandola, *King of Poisons*, pp. 1 and 9; Lane, *Encyclopaedia of Forensic Science*, pp. 30–1; Stratmann, *The Secret Poisoner*, p. 9; and Bartrip, 'A "Pennurth of Arsenic for Rat Poison"', p. 62.
20. Watson, *Poisoned Lives*, p. 6.
21. Ibid., p. 30.
22. For evidence of this see ibid., pp. 16–20; Watson, 'Criminal Poisoning in England', p. 186; and Parascandola, *King of Poisons*, pp. 10–12.
23. For further discussion see Burney, *Poison, Detection and the Victorian Imagination*, pp. 21–22, 25–6, and 30; Nagy, *Nineteenth-Century Female Poisoners*, pp. 16 and 27; Stratmann, *The Secret Poisoner*, p. 1; Robb, 'Circe in Crinoline', pp. 177–80; Ward, 'A Mania for Suspicion', p. 149; Johnston, *Crime in England*, p. 125; and Watson, *Poisoned Lives*, p. 52.
24. 14 & 15 Vict, ch. 13.
25. For further discussion see Bartrip, 'A "Pennurth of Arsenic for Rat Poison"', pp. 53–69; Nagy, *Nineteenth-Century Female Poisoners*, pp. 70–6; Parascandola, *King of Poisons*, pp. 12–15; Lane, *Encyclopaedia of Forensic Science*, pp. 31 and 33; Watson, *Poisoned Lives*, pp. 42–3.
26. *England, Select Births and Christenings, 1538–1975*, Family History Library film number 1066946 and 826466, found at <www.ancestry.com>.
27. For further discussion see P. Harrison (1993) *Hertfordshire and Bedfordshire Murders* (Newbury: Countryside Books), pp. 55–64.
28. R. Clark (2007) *Women and the Noose: A History of Female Execution* (Stroud: Tempus), p. 110.
29. *England, Select Marriages, 1538–1973*, Family History Library film number 450473, 826465, and 826466, found at <www.ancestry.com>. See also Clark, *Women and the Noose*, p. 110.
30. See P. Wilson (1971) *Murderess: A Study of Women Executed in Britain since 1843* (London: Michael Joseph), p. 17; *The Times*, 24 March 1843, p. 8, and 22 April 1843, p. 3; as well as *The Leicester Chronicle*, 8 April 1843, n.p.
31. The surname of the accused is variously presented in contemporary material as Dazley, Dazeley, and Daisley. We have decided to use Dazley in this chapter, as it is the most common spelling utilized and is the one referred to in the trial of the suspect—see for instance National Archives, Assizes: Norfolk Circuit, Gaol Books, ASSI 33/13.

32. *England, Select Marriages, 1538–1973*, Family History Library film number 1279195, found at <www.ancestry.com>. It should be noted that there is significant variation in the timing of the deaths of Simon Mead and Jonah Mead and in the marriage date of Sarah Mead to William Dazley in the scholarship and press reports of this case. I have used official registered and certificated details alongside statements made by officials presiding in this case to establish the timeline presented.
33. Clark, *Women and the Noose*, p. 111.
34. *The Times*, 15 April 1843, p. 6.
35. *The Morning Post*, 25 July 1843, p. 7.
36. *The Times*, 24 March 1843, p. 8; and *Jackson's Oxford Journal*, 25 March 1843, n.p.
37. *The Times*, 27 March 1843, p. 8; and *Freeman's Journal and Daily Commercial Advertiser*, 28 March 1843, n.p.
38. *Lloyd's Weekly London Newspaper*, 26 March 1843, p. 7; *Bedfordshire Mercury and Huntingdon Express*, 1 April 1843, n.p.
39. See the commentary provided in the *Bedfordshire Mercury and Huntingdon Express*, 1 April 1843, n.p.
40. *The Standard*, 27 March 1843, n.p. and *The Morning Chronicle*, 27 March 1843, n.p.
41. National Archives, Assize Records: Home, Norfolk and South-Eastern Circuit—Depositions, the Testimonies of Elizabeth Dazley and Henry William Sandell, ASSI 36/4/29.
42. Ibid., Testimony of Mary Carver, ASSI 36/4/29.
43. Ibid., Testimony of Sarah Freeman Gurry, ASSI 36/4/29. According to herbalists and apothecaries of the Victorian era, flour of brimstone mixed with treacle was thought to be a remedy for a wide variety of ailments—see M. Chamberlain (2010) *Old Wives' Tales: The History of Remedies, Charms and Spells* (London: History Press).
44. Ibid., Testimony of Ann Mead, ASSI 36/4/29.
45. Ibid., Testimony of Henry William Sandell, ASSI 36/4/29.
46. Ibid., the Testimonies of John Dazley and Gilbert Dazley, ASSI 36/4/29. Corroborated by the Testimony of Mary Bull, ASSI 36/4/29.
47. Ibid., the Testimonies of George Dixon Hedley and Isaac Hurst, ASSI 36/4/29. See also *Jackson's Oxford Journal*, 25 March 1843, p. 2.
48. *The Times*, 27 March 1843, 18,254, p. 8, and *Lloyd's Weekly London Newspaper*, 26 March 1843, p. 7.
49. See for instance *The Standard*, 27 March 1843, n.p.; and *Freeman's Journal and Daily Commercial Advertiser*, 28 March 1843, n.p.
50. See *The Leicester Chronicle*, 8 April 1853, n.p.
51. See *The Times*, 22 April 1843, p. 3.
52. *The Morning Post*, 22 April 1843, p. 7. See also *The Morning Chronicle*, 22 April 1843, n.p.; and *The Ipswich Journal*, 29 April 1843, n.p.
53. *The Times*, 22 April 1843, p. 3.
54. *The Times*, 15 April 1843, p. 6.
55. *The Times*, 22 April 1843, p. 3.
56. George Dixon Hedley wrote up the details of the experiments he carried out in this case for publication in a medical journal—see G. D. Hedley (1843) 'Cases of Death in Childbed and Deaths from Poisoning', *The Lancet*, 2, pp. 845–7 at pp. 846–7. See also

*The Morning Post*, 22 April 1843, p. 7; and *Freeman's Journal and Daily Commercial Advertiser*, 24 April 1843, n.p.

57. National Archives, Assize Records: Norfolk and Home Circuits—Indictment Files, 1689–1850, Inquisition Verdict 21 April 1843, ASSI 94/2388.
58. National Archives, Assize Records: Norfolk and Home Circuits—Indictment Files, 1689–1850, Bedfordshire Calendar of Prisoners, ASSI 94/2388. See also P. Heslop (2009) *Murderous Women: From Sarah Dazley to Ruth Ellis* (London: History Press), p. 16.
59. Burney, *Poison, Detection and the Victorian Imagination*, p. 17.
60. For further discussion of the complexities of the evidence surrounding poisoning cases in the nineteenth century see Forbes, *Surgeons at the Bailey*, pp. 124–5, and Robb, 'Circe in Crinoline', p. 180.
61. The use of cumulative circumstantial evidence was seemingly common in nineteenth century poisoning cases due to the evidential difficulties already outlined in this chapter—see I. A. Burney (2002) 'Testing Testimony: Toxicology and the Law of Evidence in Early Nineteenth-Century England', *Studies in History and Philosophy of* Science, 33, pp. 289–314 at p. 296.
62. It is evident that earlier in the century there had been a great deal of scepticism amongst medical professionals and judicial authorities regarding the chemical tests and other evidence presented before criminal courts in relation to poisoning cases, which had resulted in a low number of convictions for intentional homicide. However the introduction of the Marsh Test in 1836 (and to a lesser extent the Reinsch Test in 1841) largely assuaged these concerns and allowed for more definitive outcomes in criminal trials. For further discussion see Doremus, 'Can Chemical Analysis Convict Poisoners?', pp. 231 and 233–4; Watson, 'Criminal Poisoning in England', pp. 183–4, 190, and 192–7; Watson, *Poisoned Lives*, pp. 16–20; Burney, 'Testing Testimony', pp. 289–314; Forbes, *Surgeons at the Bailey*, pp. 127–8, 132, and 136–7; Lane, *Encyclopaedia of Forensic Science*, pp. 38–9; and Robb, 'Circe in Crinoline', pp. 180–2.
63. See the testimony reproduced in *The Morning Post*, 25 July 1843, 22,630, p. 7.
64. See the testimony reproduced in *The Standard*, 24 July 1843, n.p.; and *The Leeds Mercury*, 29 July 1843, n.p.
65. Sec the testimony reproduced in *The Bristol Mercury*, 29 July 1843, p. 7.
66. See the testimony reproduced in *The Bury and Norwich Post and East Anglian*, 26 July 1843, n.p.
67. See the testimony reproduced in *The Ipswich Journal*, 29 July 1843, n.p.; and *The Northern Star and Leeds General Advertiser*, 29 July 1843, p. 3.
68. For further discussion see Wilson, *Murderess*, p. 20.
69. For further discussion see for instance Nagy, *Nineteenth-Century Female Poisoners*, p. 27, and Watson, *Poisoned Lives*, pp. 56 and 59–75.
70. This was on account of the Prisoners' Counsel Act, 6 & 7 Will IV, ch. 14 (1836). For further discussion of this development see C. C. Griffiths (2014) 'The Prisoners' Counsel Act 1836: Doctrine, Advocacy and the Criminal Trial', *Law, Crime and History*, 2, pp. 28–47.
71. For further discussion see *The Bristol Mercury*, 29 July 1843, , p. 7, and Clark, *Women and the Noose*, p. 112.

72. *The Morning Post,* 25 July 1843, p. 7.
73. For further discussion of changing attitudes to convict confessions see Flanders, *Invention of Murder,* pp. 237–8.
74. National Archives, Assize Records: Norfolk Circuit—Gaol Books, ASSI 33/13. See also *The Leeds Mercury,* 29 July 1843, n.p.
75. See Bedfordshire Archives, General Report of the Justices of the Peace to the Quarter Sessions, 1842–1843, QGR/3, pp. 13–14 and Minute Book of Visiting Justices 1843, QGR/5, pp. 466–7. See also *The Times,* 8 August 1843, p. 7, and Heslop, *Murderous Women,* p. 19.
76. For evidence of the extent of the 'intense excitement' caused by the Dazley case see *The Times,* 27 March 1843, p. 8; *Freeman's Journal and Daily Commercial Advertiser,* 28 March 1843, 24 April 1843, and 9 August 1843, n.p.; *The Morning Post,* 22 April 1843, p. 7, and 25 July 1843, p. 7; *The Morning Chronicle,* 22 April 1843, n.p.; *The Ipswich Journal,* 29 April 1843, n.p.; *The Standard,* 24 July 1843, and 7 August 1843, n.p.; *The Bury and Norwich Post, and East Anglian,* 9 August 1843, n.p.; *The Bradford Observer,* 10 August 1843, p. 5; *The Newcastle Courant,* 12 August 1843, p. 3; *The Caledonian Mercury,* 14 August 1843, n.p.; and *The Belfast News-Letter,* 18 August 1843, n.p.
77. For a full description of the hanging see The Higgins Art Gallery and Museum, Bedford (1843) *The Execution of Sarah Dazley* (Bedford: J. S. & W. Merry), Special Collections BEDFM 2011.16. See also *The Morning Post,* 7 August 1843, n.p.; *Berrow's Worcester Journal,* 10 August 1843, n.p.; *The Hull Packet and East Riding Times,* 11 August 1843, n.p.; *Lloyds Weekly London Newspaper,* 13 August 1843, p. 7; and Wilson, *Murderess,* p. 20, and Clark, *Women and the Noose,* p. 114.
78. For further discussion of the ways in which female killers defied gendered expectations see Knelman, *Twisting in the Wind,* pp. 11 and 49; Nagy, *Nineteenth-Century Female Poisoners,* pp. 6 and 29–30; Ballinger, *Dead Woman Walking,* pp. 129–30; and Robb, 'Circe in Crinoline', p. 186.
79. National Archives, Home Office Registered Papers, HO 144/108/A23081, 19 December 1882.
80. For press reports referring to Sarah Dazley's actions and behaviour as 'unnatural' and 'unfeminine' see *The Morning Post,* 25 July 1843, p. 7; *The Bury and Norwich Post and East Anglian,* 26 July 1843, n.p.; *The Leeds Mercury,* 29 July 1843, n.p.; and *The Bristol Mercury,* 29 July 1843, n.p.
81. For further discussion of the typical motives amongst women who kill through poisoning see Knelman, *Twisting in the Wind,* pp. 56 and 227; Watson, *Poisoned Lives,* p. xii; K. D. Watson (2006) 'Medical and Chemical Expertise in English Trials for Criminal Poisoning, 1750–1914', *Medical History,* 50, 3, pp. 373–90 at p. 386; and Flanders, *Invention of Murder,* p. 235.
82. Clark, *Women and the Noose,* pp. 114–15. See also Robb, 'Circe in Crinoline', p. 183. There is also some suggestion of promiscuity as motive in some contemporary newspaper reports—see for instance *The Morning Post,* 7 August 1843, n.p., and *Lloyd's Weekly London Newspaper,* 13 August 1843, p. 7.
83. Anon. (1843) *Sorrowful Lamentations of Sarah Dazley, for the Murder of Her Two Husband's and Infant Son by Poison at Bedford* (London: Paul Painter), British Library, General Reference Collection, 74/1888.c.3(62).

84. Watson, *Poisoned Lives*, p. xii. See also Flanders, *Invention of Murder*, p. 237.
85. See the comments of the chaplain found at Bedfordshire Archives, General Report of the Justices of the Peace to the Quarter Sessions, 1842–1843, QGR/3, p. 13.
86. See for instance Kilday, 'Consulting the Cult of the Criminal'.
87. *Bedfordshire Mercury and Huntingdon Express*, 1 April 1843, n.p.
88. See for instance *The Times*, 24 September 1843, p. 8, and 15 April 1843, p. 6; *Jackson's Oxford Journal*, 25 March 1843, n.p.; *Freeman's Journal and Daily Commercial Advertiser*, 28 March 1843, n.p.; *The Standard*, 24 July 1843, n.p.; *The Ipswich Journal*, 29 July 1843, n.p.; *The Northern Star and Leeds General Advertiser*, 29 July 1843, p. 3 and *Hampshire Advertiser & Salisbury Guardian*, 12 August 1843, Issue 1046, n.p.
89. For further discussion see Robb, 'Circe in Crinoline', pp. 177–8.
90. For further evidence of the 'matter-of-fact' reporting of some female murders in the nineteenth century see R. D. Altink (1970) *Victorian Studies in Scarlet: Murders and Manners in the Age of Victoria* (New York: W. W. Norton & Co.), p. 43.
91. See M. J. Wiener (2004) *Men of Blood: Violence, Manliness and Criminal Justice in Victorian England* (Cambridge: Cambridge University Press), p. 123.
92. For discussion of prevailing attitudes to female poisoners amongst scholars see Watson, *Poisoned Lives*, pp. 45–6. See also D'Cruze et al., *Murder*, pp. 46–7.
93. Burney, 'A Poisoning of No Substance', p. 70.

# 6

# Desperate, Desirous, or Devious?

## Female Thieves in Early Nineteenth-Century Wales

### Introduction

The historical scholarship surrounding female criminality by individuals such as Sharon Howard and David Philips has tended to associate women with certain types of offending, namely that which was non-violent or non-confrontational and which had some sort of tangential relationship with their normative roles within the domestic sphere.[1] Theft is one such crime where women's involvement has been accepted and linked to their knowledge and participation in matters related to the household economy. Yet, even in this context, women's role in criminal activity has been relegated to that of a subsidiary participant. For instance, historians such as John Beattie and Garthine Walker have argued that women were either limited to acting as lookouts or decoys at the behest of male accomplices, or simply operated as receivers who sold on the stolen goods after the 'proper' act of criminality had occurred.[2] Women were thus rarely considered to be direct or independent actors in felonious activity more broadly and in property crime more specifically. Moreover, when evidence of women's thievery did come to light, it was typically described as being petty in nature and was said to be related to their acquisitive disposition—a specific feature of the *female* psyche.[3] Consequently, when female thieves came before the judicial system, they were believed to be treated leniently by the courts, as either their role in the perpetration of property crime was a minor one, or because their involvement could be readily explained by an inherently gendered character trait that was wholly beyond their control.

This chapter will test the veracity of the existing scholarship and gendered conclusions relating to women's involvement in property crime by exploring the experience of female theft in Wales during the early nineteenth century. There are various advantages to undertaking a study of the Welsh experience of this kind of offending in the pre-modern era. First of all, the available sources from the Court of Great Sessions offer an unparalleled and wholly complete time series of data for the period 1800–30.[4] Of course, we must consider that some acts of theft will not have been reported to the authorities and other episodes may have been heard at the proceedings of the local Quarter Sessions.[5] However, the fact that the records of the Court of Great Sessions did not distinguish between grand larceny

*Beyond Deviant Damsels: Re-evaluating Female Criminality in the Nineteenth Century.* Anne-Marie Kilday and David Nash, Oxford University Press. © Anne-Marie Kilday and David Nash 2023. DOI: 10.1093/oso/9780198830733.003.0006

and petty larceny in terms of the charges made and thus minor or mundane episodes of thievery were regularly prosecuted on its circuits, all suggests that, in the first third of the nineteenth century at least, a substantial proportion of recorded thefts were dealt with by the higher jurisdiction.[6] Consequently, it can be argued that the reach and scope of the business heard at the Court of Great Sessions is invaluable for a study of property crime in the first third of the nineteenth century.

In addition to the wealth of the prevailing primary sources, the Welsh context also offers an interesting blend of both urban and rural milieus within which to examine gendered offending. To do this analysis during the decades between 1800 and 1830, a period of significant socio-economic transition for Wales, will also make a contribution to the burgeoning scholarship by individuals such as Wynford Vaughan-Thomas, John Davies, and David Howell on the processes and experiences which resulted in the development and modernization of the Welsh nation.[7] Finally, it is evident that the history of Welsh criminality has been largely preoccupied with the explosive and prolonged series of popular disturbances that occurred over the course of the nineteenth century, rather than with more 'everyday' offending, even when theft was clearly the most commonly indicted or prosecuted offence brought before the courts.[8] Moreover, in those few studies where property crime *has* been examined, this has related to the latter part of the Victorian era and to more serious forms of theft (such as burglary or livestock theft) which were not thought to involve women. Consequently, as both John Walliss and Katherine Watson have acknowledged, Welsh women's involvement in theft during the nineteenth century has been largely ignored.[9] This study seeks to address this lacuna of historical scholarship and determine the extent to which female involvement in theft within this context was born out of desperate circumstances, an uncontrollable desire for possessions, or just plain deviousness.

## The Concept of Acquisitiveness

As scholars such as Drew Gray and Tammy Whitlock have acknowledged, acquisitiveness has long been considered a gender-specific trait and one associated with the various inherent psychological weaknesses of women.[10] From as early as Eve's fall from grace in the Garden of Eden, where she succumbed to the temptation of the forbidden fruit, women's need to acquire goods and hoard possessions has been described as something beyond their control but firmly linked to their sex.[11] Initially, in the pre-modern period, this craving was thought to be allied to the constitution and processes of the female body—pregnancy, childbirth, and menopause—which commentators had regularly blamed for a variety of female maladies such as absent-mindedness, hysteria, and other forms of mania.[12] However, as the work of Elaine Abelson and Whitlock has shown, over the course of the nineteenth century, acquisitiveness became less associated with female biology and more closely linked to specific psychological factors such as sexual desire.[13] Acquisitiveness thus came to be seen as an insatiable longing or hunger that effectively seduced women to the point where they were forced to acquire the object of their desire by any means and eventually come to fetishize it.[14]

The rise of consumerism and the development of the market for consumer goods broadened the opportunities for female acquisitiveness as there were many more items for them to crave. Moreover the fact that they could increasingly view, sample, and compare a myriad of different items as consumers, with the increased advent of shops, markets, and bazaars and the commercial advertising that went along with these emporia, only served to exacerbate the problem and increase the amount of temptation that women had to face on a daily basis.[15] Scholarship had traditionally confined scenarios such as this to the nineteenth-century period, but recent work by historians such as Maxine Berg has shown that women became independent consumers long before this time and displayed their purchasing power much earlier than had been historically acknowledged.[16] Indeed, some scholars, such as Tammy Whitlock have argued that the threat of this new-found and evidently burgeoning form of female independence, within the confines of a well-established patriarchal society, was a crucial factor in why the association between women and acquisitiveness was so loudly and so regularly articulated by fearful social commentators by the dawn of the Victorian era.[17] This discourse was particularly impactful when these concerns were voiced alongside expositions of the inherent criminal possibilities associated with uncontrollable cupidity.

What was particularly disturbing in all this, as historian Lori Ann Loeb's work has shown, is that it was middle-class women that were dominating these multifaceted nineteenth-century concerns.[18] Their acquisitive nature came to be seen as out of control in the wake of numerous well-publicized episodes of indiscriminate shoplifting and compulsive petty theft which could not be explained by basic need, want, or desperation, given the wealth and status of the protagonists involved. Instead, cultural envy, competitiveness, and a yearning to be distinctive were all said to have contributed to their compulsive behaviour, even though their base and unconstrained urge to possess was still said to have its root cause in their gendered disposition and attributes.[19]

As the work of Kerry Segrave and others has shown, kleptomania eventually came to be the accepted 'ailment' used by medical professionals to diagnose (and ultimately excuse) this kind of behaviour in the second half of the nineteenth century.[20] It was said that, in engaging too quickly with life outside the private sphere of the home, middle-class women's instability overwhelmed them and they were unable to control themselves or behave rationally when faced with the temptations that the market-place provided.[21] Through the label of kleptomaniacs, the scholar Ina Selimić contends that these women came to be considered 'incompetent and thus incapable of being an intentional thief'.[22] Not only did such a diagnosis explain away the actions of these women, but it also reinstated and reinforced traditional patriarchal boundaries and reminded women of the dangers that lurked beyond these confines.[23] Of course, all of this this stood in stark contrast to the experience of working-class women suspected of similar activity. They were not afforded the same psychological scrutiny as they were assumed to be motivated by need. Such women were simply labelled 'criminal' or 'thief' and punished accordingly upon conviction. There was to be no exculpatory diagnosis for them.[24]

The gendered link made between acquisitiveness and criminal activity has only really been considered within a certain and specific scholarly context and is now long overdue for a more careful and nuanced analysis. For instance, consideration has not been given to the female perpetration of other types of offending beyond shoplifting. Nor has the first half of the nineteenth century been looked at in relation to the extent to which cupidity was a motivating factor in criminal enterprise, largely because the kleptomania diagnosis was not widely deployed until after 1850, as Whitlock has observed.[25] However, given that that the rise of consumerism and consumer culture occurred long before that time (as we have already acknowledged), it would seem appropriate to test whether there was a change in women's felonious behaviour in the earlier decades of the nineteenth century.[26] Did they react to these broader socio-economic changes? Did men? Finally, and up until now, the scholarship which has linked acquisitiveness and criminality has been largely class-bound. Whilst the introduction of the kleptomania defence may have offered some sort of insight into the actions of respectable women, it also meant that the rationale behind the criminal activity of other women has remained largely unexplored and unexplained. It has been presumed that middle-class women stole out of greed and working-class women stole out of need, and although historians have acknowledged that the motives behind the actions of female thieves were unlikely to be as binary as this, they have done little to deconstruct this assumption.[27] This chapter will now address all of these issues and test the extent to which there was, in fact, an evident relationship between acquisitiveness and property crime in Wales between 1800 and 1830.

## Welsh Theft 1800–1830: Evidence and Analysis

### The Nature and Incidence of Welsh Theft

During the first three decades of the nineteenth century, 5,566 individuals were brought before the Court of Great Session charged with a criminal offence; 4,652 were men and, of these individuals, 1,329 were indicted for a violent offence and 3,323 were indicted for a non-violent offence. Of the latter category, there were 2,055 men indicted for some form of theftuous activity (including the receiving of

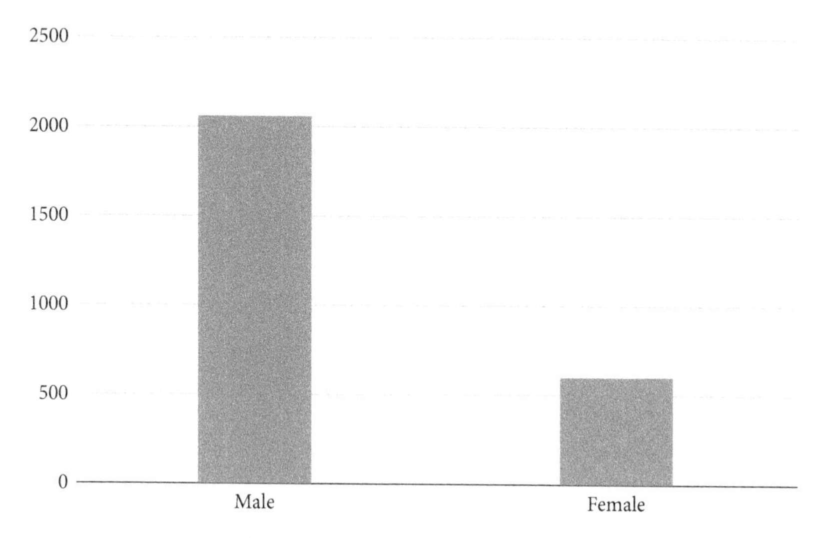


**Figure 6.1** The Gender Difference in Recorded Theft at the Welsh Court of Great Sessions 1800–1830.

stolen goods) over that thirty-year period. Women made up just 914 of the 5,566 individuals brought before the Welsh Court of Great Session between 1800 and 1830. Of these, 214 were charged with a violent offence and exactly 700 were charged with a non-violent offence. Of the latter category, there were 597 women indicted for some form of theftuous activity (including the receiving of stolen goods) during that time.[28] As is evident, this kind of criminality made up a significantly higher proportion of recorded female lawbreaking compared to male (65 per cent of the total number of indictments brought against women compared to 44 per cent of the total number of indictments levelled against men). It is also apparent that, as was the case elsewhere in Britain, both in the eighteenth and indeed the nineteenth century, forms of illegal appropriation dominated the business of the Welsh courts.[29]

Figure 6.1 reflects the dominance of male thieves at the Welsh Court of Great Sessions between 1800 and 1830 in comparison with their female counterparts. This gender disparity was not unusual according to the scholarship related to this type of property offending in either the eighteenth- or nineteenth-century period as Peter King's work has shown.[30] Figure 6.2, on the other hand, charts the perpetration of different types of theft according to gender over the same period.[31]

As is evident from the histogram, forms of larceny dominate the judicial statistics as we might have expected. In part, this dominance may be explained by the difficulties associated with bringing indictments for other types of non-violent property crime such as shoplifting, pickpocketing, and poaching which were often tricky to prove and costly to prosecute.[32] Also, as we might have predicted from what scholarship has shown us, Figure 6.2 shows that women's involvement

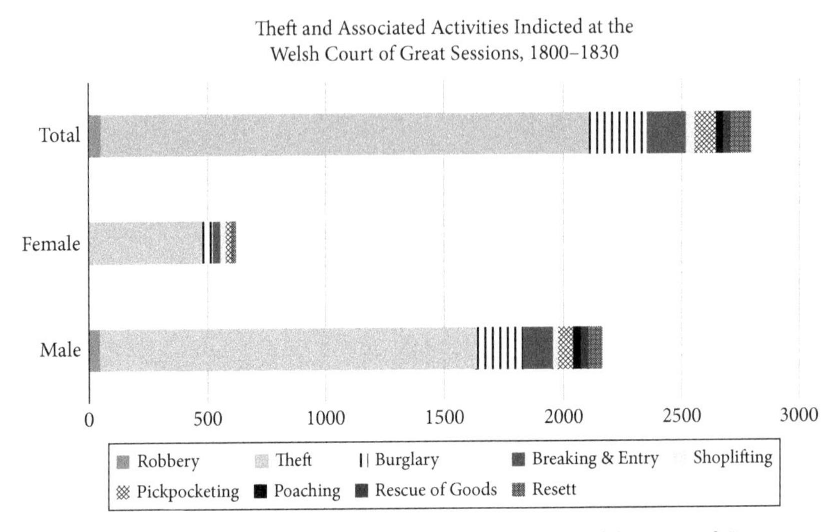


**Figure 6.2** Theft and Associated Activities Indicted at the Welsh Court of Great Sessions, 1800–1830.

in violent robbery in Wales between 1800 and 1830 was not as significant as that of their male counterparts, and the reverse was true of instances of shoplifting where accused women outnumbered accused men (although not by that much).[33] However, what is significant in the data from this survey is that proportionately, as we can see, Welsh women and Welsh men were involved in other, seemingly more serious forms of non-violent theft, to a relatively similar extent. For instance, burglaries (breaking into a property at night) made up nearly 10 per cent of the cases prosecuted against men and nearly 7 per cent against women. Episodes of breaking and entry during the day (or housebreaking) constituted 6 per cent of all male prosecutions and exactly the same proportion of female prosecutions over this period. This finding stands in sharp contrast to the conclusions of other studies of this type of offending in the pre-modern period such as that by Beattie or Walker,[34] and suggests that women were not *always* reduced to a subsidiary or unsubstantive role when non-violent property theft was committed. Furthermore, the evidence from Figure 6.2 also dispels the historiographical axiom that women were sidelined to the perpetration of resett (or receiving stolen goods) on account of their gender.[35] Despite the evident difficulties in prosecuting this offence, more Welsh men were in fact charged with this crime than Welsh women.

The nature of the different types of non-violent property crime prosecuted in Wales during the first third of the nineteenth century does not offer too many insights into whether this kind of criminality was based on acquisitiveness or not. Certainly acts of burglary and housebreaking tended to be more premeditated than episodes of regular larceny and were typically perpetrated with the aim of stealing as much profitable plunder as possible, rather than a desire to possess a

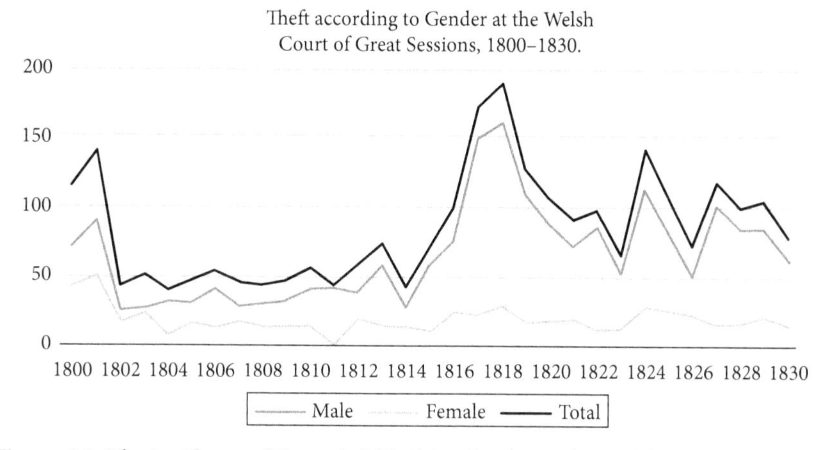


**Figure 6.3** The Incidence of Recorded Theft by Gender at the Welsh Court of Great Sessions, 1800–1830.

certain item or object.[36] Cupidity may have been more of an impetus in instances of shoplifting, pickpocketing, poaching, or the rescue of stolen goods, and in more general acts of theft, all of which tended to be more impromptu and opportunistic in nature.[37] We will return to the question of acquisitiveness as a motive for non-violent property crime as the chapter unfolds, but for now we can conclude that in Wales, between 1800 and 1830, 'most thefts, of every kind, were very ordinary affairs'.[38]

Figure 6.3 shows the rate of prosecutions for non-violent theft in Wales over the first third of the nineteenth century. We can see that, after an initial slump in indictments in the early years of the nineteenth century, the crime rate is relatively stable until 1812 when there is a pronounced spike in recorded instances of theft. This short-lived increase pales into insignificance, however, when compared with what happens in 1815, when there is a significant surge in prosecutions which is maintained for the next five years. After that time, and most notably from 1822, there are two further spikes in recorded theft, reflecting relatively dramatic fluctuations in the rate of prosecutions at the Welsh Court of Great Sessions over the remainder of our period of study.

Some of the patterns evidenced in Figure 6.3, such as the overall trend towards an increase in offending by 1830, can in part be explained by demographic change over the period. Welsh scholar and journalist Wynford Vaughan-Thomas has noted that, whilst the net in-migration of Wales in the first third of the nineteenth century was very low at just 0.4 per thousand, the natural population increase over the same period was more substantial at 13.0 per thousand.[39] Many of the other trends that emerge from the collated data may well relate to the unstable nature of changes to the socio-economic climate of Wales during this period, which historians have used to explain the persistent episodes of chronic social unrest which peppered the nation's history after 1800.[40] For instance, as John Walliss's research has highlighted, the period after the cessation of the Napoleonic Wars, which we can see marked in the graph by a significant and sustained surge in theft prosecutions, has been generally acknowledged as a particular time of economic crisis, where peacetime brought unemployment, rent increases, and a market drop in the value of saleable commodities.[41]

In Wales, although industrialization and urbanization were well under way during the 1800–30 period, the fact that the economy was still largely agricultural at this time meant that the abrupt change from a wartime economy to a peacetime economy hit the nation hard and, in some regions, utter destitution and deprivation reigned for several years.[42] This was exacerbated when bad harvests and bank failures contributed to the ongoing fiscal depression and the subsequent intensification of the crisis rendered the mechanism for the provision and distribution of Poor Law relief inadequate and unworkable.[43] As Howell's work explains in particular, the Welsh populace suffered as a result and the dire, unrelenting circumstances that they found themselves in may go some way to explain not only the prolonged growth in recorded theft immediately after 1815, but also the spasmodic statistical surges of that type of offending that occurred thereafter when remedies to the situation only provided brief abatement and temporary solace.[44]

Of course, we also have to consider that the socio-economic climate may have influenced crime statistics in a different way too, in that during times of hardship or high prices, victims of theft may have been more inclined to prosecute those who stole from them than in other periods. Not only might this be relevant to the general time series data seen in Figure 6.3, but it could also apply when we look at the seasonality of recorded theft, shown in Figure 6.4. Based on evidence regarding dates of offending rather than dates of indictment or trial, we might easily conclude that winter was the most likely time for theft to occur because it was the season when times were hardest for those who worked on the land: they were likely to be underemployed or temporarily unemployed.[45] However, we might also consider that as this season was similarly challenging for those who owned land or property, it might equally have been the case that individuals were simply more inclined to report offences committed against them in the winter months than at other times of the year.[46]

The graph at Figure 6.3 also provides a breakdown of the crime statistics by gender. At first glance, the lack of significant variation in the statistics relating to women's theft suggests that female thieves were more consistent in their criminality than male thieves and were thus arguably less responsive to the kinds of socio-economic contextual factors already discussed. Indeed, this observation might have been expected if we were to assert that acquisitiveness, rather than need, lay at the heart of this type of female offending. In that context, women would steal regardless of the prevailing economic situation. However, if we look at Figure 6.5,

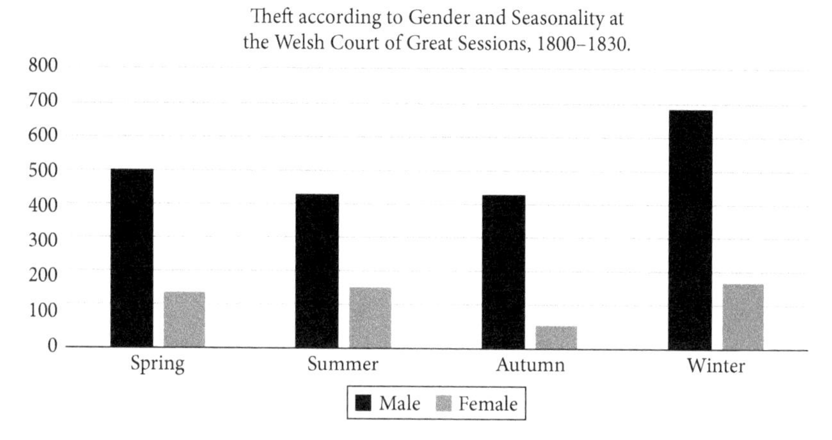


**Figure 6.4** Theft According to Gender and Seasonality at the Welsh Court of Great Sessions, 1800–1830.

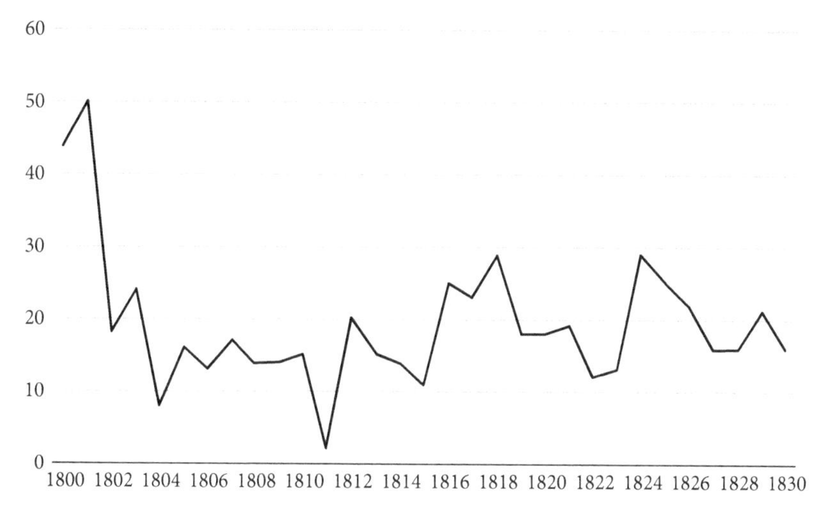


**Figure 6.5** The Incidence of Indicted Female Theft at the Welsh Court of Great Sessions, 1800–1830.

which disaggregates female theft indictments so they can be looked at in more precise detail, we can see that the indictment trends and fluctuations do, in fact, largely mirror those of the male instances of recorded theft seen in Figure 6.3.

However, this is not exact and there are two notable exceptions. The first is the noticeable downturn in female prosecutions evident in 1811 and the second is the fact that the surge in prosecutions in the post-Napoleonic War period was not as pronounced for women as it seemingly was for their light-fingered male counterparts. Certainly, what can be argued here is that the thesis propounded by the scholars Malcolm Feeley and Deborah Little, that female criminality dramatically diminished over the course of nineteenth century and beyond, is not borne out by the Welsh evidence. Instead, the number of Welsh women indicted for theft remained static at best (if we take demographic growth into account) or actually slightly increased over the 1800–30 period.[47]

The last aspect of the nature and incidence of theft for us to consider in relation to Wales during the 1800–30 period is that of *locus operandi* or where the crime took place. In order for us to better explore this aspect of offending, Figure 6.6 provides us with a map of the historical counties of Wales. This should be used

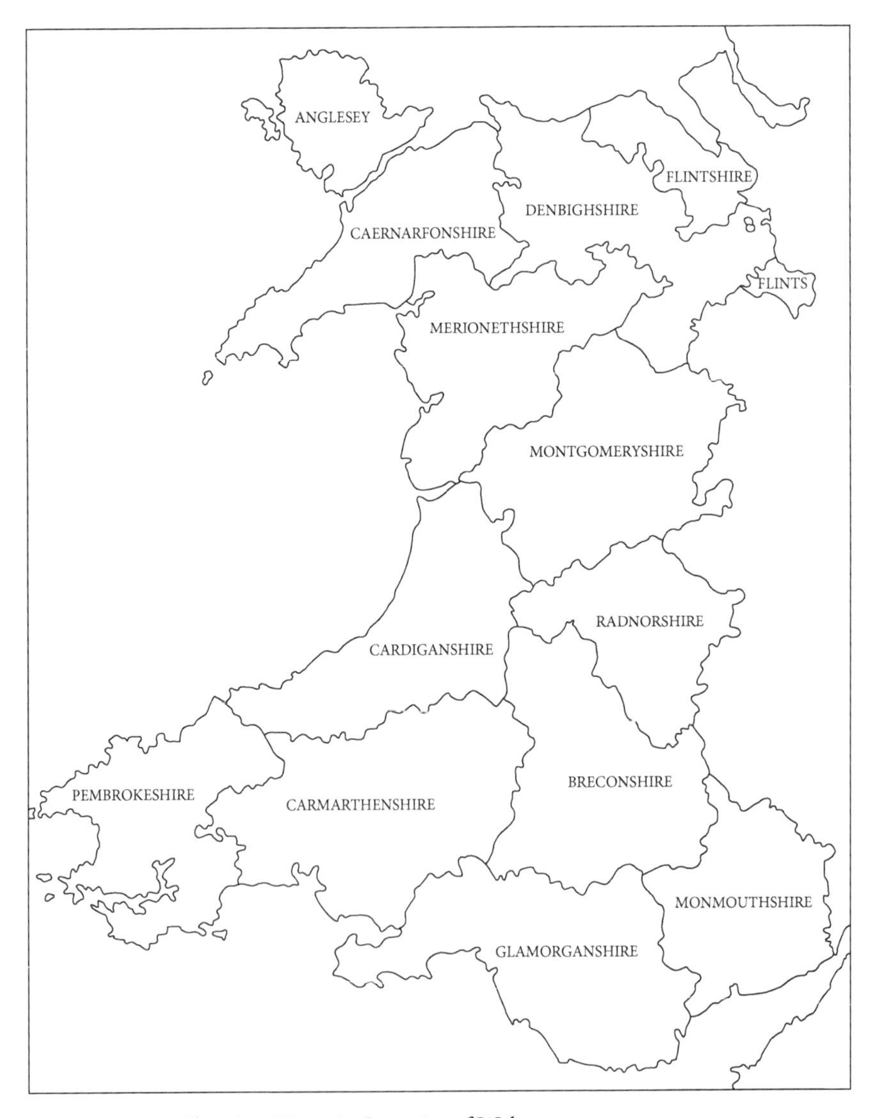


**Figure 6.6** Map Showing Historic Counties of Wales.

and aligned with Figure 6.7, which shows where the thefts indicted at the Welsh Court of Great Sessions between 1800 and 1830 were actually committed. The outer ring on the chart relates to female thefts and the inner ring relates to male thefts.

What can be seen from Figure 6.7 is that, proportionately, there was very little difference in *where* Welsh men and Welsh women committed theft. Glamorganshire dominated offending patterns but, as it was the most urbanized and most populated of the historic counties after 1800, this finding is unsurprising.[48] Certainly, some types of larceny, such as poaching or livestock theft, would be more typically found in rural counties such as Cardiganshire, rather than in more urban locations due to the prevalence and nature of the items stolen.[49] Similarly, shoplifting was more often reported in densely populated areas where retail provision was more likely to exist.[50]

In general though, and with respect to gender, the data reflect that male theft was far more broadly distributed than female theft between 1800 and 1830. The three counties of Pembrokeshire, Carmarthenshire, and Glamorganshire stand out as being the most common locations for female theft. All three are located in the southern part of the Wales (see Figure 6.6). Male theft on the other hand was more evenly dispersed, with all counties aside from Anglesey, Monmouthshire, and Merionethshire having a strong incidence of recorded offending. For men, there was no north/south divide unlike for women.[51] Whether this conclusion reflects the more opportunistic and extensive nature of male theft or simply the

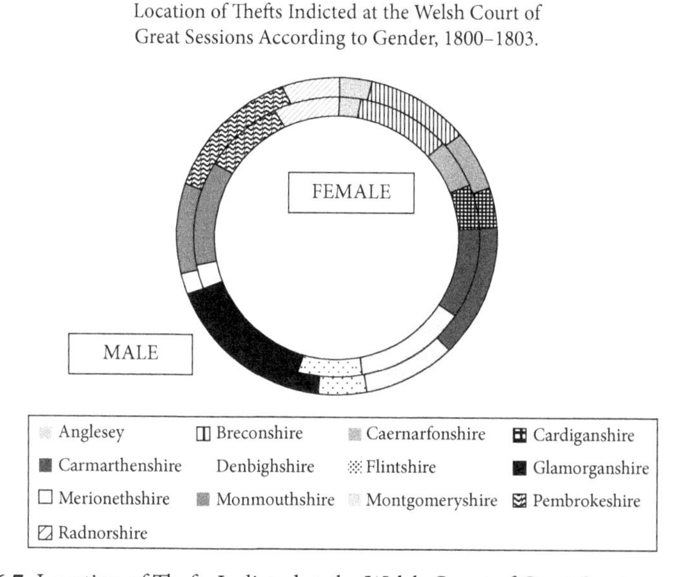


**Figure 6.7** Location of Thefts Indicted at the Welsh Court of Great Sessions According to Gender, 1800–1830.

greater freedom they had to engage in social interactions is difficult to discern from the available evidence.

## The Characteristics of Welsh Thieves and Welsh Theft

Aside from basic gender attribution, there are other characteristic markers for us to consider in relation to Welsh theft in the first third of the nineteenth century. Several of these are key to determining the extent to which acquisitiveness was a factor in the perpetration of this kind of criminality amongst women in particular.[52] As can be seen from Figure 6.8, the majority of the Welsh women indicted for acts of theft were unmarried, especially if we add the number of widowed women to the number described as being single or a spinster. These proportions in relation to marital status are roughly in line with that uncovered in other historical studies of female property crime (such as that by King or Nicholas Woodward). In these unmarried women have tended to dominate: perhaps because they had more need or want to commit theft, or perhaps because they were less protected against prosecution due to the absence of a negotiative spouse.[53]

It is also clear from Figure 6.8 that few female defendants were described as being in employment. However, we should not read too much into this, as court scribes were not systematic in their recording of women's occupations. As historian Peter King has observed, the judiciary were more concerned with 'women's status in terms of their relationships with men (married, single, widowed) rather than in terms of their relationship with the world of work'.[54] Consequently, any

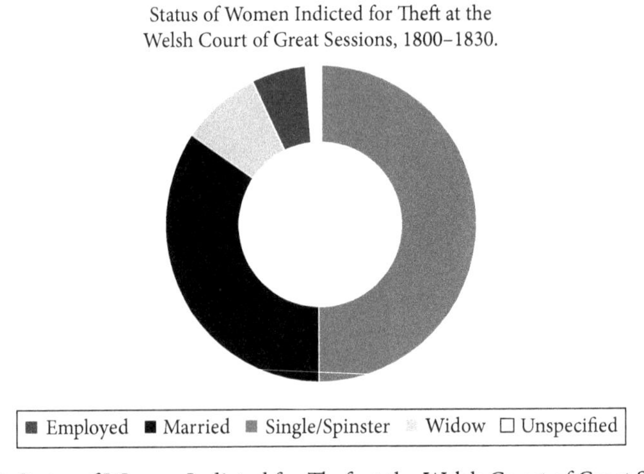


**Figure 6.8** Status of Women Indicted for Theft at the Welsh Court of Great Sessions, 1800–1830.

sort of detailed foray into the employment backgrounds or the economic status of Welsh female offenders to establish typical patterns or trends is virtually impossible to achieve. Occasionally some insights are afforded in this respect, such as occurred in the case of the unmarried Sarah Smith indicted at the court of Great Sessions in June 1802. She was accused of stealing cloth from a man in Carmarthenshire, but in her defence, she explained that the cloth had been given to her, in return for an 'illicit connection' for giving her and her child a lift from Carmarthen to Llandeilo Fair for which she could not pay. Her potentially opprobrious explanation for her possession of the cloth was rejected by the court, however, and she was found guilty and subsequently sentenced to seven years' transportation.[55] In any event, contextual details such as this were rarely revealed in the indictment evidence provided.

Figure 6.9 shows the gendered proportion of the defendants brought before the Courts of Great Sessions who were accused alongside at least one other individual. For Welsh men this occurred in 33 per cent of indictments for theft and for Welsh women in 32 per cent of cases. Historical research, such as that by Walker, has suggested that women were far more likely to work in league with other thieves than men were, but the evidence here from early nineteenth-century Wales does not support this finding.[56] It was only in more complex instances of theft—such as stealing livestock, burglary, or housebreaking—that women tended to join up with other like-minded criminals. For instance in Montgomeryshire in September 1802, Jane Roberts and her sister Martha joined forces to steal a horse from farmer Griffith Evans. The victim in this case had become so convinced a gang of thieves was stealing his livestock that he had 300 handbills printed offering a reward to anyone who could capture the culprits. It was this that led to the

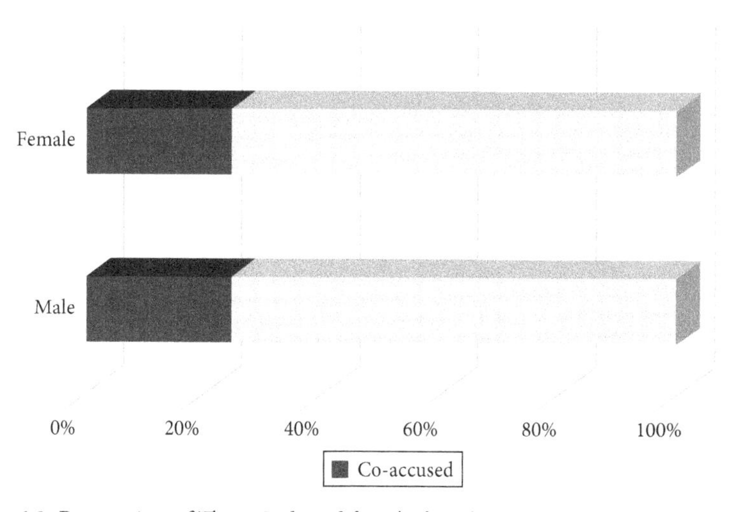


**Figure 6.9** Proportion of Those Indicted for Theft at the Welsh Court of Great Sessions with a Co-Accused, 1800–1830.

women's arrest and subsequent successful prosecution.[57] In June 1829, Hannah Evans, John Jones, and Mary Jones (no relation) were charged with working together to steal a significant quantity of iron rails that they had taken from tracks being laid in the town of Mold in Flintshire. The three were accused of carrying off 100 cast iron rails, a further 100 other iron rails, plus 200 pounds weight of iron, all belonging to a local banker called James Knight. The miscreants had seemingly struggled to move their impressive haul however, and the two women at least were caught red-handed with the heavy loot and went on to be convicted.[58] Instances such as these examples were not common amongst the Welsh evidence though, and indeed, as we saw in Figure 6.2, these kinds of offences were not ones that Welsh women engaged with in significant numbers, at least when compared with their involvement in more simple forms of theft.[59]

We might assume that, if acquisitiveness was a key motive for theft in early nineteenth-century Wales, then it would more likely result in a majority of sole offenders, given that it is a concept which tends to be ascribed to individualized personal tastes, preferences, or desires. However, whilst the evidence from the Court of Great Sessions does suggest that theft—for both men and women—was an act typically perpetrated by individuals rather than partners or gangs, it is difficult to establish the motive or rationale behind these criminal endeavours simply from the number of perpetrators involved. Nonetheless, the similarity in the gendered proportions of this evidence is noteworthy and, in general, the findings of this study support that of other scholarship that has suggested that professional gangs of thieves were rare in the nineteenth-century Welsh context.[60]

Similarly, the same complications arise when we consider recidivism or repeat offending. As Figure 6.10 illustrates, just 9 per cent of female offenders brought

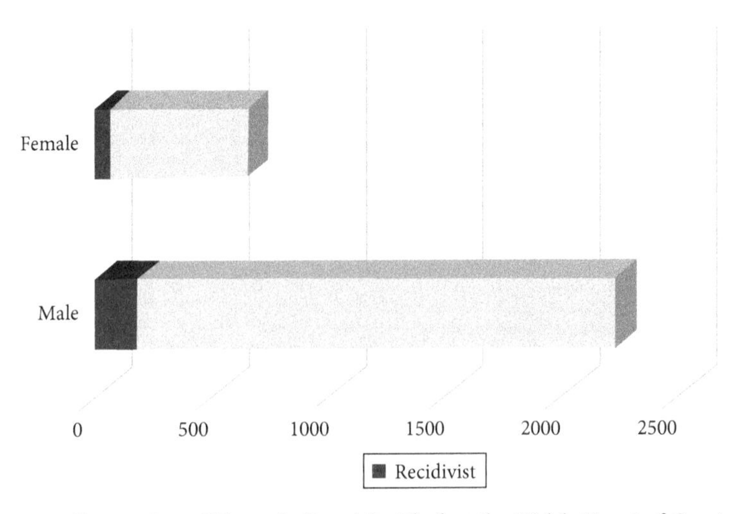


**Figure 6.10** Proportion of Those Indicted for Theft at the Welsh Court of Great Sessions and Named as a Recidivist, 1800–1830.

before the Court of Great Sessions were described in the records as being a recidivist or having a prior criminal record. The same was true of exactly the same proportion of male defendants.[61] Given the provenance of the Court of Great Sessions, we might have expected many more of the defendants to have been described in this fashion, as recidivists tended to be sent to the highest judiciary context when facing a subsequent trial. This was true in the case of Breconshire spinster Elizabeth Games who was indicted on four separate occasions at the Court of Great Sessions in May 1830 alone, all for shoplifting items of wearing apparel.[62] Whilst some of the cases brought to the Court of Great Sessions demonstrate prior planning and preparation on the part of the thieves involved, few point to the kind of repeat offending or criminal 'professionalism' demonstrated by Miss Games.[63] Once again, it is difficult to discern anything with regard to motive from this evidence, as acquisitiveness could surely be both fleeting and/or more persistent as a driver for the activity of theft, depending on the thief and their socio-economic or personal context. Consequently, it is the repeated gender disparity in relation to this characteristic of offending that is more worthy of note here.

So, do we get any closer to understanding the motives behind acts of theft in Wales between 1800 and 1830 if we examine the type of item or items stolen by Welsh thieves? The evidence in this respect can be seen in Figure 6.11.

Whilst of course we have to take into account the potential for these findings to not be wholly representative of the nature of theft in Wales between 1800 and 1830, due to the influence of the so-called 'dark figure' of unknown or unrecorded

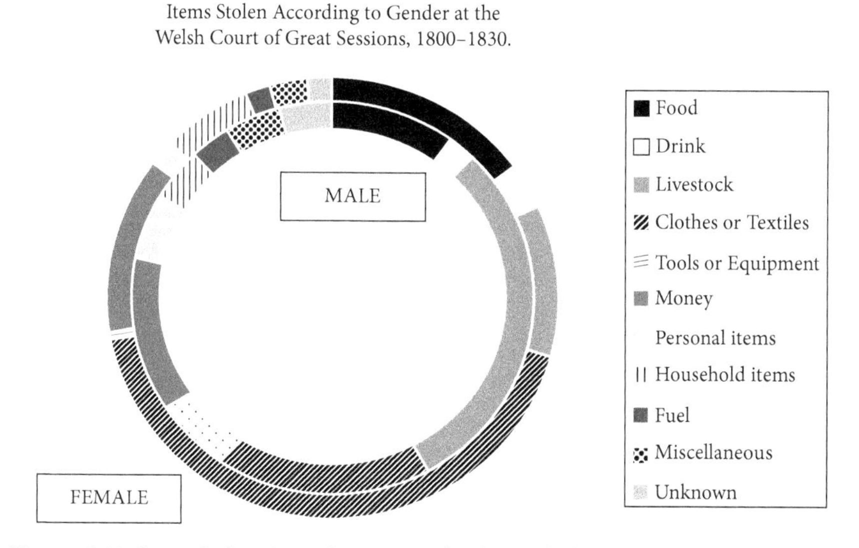


**Figure 6.11** Items Stolen According to Gender from Theft Prosecutions at the Welsh Court of Great Sessions, 1800–1830.

crime, the results of this survey are nonetheless significant and somewhat surprising.[64] This is because the established historiography of property offending in the pre-modern period has identified a significant gender difference in the types of goods stolen by male thieves compared to female thieves. Historians such as Daniel Gray have argued that male thieves were much more likely to steal types of fuel, household valuables, tools, and livestock.[65] Female thieves, on the other hand, were much more likely to take foodstuffs, items of wearing apparel, or money.[66] Yet the evidence from the Welsh context from the first third of the nineteenth century suggests that, with the exception of clothing or textiles (which women were proportionately more likely to steal) and livestock (which men were proportionately more likely to steal), there was no significant gender difference in terms of the kinds of items that thieves took. It is likely that this is a reflection of the opportunistic nature of larceny and has as much to do with *where* the items were at the time they were stolen, as *what* they were.[67]

Acquisitiveness may well have had a part to play in the *selection* of goods stolen by Welsh thieves. This could have been the case when Mrs Mary Morgan stole a promissory note, a silver cigarette case, and a jewelled comb from a locked drawer in the house of Merthyr Tydfil shopkeeper, William Jones, in August 1804 using a false key.[68] It also may well have applied to Mary Miller and her husband Alexander who stole thirteen hats from a shop in Wrexham, Denbighshire, in April 1822.[69] But equally, other factors may have been involved in the thefts that occurred, such as criminality with profit in mind or basic need. For instance when Carmarthenshire women Anne Harries and her daughter Mary were indicted at the Court of Great Sessions in January 1813, they were accused of stealing four turkeys and two geese from Thomas Jones and then selling them on at a market at Llansadwrn the next day for the princely sum of five shillings.[70] Then, right at the end of period, in 1830, Ann Tunley was accused of the elaborate theft of a bee hive from the garden of William Owens in Llanbister, Radnorshire. After carrying off the hive, she smoked out the bees by setting fire to some straw that she had placed underneath it. She removed the combs and smashed up the hive to destroy any incriminatory evidence. Ann Tunley then sat down to a feast of honey that she enjoyed along with several onions and carrots that she had also cheekily purloined from Mr Owens' garden![71] Like the majority of indicted Welsh thieves, Tunley made her theft worthwhile, stealing more than one item. Whilst Welsh thieves may have craved a particular item initially on the basis of their own cupidity, unless they stole something for immediate use (such as was evidently the case with the hungry Ann Tunley), most of the time it would seem that thieves tended to steal items that they knew had retail value.[72] After the theft was completed, they then decided to either keep their plunder or sell it on.

## Motives for Theft

Historical scholarship on crime and criminality during the pre-modern period, such as that by Anne-Marie Kilday and Drew Gray, has been quick to point out how difficult it is to ascertain the motive of offenders from the information provided in judicial records. The question of why a crime was committed was rarely seen as being pivotal to the outcome of a case, and instead, all efforts were expended into determining whether or not the accused individual had committed the crime for which they were indicted or not.[73] This seems to have been especially the case in prosecutions for theft where motive was rarely of interest to judicial officials. Consequently, it is difficult to determine with any accuracy the extent to which instances of theft in Wales in the first of the nineteenth century were committed in the pursuit of acquisitiveness. Instead, supposition as to purpose and intent, on the basis of testimony and other evidence provided to the Court of Great Sessions, has to suffice. Even then, we need to bear in mind the degree to which motivation is determined by highly personal and subjective thoughts which sit within individualized contexts and lived experiences that we can never fully know or appreciate.

In the main, it is possible to glean three key motives for theft amongst the accused brought before the Welsh Court of Great Sessions: first, acquisitiveness; second, a desire for profit; and third, basic want or need. These motives were not necessarily mutually exclusive. In some episodes of theft one of these motives clearly dominated, others involved two of the motives, and many involved all three. It is evident from some of the cases in our study that, to some extent, acquisitiveness or cupidity did act as a trigger for the perpetration of theftuous activities. Historians such as John Styles have written about how the possession of certain goods, usually clothes or items of physical adornment (hats, jewellery, ribbons, buckles, watches), were just as important to plebeian society as to their social betters. This was because such items signified material advancement and maturity, they were 'a currency in sexual competition and a source of self-regarding pleasure'.[74] This may explain why these types of goods were so commonly stolen in Wales between 1800 and 1830 by men, and especially by women, as Figure 6.11 clearly demonstrates. Although some of these episodes were likely committed for immediate financial gain through the selling on of the goods purloined, there are also some examples where Welsh women, in particular, stole the items concerned for their own personal use, titillation, and adornment.[75]

A good example of many that could be offered to illustrate this finding is the case of recidivist thief Eleanor Prichard, who was prosecuted under four different indictments in May 1815 by her employer David Price. Mr Price started to notice things going missing from around his house and his larder and he asked each of his employees about the whereabouts of these items. Samuel Powell, who worked as a gardener, told Mr Price (and later testified in court) that he had seen Eleanor Prichard carry bags of items away from the house but did not know what the bags contained. Eleanor had worked as Mr Price's domestic servant at Trallong in Breconshire for quite some time, and he did not believe her to be the thief. However, when he went to ask her about the matter, he found her in a room, 'ambling as if on a promenade, wearing a fine calico blouse and a blue woollen cloak' both of which belonged to his wife. Beneath Eleanor's bed in the room he found various other items of wearing apparel (ribbons, a linen shift, two silk dresses, and three petticoats) and it became clear to Mr Price that Eleanor had been pilfering from him for some time. In addition to the clothing items which she had kept to try on or wear in secret, Eleanor Prichard was also accused of stealing food (some flour, oatmeal, beef, and bacon) and a few household goods (earthen teacups and saucers). It was thought that she had disposed of these goods in the nearby town of Brecon, but there was no evidence to substantiate that claim.[76] Eleanor Prichard was found guilty of theft and sentenced to two years' imprisonment.

Although acts of theft such as that by Eleanor Prichard point to acquisitiveness as a key motive which spurred theft, we also have to consider that the theft of items such as these could also have been induced by a longer term consideration. As historian Beverley Lemire has described, the theft of garments and fashionable decorative items was seen by many to be the 'equivalent to a savings account, as articles of clothing were commonly used as a ready source of cash in emergencies'.[77] So whilst cupidity could have been the original motive for certain thefts in the short term, such activities could also prove beneficial in the longer term to the perpetrator if the circumstances warranted it.

Another way in which acquisitiveness could act as a motive for theft is demonstrated in the case brought against another domestic servant, Elizabeth Lloyd, in 1825. The Court of Great Sessions heard how Elizabeth had stolen no less than fifteen gold sovereigns from her employer Anne Roberts, in the parish of Gyffin in Caernarfonshire. The money had been in a locked drawer inside a press cupboard within Roberts' home. Suspicion against Elizabeth Lloyd started to be aroused when her purchasing capabilities dramatically improved overnight. Her first purchase was a pair of wooden clogs that friends knew she had coveted for some time, but had been unable to afford. She then bought some patterns, tea, and sugar from a shop in Llanrwst in Denbighshire and paid for them with a sovereign and she also gave her brother money to go and buy several lambs at a local fair and give them to her parents.

According to witnesses, though, the most damning evidence against Elizabeth Lloyd was her own personal transformation. One witness, Robert Roberts described how he had known the accused for some time and that she 'was very poor...and had very poor clothes and ragged stockings and no shoes worth wearing'. However, not long after the theft of the money had been reported to the authorities, things changed substantially. Elizabeth 'became very tidy in her clothes, first getting a bonnet, new pumps (and said two other pairs were in the making), three new aprons, a new beaver hat, a new bed gown and several other new clothes'. Robert Roberts said that this metamorphosis of his acquaintance's appearance 'caused in him a suspicion that she was a thief'. Elizabeth Lloyd, for her part, could offer no explanation for her reversal of fortunes. She was arrested, prosecuted, and convicted. Initially sentenced to death for her crimes, she was later pardoned and sentenced to transportation for life.[78]

Motives for theft, as we know, were regularly influenced and ignited by the prevailing economic conditions at any given time in a given place, but this was not necessarily always the case. As we have already seen in this chapter, many episodes of larceny were prompted by the opportunity that presented itself to the thief concerned, as much as by the specific fiscal circumstances of that individual or indeed their family and kin. Yet as we saw from the early section of the chapter relating to the instances of theft, the early part of the nineteenth century, and the post-Napoleonic War period in particular, was an exceptionally desperate time for many Welsh men and Welsh women. The lack of resources to support the population expansion that occurred at this time, along with high levels of unemployment, a stark increase in the cost of living, and a sizeable slump in the value of saleable goods, must have meant that, for some, theft became a way to generate an income through the sale of stolen goods. This became an inescapable course of action when alternative ways of making a living had become unpredictable or had significantly contracted. Making money from criminality was undoubtedly in the mind of Elizabeth Oliver who stole three watches (one in a silver case) from a blacksmith's shop in Llanfyllin, Montgomeryshire, in 1802. She was caught outside her own dwelling place trying to sell the watches for thirty shillings each to passers-by!

For others in more dire circumstances, and as the work of Howell and Davies has shown, theft became the only practical remedy that they could deploy to try to mitigate against the relentless penury and destitution they were having to endure.[79] This probably goes some way to explaining why animal theft and fuel and foodstuffs were common targets for theft by Welsh men and women in the 1800–30 period, as shown in Figure 6.11.[80] Consider for example the case of unmarried mother Jane Collins who was accused of stealing a bushel of coal and a bushel of culm[81] from a merchant in Prendergast in Pembrokeshire during the harsh winter of 1808. In an attempt to secure clemency, witnesses spoke in her defence and asked the Court of Great Sessions to have mercy on her as she was 'done with cold and done with life and needed to tend to her child'. The authorities still found her guilty and she was ordered to be imprisoned for a month in the gaol at Haverfordwest.[82] Then in 1819, Ann Jones, a woman from Welshpool in Montgomeryshire was indicted for stealing a piece of cheese weighing 12 pounds from her neighbour William Griffiths. Witnesses testified to Ann's devastation and enduring destitution in the wake of the deaths of her father and both her brothers at the Battle of Waterloo. She had no income, no inheritance, and no future. Yet the court was similarly unsympathetic to Ann's plight as it had been in relation to Jane Collins. Ann Jones was convicted and sentenced to eighteen months' hard labour in the House of Correction.[83]

## Reactions to Theft

The final section of this chapter will explore how individuals accused of theft were regarded and treated by the Welsh Court of Great Sessions in the first third of the nineteenth century. It will ascertain the key factors which determined the nature and degree of punishment given to those convicted of this crime. In particular, we will consider whether there is any evidence to suggest that motive was a determinant in the outcomes of the judicial process. Figure 6.12 shows the verdicts that resulted against those prosecuted for theft at the Court of Great Sessions between 1800 and 1830 by gender. One thing that is evident straight away is the significant proportion of 'no true bills' found in relation to the individuals accused. Declaring an indictment to be a 'no true bill' occurred when there was insufficient evidence to proceed with a given case, and the defendant was discharged. This happened in 20 per cent of the cases against Welsh men and 21 per cent of the cases against Welsh women. When added together with the verdicts of not guilty, we can conclude that a significant proportion of the men and women accused of theft in Wales during our period of study were not convicted of the charges against them. However, what Figure 6.12 also shows is that the majority

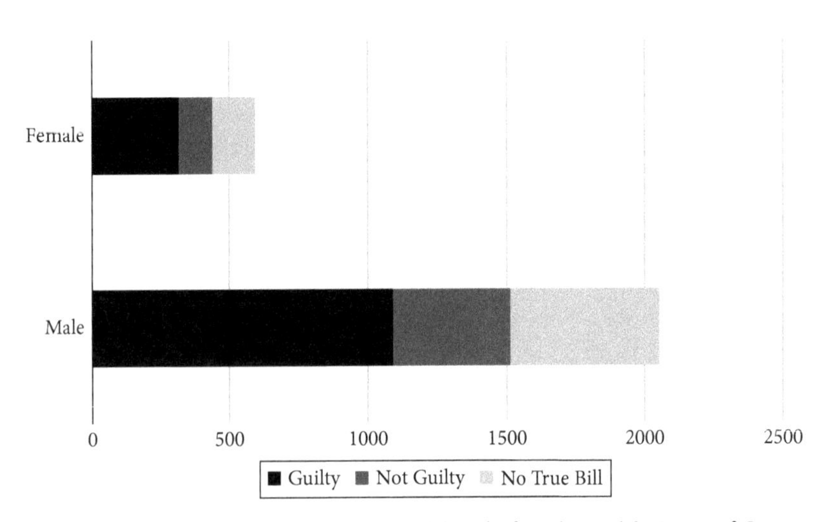


**Figure 6.12** Verdicts Against Those Indicted for Theft at the Welsh Court of Great Sessions, 1800–1830.

of defendants were, in fact, *convicted* of a property offence. Moreover, what is significant is that the proportions between men and women with regard to this low conviction rate were exactly the same: 53 per cent of Welsh men and Welsh women were deemed to be guilty of their offences.[84] As we have already seen in the previous section of this chapter, in coming to this determination, the motive for offending was not a key consideration. Instead, establishing whether the accused individual had been involved, and was thus guilty as charged, was the primary concern of the courts.

Figure 6.13 shows the different types of punishment meted out by the Welsh Court of Great Sessions against those found guilty of theft between 1800 and 1830. Numerically and proportionately it was rare for a Welsh woman to be executed for theft unless she was a proven recidivist. Only 5 per cent of female convicts were executed over the thirty-year period.[85] Although some women were sentenced to corporal punishment or fines and more to transportation, it was far more common for female Welsh thieves to receive a sentence of imprisonment of up to two years. Welsh men, on the other hand, were more likely than Welsh women to be executed for theft (22 per cent of those convicted), and were proportionately less likely to be pardoned or to receive a commutation of a capital sentence to a lesser punishment (this occurred in 31 per cent of male cases compared to 67 per cent of female cases). Men were numerically and proportionately more likely to be transported than women (usually for a period of seven years) but again, it was imprisonment that evidently dominated as the punishment of choice at the Welsh Court of Great Sessions in these instances. Incarceration for male thieves was typically up to two years (as was the case for women), but Welsh male convicts were far more likely than females to be ordered to hard labour.[86]

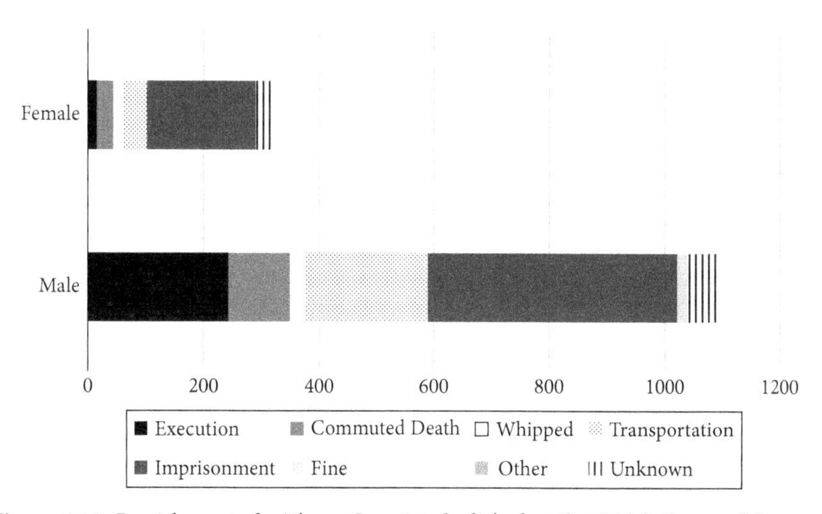


**Figure 6.13** Punishments for Those Convicted of Theft at the Welsh Court of Great Sessions, 1800–1830.

The main reason for the gendered disparity in the evidence of punishments at the Welsh Court of Great Sessions had little to do with the motives behind the thefts proven to have occurred, and instead much more to do with the type of theft committed and the precise nature of the item or items stolen. What were considered more serious or threatening forms of theft (for instance burglary or housebreaking) were prosecuted under more stringent legal provisions where it was difficult for the courts to avoid anything other than a capital sentence upon conviction.[87] Similarly, certain types of plunder (such as livestock) were considered to merit more serious punishments. As we have already established earlier on in this chapter, although the number of Welsh women who engaged in more serious forms of theft and who stole more serious types of loot were more numerous than we might have expected based on the established scholarship on this subject, they were nonetheless in the minority when compared to men. This must go some of the way to explaining why women were rarely in receipt of a capital sentence from the courts. However, if we consider the remarkably similar treatment of convicted male and female Welsh thieves, in relation to non-capital sentences, then it is clear that the gendered leniency that historians have agreed was afforded convicted female criminals in the pre-modern period was seemingly not given to the Welsh women proven to be involved in non-violent property crime during the early nineteenth century.[88] The close correlation between the punishments given to Welsh male and female thieves is likely a reflection of the fact that Welsh women, whilst numerically fewer in number than Welsh men, did nevertheless participate in the same kinds of theft and stole the same kinds of plunder as their male counterparts. It is also likely that they did so for the same reasons.

## Conclusion

Historical scholarship on female criminality has tended to narrow women's involvement in criminal activity to non-violent and non-direct action of a kind which fits well with the stereotypical traits of femininity and women's roles within the domestic context. When female offending *has* been discussed, it has tended to relate to minor forms of illegality and to subsidiary roles within the criminal process conducted at the instigation of others. Women were not deemed to be independent direct actors in criminal offending. If evidence of this did come to the fore, it was explained away by a flaw of some sort in the psyche of the female species. In relation to property crime, this gendered flaw was acquisitiveness: a compulsion or excessive desire to possess material goods. The use of this medicalized explanation, especially in the second half of the nineteenth century, enabled the authorities to restate their view that women could not be overtly criminal of their own free will. It was also said to have facilitated a corresponding judicial leniency towards some female offenders as there was now a ready-made excuse for their illegality. This chapter explored the extent to which acquisitiveness was evident amongst accused Welsh female thieves in the first third of the nineteenth century and whether that was a key determinant in how they were treated within the judicial process.

Forms of illegal appropriation certainly dominated the work of the Welsh Court of Great Sessions between 1800 and 1830. Male thieves predominated, but men and women engaged in the same *kinds* of property crime in similar proportions. To some degree, this finding asks questions of the conclusions of historians such as Drew Gray who have pointed to the strict gendered distinctions in the nature of this type of offending.[89] Yet in the Welsh context, serious forms of theft such as robbery, burglary, and housebreaking were relatively rare amongst the men and women accused, whereas ordinary larceny was far more common. The rates of non-violent property offending across the first three decades of the nineteenth century show a general overall increase in recorded offending over time, which is punctuated by peaks and troughs which can be broadly explained by the prevailing socio-economic context rather than being driven by any particular motive. These fluctuations are more marked amongst Welsh men accused of theft and less so amongst Welsh women.

Welsh theft between 1800 and 1830 tended to be conducted by individuals rather than by criminal gangs and most recorded episodes were seemingly opportunistic in nature, rather than planned and forensically premeditated. Certainly recidivism or persistent offending by more 'professional' thieves of either gender was uncommon at the Welsh Court of Great Sessions before 1830 and suggests that, in the Welsh context at least, theft was not an option that was routinely deployed within the economy of makeshifts resorted to when times were tough.[90] The fact that this was true of both the men *and* the women accused of theft provides yet another example of the uniqueness of the Welsh criminal context and its contrast with the English experience at this time.[91]

When we look at the types of goods stolen by Welsh thieves for signs of acquisitiveness, we find that there was not a marked difference in what was stolen amongst accused individuals, save for the preponderance of livestock amongst men and clothing amongst women. Once again, the expected gender disparity that scholars of other contexts have described in relation to this kind of offending was not evident in early nineteenth-century Wales.[92] It is difficult to discern from the evidence *why* specific items were selected for theft, but the fact that, amongst women, most of the items purloined were sold on, rather than kept and adored, would suggest that basic need or the want of lucre were the foremost rationales for perpetrating this form of illegality. Certainly, there was little evidence of Welsh women thieving just to be devious or in order to show some sort of gender-defying bravado and only a few suspects evidenced basic cupidity. Theft amongst Welsh women, whilst often opportunistic, was still purposeful and intentional. The same was true of Welsh men and, once again, we see a parity between the two sexes, which contrasts sharply with existing historical scholarship.[93] Perhaps because there was almost a fifty-fifty chance of conviction and an evident lack of leniency for the majority of Welsh men and Welsh women facing the determination of judges at the Court of Great Sessions, an act of theft really had to be seen to be worth the risk, in order for it to be undertaken.[94] For Welsh women thieves in particular, and indeed thieves more generally in the Welsh context between 1800 and 1830, acquisitiveness was a fanciful desire that few could afford to entertain amidst the harsh realities of pre-modern life.

## Notes

1. For further discussion see S. Howard (2008) Law and Disorder in Early Modern Wales: Crime and Authority in the Denbighshire Courts, c.1660–1730 (Cardiff: University of Wales Press), p. 128; A.-M. Kilday (2007) *Women and Violent Crime in Enlightenment Scotland* (Woodbridge: Boydell), *passim*; and D. Philips (1977) *Crime and Authority in Victorian England: The Black Country 1835–1860* (London: Croom Helm), p. 148.
2. See for instance J. M. Beattie (2002 edition) *Crime and the Courts in England 1660–1800* (Oxford: Clarendon Press), p. 238; and G. Walker (2003) *Crime, Gender and Social Order in Early Modern England* (Cambridge: Cambridge University Press), p. 159.
3. See for instance D. Palk (2003) 'Private Crime in Public and Private Places: Pickpockets and Shoplifters in London, 1780–1823', in T. Hitchcock and H. Shore (eds), *The Streets of London: From the Great Fire to the Great Stink* (London: Rivers Oram Press), pp. 135–50 at p. 137.
4. The Court of Great Sessions in Wales existed from between 1538 and 1830 and was essentially equivalent to the English assize courts. It had four circuits: Brecon (which incorporated the counties of Brecon, Glamorgan, and Radnor), Carmarthen (which incorporated Carmarthen, Cardigan, and Pembroke), Chester (which incorporated Denbigh, Flint, and Montgomery) and North Wales (which incorporated Anglesey, Caernarvon, and Merioneth). These districts or regions can be seen in the map at Figure 6.6. For further discussion see N. Woodward (2008) 'Seasonality and Sheep-Stealing: Wales, 1730–1830', *Agricultural History Review*, 56, I, pp. 24–47 at p. 27.
5. For more on the likely contribution of theft to the levels of unknown or unrecorded crime referred to as the 'dark figure' of criminal statistics see A.-M. Kilday (2014) '"Criminally Poor?" Investigating the Link between Crime and Poverty in Eighteenth Century England', *Cultural and Social History*, 11, 4, pp. 507–26 at pp. 509–10; P. King (1996) 'Female Offenders, Work and Life-cycle Change in Late-Eighteenth-Century London', *Continuity and Change*, 11, 1, pp. 61–90 at p. 63; N. Woodward (2008) 'Burglary in Wales, 1730–1830: Evidence from the Great Sessions', *Welsh History Review*, 24, pp. 60–91 at pp. 62 and 76; T. C. Whitlock (2005) *Crime, Gender and Consumer Culture in Nineteenth-Century England* (Aldershot: Ashgate), p. 128; and D. J. V. Jones (1992) *Crime in Nineteenth-Century Wales* (Cardiff: University of Wales Press), pp. 4–6.

6. Grand larceny was the theft of items worth more than one shilling or 12 pence. This was deemed more serious and typically dealt with in courts of higher jurisdiction in the English context at least. Petty larceny was the theft of items worth less than one shilling or 12 pence and was deemed a minor offence typically prosecuted at Quarter Sessions in England. In the Welsh context, this distinction was seemingly not made in any explicitly articulated sense and so more prosecutions related to stealing and pilfering came to the higher Court of Great Sessions, regardless of the nature of theft conducted or the value of the goods stolen. In any event, in 1827 these two categories of offence were assimilated into one, entitled 'simple larceny'. For further discussion of the legal distinction between grand and petty larceny see S. Horrell, J. Humphries, and K. Sneath (2013) 'Cupidity and Crime: Consumption as Revealed by Insights from the Old Bailey Records of Thefts in the Eighteenth and Nineteenth Centuries', in M. Casson and N. Hashimzade (eds), *Large Databases in Economic History: Research Methods and Case Studies* (London: Routledge), pp. 246–67 at p. 254.
7. For further discussion of this period in Welsh history see W. Vaughan-Thomas (1985) *Wales: A History* (London: Michael Joseph), pp. 199–201; J. Davies (2007 edition) *A History of Wales* (London: Penguin), pp. 310–72; and D. W. Howell (2016 edition) *Land and People in Nineteenth-Century Wales* (London: Routledge), *passim*.
8. For an acknowledgement of the preoccupation with popular disturbances in the historiography of Welsh criminal history see Howell, *Land and People*, p. xli, and Davies, *A History of Wales*, pp. 354–72. For evidence that theft was the most commonly prosecuted crime within the Welsh judiciary in both the eighteenth and nineteenth centuries see for instance D. W. Howell (2000) *The Rural Poor in Eighteenth-Century Wales* (Cardiff: University of Wales Press), p. 210; J. Walliss (2018) *The Bloody Code in England and Wales, 1760–1830* (Basingstoke: Palgrave), p. 104; R. Jones (2018) *Crime, Courts and Community in Mid-Victorian Wales: Montgomeryshire, People and Places* (Cardiff: University of Wales Press), p. 150; and Jones, *Crime in Nineteenth-Century Wales*, p. 45.
9. For commentary relating to the dearth of scholarship on the history of Welsh criminality and gendered criminality in particular see Walliss, *Bloody Code*, p. 90, and K. D. Watson (2013) 'Women, Violent Crime and Justice in Georgian Wales', *Continuity and Change*, 28, 2, pp. 245–72 at p. 246.
10. See for instance D. G. Gray (2016) *Crime, Policing and Punishment in England, 1660–1914* (London: Bloomsbury), p. 143; T. C. Whitlock (1999) 'Gender, Medicine and Consumer Culture in Victorian England: Creating the Kleptomaniac', *Albion*, 31, 3, pp. 413–37 at p. 419; and E. S. Abelson (1989) 'The Invention of Kleptomania', *Signs*, 15, 1, pp. 123–43 at p. 126.
11. See L. Coar (2012) 'Sugar and Spice and All Things Nice: The Victorian Woman's All-Consuming Predicament', *Victorian Network*, 4, 1, pp. 48–72 at p. 66.
12. For further discussion see P. O'Brien (1983) 'The Kleptomania Diagnosis: Bourgeois Women and Theft in Late Nineteenth-Century France', *Journal of Social History*, 17, 1, pp. 65–77 at pp. 68–9.
13. Ibid., p. 71; Abelson, 'Invention of Kleptomania', pp. 134 and 143; Whitlock, 'Gender, Medicine and Consumer Culture', pp. 424 and 435; and S. L. Steinbach (2012)

*Understanding the Victorians: Politics, Culture and Society in Nineteenth-Century Britain* (London and New York: Routledge), p. 109.

14. For further discussion see J. A. N. Bamfield (2012) *Shopping and Crime* (Basingstoke: Palgrave), pp. 25 and 29; Coar, 'Sugar and Spice', p. 48; and S. Sloboda (2009) 'Porcelain Bodies: Gender, Acquisitiveness, and Taste in Eighteenth-Century England', in A. Myzelev and J. Potvin (eds), *Material Cultures, 1740–1920: The Meanings and Pleasures of Collecting* (Burlington, VT: Ashgate), pp. 19–36 at pp. 19 and 29.
15. See K. Lysack (2008) *Come Buy, Come Buy: Shopping and the Culture of Consumption* (Athens, OH: Ohio University Press), p. 49; E. Kowaleski-Wallace (1997) *Consuming Subjects: Women, Shopping and Business in the Eighteenth Century* (New York: Columbia University Press), pp. 4–5; L. A. Loeb (1994) *Consuming Angels: Advertising and Victorian Women* (New York: Oxford University Press), p. 26; Steinbach (2012) *Understanding the Victorians*, pp. 99–100; and J. D. Walkowitz (1998) 'Going Public: Shopping, Street Harassment, and Streetwalking in Late Victorian London', *Representations*, 62, pp. 1–30 at pp. 4–6.
16. See for instance M. Berg (2005) *Luxury and Pleasure in Eighteenth-Century Britain* (Oxford: Oxford University Press), pp. ix–x, 3–4, and 235; Kowaleski-Wallace, *Consuming Subjects*, p. 6; and esp. M. Finn (1996) 'Women, Consumption and Coverture in England, 1760–1860', *Historical Journal*, 39, 3, pp. 703–22 at pp. 703–4 and 706.
17. Whitlock, *Crime, Gender and Consumer Culture*, p. 5.
18. Loeb, *Consuming Angels*, pp. vii–viii.
19. Ibid., pp. 3–4; Lysack, *Come Buy*, pp. 56–7; I. Selimić (2016) 'Female Criminality, Class, and Deviance during the Rise of the Twentieth Century Department Store', *LSE Law Review*, 1, pp. 1–30 at p. 23; and D. Hussey (2008) 'Guns, Horses and Stylish Waistcoats? Male Consumer Activity and Domestic Shopping in Late-Eighteenth and Early-Nineteenth-Century England', in D. Hussey and M. Ponsonby (eds), *Buying for the Home: Shopping for the Domestic from the Seventeenth Century to the Present* (Aldershot: Ashgate), pp. 47–69 at p. 48.
20. For further discussion of the origins and reach of the kleptomania diagnosis see for instance K. Segrave (2001) *Shoplifting: A Social History* (Jefferson, NC: McFarland & Co.); E. S. Abelson (1989) *When Ladies Go A-Thieving: Middle-Class Shoplifters in the Victorian Department Store* (New York and Oxford: Oxford University Press), pp. 8–9 and 174; R. A. Fullerton and G. N. Punj (2004) 'Shoplifting as Moral Insanity: Historical Perspectives on Kleptomania', *Journal of Macromarketing*, 24, 1, pp. 8–16; Whitlock, *Crime, Gender and Consumer Culture*, chapter 7; Abelson, 'Invention of Kleptomania', pp. 123–4, 126, and 133; P. Gurney (2019 edition) *The Making of Consumer Culture in Modern Britain* (London: Bloomsbury), pp. 95–7; T. Whitlock (2016) 'Forms of Crime: Crime and Retail Theft', in P. Knepper and A. Johansen (eds), *The Oxford Handbook of the History of Crime and Criminal Justice* (Oxford: Oxford University Press), pp. 155–69 at pp. 162–4; Whitlock, 'Gender, Medicine and Consumer Culture', pp. 413–14, 418–19, and 430; and Selimić, 'Female Criminality', p. 16.
21. For further discussion see Whitlock, *Crime, Gender and Consumer Culture*, p. 7, and Lysack, *Come Buy*, p. 47.
22. Selimić, 'Female Criminality', p. 17.

23. See Loeb, *Consuming Angels*, p. 18; Whitlock, 'Gender, Medicine and Consumer Culture', p. 414; Selimić, 'Female Criminality', p. 19; Walkowitz, 'Going Public', p. 5; Steinbach, *Understanding the Victorians*, p. 109; and Coar, 'Sugar and Spice', pp. 53 and 69.
24. See Gurney, *The Making of Consumer* Culture, p. 96; Whitlock, *Crime, Gender and Consumer Culture*, p. 129; Abelson, *When Ladies Go A-Thieving*, p. 191; and Steinbach, *Understanding the Victorians*, p. 107.
25. See Whitlock, 'Gender, Medicine and Consumer Culture', p. 433.
26. For the suggestion that such an academic endeavour is warranted see M. Finn (2000) 'Men's Things: Masculine Possession in the Consumer Revolution', *Social History*, 25, 2, pp. 133–55 at pp. 133–5; J. Flanders (2007 edition) *Consuming Passions: Leisure and Pleasure in Victorian Britain* (London: Harper Perennial), pp. xv–xvi and esp. p. 42; D. Cohen (2006) *Household Gods: The British and their Possessions* (New Haven: Yale University Press), pp. x–xii; K. Graham (2008) *'Gone to the Shops': Shopping in Victorian England* (Westport, CT: Praeger); Berg, *Luxury and Pleasure*, pp. 9–11; and Hussey, 'Guns, Horses and Stylish Waistcoats?', p. 47.
27. The suggestion of acquisitiveness being a factor in theft outside the boundaries of respectable society is provided in J. Styles (2003) 'Custom or Consumption? Plebeian Fashion in Eighteenth-Century England', in M. Berg and E. Eger (eds), *Luxury in the Eighteenth Century: Debates, Desires and Delectable Goods* (Basingstoke: Palgrave), pp. 103–15 at pp. 105, 110, and 113; and in Gurney, *The Making of Consumer Culture*, p. 96.
28. For the purposes of this study, the crime of resett or receiving stolen goods has been included in all the calculations of Welsh theiving activity between 1800 and 1830. Figure 6.2 shows the contribution that resett made to the overall dataset.
29. See for instance Walker, *Crime, Gender and Social Order*, p. 159; Beattie, *Crime and the Courts*, p. 140; Walliss, *Bloody Code*, pp. 32 and 68; Kilday (2014) 'Criminally Poor?', p. 509; Howell, *Land and People*, p. 106; Jones, *Crime, Courts and Community*, p. 150; and A.-M. Kilday (2019) *Crime in Scotland 1660–1960: The Violent North?* (London: Routledge), pp. 243–4.
30. For further discussion see Walker, *Crime, Gender and Social Order*, p. 159; Beattie, *Crime and the Courts*, p. 239; Walliss, *Bloody Code*, pp. 38–9; Kilday, 'Criminally Poor?', p. 512; Howell, *The Rural Poor*, pp. 228 and 234; P. King (2006) *Crime and Law in England, 1750–1840* (Cambridge: Cambridge University Press), p. 167; Jones, *Crime in Nineteenth-Century Wales*, p. 171; and Kilday, *Crime in Scotland*, pp. 248–50 and 257.
31. It should be noted that from 1808 pickpocketing was no longer a capital offence and in 1823 shoplifting and poaching were no longer deemed to be capital either, as part of the changes enforced by the Judgement of Death Act (4 Geo IV, ch. 48). As there was an evident blurring of the use of grand and petty larceny too in the Welsh context, in practical terms the capital non-violent thieving offences which remained on the statute book and were applied in the 1800–30 period were animal theft, burglary, housebreaking, and occasional significant or repeated acts of larceny.
32. See for instance S. Tickell (2018) *Shoplifting in Eighteenth-Century England* (Woodbridge: Boydell), p. 4; Palk, 'Private Crime', p. 135; Kilday, *Crime in Scotland*, pp. 248–9; and Jones, *Crime in Nineteenth-Century Wales*, p. 131.

33. For discussion of the gender disparity in recorded instances of robbery in the pre-modern period see Beattie, *Crime and the Courts*, p. 239, and King, *Crime and Law*, pp. 171–2. For discussion of the gender disparity in shoplifting in the pre-modern period see Tickell, *Shoplifting*, p. 18, and Gurney, *The Making of Consumer Culture*, p. 96.
34. For scholarship that argues that women had a limited role in the direct perpetration of more serious forms of non-violent property crime in the pre-modern period see Walker, *Crime, Gender and Social Order*, pp. 159–60; Beattie, *Crime and the Courts*, p. 239; King, 'Female Offenders', p. 62; Gray, *Crime, Policing and Punishment*, p. 159; Walliss, *Bloody Code*, pp. 37–9 and 112; Woodward, 'Burglary in Wales', pp. 78–9; and Jones, *Crime in Nineteenth-Century Wales*, pp. 171–2.
35. For further discussion of women's role in the crime of receiving stolen goods (or resett) see Walker, *Crime, Gender and Social Order*, p. 165; Kilday, *Crime in Scotland*, pp. 250–1, 254–5, and 257; and esp. Philips, *Crime and Authority*, pp. 219–21.
36. See for instance Beattie, *Crime and the Courts*, p. 163; Gray, *Crime, Policing and Punishment*, p. 100; and Jones, *Crime in Nineteenth-Century Wales*, pp. 119–20.
37. See for instance Tickell, *Shoplifting*, p. 81; Philips, *Crime and Authority*, p. 211; and Jones, *Crime in Nineteenth-Century Wales*, p. 123.
38. Jones, *Crime in Nineteenth-Century Wales*, p. 137, and see also his comments at p. 140. See also Philips, *Crime and Authority*, p. 178; and Howell, *Land and People*, p. 211.
39. Vaughan-Thomas, *Wales*, p. 199. See also Davies, *A History of Wales*, pp. 310–14.
40. See for instance Howell, *Land and People*, p. xii; Davies, *A History of Wales*, pp. 354–72; and Vaughan-Thomas, *Wales*, p. 200.
41. See Walliss, *Bloody Code*, p. 21; Gray, *Crime, Policing and Punishment*, pp. 123–4; Jones, *Crime in Nineteenth-Century Wales*, p. 31; Davies, *A History of Wales*, pp. 338 and 345.
42. See Howell, *Land and People*, pp. xi and xiii as well as Davies, *A History of Wales*, pp. 343 and 345.
43. See Davies, *A History of Wales*, pp. 345–7; Jones, *Crime in Nineteenth-Century Wales*, pp. 52 and 54; and Howell, *Land and People*, pp. xiii and 3.
44. For evidence that the socio-economic crisis continued, albeit not as incessantly after the 1820s, see Howell, *Land and People*, pp. 4–5, 9–11, and 158. For scholarship that has linked socio-economic change to criminal activity in Wales see Jones, *Crime in Nineteenth-Century Wales*, pp. 55–6; Woodward, 'Burglary in Wales', pp. 87–90; Woodward, 'Seasonality and Sheep-Stealing', pp. 26 and 35–6; and N. Woodward (2009) 'Horse-Stealing in Wales, 1730–1830', *Agricultural History Review*, 57, I, pp. 70–108 at p. 92.
45. The high instance of theft in the winter months compared to the remaining seasons of the year is an observation also made by the Welsh crime historian David J. V. Jones for the whole of the nineteenth-century period; see Jones, *Crime in Nineteenth-Century Wales*, p. 58.
46. The evidence uncovered for this study relating to the seasonality of theft in Wales between 1800 and 1830 does not align with the work done on sheep-stealing or burglary carried out for the same period and place by historian Nick Woodward: see Woodward, 'Seasonality and Sheep-Stealing', pp. 25 and 41–2, as well as Woodward, 'Burglary in Wales', pp. 85–6. However, his data related to specific offences whereas

the data here are an aggregate of all acts of non-violent property theft brought before the Court of Great Sessions.

47. See M. Feeley and D. Little (1991) 'The Vanishing Female: The Decline of Women in the Criminal Process 1687–1912', *Law and Society Review*, 25, pp. 719–57. For further discussion of the lack of support for their thesis see Walliss, *Bloody Code*, p. 114, and esp. King, *Crime and Law*, chapter 6.
48. For further discussion of the link between urbanization and crime, particularly for women thieves, see Kilday, 'Criminally Poor?', p. 511; Beattie, *Crime and the Courts*, pp. 240–1; King, 'Female Offenders', p. 82; Gray, *Crime, Policing and Punishment*, pp. 113 and 122; King, *Crime and Law*, p. 217; Jones, *Crime, Courts and Community*, p. 153, and esp. Jones, *Crime in Nineteenth-Century Wales*, pp. 37, 39, 111–13, and 173.
49. For further discussion of the rural milieu and offences specific to that context see R. W. Ireland (2015) *Land of White Gloves? A History of Crime and Punishment in Wales* (Abingdon: Routledge), p. 70.
50. For further discussion see D. J. I. Murphy (1986) *Customers and Thieves: An Ethnography of Shoplifting* (Aldershot: Gower), chapter 4; and Philips, *Crime and Authority*, p. 199.
51. Historian Nick Woodward writes of there being an east/west divide in the perpetration of burglary in Wales between 1730 and 1830, but such a distribution in recorded theft more generally is not evident from this analysis either in relation to male offenders or female offenders—see Woodward, 'Burglary in Wales', p. 65. For further discussion of the historical tendency towards a broad geographical distribution of thieving episodes see Howell, *The Rural Poor*, p. 227.
52. Unfortunately, as the age of the defendant was only provided in a small number of the cases brought against women at the Court of Great Sessions, this variable was not included in the data characteristics of this study. When age was recorded, it was typically provided in relation to the very elderly or to juveniles. It is unclear whether such information was recorded in random or routine fashion by the court authorities in Wales, but in any event, age extremes in offender profiles were not prominent in the indictment evidence uncovered.
53. See for instance King, 'Female Offenders', pp. 69–70; Kilday, 'Criminally Poor?', p. 512; Woodward, 'Burglary in Wales', p. 79; Whitlock, 'Gender, Medicine and Consumer Culture', p. 416; and Jones, *Crime in Nineteenth-Century Wales*, p. 172.
54. King, 'Female Offenders', p. 63.
55. National Library of Wales (NLW), Records of the Court of Great Sessions, 4/753/4. For further discussion of the link between sexual encounters and women's involvement in theft see Palk, 'Private Crime', p. 137, and Philips, *Crime and Authority*, p. 208.
56. For studies which suggest that women were more inclined to participate in theft with others than men see Walker, *Crime, Gender and Social Order*, p. 171; J. Diski (2011) 'The Secret Shopper', *The New Yorker*, 87, 29, pp. 115–20 at p. 118; Murphy, *Customers and Thieves*, p. 88; and Selimić, 'Female Criminality', p. 12.
57. NLW, Records of the Court of Great Sessions, 4/197/6.
58. NLW, Records of the Court of Great Sessions, 4/74/5A.
59. For further scholarly discussion of the engagement of professional gangs in more serious/complex forms of theft see Beattie, *Crime and the Courts*, pp. 163–4; Horrell

et al., 'Cupidity and Crime', p. 253; Woodward, 'Horse-Stealing in Wales', pp. 93–4; and Philips, *Crime and Authority*, p. 206.

60. See for instance the conclusions of Woodward, 'Burglary in Wales', p. 84, and Jones, *Crime in Nineteenth-Century Wales*, pp. 119 and 139.
61. For further discussion of the paucity of recidivism in studies of theft in the pre-modern era see Kilday, 'Criminally Poor?', p. 512; Kilday, *Crime in Scotland*, pp. 251–2 and 256; and Jones, *Crime in Nineteenth-Century Wales*, p. 119.
62. NLW, Records of the Court of Great Sessions, 4/398/8.
63. For scholarship that points to evidence of professionalism in theft in relation to the *way* the crime was carried out and the planning and preparation involved, rather than to evidence of repeated instances of this kind of property crime by known offenders, see Palk, 'Private Crime', p. 140, and Woodward, 'Burglary in Wales', p. 83.
64. For further discussion of the influence of the 'dark figure' of unknown or unreported crime in relation to non-violent property crime see Palk, 'Private Crime', p. 135; Woodward, 'Seasonality and Sheep-Stealing', p. 30; and Jones, *Crime in Nineteenth-Century Wales*, p. 5.
65. See for instance Gray, *Crime, Policing and Punishment*, pp. 136 and 158; Walker, *Crime, Gender and Social Order*, p. 162; Kilday, 'Criminally Poor?', pp. 514 and 516; Howell, *The Rural Poor*, p. 234; Woodward, 'Burglary in Wales', p. 68; Woodward, 'Horse-Stealing in Wales', p. 84; and Jones, *Crime, Courts and Community*, p. 158.
66. See for instance Gray, *Crime, Policing and Punishment*, p. 158; C. Walsh (2008) 'Shopping at First Hand? Mistresses, Servants and Shopping for the Household in Early-Modern England', in D. Hussey and M. Ponsonby (eds), *Buying for the Home: Shopping for the Domestic from the Seventeenth Century to the Present* (Aldershot: Ashgate), pp. 13–26 at p. 15; Walker, *Crime, Gender and Social Order*, pp. 162–4 and 169; G. Walker (1994) 'Women, Theft and the World of Stolen Goods', in J. Kermode and G. Walker (eds), *Women, Crime and the Courts in Early Modern England* (Chapel Hill, NC, and London: University of North Carolina Press), pp. 81–105; B. Lemire (1990) 'The Theft of Clothes and Popular Consumerism in Early Modern England', *Journal of Social History*, 24, 2, pp. 255–76 at p. 257; Kilday, 'Criminally Poor?', pp. 514–15; Woodward, 'Burglary in Wales', p. 68; Jones, *Crime, Courts and Community*, p. 154; and Gurney, *The Making of Consumer Culture*, p. 96.
67. For further discussion of the opportunistic nature of theft in the pre-modern period and the importance of context see Walker, *Crime, Gender and Social Order*, p. 170; Beattie, *Crime and the Courts*, p. 186; Gray, *Crime, Policing and Punishment*, p. 112; Horrell et al., 'Cupidity and Crime', p. 254; and Jones, *Crime, Courts and Community*, p. 154.
68. NLW, Records of the Court of Great Sessions, 4/631/6.
69. NLW, Records of the Court of Great Sessions, 4/72/5A.
70. NLW, Records of the Court of Great Sessions, 4/759/1.
71. NLW, Records of the Court of Great Sessions, 4/538/8.
72. For evidence to support this contention in wider scholarship see Walker, *Crime, Gender and Social Order*, pp. 161 and 163; Lemire, 'The Theft of Clothes', p. 270; Tickell, *Shoplifting*, pp. 94–6; D. W. Howell, *Land and People*, p. 3 and Flanders, *Consuming Passions*, p. 86.
73. For further discussion see for instance Kilday, *Women and Violent* Crime, pp. 52 and 77–8, and Gray, *Crime, Policing and Punishment*, pp. 121–2.

74. Styles, 'Custom or Consumption?', p. 111. See also Lemire, 'The Theft of Clothes', p. 257.
75. For further evidence of these motives in theftuous activity during the pre-modern period see Beattie, *Crime and the Courts*, pp. 242–3; Tickell, *Shoplifting*, p. 5; Lemire, 'The Theft of Clothes', pp. 257–8 and 264; Jones, *Crime, Courts and Community*, pp. 155 and 157; and Whitlock, *Crime, Gender and Consumer Culture*, p. 140.
76. NLW, Records of the Court of Great Sessions, 4/394/2.
77. Lemire, 'The Theft of Clothes', p. 270.
78. NLW, Records of the Court of Great Sessions, 4/283/1.
79. For more on the economic context within Wales at this time see Davies, *A History of Wales*, pp. 312–14, 338, and 343–53, and Howell, *Land and People*, p. xi–xiii, 1–11, and the data shared at p. 158. For further discussion of the economic instability of this period and its impact on property offending more generally see Horrell et al., 'Cupidity and Crime', pp. 257–8, and esp. Philips, *Crime and Authority*, pp. 148–9, 201, and 204.
80. For further evidence of these motives in theftuous activity during the pre-modern period see Beattie, *Crime and the Courts*, pp. 170–1 and 188–9; Tickell, *Shoplifting*, pp. 5, 95, and 124; Kilday, 'Criminally Poor?', pp. 507 and 520; Howell, *The Rural Poor*, pp. 231–2; King, 'Female Offenders', pp. 81–2; Gray, *Crime, Policing and Punishment*, p. 130; Woodward, 'Burglary in Wales', p. 72; and A. W. Ager (2014) *Crime and Poverty in Nineteenth-Century England: The Economy of Makeshifts* (London: Bloomsbury), pp. 60–2 and 139.
81. Culm is a fine anthracite dust generated as a by-product of the coal-mining process. Historically, it was often mixed with wet clay, rolled into a ball and then dried and used for fuel. See Revd J. Evans (1813) *The Topographical Description of North Wales by Rev Mr Evans for the Beauties of England and Wales: Delineations, Topographical, Historical and Descriptive*, vol. 17 (London: Thomas Maiden), p. 92.
82. NLW, Records of the Court of Great Sessions, 4/830/4.
83. NLW, Records of the Court of Great Sessions, 4/200/9.
84. For further discussion of the low conviction rate in relation to the theft in the pre-modern period and the lengths the authorities went to avoid prosecutions and condemnatory verdicts see Howard, *Law and Disorder*, p. 134; Woodward, 'Burglary in Wales', p. 77; Woodward, 'Seasonality and Sheep-Stealing', p. 31; Gray, *Crime, Policing and Punishment*, p. 122; Walliss, *Bloody Code*, p. 108; Ireland, *Land of White Gloves?*, p. 51; and Jones, *Crime in Nineteenth-Century Wales*, p. 7.
85. For evidence of a low execution rate in relation to theft in the pre-modern period in general see Howard, *Law and Disorder*, pp. 133 and 135; Walliss, *Bloody Code*, pp. 69, 91, 126–237, and 151–2; and Ager, *Crime and Poverty*, p. 63. For discussion of this in relation to women in particular see Walker, *Crime, Gender and Social Order*, p. 182, and Walliss, *Bloody Code*, p. 77.
86. For further discussion of the increasing dominance of imprisonment in theft convictions in the pre-modern period see Philips, *Crime and Authority*, p. 179.
87. See for instance Walker, *Crime, Gender and Social Order*, pp. 181 and 195; Walliss, *Bloody Code*, p. 70; and Gray, *Crime, Policing and Punishment*, p. 122.
88. For evidence of the acceptance of gendered leniency amongst scholars of the pre-modern period see Jones, *Crime in Nineteenth-Century Wales*, p. 174; Walliss, *The Bloody Code*, p. 77 and especially King (2006) *Crime and Law*, pp. 167–169, p. 178 and pp. 192–3.

89. See for instance Gray (2016) *Crime, Policing and Punishment*, p. 158.
90. For the contrasting English experience in this respect see for instance the various chapters in S. King and A. Tomkins (2003) (eds) *The Poor in England 1700–1850: An Economy of Makeshifts* (Manchester: Manchester University Press) and also Ager (2014) *Crime and Poverty, passim.*
91. See for instance Gray (2016) *Crime, Policing and Punishment*, p. 136.
92. Ibid.
93. Ibid, p. 158.
94. Again this finding contrasts with the English experience of non-violent property crime in the early nineteenth century where gendered leniency seemingly abounded. See for instance King (2006) *Crime and Law*, pp. 167–79, p. 178 and pp. 192–3.

# 7

# 'Tigerish in their Ferocity' and 'Traitors to their Sex'?

## Violent Female Robbers in Nineteenth-Century Scotland

### Introduction

It has long been believed that, due to the specific characteristics associated with the female sex, women's only meaningful engagement with crime, and with violent crime more specifically, was in the role of victim rather than perpetrator.[1] This view certainly prevailed in the nineteenth century, and as we have seen elsewhere in this volume, there was a fair degree of confusion and anxiety when state authorities and the British public more generally were confronted with women who appeared to have broken the boundaries of what was considered normal, gendered behaviour. Whilst there was some eventual acknowledgement that women could be capable of aggressive criminal behaviour, it was only deemed to be possible under certain conditions and in specific contexts. So for instance, women's violence came to be associated solely with forms of private or hidden malevolence which emanated from their prevailing passions, rather than being based on any innate capacity for wrong-doing. The poisoning and infanticidal episodes used as case studies in some of the previous chapters in this volume are indicative of the kind of covert or cloaked criminality said to have been perpetrated by members of the 'fairer sex'.[2] In addition, women were not considered to be autonomous or direct actors in crime. Instead, and on account of their submissive feminine traits, it was believed that they only played subsidiary roles in illegality (such as acting as decoys or lookouts) and they did so purely at the behest of men rather than on account of their own personal motivations or desires.[3]

Using a Scottish case study from the middle of the nineteenth century, this chapter will explore how Victorians reacted when they were faced with overt violence, carried out by experienced female felons, with the declared objective of deriving personal gain. Although the gang of women involved in this particular instance of robbery were relatively unusual in that a fatality resulted from their actions, their calculated attitudes, their explicit behaviour, and the independent nature of their activities still represented the antithesis of the meek, genteel, and

*Beyond Deviant Damsels: Re-evaluating Female Criminality in the Nineteenth Century.* Anne-Marie Kilday and David Nash, Oxford University Press. © Anne-Marie Kilday and David Nash 2023. DOI: 10.1093/oso/9780198830733.003.0007

courteous woman. They were a challenge to attitudes that had become so firmly entrenched in notions of respectability by the nineteenth-century era.[4] So why had these women so refused to conform to the social expectations linked to their sex? How did the judicial system regard women who had patently stepped outside the boundaries of civilized feminine behaviour? And finally, what did the wider public have to say about harridans and viragoes such as these?

## The Accepted Traits of Femininity

In order to fully appreciate the extent to which the women in the forthcoming case study could be deemed 'traitors to their sex' in the way that they behaved, and through their perpetration of violent criminal activity, we first need to better understand what the acceptable traits of femininity were. Part of this is appreciating how they came to be derived, and the extent to which they still prevailed by the Victorian era. A belief in the innate inferiority and essential subordination of women was first suggested by various Bible references. The fact that, in the Old Testament, God created Adam first rather than Eve was held to be significant, as was the fact that Eve's punishment after the 'fall' rendered her, and all women after her, under the rule of man. This opinion was then reinforced in the New Testament and the writings of St Paul in particular, who famously described women as 'the weaker vessel'. Over time, as historian Robert Shoemaker has explained, Protestant scholars and commentators adopted these attitudes and so these views became further entrenched as a result.[5]

By the early modern period, observations about female characteristics were dominated by the belief that women possessed inferior attributes to their male counterparts and were thus perpetually subordinate to them. According to Shoemaker, even when women were ascribed affirmative virtues, such as humility, these qualities only served to reinforce their inferiority in comparison to men.[6] By the seventeenth and eighteenth centuries, scriptural directives were overtaken by nascent medical opinion which sought to develop an additional hierarchical view of gender. The humoral theories, which had originated with the work of Aristotle (384–322 BC), had been refined by Galen (AD 130–210), and were then rearticulated with some adaptations by early and pre-modern scholars, proposed that the body was composed of four different types of fluids. As men were hotter and drier in this analysis compared to women who were cooler and moister, the former were deemed to be complete and perfect in formation, whilst the latter were considered weak, passive, and suited to a more sedentary-type lifestyle.[7] Women, it was believed, were more susceptible to irrationality, mental inconsistency, and deviousness on account of their possession of a range of superfluous fluids. Their anatomical limitations meant that they needed to be protected and their ambitions restricted. Men on the other hand possessed a toughness, a vigour, and an intelligence which enabled them to be active, brave, and honourable.[8] These humoral theories, which had seemingly exposed tangible differences between the sexes, came to be replaced by fresh and evolving medical knowledge which concentrated upon the concept of 'sensational psychology' and the contrasting nervous system anatomies which prevailed in each gender.[9] Once again, however, this medical evidence was used to stress female inferiority and reinforce notions of women's weakness, frailty, and limitations—in both a physical and a mental sense—in comparison to men's strength, acumen, and potential.[10]

All of the initial, rudimentary scholarship about the construction of gender norms, and the restrictions that ought to be placed upon gender roles, were given a 'popular' voice (under the cover of moral instruction) in conduct books which existed from as early as the pre-Reformation period. Largely produced for a middle-class, literate audience, these works grew in popularity and in circulation from the end of the seventeenth century period onwards and served, alongside other forms of print culture such as plays, poetry, chapbooks, ballads, periodicals, and other writings, to promulgate and further entrench common understandings of the subordinate place and position of women in society.[11] Writers and commentators assigned what they believed to be the characteristic failings and virtues of each sex. For women, their faults included 'vanity, affectation, ambition, artifice, impatience, confidence and stubbornness'. Conversely, their qualities comprised 'purity, modesty, meekness, patience, tenderness, charity, piety and devotion'.[12] These notions evidently perpetuated beliefs in women's innate inferiority to men and meant that any desire for intellectual improvement or any perceived need for education was rendered redundant and unnecessary. Not only did this serve to maintain women's subordinate position in society more generally, but it also helped to establish—particularly by the eighteenth century—that their appropriate sphere of operation and influence should be that of the home. As scholars such as Anthony Fletcher have argued, the domestic domain not only afforded women protection from others and from themselves (given the apparently limited nature of their capabilities), but it was also seen to be the most appropriate context within which to nurture their positive virtues. From here these qualities supposedly became inculcated in the minds and behaviours of future generations.[13] Women's confinement to the domestic sphere thus went hand in hand with a renewed preoccupation with their roles as wife and mother, and during the nineteenth century, as we have seen in other chapters in this volume, a series of socio-religious campaigns were launched to ensure that women habitually embodied moral integrity and routinely practised 'good motherhood'.[14]

By the nineteenth century, as historian Carl Chinn explains, there was a further rearticulation of gendered identities and gender roles once again. In large part this was caused by a panic over seemingly significant numbers of working-class women entering the labour market and acting as a cheap source of labour.[15] As a consequence of this, attempts were made to reinforce the notion amongst the middle classes at least that a respectable woman's place was in the home and, by abandoning the domestic environment for the world of work, a woman abandoned the natural virtues of femininity and maternity which had been afforded to her by God himself.[16] By the Victorian era then, the discussed lines of delineation were less to do with defining the characteristics of binary gender types and more to do with distinguishing 'good' women from 'bad'.[17] Of course, many working-class women did not have the luxury of choice when it came to the practicalities of their everyday lives. Many had to work to make ends meet and did this in combination with strenuous domestic duties, trying to attain their own version of respectability in the process, as research by historians such as Elizabeth Roberts and Anne Digby has highlighted.[18] Yet undoubtedly there were other women who were wholly disinterested in propriety and decorum and who chose an entirely different path to survival whereby they shunned all the virtuous characteristics associated with the members of the 'fairer sex' and instead embraced deviance, immorality, bad behaviour, and/or crime.[19]

## The Accepted Traits of Robbery

The crime of robbery can be defined as 'the taking and carrying away of [the] personal property of another, from the person and against his will, by force or violence or by assault and putting in fear with intent to steal'.[20] Perhaps because of the deliberate intent involved in the crime's perpetration and on account of the evident combination between an attack on the person and an attack on property, the incidence of robbery offending has historically been regarded as a useful gauge or barometer of levels of 'true' violence in a given place during a specific period of time.[21] Rates of fatal violence, or homicide, for instance, cannot offer the same degree of accuracy in this regard, as many episodes may have been accidental or at least involved violence committed with unintended consequences. Robbery, on the other hand, whilst often opportunistic in terms of the timing of its perpetration or the victim targeted, was an indisputably deliberate act of violence. The acknowledgement of this aspect of the offence resulted in episodic moral panics over its commission, which were fuelled by the machinations of the press media, either when the incidence of robbery had seemingly increased, or when the nature of its perpetration had changed in some way. As historian Rob Sindall has pointed out, the nineteenth century was one era where social and state anxiety over robbery offending and the individuals who perpetrated it was almost ubiquitous.[22]

In Scotland, robbery was deemed a capital crime at common law and there were just two simple and logical qualifications that had to be met in order for a charge of this nature to arise. The first was that something had to be stolen and the second was that the thief in question had to have deployed violence to attain the loot in question. A robbery indictment did not require that violence be directly applied to the victim. If he or she had simply surrendered their possessions on account of the threat of being assaulted, this was sufficient to constitute a robbery under the parameters of Scots Law.[23] As robbery often involved direct physical confrontation between victim and offender, as has been described above, it was deemed to be a very serious offence within the judicial context. Moreover, its gravitas was assured if we consider the threat that the crime posed to personal and wider economic security, and the extent to which its prevalence came to be regarded an indicator of regional or even national stability.[24]

In consequence of all this, the punishments meted out to the individuals convicted of robbery in the Scottish context were severe. So much so that, even by the middle of the nineteenth century, when our case study for this chapter is set and when capital punishment was used relatively sparingly especially in a Scottish context, a death sentence still remained the most likely outcome following a guilty verdict in a robbery trial.[25] The reason for these harsh sanctions appears to be related to the fact that, in the Scottish context at this time, the number of reported robberies was far higher than the recorded instances of other types of serious violent crime. Moreover, the reported rates of robbery offending evidently intensified from the mid-point of the nineteenth century onwards. This trend was counter to that evident in all other forms of violent offending where indictment levels were either static or in decline during the same period.[26]

By the nineteenth century, and the mid-point of that period, the nature of robbery had changed substantially from earlier eras. Gone were the 'romantic' days of the highway robber, who hijacked wealthy victims travelling in coaches upon the roads and byways of the country, relieved them of their money, jewellery, and possessions, and who became legendary folk heroes to 'popular' society in the process. Yet, as the work of Anne-Marie Kilday has shown, such individuals were never hugely prevalent in a Scottish context, aside from a few reported episodes in the Lowland part of the country in the late seventeenth and early eighteenth centuries.[27] Far more common, especially by the Victorian era, were street robbers who operated on foot and who deployed a wide variety of ruses and techniques to facilitate their crimes. These individuals were regarded as far more threatening than the robbers who rode on horseback, as typically they could not make an easy getaway from a crime scene and thus had to employ a fair degree of violence and brutality towards their selected victim in order to achieve subjugation and effect an escape. In some instances, the robbery was conducted in public where the victim was first observed and in a rather unsophisticated manner: the robbers launched an attack, took what they could, and ran off. In other instances (such as in the case study below) the victim was lured elsewhere and was then hustled, assaulted, and robbed in private.[28]

As David Philips and Robert Hopps have shown in their research, robbery of this nature was almost exclusively an urban phenomenon and was perpetrated by lower class criminals trying to make crime pay quickly.[29] As a result of the largely opportunistic nature of the victim selection in these instances, the nature of the loot retrieved varied enormously from robbery to robbery. It was typical for money to be stolen, but it was not uncommon for other items such as watches, jewellery, hats, gloves, and pocket-books to be taken and then converted to cash later via the substantial market for second-hand goods which prevailed within the Victorian urban milieu.[30] The value of the goods plundered was never very substantial in these instances, however, and this goes some way to explain why most of the individuals involved in this type of criminality were hardened recidivists. In order to make this kind of felonious activity worthwhile in the short to medium term, it had to be repeated time and time again.[31]

The recidivist nature of robbery in nineteenth-century Scotland sets this offence apart from many of the other crimes prosecuted before the judicial system. It also implies that there was a certain element of professionalism involved in the perpetration of this offence, as some robbers (such as those we meet in the case study below) were able to review and refine their techniques after each episode to improve their chances of success. Some used weapons as the tools of their trade, whilst others were content to use their fists or threaten their victims into parting with their possessions.[32] Explicit violence was a typical feature of robbery incidents in nineteenth-century Scotland, with one judge describing the assailants of this offence as being 'tigerish in their ferocity'.[33] Evidence to suggest that this may well have been an accurate description rather than establishment overstatement comes with the knowledge that most of the individuals accused of this offence in the Scottish context were indicted for aggravated assault alongside the more serious charge.[34] In some instances, such as in our case study, the aggression and brutishness afforded robbery victims could have fatal consequences. The other element which points to the seemingly professional nature of Scottish robberies was that they seem to have involved a fair degree of forethought relating to knowledge of targets, techniques of appropriation, methods of flight, and means of disposal. Planning was evidently essential to ensure the effective perpetration of this particular offence.[35]

Robbers rarely worked alone. They were far more likely to operate with an accomplice or as part of a larger group and they did so not only to plan an attack on a would-be victim, but also to perpetrate the actual act of violence for gain itself. As we have seen, this was usually because the practical requirements of a successful robbery necessitated multiple participants. With interpersonal 'smash-and-grab' attacks for instance, at least one individual was needed to subdue the victim and one to purloin his or her property or possessions. As Gillian Spraggs explains, working in a group also offered extra pairs of hands in those situations where the victim offered more resistance than had been predicted and to expedite a clean escape.[36] Planning was thus essential, in order to maximize the benefits of engaging multiple assailants in the crime, even though the selection of the victim was often relatively random. The majority of robbers in nineteenth-century Scotland were men, but there is plenty of evidence to suggest that more women participated in this type of offence during this period than seemed to be the case elsewhere. Certainly, the indicted Scottish female robbers did not engage in the offence according to the prescribed notions of how their gender was expected to behave. They were *not* routinely timorous, genteel, or lacklustre in their actions. Nor did they take minor or subsidiary roles, such as acting as a decoy or lookout, as some historians have suggested was the case. Rather, these women were direct, independent, and autonomous criminal actors who regularly perpetrated violence with enthusiasm and with relish, as is evident from the case study in the section to follow.[37] But how were these women and their blatantly aggressive and non-feminine behaviours regarded by the Scottish authorities and by wider Victorian society?

## Fiery Femme Fatales: The Robbery and Murder of Alexander Boyd (1853)

In the middle of June 1853, newspapers reported that 'a murder and robbery of the most savage character' had occurred at a residence in the infamous Croiley's Land area off New Vennel Street in Glasgow.[38] Originally, five individuals were arrested for their involvement in the crime: Hans Smith MacFarlane, Ann Young (or Marshall), Helen Blackwood, Mary Hamilton, and a woman called Margaret Cunningham (or Thomson), whose multiple previous convictions for theft at Edinburgh's Sheriff Court had rendered her someone already known to the authorities.[39] Recidivist criminal Cunningham was not, however, indicted for the offence when the episode came to be formally prosecuted at the trial heard at the High Court on Edinburgh a month later, unlike her four erstwhile companions.[40]

The court heard that on Friday 10 June 1853, two companions and co-workers, 38-year-old James Law and 40-year-old Alexander Boyd, were at a bit of a loose end, as a strike at the shipyard where they worked as carpenters had entered its fourth week. The men decided to pass the time by going to several public houses together, where they engaged in a prolonged drinking spree—this continued throughout the night and into the next day.[41] As a result of his acute inebriation, James Law could not recollect any other details of what further transpired. The accused in this case probably believed that they had nothing to worry about with regard to the prosecution's case, given that their victim was now deceased, and his companion was suffering from alcohol-induced amnesia. However, they and their defence team had not counted on several individuals coming forward who had clearly seen the events that unfolded in the room on the evening in question.

Amazingly, *four* different eye-witnesses, two young brothers (distantly related to one of the accused) who were under a bed and two young women voyeuristically observing through the chinks in the door were all able to provide precise, damning, and corroboratory evidence of what transpired.

Initially, the court heard from 14-year-old William Shillinglaw and his brother James (aged 9), who explained that every evening they were permitted to sleep under one of the beds in a room at No. 77 New Vennel Street as they had nowhere else to go. William explained how the accused Helen Blackwood, Ann Young, and Mary Hamilton 'generally came home tipsy and commonly brought strange men with them; and then drinking and carousing would follow and sometimes fighting and disorder'.[42] He said that the women always slept with the men they brought home, that they were 'bad women', and that Hans Smith MacFarlane was their 'bully' or pimp. William further observed how the clients that came to the house 'were made to send for drink and give money' to the women and if they did not do this, 'they were soon abused and they did not often escape, even when they had spent their money'. He added that 'the women usually left the men drunk on the floor' and that he 'frequently saw them put their hands into the men's pockets'.[43] Evidence to substantiate William Shillinglaw's observations in this regard comes from contemporary commentaries and from historical scholarship, which explains that such activities were a commonly deployed ruse amongst nineteenth-century prostitute thieves.[44]

William Shillinglaw testified before the court that on Saturday, 11 June 1853, he and his brother James were asleep under the bed as usual, when they were awakened 'by bawling and noise' in the room which was lit by several candles placed on the mantelpiece. William recounted seeing the witness James Law sitting in Mary Hamilton's lap by the fireside. He appeared to both boys to be 'very drunk' and his consort was 'touched with drink too'.[45] Despite this, Mary Hamilton left Law sleeping and turned her attention to the equally inebriated Alexander Boyd. William Shillinglaw, along with 14-year-old Mary Keelan and 16-year-old Jane Leitch who both observed the scene unfolding through chinks in the door of the room where the wood was broken, saw Hamilton prepare some whisky in a cup and then add some 'brown grains like snuff' to it and gave it to Boyd to drink. Immediately prior to Mary Hamilton's intervention in this way, Mary Keelan testified that she had specifically heard Helen Blackwood say to Hamilton, 'Mary, that's a damned good chance'—implying that there was potentially money to be made from whatever endeavours the women had planned (legitimate or otherwise).[46] In any event, after consuming the concoction given to him, Boyd 'became quite sick, retched and hung his head' but seemed to immediately suspect that something was amiss.[47] William saw that 'he started up' and tried to strike Helen Blackwood who was then sitting beside him. Blackwood was incensed by this move on the part of Alexander Boyd, and she reacted by lifting up a chamber-pot which was beside her and struck him 'with such a blow on the forehead that the utensil was shattered in pieces and the fragments flew thro' [through] the room like sparks'.[48] William Shillinglaw described how, as a result of this assault, Boyd 'staggered backwards and dropped his whole length on the floor near the window where the back of his head struck hard upon a heavy square stone there which was used as a seat'. Boyd 'lay gasping and moaning like a dying man' but neither the witness nor his younger brother saw any blood emanate from him.[49]

William Shillinglaw then heard Helen Blackwood say in a low voice 'Let's have his clothes!' and she and Ann Young proceeded to remove the victim's cap, jacket, trousers, and boots (whilst Hans Smith MacFarlane and Mary Hamilton looked on). During this time, according to the young witness at least, Alexander Boyd was 'quite a dead mass in their hands'.[50] Blackwood rifled through Boyd's pockets and the young witnesses saw her remove some coins and secrete them on her person.[51] Boyd continued to gasp, moan, and turn about in pain at this juncture, and the women present could tell that their victim was in a bad way; thus, according to witnesses William Shillinglaw and Jane Leitch at least, 'a state of alarm' began to spread amongst the women about what to do next. After a brief discussion with Mary Hamilton, Hans Smith MacFarlane resolved the matter by declaring 'It's dark—Who sees?—Pitch the Buggar [Bugger] over!'[52] Straight after hearing this instruction, Helen Blackwood and Ann Young (with partial assistance from Hans Smith MacFarlane) lifted Alexander Boyd by the legs, shoulders, and testicles and 'pitched him over the window head'.[53] William Shillinglaw and his brother James both testified that Boyd 'made no resistance in their hands' and that they 'saw his feet disappear last out of the window'. They then 'heard the sug [thud] of a heavy fall in the back Court or Close'.[54] The body of Alexander Boyd must have fallen at significant speed from the window as neighbour Thomas McClymont, who happened to be looking out of his window on the floor below at the time of the incident, described to the court how the victim 'shot down like a dark shadow and was past in a twinkling'.[55]

Immediately after the deed had been done, both Hans Smith MacFarlane and Mary Hamilton rapidly fled the scene, with the former desperately trying to seek refuge with other acquaintances within the tenement building. However, given the noisy horde assembling outside of the premises, and the likelihood of the authorities' imminent arrival to investigate the cause of the rabble's assembly, no one was particularly keen to harbour a suspected fugitive and he was forced to depart.[56] Back at the scene of the assault and robbery of Alexander Boyd, the witnesses told the court how they observed Helen Blackwood pacing the room in an agitated state, moving backwards and forwards whilst wringing her hands. They also recounted seeing Ann Young throw the fragments of the broken chamber-pot out of the window after the victim. She then 'flung up her hands, ran to the open window and cried over it... "O my man's dead! He came to the window to make water and fell over!"' She then bolted out of the room and ran down the stairs. Upon seeing this, Helen Blackwood abruptly halted her pacing, blew out the candles, and followed her colleague, but not before locking the door of the room, leaving the aforementioned James Law passed out drunk on the floor and the two young boys still lying under the bed feeling rather bewildered by what they had just seen.[57]

The first person to happen upon the victim was a neighbour of the accused individuals, 37-year-old John McGinnis. McGinnis had heard a commotion and went to investigate. He found a partially clothed Alexander Boyd lying directly beneath Hans Smith MacFarlane's window 'upon the stone flags of the area'. According to McGinnins, Boyd 'was quite dead tho' still warm and his head was covered with blood'.[58] Very soon after his discovery, McGinnis was joined by Night Constables Robert Campbell and Darren Henderson from the A Division of Glasgow Police. Both policemen saw the body of the victim and confirmed him as deceased. They then went to seek additional help from colleagues as both the crime scene and the area where the victim's body lay 'were swarming with men and women'.[59] They were soon joined by Night Sergeant George Thomson and Constable John Smith and their preliminary investigations began.[60]

Constable Henderson broke open the door of Hans Smith MacFarlane's room in the tenement building and found witness James Law 'in a drunken sleep on the floor' and the two young Shillinglaw boys still under the bed. He also discovered 'a pair of boots wrapped in a man's dark cloth jacket, along with a vest, cap and light moleskin trousers all concealed under the bed clothes'.[61] From listening to the accounts of William and James Shillinglaw and knowing from previous interactions of the typical criminal habits deployed by the dwellers of the particular abode, the constable guessed what had transpired and told his colleagues the details of the suspects he thought they should capture. Word was accordingly spread amongst A Division to seek the arrest of Mary Hamilton, Ann Young, Helen Blackwood, and Hans Smith MacFarlane.[62]

Inspector of Day Constables Thomas Harding was the first to fulfil this directive when he arrested 27-year-old Mary Hamilton in College Street at 3 a.m. on the morning of 12 June 1853. When the witness was later searched by Night Detective Officer Bernard McLachlan at the police station, she was found to have some copper coins of small value on her person as well as a small paper packet containing snuff.[63] Hamilton claimed in her sworn declaration to the investigating officers that she was accustomed to being employed as a straw-hat maker, but for the last three months she had lodged with Hans Smith MacFarlane and the others at New Vennel Street. She admitted that she and Ann Young had happened to meet two men in Glasgow's Exchange Square and decided to go with them to a 'spirit cellar' where they drank liquor together for a couple of hours, before taking their new companions back to the house in Croiley's Land where they met up with Helen Blackwood.[64] Mary Hamilton recollected that one of the men was so drunk he immediately fell asleep on the floor. The other man, who wasn't quite as inebriated as his friend, gave Blackwood and Hamilton money for more alcohol and so they went out to purchase some, leaving the man and Ann Young to retire to bed together.[65] When the two women returned, Mary Hamilton saw the man get out of bed and go towards the window 'which was open, as it always is for air, the House being so close' and he fell out. Hamilton surmised that the man must have 'thought it was a door' and was at pains to point out that 'there was no person beside him and no-one doing anything to him'.[66] She was adamant that no robbery or assault was conducted on the victim prior to his falling from the window.[67]

Night Constable Duncan McInnes was walking his usual beat on the outskirts of the city on 12 June 1853, after receiving a report of a robbery and murder in the vicinity alongside descriptions of the likely suspects. McInnes knew exactly who he was looking for, as the individuals from Croiley's Land were 'women of the town' and 'confirmed troublemakers' who were well known to him.[68] At around 5 a.m. that morning, he spotted the suspect Hans Smith MacFarlane walking 'at a sharp pace' down Reid Street, closely followed by Helen Blackwood, just a few yards behind. In McInnes' view, the suspects appeared to be trying to leave the city by stealth because Blackwood was only wearing 'a pink bed-gown over a lilac one' and because 'both of them had an eager and anxious appearance'.[69] When the constable finally caught up with them and enquired where they were going, neither could offer a reply and they also denied knowing one another.

Twenty-two-year-old Helen Blackwood and 25-year-old Hans Smith MacFarlane were promptly arrested and taken into custody where MacFarlane eventually admitted to the authorities 'in a rather arrogant tone' that they 'were Comrades and Inmates of "the House" at Croiley's Land. But as he had been drinking elsewhere all night with his friends, he knew nothing about any bad business.'[70] Blackwood, when examined, also proudly acknowledged to the authorities that she lodged in the house at Croiley's Land. However, unlike MacFarlane, she disclosed that she had been in the house in New Vennel on the evening of Saturday 11 June 1853, when Mary Hamilton and Ann Young brought in two 'very drunk' individuals. Blackwood's testimony largely mirrored that of Mary Hamilton's, save for a few important details. First, unlike Mary Hamilton, Helen Blackwood made explicit reference to a transaction for sexual services being part of the prelude to Alexander Boyd's demise. She explained that the victim paid her two shillings and that amount meant that not only could she could go and purchase some more alcohol but it also enabled him to stay with the women until Monday 13 June as 'he intended to make them happy' for the rest of the night and all of the next day.[71]

The second variance from Mary Hamilton's testimony came when Helen Blackwood described that, after she and Hamilton had returned from purchasing the alcohol, a loud altercation broke out between Mary Hamilton and Ann Young over money, which roused the man who had been in bed with Young and he asked Blackwood for a water pot to relieve himself.[72] On receipt of this, he went with it to the window, 'lost his balance and fell over'. Blackwood insisted that the incident had been nothing more than an unfortunate accident, that 'no-one put a hand upon the victim' or robbed him of his possessions, and she obdurately maintained that Hans Smith MacFarlane had not been present for any of the events she had just described.[73] This latter detail was an additional deviation from the statement made by Mary Hamilton who, whilst making no mention of MacFarlane in what she said to the authorities, did not go as far as to explicitly deny his presence as Blackwood did.

The last of the suspects to be apprehended was 25-year-old widow Ann Young, who 'took to her heels' the minute she saw Day Constable Donald Carmichael recognizing her on the city's King Street at around noon on 12 June.[74] Carmichael was resilient in his duty, however, and pursued Ann Young until he caught up with her. Upon arresting the suspect, the policeman asked Young if she lodged in the house at New Vennel. Young acknowledged that she did lodge at the address in question with Mary Hamilton and Helen Blackwood, but she was adamant that no violence had been perpetrated on the premises.[75] Upon subsequent examination, the authorities asked Ann Young if she knew the victim Alexander Boyd. Young admitted that it was *she* who invited both Boyd and his companion up to the house in Croiley's Land, but she denied having sexual relations with the deceased, explaining that although he had stripped to go to bed, he met his end before intercourse had taken place.[76] In this respect, Young's statement diverged from that of both Hamilton and Blackwood with regard to the sequence of events. Ann Young also presented a slightly modified version of what ultimately happened to Alexander Boyd. She recounted that on his way back from using a water pot at the window, Boyd tripped over the legs of the recumbent James Law and proceeded to fall backwards out of the open window.[77] This account seems flawed, however, if we consider that most tripping hazards cause individuals to fall forwards, rather than backwards. In any event, there was at least some consistency between the stories of the three women as Young, like her erstwhile roommates, made no reference to Boyd being assaulted or robbed prior to falling to his death.[78]

When the body of Alexander Boyd was examined post-mortem by medical professionals, John Alexander Easton and Robert McGregor, it was noted 'that the deceased was a strong muscular man, who had not been the subject of a lingering illness but had died while in the prime and vigour of life'.[79] The first abnormality on the cadaver that the medical men focused on was the extensive bruising evident on both of Alexander Boyd's testicles, which in their view had been 'caused by the parts being rudely grasped by an adult hand'.[80] This conclusion clearly corroborates the eye-witness testimony of the Shillinglaw brothers and Jane Leitch, regarding the methodology used to pitch Alexander Boyd out of the window. Conversely, on the other hand, the post-mortem examination and associated chemical analyses did not indicate the presence of snuff in the victim's stomach contents. Drs Easton and McGregor did acknowledge, however, that 'narcotic poisons derived from the animal kingdom were detected with comparative difficulty and often elude discovery... due to the transformative influences of the digestive process'.[81] Moreover, they did explain that 'the effects produced by even a small quantity of tobacco in the stomach were stupor, giddiness, depression of nervous energy, relaxation of muscular power and necessary diminution of strength'. If these symptoms were combined with that of inebriation, then an individual would likely be rendered compliant and submissive.[82]

The doctors then turned their attention to a portion of the right side of the victim's head (about three inches in length) which had effectively been scalped or removed and where they noted 'a large surface of the right temporal and parietal bones was exposed'.[83] On further examination 'several severe fractures in the bones of the deceased's head were seen to radiate from this site too'.[84] It was their contention that this wound was most likely caused by the impact from the blow using the chamber-pot, rather than from Boyd hitting his head on the projecting stone in the room whilst falling backwards or falling from the window as previous testimony might have suggested. This was because the affected area was near the temple, rather than the back of the head. The medical men did think that more blood should have been present at the crime scene based upon the degree of damage they observed in relation to this specific injury, but no haemorrhaging had been evident upon examination of the room in question.[85]

Significantly, when Drs Easton and McGregor investigated the rest of the victim's head, they discovered a considerable amount of clotted blood 'over the right side and at the base of the Brain... compressing that organ and thereby interrupting its functions'.[86] They determined, based on the evidence before them, that this particular injury 'could only have resulted from the application of very great violence, such as a heavy blow, or blows by some ponderous lethal weapon, or what is more likely, by the precipitation of the body to the ground from a considerable height'.[87] But, they admitted, the precise kind of violence involved was impossible to specify.'[88] James Morris Gale, civil engineer and surveyor, was then called before the court to give supplementary evidence as to the distance that Alexander Boyd had fallen from the window. Gale explained that he had measured this very carefully and was able to testify that the man had fallen precisely 23 feet and 9 inches. The court agreed that this fall ought to be regarded as one from a 'considerable height'.[89]

Upon opening Alexander Boyd's belly, Drs Easton and McGregor discovered 'a large quantity of bloody fluid, a deviation from the natural state', which they traced 'to a tear on the under or concave side of the liver, more than an inch in length and fully half an inch in depth'.[90] As the laceration of the liver had not been occasioned by disease and there was no evidence of local violence or bruising around the organ itself or the ribs encasing it, the only explanation as far as the medical men were concerned was

> to suggest some general agency at play, which had subjected not only this organ, but the whole body, to a simultaneous and severe concussion, the effects of which, of course, would be the most injurious and the most palpable on those organs, which, like the liver, offer from the nature of their structure, but a feeble resistance to a violently acting extraneous force. A fall to the ground from a high elevation would exert that requisite force, of which rupture of the liver was a very likely result.[91]

In their summation of the examination, Dr Easton and Dr McGregor concluded 'there can be no doubt that the death of this man was caused either by the fracture of the skull, by the extravasation of blood on the brain, by the laceration of the liver, or by two or three of these causes combined'.[92]

The extensive and substantiated eye-witness testimony provided in this case meant that the prosecution's task was a relatively straightforward one, aside that is, from determining degrees of culpability between the assailants involved. No evidence was offered in defence; not even character witness testimony or statements of regret or remorse.[93] After some deliberation, the assize found the case against Mary Hamilton not proven, but it did convict Ann Young, Helen Blackwood, and Hans Smith MacFarlane of the robbery and murder charges against them.[94] Despite having reached this decision, the assize did recommend that mercy be shown to Ann Young as they believed her to be 'less deeply implicated'.[95] They offered no such clement suggestion in relation to the other two felons. In any event, it would seem that the judge in this case was in no mood to be temperate. He decreed that 'blood for blood was required in this case' and sentenced the three prisoners to death, ordering them to be executed at Glasgow on Thursday 11 August 1853.[96]

## Reactions to Violent Women

Historian Lucia Zedner has noted that, in the Victorian era, 'Criminal women were perceived and judged against complex, carefully constructed notions of ideal womanhood.'[97] As she further explains:

> The ideal of femininity was invested in the middle-class wife and mother whose asexual, morally uplifting influence was held as a vital bulwark against the sordid intrusions of industrial life. Her antithesis was the epitome of female corruption—fallen from innocence, she had plummeted to the depths of degradation and contaminated all who came near her. Although Christianity taught that everyone was fallen from an original state of grace, the notion of the 'fallen woman' suggested a decent to a far greater depths.[98]

Moreover, the woman who had 'fallen', whether it be through drunkenness, sexual misconduct, or criminality, could never attain the coveted status of respectability which would enable her to align, at least in part, with 'decent' society.[99] Given what has already been said in this chapter about how women were expected to behave in this period, we could predict then that the responses to the behaviour of Mary Hamilton, Ann Young and Helen Blackwood would be uniform, strident, and unremittingly condemnatory in nature. However, reactions to this case were far more nuanced and complicated than this—a pattern we have seen repeated in other chapters elsewhere in this volume.

Although there is some evidence to suggest that Hans Smith MacFarlane was the ring-leader or puppet-master of this particular Croiley's Land gang of thieves,[100] the three women involved still offered various challenges to Victorian expectations of femininity through their participation in the robbery and murder of Alexander Boyd. First, there is no question that they displayed criminal autonomy in their endeavours. We see this particularly in their efforts to render their victim compliant, in their suggestion and perpetration of the act of robbery itself, and in their various machinations and attempts to cover up their criminality after the fact. Then there is the evidence that points to their explicit display of physical strength with regard to the dispatch of Alexander Boyd. For two of the women to lift a man who was 5 foot 8 and described as 'strong and muscular'[101] (with only minimal help from MacFarlane), and to do this whilst he was drugged, intoxicated, and thus something of a 'dead-weight', was quite an impressive feat. Moreover, the fact that one of the women used Boyd's testicles as the lifting point to facilitate the removal of his body from the room, further distancess the actions of these women from Victorian notions of gentility!

Yet, contrary to what we might expect, gender was not a particular focus of the reactions to this well-publicized case.[102] The individuals involved were not even described using gendered language and, instead, were referred to in generic, androgynous terms such as 'miscreants', 'barbarian robbers', 'powerful savages', or 'hardened individuals' possessing an 'abandoned character'.[103] Was this because there was a commonly held belief that recidivist offenders and immoral women like Helen Blackwood, Ann Young, and Mary Hamilton had 'fallen' too far to be saved? Whilst this may be true to some extent there seems to have been a tacit acceptance, at least amongst some Victorians according to the work of Chinn, that women from the lower orders 'retained a physical hardness' due to the strenuous nature of the daily tasks they performed (both in terms of paid employment and in relation to their domestic duties). Although they were thus quite capable of being violent or aggressive on occasion, the muted reaction to the criminality of the women in this case still seems strange.[104] This is especially so if we consider that the defiant objective of the judicial process and the stark purpose of punishment in the mid-nineteenth century remained one of deterrence.

Why did the Scottish authorities not use this instance as a preventative exemplar for other would-be criminal women? Instead, not only were the accused women almost invisible in the portrayal of the case to the general public, but their treatment at the hands of the authorities erred more towards forbearance and moderation, rather than to a more uncompromising and austere approach which we might have expected to see.

For one thing, as we know from the evidence above, the case against Mary Hamilton was found to be not proven and she was released without punishment. In addition to this, Ann Young (who was recommended to mercy by the assize) was latterly granted a remission from the sentence of capital punishment against her and, instead, she was condemned to a prolonged period of banishment.[105] This seems an extraordinarily lenient judicial decision, given the patent extent of Young's culpability in the robbery and murder of Alexander Boyd. However, if the Victorians believed women to be less prone to committing crime, then it would appear to make little sense to publicly punish female convicts to act as deterrent examples, as this would be both unwarranted and unnecessary.[106] This may go some way to explain why, by the mid-point of the nineteenth century, as the work of John Kellie, Kilday, and Martin Wiener has shown, there was a growing reluctance to execute female offenders in Scotland, as indeed elsewhere.[107]

The violent nature of this case still needed justice to be served however, and so the two convicts (and lovers) Helen Blackwood and Hans Smith MacFarlane were ordered to meet their fate on the gallows. Typically, in the run-up to such a public spectacle, there would be a wave of publicity where the public would hear in great detail about the life histories of the individuals concerned, in part, of course, to justify the severity of the sentence to be carried out. Particular attention would always be given to any female convict facing the hangman's noose, as not only was her plight becoming increasingly rare, but also, and as we have seen in other chapters in this volume, violent women were considered especially enthralling to a Victorian public who revelled in the morbid and the macabre as Kilday has highlighted elsewhere.[108] However, the executions of Helen Blackwood and Hans Smith MacFarlane were *not* carried out with anything like the usual popular fanfare, ritualized fuss, or voyeuristic fascination of other contemporary executions. Quite the opposite. Relatively few press reports covered either the run-up to the event, or the execution day itself, and those that did were brief and to the point, despite double hangings being exceedingly rare phenomena.[109] Indeed, rather than the judicial message of this event being one of deterrence, or the power of state authority against two habitually violent offenders, it instead came across as something of a farce. This was because the main element involving the two protagonists that newspapers reported upon was that MacFarlane and Blackwood became engaged to be married whilst standing on the gallows before both were swiftly dispatched by the executioner William Calcraft![110]

We should not conclude from this evidence that the crimes of the four accused individuals were somehow condoned by the authorities or by wider society. Clearly this was not the case, as two individuals were executed for the offences as described. Moreover, the press coverage of this incident was significant and substantial and it did have much to say on the events that transpired. However, Mary Hamilton, Ann Young, and Helen Blackwood were not the centre of attention in the ongoing dialogue that emerged from these events as we might have expected, given the extent of blatant female criminality in evidence. Rather their violent actions, and indeed their unambiguous immorality as 'fallen women' or prostitutes, were largely ignored; this seems somewhat curious given the Victorian preoccupation with efforts to suppress vice and illicit sexual practices of the very type these three women were engaged in. So, we may ask, what *was* the focus of public interest? For some, a lack of religious observance and a predilection for alcohol were seen to be the key discussion points and causes of this crime, but not with regard to the reasons for its perpetration amongst the protagonists involved. Rather, commentators wrote about these deficiencies as an explanation for the *victim's* demise, and suggested that, without religious adherence and sustained temperance, other individuals would follow in the stumbling footsteps of Alexander Boyd and meet an unfortunate and unnecessary end.[111] Other writers concentrated on the plight of the two young Shillinglaw boys who had witnessed the violent and murderous episode unfold before their very eyes. Newspapers offered conjecture over their eventual fate and some publications even encouraged their readers to home them or to donate money for their upkeep.[112] It would seem that, for some Victorians, the two boys offered the only hope for any sort of redemption in this case.

In addition to these fleeting observations mentioned in just a few areas of the burgeoning nineteenth-century press corps, there was one constant and ubiquitous theme that was arguably the true focal point for reactions to this particular criminal case: the infamous area where the crime occurred, the irredeemable nature of its inhabitants, and the evidential need to clearly demarcate 'rough' society from that of 'respectable'.[113] The area around No. 77 New Vennel in the City of Glasgow was known as Croiley's Land and is seen in the highlighted section of the map at Figure 7.1.

By the middle of the nineteenth century, not only did locals deem Croiley's Land to be the worst area of Glasgow, but they also deemed it to be 'the worst place in the world' due to the high density of population that lived there.[114] According to contemporaries, Croiley's Land was 'an accursed place haunted by evil spirits' which was made up of 'a nest of tall gaunt houses cramped together, of some three or four stories high, each room of which was occupied by one or more proprietors'.[115] Typically rooms (measuring 8 feet by 6 feet) had four or five occupants, but several rooms had eleven or twelve individual lodgers crammed together.[116] More than this, the area was a haven for criminals, 'a wild beast's den',

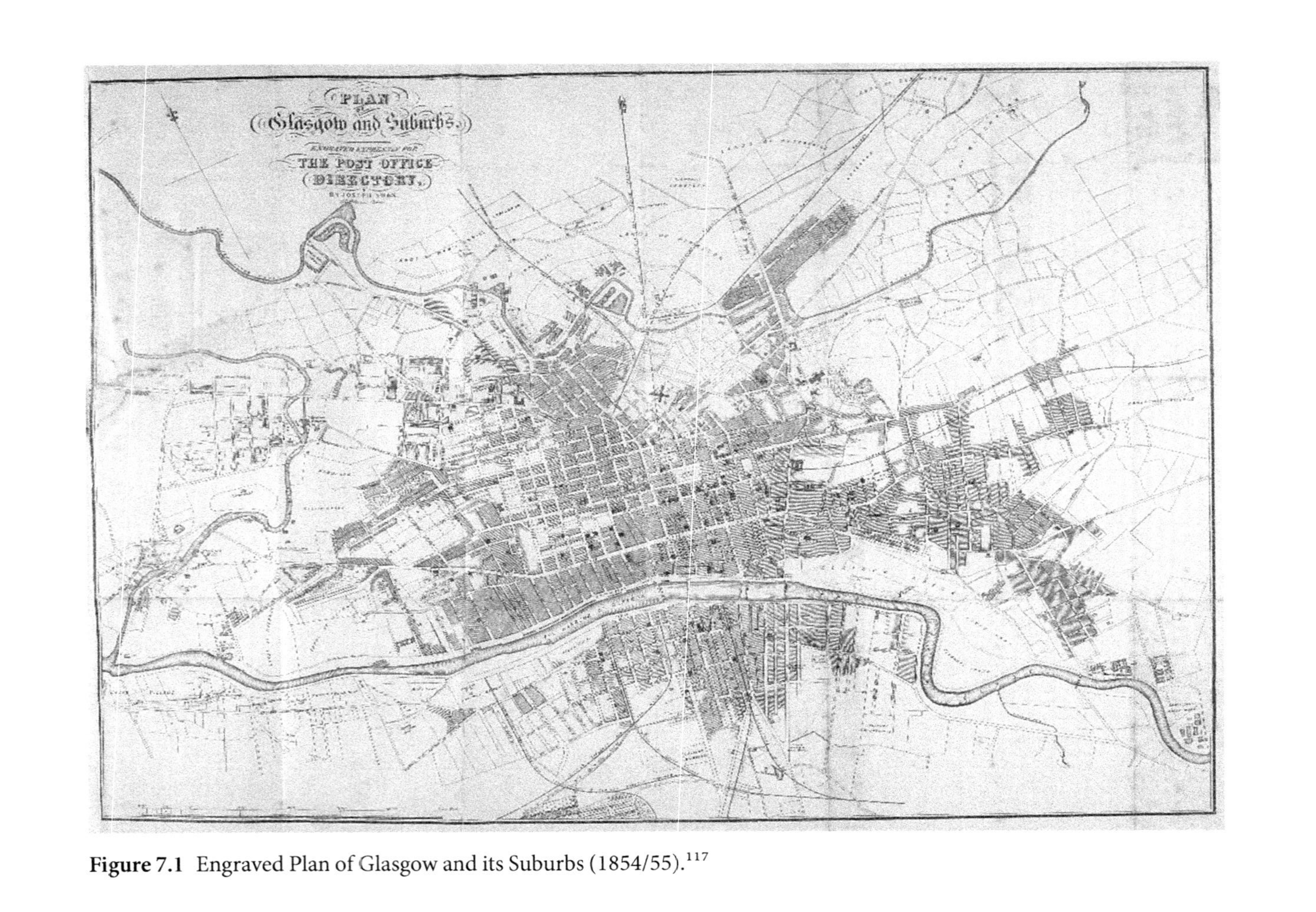


**Figure 7.1** Engraved Plan of Glasgow and its Suburbs (1854/55).[117]

'a neighbourhood for thieves and worse than thieves', and 'a place where honest poverty seldom troubled itself to seek refuge'.[118] It was reported that in the 1850s the average number or robberies per room of this densely populated quarter was twelve a week.[119]

One contemporary commentator vividly described the area, saying:

> From Croiley's Land stole forth at night the thieves and prostitutes who made night hideous—into Croiley's Land were decoyed the dupes and dragged the resisting, and dark work was done there after sun-down. All the crimes which shock humanity have had existence there...in that sin-haunted labyrinth. Robbery with violence still occurs too frequently in the New Vennel to call for any special remark: the most desperate of a desperate class are caught here, or in the adjacent closes...[120]

Evidently, Croiley's Land was a place set apart and this conclusion is reinforced by the testimony of the police officers in the trial against Hamilton, Young, Blackwood, and MacFarlane, who described it variously as an area 'peopled by a swarm of loose women and profligate men' which in terms of 'vice and squalid wretchedness was unequalled in Glasgow or elsewhere'.[121] The rapid response of the police at the site of Alexander Boyd's robbery and murder, alongside the effectiveness of their investigations in bringing about the arrests of the suspects involved, attested not only to the fact that the area was heavily policed at the time, but also to the fact that the authorities were relatively successful at containing the apparent 'contagion of criminality' within the confines of Croiley's Land.[122] Signposting this visible demonstration of the effectiveness of the new police went hand in hand with the articulation of renewed requests for the containment of the criminal classes to be maintained, and it was this leitmotif that lay at the heart of reactions to this case amongst contemporary commentators and newspaper reportage.

Victorians soon recognized that the individuals who resided within areas like Croiley's Land could not and should not be saved. That is why only scant attention is given to the individual protagonists involved in this case and why press reports say next to nothing of the actions, demeanours, and personal histories of the three women robbers involved. The ways in which these women so obviously deviated from accepted gender norms was rendered insignificant in this case. This was because, increasingly, the burgeoning middle classes came to believe that Croiley's Land residents (and their contemporaries elsewhere) had made an active choice to exist or subsist within that particular context. As such, they should no longer be considered as vulnerable individuals in need of establishment protection, state support, or popular sympathy.[123] Rather, they should be more routinely regarded as a pressing threat to 'civilized' society and ought to be kept in check and prevented from polluting other areas and other peoples with their crime, vice, immorality, and unnaturally aggressive tendencies.[124] The criminal underworld—regardless of the gender of its inhabitants—had to be segregated from the rest of society and confined to one place, in order to protect the majority of the population who were either 'respectable' citizens, or were individuals who had at least the potential for redemption and self-improvement. The conspicuous bravado of Helen Blackwood and Hans Smith MacFarlane over their residency of Croiley's Land, more than their criminal recidivism, more than their actions against Alexander Boyd, more than their gender, or the various lies they told to the authorities, may well have been the crucial factor which determined why *they* were the two individuals chosen for exemplary punishment rather than their erstwhile roommates. They had unwittingly made themselves the living embodiment of the irretrievable and unredeemable criminal underworld. Even within the seemingly dominant patriarchal structures of Victorian Britain it would seem that concerns regarding violent women who overtly betrayed the qualities of their sex could be readily superseded by contemporary fears over criminality more generally, or by the need to score political points over a given issue (such as the justification for the introduction of a new mechanism of social control). Clearly, gendered ideologies were not as dominant or as imperative as many nineteenth-century commentators would have had us believe.

## Conclusion

We have seen in this chapter how certain characteristics or traits came to be associated with women over the course of history. These behavioural norms seemingly rendered women less prone to criminality and effectively incapable of conduct that was violent or aggressive. Whilst acknowledging a few aberrant examples, historians have largely reinforced this perspective by arguing that, by the nineteenth century, the focus of judicial and state attention had turned to the curtailing of male villainy alone.[125] Female criminality was deemed to be so unnatural and so anomalous that it was not worth discussion and did not require efforts to curb its committal. In the case study in this chapter for instance, we do not find out why the women involved failed to conform to gendered notions of behaviour and we get very little insight into how the authorities or the public regarded them.

Yet what this chapter and others in this volume show is that, although there might have been more of a concentration on male criminality by the Victorian era as such offending was far more typical, there was also much more of a deliberate ploy to ignore female criminality than we may have first assumed. Not because contemporary society thought it unimportant or insignificant, but because neither the public nor the authorities could rationalize its existence or prevent its occurrence. Despite all of the best efforts of numerous scholars, scientists, social commentators, religious leaders, and state authorities, women *did* commit crime. They perpetrated it in public and in private on a relatively regular basis and they did so of their own volition. On occasion, women deployed violence against others too. They also did this out of choice and some even savoured their own aggressive and brutalizing tendencies. Victorian society had tried everything they could to control women's behaviour, to limit their spheres of interaction, and to reinforce the subordinate position of women in society. By the nineteenth century, however, they could see that their efforts had failed. Not only had they failed in relation to working-class women and their entry into the world of work as we have seen, but they had also failed in relation to women's criminality. More importantly perhaps, the Victorians could offer no further solutions to the problem of female offending, aside from pretending that it did not exist in the first place.

Female criminality became deliberately concealed by Victorians who could neither explain its presence nor curb its committal. Women's violence, and their offending more generally, came to be portrayed as something unfeminine or unwomanly, rather than as something deliberately felonious or nefarious.[126] Yet the same treatment was not afforded to male offending which was never described according to gendered norms or expectations. Evidently by the nineteenth century there was a dawning recognition that society was losing the ideological battle over women's subservience and compliance in a number of contexts.[127] The realm of female criminality was one such example.[128] As we saw in the reaction to the crimes of Helen Blackwood, Mary Hamilton, and Ann Young in 1853, by focusing on effective policing and the need to segregate the criminal classes from respectable society, nineteenth-century commentators conveniently avoided the need to explain the murderous actions of these women. Seemingly, it had become a pointless and thankless task to protect and redeem some individuals, particularly morally repugnant recidivists. The Victorians came to realize that they could only save those who were saveable. The rest were not worth the effort or worth speaking about.

## Notes

1. For further discussion see L. Zedner (1991) *Women, Crime and Custody in Victorian England* (Oxford: Clarendon Press), pp. 23–6; R. B. Shoemaker (1998) *Gender in English Society 1650–1850* (Harlow: Pearson), pp. 297–301; M. Wiener (2004) *Men of Blood: Violence, Manliness and Criminal Justice in Victorian England* (Cambridge: Cambridge University Press), p. 38; and M. J. Wiener (2001) 'Alice Arden to Bill Sikes: Changing Nightmares of Intimate Violence in England, 1558–1869', *Journal of British* Studies, 40, 2, pp. 184–212 at p. 195.
2. See for instance A.-M. Kilday (2007) *Women and Violent Crime in Enlightenment Scotland* (Woodbridge: Boydell & Brewer), pp. 19–20; A. Mangham (2007) *Violent Women and Sensation Fiction: Crime, Medicine and Victorian Popular Culture*

(Basingstoke: Palgrave MacMillan), pp. 9 and 15; Wiener, 'Alice Arden to Bill Sikes', p. 189; and A. Davies (1999) '"These Viragoes are No Less Cruel than the Lads": Young Women, Gangs and Violence in Late Victorian Manchester and Salford', *British Journal of Criminology*, 39, 1, pp. 72–89 at p. 76.

3. For further discussion see Kilday, *Women and Violent Crime*, pp. 20–1, and Wiener, 'Alice Arden to Bill Sikes', pp. 186–7.
4. See for instance Zedner, *Women, Crime and Custody*, p. 2, and Davies, 'These Viragoes', p. 79.
5. Shoemaker, *Gender in English Society*, pp. 16–17. See also A. Fletcher (1995) *Gender, Sex and Subordination in England 1500–1800* (New Haven: Yale University Press), p. xvii.
6. Shoemaker, *Gender in English Society*, p. 18.
7. For further discussion see ibid. See also Fletcher, *Gender, Sex and Subordination*, pp. xvi, 30–43, and 44–59, and A. Digby (1992) 'Victorian Values and Women in Public and Private', *Proceedings of the British Academy*, 78, pp. 195–215 at p. 195.
8. Shoemaker, *Gender in English Society*, pp. 18–19.
9. Ibid., p. 20.
10. Ibid. See also Fletcher, *Gender, Sex and Subordination*, pp. 30–43 and 44–59.
11. Shoemaker, *Gender in English Society*, pp. 21–2 and 36.
12. Ibid., pp. 23–8.
13. Ibid., p. 28. See also Fletcher, *Gender, Sex and Subordination*, pp. 60–2, 71, 73, and 204; Wiener, *Men of Blood*, pp. 29–30; and H. Barker and E. Chalus (1997) 'Introduction', in H. Barker and E. Chalus (eds), *Gender in Eighteenth-Century England: Roles, Representations and Responsibilities* (London: Longman), pp. 1–28 at pp. 1–2.
14. See for instance Shoemaker, *Gender in English Society*, p. 7; Fletcher, *Gender, Sex and Subordination*, p. 378; and S. K. Kent (2006) *Gender and Power in Britain, 1640–1990* (London: Routledge), pp. 68–9.
15. See for instance C. Chinn (1988) *They Worked All their Lives: Women of the Urban Poor in England, 1880–1939* (Manchester and New York: Manchester University Press), *passim* and esp. p. 86.
16. For further discussion in relation to the nineteenth-century context see Shoemaker, *Gender in English Society*, pp. 32–3; Zedner, *Women, Crime and Custody*, pp. 14–17; Digby, 'Victorian Values', p. 200; L. Davidoff and C. Hall (2002 edition) *Family Fortunes: Men and Women of the English Middle Class, 1780–1850* (London: Routledge); L. Davidoff and C. Hall (2007) 'Separate Spheres', in K. Boyd and R. McWilliam (eds), *The Victorian Studies Reader* (London: Routledge), pp. 307–17; C. Hall (1998) 'The Early Formation of Victorian Domestic Ideology', in R. Shoemaker and M. Vincent (eds), *Gender and History in Western Europe* (London: Arnold), pp. 182–96; C. Christ (1977) 'Victorian Masculinity and the Angel in the House', in M. Vicinus (ed.), *A Widening Sphere: Changing Roles of Victorian Women* (London: Methuen & Co.), pp. 146–62 at p. 149 and A. Vickery (1998) 'Golden Age to Separate Spheres? A Review of the Categories and Chronology of English Women's History', in R. Shoemaker and M. Vincent (eds), *Gender and History in Western Europe* (London: Arnold), pp. 197–225 at pp. 197 and 201. For evidence of middle-class women

rejecting the ideology of domesticity see E. Langland (1995) *Nobody's Angels: Middle-Class Women and Domestic Ideology in Victorian Culture* (Ithaca, NY, and London: Cornell University Press); and M. Vicinus (1977) 'Introduction: New Trends in the Study of Victorian Women', in M. Vicinus (ed.), *A Widening Sphere: Changing Roles of Victorian Women* (London: Methuen & Co.), pp. ix–xix at p. ix.

17. See Zedner, *Women, Crime and Custody*, pp. 11–12, and L. Davidoff (1995) *Worlds Between: Historical Perspectives on Gender and Class* (London: Polity Press), pp. 53–4 and 56.
18. For further discussion see C. Chinn (1995) *Poverty amidst Prosperity: The Urban Poor in England 1834–1914* (Manchester: Manchester University Press), *passim* and esp. pp. 60–2; E. Roberts (1988) *Women's Work 1840–1940* (Basingstoke: Macmillan Education); Digby, 'Victorian Values', pp. 196–8 and 201–4; Kent, *Gender and Power*, pp. 70–1; Vicinus, 'Introduction', pp. x, xv, and xix and J. Lewis (1984) *Women in England 1870–1950: Sexual Divisions and Social Change* (Brighton: Wheatsheaf Books), pp. x and 55–62.
19. For further discussion see for instance Vickery, 'Golden Age to Separate Spheres?', p. 220, and J. Walkowitz (1977) 'The Making of an Outcast Group: Prostitutes and Working Women in Nineteenth-Century Plymouth and Southampton', in M. Vicinus (ed.), *A Widening Sphere: Changing Roles of Victorian Women* (London: Methuen & Co.), pp. 72–93 at p. 74.
20. J. E. Conklin (1972) *Robbery and the Criminal Justice System* (Philadelphia: J. B. Lippincott Co.), p. 4. [Authors' addition in parentheses.] See also R. Sindall (1990) *Street Violence in the Nineteenth Century: Media Panic or Real Danger?* (Leicester: Leicester University Press), p. 9; and D. Philips (1977) *Crime and Authority in Victorian England: The Black Country 1835–1860* (London: Croom Helm), p. 246.
21. For further discussion see A.-M. Kilday (2019) *Crime in Scotland 1660–1960: The Violent North?* (Abingdon: Routledge), pp. 200–1.
22. For further discussion see Sindall, *Street Violence*, pp. 1 and 6; R. Sindall (1987) 'The London Garotting Panics of 1856 and 1862', *Social History*, 12, 3, pp. 351–9 and J. Davis (1980) 'The London Garotting Panic of 1862: A Moral Panic and the Creation of a Criminal Class in Mid-Victorian England', in V. A. C. Gatrell, B. Lenman, and G. Parker (eds), *Crime and the Law: The Social History of Crime in Western Europe since 1500* (London: Europa Publications), pp. 190–213.
23. For further discussion see Kilday, *Crime in Scotland*, p. 202. See also Baron D. Hume (1797) *Commentaries on the Laws of Scotland Respecting the Description and Punishment of Crimes—Volume I* (Edinburgh: Bell & Bradfute), pp. 139–46; and A. M. Anderson (1904 edition) *Criminal Law of Scotland* (Edinburgh: Bell & Bradfute), Part II, p. 183.
24. For more on the persistent nature of the serious regard for robbery amongst socio-political and judicial authorities in Britain see T. Duke (2014) *Rogues of the Road: Highwaymen and Highway Robbery in Eighteenth Century England* (Union Bay, BC: Duke Publications), p. 8; J. M. Beattie (1986) *Crime and the Courts in England 1660–1800* (Oxford: Princeton University Press), p. 148; F. McLynn (1991) *Crime and Punishment in Eighteenth-Century England* (Oxford: Oxford University Press), pp. 25–7 and 58;

Kilday, *Crime in Scotland*, p. 202; Sindall, *Street Violence*, pp. 146–7; and H. Croall (1998) *Crime and Society in Britain* (London and New York: Longman), p. 224.

25. See Kilday, *Crime in Scotland*, p. 202. For further discussion of the historically tough sanctions applied to robbery convicts in Scotland and elsewhere see G. Walker (2003) *Crime, Gender and Social Order in Early Modern England* (Cambridge: Cambridge University Press), p. 194; P. Newark (1979) *The Crimson Book of Highwaymen* (London: Juniper Books), pp. 35 and 40; Kilday, *Women and Violent Crime*, p. 133; Beattie, *Crime and the Courts*, p. 148; McLynn, *Crime and Punishment*, pp. 75 and 77; G. Morgan and P. Rushton (1998) *Rogues, Thieves and the Rule of Law* (London: Routledge), pp. 149–50; Philips, *Crime and Authority*, pp. 248 and 252; C. Emsley (2005 edition) *Crime and Society in England, 1750–1900* (Harlow: Longman), p. 260; and H. Shore (2010) 'Criminality, Deviance and the Underworld since 1750', in A-M. Kilday and D.S. Nash (eds), *Histories of Crime: Britain 1600–2000* (Basingstoke: Palgrave Macmillan), pp. 120–40 at p. 122.
26. For further discussion see Kilday, *Crime in Scotland*, pp. 203–8.
27. For further discussion see ibid., p. 209. See also A.-M. Kilday (2013) 'Hell-Raising and Hair-Razing: Violent Robbery in Nineteenth Century Scotland', *Scottish Historical Review*, 92, 235, pp. 255–74 at p. 261.
28. For further discussion of this kind of violent pickpocketing see Kilday, *Crime in Scotland*, pp. 211–12 and 215; Kilday, 'Hell-Raising', p. 262; Sindall, *Street Violence*, p. 6; Philips, *Crime and Authority*, p. 249; D. Brandon (2001) *Stand and Deliver: A History of Highway Robbery* (London: Sutton Publishing), p. 165; and R. S. Hopps (2017) 'Narratives of Crime and Disorder: Representations of Robbery and Burglary in the London Press, 1780–1830' (PhD thesis, The Open University), pp. 135, 147–50, and 155.
29. See Philips, *Crime and Authority*, p. 126, and Hopps, 'Narratives of Crime and Disorder', pp. 148–9.
30. See Kilday, *Crime in Scotland*, p. 213, and Sindall, *Street Violence*, p. 51.
31. See Kilday, *Crime in Scotland*, p. 212; Duke, *Rogues of the Road*, p. 110; Shore, 'Criminality, Deviance and the Underworld', p. 122; and M. Archibald (2014 edition) *Glasgow: The Real Mean City—True Crime and Punishment in the Second City of the Empire* (Edinburgh: Black and White Publishing), pp. 49–50.
32. For more on this see Kilday, *Crime in Scotland*, p. 211; Kilday, *Women and Violent Crime*, p. 138; Brandon, *Stand and Deliver*, p. 165; Kilday, 'Hell-Raising', p. 266; Philips, *Crime and Authority*, pp. 250–1; G. Spraggs (2001) *Outlaws and Highwaymen: The Cult of the Robber in England from the Middle Ages to the Nineteenth Century* (London: Pimlico), p. 89; and F. McDonald (2012) *Gentlemen Rogues and Wicked Ladies: A Guide to British Highwaymen and Highwaywomen* (Stroud: History Press), pp. 43–9.
33. See the trial papers from the High Court heard at Stirling on 1 September 1840 against John McKenzie and Ann Ure for robbery and aggravated assault—NRS, Justiciary Court, Process Papers, JC/1840/292D.
34. For further discussion of the commonplace of violence in robbery offences generally see Brandon, *Stand and Deliver*, pp. 23–4; Duke, *Rogues of the Road*, pp. 3 and 9–10; and R. Shoemaker (2006) 'The Street Robber and the Gentleman Highwayman: Changing Representations and Perceptions of Robbery in London 1600–1800',

*Cultural and Social History*, 3, 4, pp. 381–405 at p. 387. For the Scottish experience see Kilday, *Women and Violent Crime*, p. 138; Kilday, 'Hell-Raising', pp. 262 and 266; Archibald, *Glasgow*, p. 234; and Kilday, *Crime in Scotland*, p. 211.

35. See Kilday, *Women and Violent Crime*, p. 131; Kilday, 'Hell-Raising', p. 265; Kilday, *Crime in Scotland*, p. 212; M. Archibald (2012) *A Sink of Atrocity: Crime in Nineteenth Century Dundee* (Edinburgh: Black and White Publishing), p. 167; Archibald, *Glasgow*, pp. 234–5; and M. Archibald (2014) *Bloody Scotland: Crime in Nineteenth Century Scotland* (Edinburgh: Black and White Publishing), pp. 21–7 and 45.
36. For further discussion see Spraggs, *Outlaws and Highwaymen*, p. 94; Sindall, *Street Violence*, p. 100; Kilday, *Crime in Scotland*, p. 212; Hopps, 'Narratives of Crime and Disorder', p. 149; and R. M. Ward (2014) *Print Culture, Crime and Justice in Eighteenth-Century London* (London: Bloomsbury), p. 99.
37. For further discussion of historians' views on the subsidiary role women played in robbery see J. A. Sharpe (1999 edition) *Crime in Early Modern England 1550–1750* (Harlow: Longman), p. 109; E. Hobsbawm (2000) *Bandits* (London: Abacus), p. 147; Philips, *Crime and Authority*, p. 252; and Hopps, 'Narratives of Crime and Disorder', pp. 168–72. For evidence to dispute these conclusions in the Scottish context see Kilday, *Crime in Scotland*, pp. 204–8 and 210–11; Kilday, 'Hell-Raising', pp. 264–5; and Kilday, *Women and Violent Crime*, pp. 136–7.
38. See *The Times*, 15 June 1853, p. 8, and *The Ipswich Journal*, 18 June 1853.
39. For details of the previous convictions against Margaret Cunningham see National Records of Scotland (NRS), Justiciary Court, Process Papers, JC26/1853/525.
40. NRS, Justiciary Court, Process Papers, Indictment, JC26/1853/525/1. It is important to note that Margaret Cunningham was not mentioned in *any* of the testimony or evidence presented to the High Court as part of this trial. Perhaps she was a known associate of the accused individuals or had formerly resided at the address where the crime took place.
41. NRS, Justiciary Court, Precognition Papers, AD14/53/448/2, the Testimony of James Law. See also the account of the trial in *The Glasgow Herald*, 22 July 1853.
42. NRS, Justiciary Court, Precognition Papers, AD14/53/448/2, the Testimony of William Shillinglaw.
43. Ibid. See also the account of the trial in *The Times*, 23 July 1853, p. 8, as well as the testimony of a neighbour of the accused, who corroborated that the women had a particular ruse to rob clients of their money and possessions—NRS, Justiciary Court, Precognition Papers, AD14/53/448/2, the Testimony of Thomas Clymont.
44. See for instance H. Mayhew (1968 edition) *London Labour and the London Poor—Volume IV* (New York: Dover), pp. 359–60 and 364; L. Mahood (2013 edition) *The Magdalenes: Prostitution in the Nineteenth Century* (London: Routledge), p. 143; K. Chesney (1970) *The Victorian Underworld* (Trowbridge: Readers Union), pp. 333–4; and D. Palk (2003) 'Private Crime and Public and Private Places: Pickpockets and Shoplifters in London, 1780–1823' in T. Hitchcock and H. Shore (2003) (eds) *The Streets of London: From the Great Fire to the Great Stink* (London: Rivers Oram Press), pp. 135–50 at p. 145.
45. NRS, Justiciary Court, Precognition Papers, AD14/53/448/2, the Testimony of William Shillinglaw. See too the account of the crime in *The Times*, 15 June 1853, p. 8,

and also the corroboration of this evidence found in NRS, Justiciary Court, Precognition Papers, AD14/53/448/2, the Testimony of James Shillinglaw.

46. NRS, Justiciary Court, Precognition Papers, AD14/53/448/2, the Testimony of Mary Keelan. See too the account of the crime in *The Ipswich Journal*, 18 June 1853, and the evidence from the trial proceedings recounted in *The Bristol Mercury*, 30 July 1853.
47. NRS, Justiciary Court, Precognition Papers, AD14/53/448/2, the Testimonies of William Shillinglaw, Mary Keelan, and Jane Leitch.
48. Ibid., although neither Mary Keelan nor Jane Leitch could not determine which of the women had inflicted the blow to Alexander Boyd as their view was obstructed, whereas William Shillinglaw was clear on this point. See too the evidence from the trial proceedings recounted in *The Newcastle Courant*, 29 July 1853.
49. NRS, Justiciary Court, Precognition Papers, AD14/53/448/2, the Testimonies of William Shillinglaw, Mary Keelan, and Jane Leitch. See too the account of the crime in *The Bristol Mercury*, 18 June 1853, and also NRS, Justiciary Court, Precognition Papers, AD14/53/448/2, the Testimony of James Shillinglaw.
50. NRS, Justiciary Court, Precognition Papers, AD14/53/448/2, the Testimony of William Shillinglaw. See too the evidence from the trial proceedings recounted in *The Bristol Mercury*, 30 July 1853, and *The Lancaster Gazette*, 30 July 1853.
51. NRS, Justiciary Court, Precognition Papers, AD14/53/448/2, the Testimony of William Shillinglaw. See too the account of the crime in *The Preston Guardian*, 18 June 1853, and also NRS, Justiciary Court, Precognition Papers, AD14/53/448/2, the Testimonies of James Shillinglaw and Mary Keelan.
52. NRS, Justiciary Court, Precognition Papers, AD14/53/448/2, the Testimonies of William Shillinglaw and Jane Leitch. (Authors' addition in parentheses.) See too the evidence from the trial proceedings recounted in *Berrow's Worcester Journal*, 30 July 1853, p. 6.
53. NRS, Justiciary Court, Precognition Papers, AD14/53/448/2, the Testimonies of William Shillinglaw and Jane Leitch. Although as before Jane Leitch could not be sure which of the accused had thrown the victim out of the window. William Shillinglaw, on the other hand, was very definitive about the participants involved. See too the account of the crime in *The York Herald*, 18 June 1853.
54. NRS, Justiciary Court, Precognition Papers, AD14/53/448/2, the Testimonies of William Shillinglaw and Jane Leitch. (Authors' addition in parentheses after referral to (2017 edition) *Concise Scots Dictionary* (Edinburgh: Edinburgh University Press), pp. 660 and 705.) See also NRS, Justiciary Court, Precognition Papers, AD14/53/448/2, the Testimony of James Shillinglaw.
55. NRS, Justiciary Court, Precognition Papers, AD14/53/448/2, the Testimony of Thomas Clymont.
56. NRS, Justiciary Court, Precognition Papers, AD14/53/448/2, the Testimonies of neighbours Charles Scott and Hugh Gray.
57. NRS, Justiciary Court, Precognition Papers, AD14/53/448/2, the Testimonies of William Shillinglaw, James Shillinglaw, and Jane Leitch. See also the account of the trial proceedings and the evidence presented in *The Glasgow Herald*, 22 July 1853, and *The Times*, 23 July 1853, p. 8.
58. NRS, Justiciary Court, Precognition Papers, AD14/53/448/2, the Testimony of John McGinnis.

59. NRS, Justiciary Court, Precognition Papers, AD14/53/448/2, the Testimonies of Constable Robert Campbell and Constable David Henderson.
60. NRS, Justiciary Court, Precognition Papers, AD14/53/448/2, the Testimonies of Night Sergeant George Thomson and Constable John Smith.
61. NRS, Justiciary Court, Precognition Papers, AD14/53/448/2, the Testimony of Constable Darren Henderson. For corroborating evidence of the victim's recovered property see NRS, Justiciary Court, Precognition Papers, AD14/53/448/2, the Testimony of Detective Robert Mitchell. See too the evidence from the trial proceedings recounted in *The York Herald*, 30 July 1853, p. 5.
62. NRS, Justiciary Court, Precognition Papers, AD14/53/448/2, the Testimony of Constable Darren Henderson.
63. NRS, Justiciary Court, Precognition Papers, AD14/53/448/2, the Testimonies of Inspector Thomas Harding and Night Detective Officer Bernard McLachlan. See also the report of her capture featured in *The Newcastle Courant*, 17 June 1853, and *The Era*, 19 June 1853.
64. NRS, Justiciary Court, Process Papers, JC26/1853/525/4, the Declaration of Mary Hamilton.
65. Ibid.
66. Ibid.
67. Ibid.
68. NRS, Justiciary Court, Precognition Papers, AD14/53/448/2, the Testimony of Constable Duncan McInnes. For further corroboration that the accused women in particular were well known to the police see NRS, Justiciary Court, Precognition Papers, AD14/53/448/2, the Testimony of Assistant Superintendent of the Glasgow Police, George Mackay.
69. NRS, Justiciary Court, Precognition Papers, AD14/53/448/2, the Testimony of Constable Duncan McInnes. See also the report of their capture featured in *The Times*, 15 June 1853, p. 8, and *The Morning Post*, 17 June 1853, p. 7.
70. NRS, Justiciary Court, Precognition Papers, AD14/53/448/2, the Testimony of Constable Duncan McInnes. See also NRS, Justiciary Court, Process Papers, JC26/1853/525/2, the Declaration of Hans Smith MacFarlane.
71. NRS, Justiciary Court, Process Papers, JC26/1853/525/4, the Declaration of Helen Blackwood.
72. Ibid.
73. Ibid.
74. NRS, Justiciary Court, Precognition Papers, AD14/53/448/2, the Testimony of Constable Donald Carmichael.
75. Ibid.
76. NRS, Justiciary Court, Process Papers, JC26/1853/525/5, the Declaration of Ann Young.
77. Ibid.
78. Ibid.
79. NRS, Justiciary Court, Process Papers, JC26/1853/526/6, Post-Mortem Examination of Alexander Boyd, 13 June 1853.
80. Ibid.
81. Ibid.

82. Ibid.
83. Ibid.
84. NRS, Justiciary Court, Precognition Papers, AD14/53/448/2, the Testimonies of Dr John Alexander Easton, Medical Officer to the Glasgow Police, and Dr Robert McGregor, Physician to the Glasgow Royal Infirmary.
85. Ibid.
86. NRS, Justiciary Court, Process Papers, JC26/1853/526/6, Post-Mortem Examination of Alexander Boyd, 13 June 1853.
87. Ibid.
88. Ibid.
89. NRS, Justiciary Court, Precognition Papers, AD14/53/448/2, the Testimony of James Morris Gale, Assistant to William Gale, Civil Engineer and Surveyor in Glasgow.
90. NRS, Justiciary Court, Process Papers, JC26/1853/526/6, Post-Mortem Examination of Alexander Boyd, 13 June 1853.
91. Ibid.
92. Ibid.
93. See the report of the conclusion of the trial in *The Aberdeen Journal*, 27 July 1853, and *The Derby Mercury*, 27 July 1853.
94. See the report of the assize verdict in *The Ipswich Journal*, 30 July 1853.
95. See the report of the verdict in *Daily News*, 23 July 1853; *The Morning Chronicle*, 23 July 1853; *The Standard*, 23 July 1853; and *The Liverpool Mercury*, 26 July 1853.
96. See the details of the Lord Justice-General's sentencing oration in National Library of Scotland (NLS), (1853) *The Lamentations of McFarlane, Blackwood and Young* (Glasgow: n.p.), Special Collections, L.C. Fol. 73 (125) and also reported in *The Morning Post*, 25 July 1853, p. 3; *Freeman's Journal and Daily Commercial Advertiser*, 26 July 1853; and *Dundee Courtier*, 27 July 1853. *Freeman's Journal and Daily Commercial Advertiser*, 26 July 1853.
97. Zedner, *Women, Crime and Custody*, p. 11.
98. Ibid.
99. Ibid., pp. 2 and 11.
100. A suggestion made in *The Dundee Courier*, 27 July 1853.
101. NRS, Justiciary Court, Precognition Papers, AD14/53/448/2, the Testimony of James Law.
102. Historian Andrew Davies has suggested that female participants in English Victorian gangs were picked out and set upon by the press who described them using 'exotic language' to distinguish them as 'fallen' women—see Davies, 'These Viragoes', p. 88. This tactic was most certainly not deployed in this present Glaswegian example from 1853 and in similar gang-related cases from Scotland in the nineteenth-century period.
103. See respectively *The Dundee Courier*, 15 June 1853; NLS (1853) *The Lamentations of McFarlane, Blackwood and Young*; *The Times*, 15 June 1853, p. 8; *Daily News*, 23 July 1853; and *The Liverpool Mercury*, 26 July 1853.
104. See for instance Chinn, *They Worked All their Lives*, pp. 160–3.
105. See the remission dated 30 August 1853 and found in NRS, Justiciary Court, High Court Minute Books—Series E, JC8/61, 88v. See also *Daily News*, 8 August 1853;

*The Morning Post*, 8 August 1853, p. 3; *The Dundee Courier*, 10 August 1853; and *The Glasgow Herald*, 12 August 1853. Historian David Leslie suggests that the decision to grant Ann Young remission 'caused outrage and considerable comment in a number of the newspapers'—see D. Leslie (2017) *Launched into Eternity: Crime and Punishment, Hitmen and Hangmen* (Edinburgh: Black and White Publishing), p. 76. The authors of this present volume wholly disagree with this contention as our research shows that the decision was barely reported in the press and little comment was made thereon.

106. For further discussion see Shoemaker, *Gender in English Society*, p. 297, and Wiener, 'Alice Arden to Bill Sikes', p. 187.
107. For evidence of the decline in female executions see J. Kellie (2018) *Hanged Until Dead: Men and Women Hanged in Nineteenth-century Scotland* (Cumnock: Carn Publishing); Kilday, *Crime in Scotland, passim*; and Wiener, 'Alice Arden to Bill Sikes', p. 198.
108. For further discussion see A.-M. Kilday (2016) 'Constructing the Cult of the Criminal: Kate Webster—Victorian Murderess and Media Sensation', in A.-M. Kilday and D. S. Nash (eds), *Law, Crime and Deviance since 1700: Micro-Studies in the History of Crime* (London: Bloomsbury), pp. 125–48; and J. Flanders (2011) *The Invention of Murder: How the Victorians Revelled in Death and Detection and Created Modern Crime* (London: Harper Press).
109. The lack of fuss over the double execution is evident from the limited and matter-of-fact newspaper reporting prior to and after the event, see for instance *The Bristol Mercury*, 30 July 1853; *Daily News*, 12 August 1853; *The Morning Chronicle*, 13 August 1853; *The Hampshire Telegraph and Sussex* Chronicle, 13 August 1853; *The Era*, 14 August 1853; *The Aberdeen* Journal, 17 August 1853; *The Dundee Courier*, 17 August 1853; *The Manchester Times*, 17 August 1853; and *Reynolds' Newspaper*, 21 August 1853. Only three broadsides were produced on the case and none of them contain the usual sensational reporting and sentiment typically directed towards the accused—see NLS (1853) *Lament of MacFarlane, Blackwood and Young I*, Special Collections, L.C. Fol. 73 (124); NLS (1853) *Lament of MacFarlane, Blackwood and Young II*, Special Collections, L.C. Fol. 73 (124); and NLS (1853) *Widow MacFarlane's Lamentation For Her Son*, Special Collections, L.C. Fol. 178 A.2. (096).
110. See the dead warrant confirming the executions were carried out—NRS, Justiciary Court, Process Papers, JC26/1853/525. For further discussion of MacFarlane's rather farcical ill-timed proposal see T. M. Tod (1938) *The- Scots Black Kalendar: A Record of Criminal Trials and Executions in Scotland 1800–1910* (Perth: Munro & Scott Ltd), p. 62; *The Bury and Norwich Post and Suffolk Herald*, 17 August 1853, p. 1; *The Bradford Observer*, 18 August 1853, p. 3; *The Preston Guardian*, 20 August 1853; *Jackson's Oxford Journal*, 20 August 1853; D. Skelton (2003) *Deadlier than the Male: Scotland's Most Wicked Women* (Edinburgh: Black and White Publishing), pp. 144–5; and D. Skelton (2009) *Glasgow's Black Heart: A City's Life of Crime* (Edinburgh and London: Mainstream Publishing), pp. 45–6.
111. See *The Glasgow Herald*, 12 August 1853; *The Bury and Norwich Post and Suffolk Herald*, 17 August 1853, p. 1 and *Jackson's Oxford Journal*, 20 August 1853. For some background reporting provided in relation to the victim in this case see *The Era*, 19 June 1853.

112. See for instance *The Glasgow Herald*, 22 July 1853.
113. For further discussion of Victorian campaigns to segregate the perceived 'criminal classes' from the rest of society (with particular reference to prostitution) see Zedner, *Women, Crime and Custody*, p. 77, and Mahood, *The Magdalenes*, pp. 142 and 144.
114. Anon. (1864) *Memoirs of Jane Cameron, Female Convict, By a Prison Matron* (London: Hurst & Blackett Publishers), p. 11. (This work is believed to have been written by Frederick William Robinson (1830–1901).) This work was retrieved from <https://archive.org/details/memoirsjanecame01robigoog/page/n9> on 22 April 2019.
115. See *The Glasgow Herald*, 12 August 1853 and Anon., *Memoirs of Jane Cameron*, p. 10.
116. Anon., *Memoirs of Jane Cameron.*, p. 13. See also *The Dundee Courier*, 15 June 1863.
117. NLS, Joseph Swan (1854/1855) *Plan of Glasgow and Suburbs: Engraved Expressly for the Post Office Directory*, Map Collection, Reference ID 117744183.
118. Anon., *Memoirs of Jane Cameron.*, pp. 11 and 13.
119. Ibid., p. 12.
120. Ibid., pp. 11–12.
121. See respectively NRS, Justiciary Court, Precognition Records, AD14/53/448/2 the Testimonies of Constable Robert Campbell, Constable Darren Henderson, and Assistant Superintendent George Mackay all of the Glasgow Police.
122. For newspaper reports which strongly praised the effectiveness of the police involved in the case see *The Morning Post*, 17 June 1853, p. 7, and *The Newcastle Courant*, 17 June 1853.
123. For further discussion of this transition in attitudes see Mayhew, *London Labour and the London Poor—Volume IV*, pp. 358–61 and 364; Chesney, *The Victorian Underworld*, pp. 333–4; Palk, 'Private Crime', pp. 137–9 and 141–2; and Walkowitz, 'The Making of an Outcast Group', p. 76.
124. For further discussion in the Scottish context see J. Miller (1859) *Prostitution Considered in Relation to its Cause and Cure* (Edinburgh: Sutherland & Knox). This work was retrieved from <https://archive.org/details/prostitutioncons00milluoft/page/n2> on 22 April 2019. See also Mahood, *The Magdalenes*, pp. 64, 120–1, and 123; Chinn, *They Worked All their Lives*, p. 164; Hopps, 'Narratives of Crime and Disorder', p. 178; and Davidoff, *Worlds Between*, p. 55.
125. See for instance Wiener, 'Alice Arden to Bill Sikes', p. 211, and Shoemaker, *Gender in English Society*, pp. 302–4.
126. See for further discussion Zedner, *Women, Crime and Custody*, p. 29.
127. See for instance Chinn, *They Worked All their Lives*, pp. 84 and 164–5; Chinn, *Poverty amidst Prosperity*, *passim*; E. Roberts (1984) *A Woman's Place: An Oral History of Working Class Women 1890–1914* (Oxford and New York: John Wiley); E. Ross (1982) 'Fierce Questions and Taunts: Married Life in Working-Class London, 1870–1915', *Feminist Studies*, 8, 3, pp. 575–602; and L. Jamieson (1986) 'Limited Resources and Limiting Conventions: Working-Class Mothers and Daughters in Urban Scotland c. 1890–1925', in J. Lewis (ed.) *Labour and Love: Women's Experience of Home and Family 1850–1940* (Oxford: Basil Blackwell), pp. 55–62.
128. For a very brief acknowledgement of this see Davidoff, *Worlds Between*, p. 9, and Chinn, *They Worked All their Lives*, pp. 160–3.

# 8

# 'When a Man Cries, it is called Crying; when a Woman Cries it is called Hysterics'

## Lady Harriett Mordaunt—Mad or Bad? Gendering the Behaviour of a 'Wayward' Aristocratic Wife

### Introduction

This book has been concerned with the categorization of women's behaviour by nineteenth-century and modern commentators—the latter as contemporary historians of behaviour within the period. It has consistently argued that these categories have been needlessly rigid, and have too readily created accepted stereotypes of such behaviour. Their ubiquity means that they are too easily reached for as tools of analysis and understanding of female behaviour in the period. This book, through an array of wide-ranging examples, has observed how frequently this happened in the period 1800–1900. Through its engagement with historiography, it has also demonstrated how stubbornly persistent this view remains amongst those historians who analyse the deviant behaviour of women in past societies. In previous chapters we have seen how decisions about and views of deviant women sought to label them ostensibly as forms of 'bad' or forms of 'mad'. Where 'mad' or 'bad' were inconvenient or uncomfortable labels due to other factors, or they proved unsuccessful in disciplining such women, these polar categories would enter a state of suspension. This third indeterminate limbo state would either hope such actions would be ignored, or that their perpetrator would experience some form of comeuppance that would subsequently overwhelm or even serve to re-engender the woman concerned, reminding her of the expectations surrounding the so-called 'fairer sex'.

This final chapter places the socially constructed dichotomy of 'mad' versus 'bad' centre stage and constitutes the behavioural 'norm' and 'expectation' investigated here. Some of the women investigated earlier in this book were deemed to have stepped outside the boundaries of acceptable behaviour for the female sex at this time. Such behaviour could very obviously also be further constrained by expectations around the class of such women, often with class and gender expectations intersecting with one another. In this final chapter, we see similar constraints placed upon an aristocratic female protagonist, an individual considerably higher up the social scale than those considered earlier. Expectations of

*Beyond Deviant Damsels: Re-evaluating Female Criminality in the Nineteenth Century.* Anne-Marie Kilday and David Nash, Oxford University Press. © Anne-Marie Kilday and David Nash 2023. DOI: 10.1093/oso/9780198830733.003.0008

'correct' regulated behaviour followed such women from the cradle to the grave as they, by turns, accommodated the behavioural expectations of parents, siblings, friends, spouses, and even servants.[1]

Nonconforming behaviour amongst this class existed in a clandestine manner, very self-consciously hidden from view. This ensured it would not attract attention, comment, or judgement. The key to this obverse world is that it did not disturb the social and cultural system established by this elevated class. We may wonder precisely how this clandestine subculture flourished, but at this point it is important to remember the spaciousness of aristocratic houses and grounds. When we add to this the ingrained habits of visiting and staying with compatriots from one's own social circle, and trips to the capital with nights staying in numerous hotels, the opportunities to misbehave privately emerge in earnest. One disadvantage that aristocratic women (and to a far lesser extent men) had to contend with was the presence of servants.[2] As we shall see, this element was to prove severely detrimental to the welfare of this chapter's protagonist. Those who observed this individual's lifestyle, or were intimately involved in her story, inevitably reacted to what they saw. What is important here is that all forms of judgement upon her behaviour utilized the narratives of 'bad' or 'mad', placing all aspects of her behaviour and its manifestations into one of these categories. As such, these archetypal reactions served to ignore aspects of her own character, autonomy, agency, and choices—all aspects that are so rarely mentioned or discussed in relation to the men in her story.

As a concluding chapter in this book, it is a fitting illustration of the pervasive nature of the 'bad' versus 'mad' dichotomous narrative. Moreover, it demonstrates its operation at the highest social levels and thus constitutes the final piece of the socially heterogeneous jigsaw this volume seeks to complete. By investigating behaviour much higher up the social scale, the chapter seeks to see the 'bad'/'mad' dichotomy at work amongst a stratum of women who are often seen as having even less autonomy than those at the bottom of the social scale. What also emerges is the sustained nature and surprising prevalence of these dichotomous narratives in the judgement of twentieth- and twenty-first-century commentators upon the life and choices of Harriet Mordaunt. In their collective failure to move beyond these two categories, they have collectively damaged the history of women's behaviour.

The case is important, since after her infidelity was exposed contemporaries were unsure whether Harriett Mordaunt eventually became insane or in fact may have feigned this.[3] Was a diagnosis of 'puerperal insanity' one that could be sustained? Or were there two psychological conditions at work, at different times? Was she simply 'bad' rather than 'mad' and was she made to pay the 'price' for her poor behaviour or lifestyle choices in an age of prudery? Or did Lady Mordaunt make 'use' of the concept of insanity to protect herself as best she could, leaving her husband with an ongoing dilemma that would last several years? Beyond this, how far did the respective 'mad' and 'bad' labels themselves unwittingly operate as a cloak to hide opportunities for female choice and agency. Historians have taken mixed views on this whole affair and its significance. Consequently, the chapter investigates these different views of the agency of aristocratic women and maps these onto the 'archaeology of reputation' of Harriett Mordaunt.[4] Each subsequent generation formed its own judgement about her actions and her representativeness as an icon of the 'wronged woman' and the likelihood that she was the victim of a conspiracy to remove an inconvenience.

In effect, this chapter makes us think more deeply about the agency and autonomy of aristocratic women. This emerges as the case is analysed by those who saw it through the sensibilities and issues of their own age around such things as fashion, the changing perceptions of women's legitimate desires and appetites, and the appropriateness of their interactions with men of their own class.[5] It also, finally, asks questions about the emergence and exercise of a public sphere in which a much wider 'archaeology of reputation' consciously scrutinized and scrutinizes the conduct of women, sometimes perhaps uncomfortably, using some of the same tools and assumptions displayed by the very first generation of commentators.

## Creating the 'Mad' and the 'Bad'

The nineteenth century was the period where the science of women's medicine was rapidly developing to create new specialisms, but notably the science of gynaecology.[6] These new specialists, the gynaecologists, used two models of analysis to explain the function of the female nervous system. One of these was termed 'economic' which saw the body as a finite system which had to conserve energy so one organ did not suffer depletion at the expense of another. This saw ailments as functions of, respectively, overload and starvation. The other was a 'reflex' theory where higher and lower functions were controlled differently in men and women, with the latter having an imbalance of physical over mental. This sometimes struggled to consider women's psychological ailments as having anything but physiological causes. By the end of the century, medical practitioners advocated the employment of gynaecologists in lunatic asylums with a brief to conduct more examinations, seeking to diagnose women's mental disorders.[7]

This new science and basket of explanations linked woman's behaviour to sexual and reproductive functionality which differentiated her from the male. As historian Ornella Moscucci puts it 'women's sexual physiology and pathology affected their behaviour, and thus had social and moral consequences which had no parallel in the pathology of the male'.[8] This apparent custody of reproduction was turned by such scientific explanations to determinedly wholesome and moral ends, since it was considered to shape women solely to desire men for procreation within marriage and it was 'mutual sexual attraction which bound man and wife into an exclusive society of interests and affections'.[9] Such ideas were further reinforced by aesthetic descriptions of the female body, highlighting woman's 'charms' as signifying 'life-giving capacities', which also meant 'menopausal ovariotomised women, whose sexual functions were in abeyance... becoming... the least beautiful and also the least moral of all'.[10]

Giving birth supposedly awakened women's lasting moral trajectory even further so that they would instinctively become a 'benign and humanising influence over the offspring'.[11] Those whose expertise investigated the sexual development of the female body were also at this time pursuing the definition of what was a 'normal' pattern of sexual development and behaviour. This also occurred alongside attempts to advocate self-control, which Victoria Bates argues was 'increasingly valorised'.[12] This virtue appeared especially important alongside the growing study of the apparently 'precocious girl'.[13] The development of this science of women's physiology and the investigation of physiological sexual developments was contemporary with Harriet Mordaunt's story. This meant there was a considerable range of ideas that could be shaped to explain episodes in what follows.

It also seems to be the case that, whilst the duties facing mid/late nineteenth-century aristocratic women seemed relatively straightforward and obvious, this was scarcely the case around the issue of individual freedom. This concept may even have been alien to many aristocratic women, but perhaps importantly, it was ambiguous and ambivalent for many others.[14] The image of such women as birds in a gilded cage, which prevailed in the first half of the twentieth century, has long been successfully qualified.[15] Investigation of a number of women's lives and a number of estate papers has also demonstrated that inclination or circumstance could create very active roles for aristocratic women. As the wives and daughters of substantial landowners, they were often able to maintain links with the local community, operating forms of patronage and philanthropy. This was not independence as such, but it was part of an accepted 'feminine domain'.[16]

Although this points to aristocratic women having some agency within their lives, this was within an ideal of the aristocratic family. A cornerstone of this institution was the emotional and sexual propriety of its female members. Wives and daughters were expected to be pillars of virtue, maintaining a status as moral exemplars for those in the local communities they were a part of. This regulated behavioural system safeguarded the Victorian aristocratic family from scandal, but more importantly, it protected this same family from thorny issues surrounding legitimacy and inheritance.[17] Many have noted that the maintenance of lineage and landed estates was not surprisingly a significant preoccupation of many aristocratic families.[18] Thus the role of the aristocratic woman specifically within this institution was to nurture the next generation for their role in society and perhaps in government, all the while maintaining the integrity of family lineage and legitimate ownership of its assets. To do so, they had to absorb years of 'training, practice and control' in which a culture of selflessness would flourish.[19] Harriett, almost consciously or instinctively (depending on interpretation), distanced herself from the stereotypes listed above. Such decisions ensured she would be judged by the categories of 'mad' or 'bad'.

## Harriett Mordaunt—Negotiating the World of Men

Harriett Mordaunt, the daughter of an aristocratic Scottish family (the Moncrieffs), was brought up with the expectations of a woman of this background. She avidly took part in the social side of aristocratic society and eventually attracted the attention of Sir Charles Mordaunt, a man sixteen years older than her.[20] When marriage was proposed, Harriett immediately bargained with her prospective husband. She made it plain that she had no intention of merely becoming the household steward, overseer of her husband's estates, local philanthropist, or indeed leisured bird in a gilded cage.

Harriett refused to go forward with the marriage unless she received assurances that her way of life would not substantially alter.[21] Sir Charles was made to agree that Harriett could have as many visitors as she wished, thereby maintaining the giddy social life she enjoyed.[22] This bargain might have masqueraded as the wish of every eligible young aristocratic woman forced to bite the bullet and marry the older man with the resources previously described, but obviously without the necessary attractions she had lived for.[23] But Harriett wanted more. She extracted from her husband-to-be a promise that he would never be jealous of her talking to other men, or even dancing with them if it was appropriate.[24] This bargain was driven particularly hard, by Harriett declaring she would not marry Sir Charles if he was unwilling to accept these provisions.[25] Sir Charles Mordaunt appears to have been 'infatuated' with Harriett and readily agreed to this very important proviso. Standing back from this abortive, verbal 'pre-nuptial agreement' made over 150 years ago, it is difficult to uncover what the two parties might have felt about this.[26] Certainly to modern analysts, it was an utterly important moment in the story.

To Sir Charles Mordaunt, this conceivably signalled that both he and his future wife were defining the separate worlds that would govern their lives and the smooth running of their marriage and estate. After all, this potential bargain might well have attracted Sir Charles. Elsewhere in orthodox accounts of the affair, he is portrayed as fond of shooting, riding, and fishing, with an instinct to frequent sportingly inclined male company.[27] To Sir Charles this probably looked like an amiable and equitable arrangement which did not, at least on the surface, appear to spell out anything obviously untoward.

It is possible to speculate just how many ancestors of such 'pre-nuptial agreements' the British aristocracy might have made. This was certainly not the ideal companionate marriage envisaged and invoked by writers like Coventry Patmore, nor the choreographed courtship envisaged by epistolary conduct literature.[28] For some, who found themselves perhaps otherwise ill-matched by overenthusiastic families, this might have been a welcome consolation. It would also allow privacy and amiable part-separation rather than unhappiness and potentially broken lives. For the aristocracy, such damage had an impact upon their immediate economic assets and the nature of inheritance. How many convenient arrangements of this nature did such couples decide to enter into in the late nineteenth-century heyday of the British gentry? We may never know, since if such arrangements did exist, almost all of these must have remained secret for the duration of the marriage. Indeed this whole equation might be reformulated when we consider that the arrangement between Sir Charles and Harriett Mordaunt only surfaced because it went spectacularly wrong.

Many married couples must have felt outflanked by two powerful families using their power and influence in the bruising arena of social climbing and dynasty consolidation. Of course, both parties in such an agreement were conceivably taking a gamble in presuming they fully understood the other party's requirements and promises. Joan Perkin has noted that such understandings did exist where personal lives became segregated and both parties were free to indulge in extra-marital sexual behaviour. However, this was supposedly not intended to happen until the marriage had produced children. Perkin argues, 'when the nursery was well stocked, a husband was likely to turn a blind eye to his wife's amours, so that he could look at other men's wives'.[29] All of this was permitted under the crucial watchword of discretion and, as we will discover, Harriett, her husband, and the Prince of Wales all broke these particular rules.

Harriett Mordaunt's thoughts about this bargaining episode might well have been another matter. Her desire to sustain friendships, lively company, and her former social life might be understandable, but there is more to ponder here. Harriett's own pleasure-seeking and desires make the historian contrast these with what we know about the mainstream experiences of aristocratic Victorian women. Harriett Mordaunt's departure from conceptions of duty, philanthropy, or leisured dissipation mark her out as a young woman flouting the rules of her social situation to defy previous convention. As such, Harriet's divergence from the norms of her gender and social position takes on a different texture from the other examples outlined in this volume. Harriett did not flee from her predetermined life path or narrative to take on a wholly new and uncharted route away from the expectations of her gender and social class. After all, what she wanted was to actually maintain her previous lifestyle to avoid the monogamy of a marriage OR a single sustained extra-marital affair. Whilst there is no doubt that Harriett refused to accept a new life which clearly did not enthral her, we have no way of knowing just how far she envisaged taking this.

In the weeks leading up to the marriage, Harriett tested out their agreement by seeking to be relatively intimate in public with a number of men. Although her leading historian Elizabeth Hamilton notes that Harriett made conciliatory noises, a number of third parties made their own judgement about her behaviour and warned Sir Charles accordingly.[30] Nevertheless, soon after the marriage, Harriett was caught in an intimate embrace with a male confidant by one of the estate's gardeners.[31] Around the same time, she was noted to have thrown herself into the arms of her brother-in-law in an inappropriate fashion.[32] Harriett was also selective in showing Sir Charles the letters that she received from gentlemen within her circle. This was both deceitful and seeking to preserve the fundamental nature of her agreement with Sir Charles.[33] Meanwhile Harriett soon renewed her close relationship with the Prince of Wales. She tried to engineer a trip to Paris with her husband to coincide with the visit of the Prince. Their meeting did not occur, but the Prince contented himself with asking her to procure a lady's umbrella, which was widely seen as a symbol of male incompetence in the bedroom. This was a slight clearly aimed at Sir Charles, since Harriett had been unable to conceive a child by this point.[34]

As Harriett threw herself into the giddy social whirl, she began to accumulate adverse internal reactions from, and debts she owed to, servants for their service above and beyond the call of duty—a consequence of her activities which she would pay dearly for. One of these recorded the first instance of the Prince of Wales calling on Lady Mordaunt at the family's London address in Chesham Street. During this time Harriett also visited other friends in London where the Prince was also almost certainly present.[35]

The effects of the company she kept was rubbing off on Harriett and Sir Charles Mordaunt was shocked by her behaviour, her impolite language, and the indelicate subjects she sometimes spoke of.[36] We might here speculate how far this might have been viewed as a temporary or small breach of the 'separate lives' agreement that they had only recently concluded, or whether this was regarded as something more substantive. Harriet could here have been indulging her freedom only to be labelled as 'bad' when she broke the sense of decorum championed by certain observers. In any case, the frivolity continued, when she was over-familiar with male guests invited to stay at Walton Hall, the Mordaunt family home in Warwickshire. The first of these was a Moncrieff family friend, Captain Arthur Farquhar, who was considered acceptable by Sir Charles, since he seemingly had the approval of his wife's family.[37] Servants again reported a number of incidents that suggested a considerable degree of intimacy between Arthur and Harriet. This took on an even darker complexion when servants unexpectedly met him when Harriett stayed at a London hotel, ostensibly on a shopping trip. The following day, her servant Jesse Clark was unable to resist reading a letter that Harriett had carelessly left lying around. This indicated that Farquhar had registered in the hotel under the assumed name of 'Farmer', a ruse to avoid Sir Charles Mordaunt reading his real name in the hotel register which would appear in the newspapers. It later emerged in a letter that this assignation had been prearranged between Harriett and Arthur.[38]

Harriett attracted the renewed attention of the Prince of Wales who took the opportunity of Harriett's brief bout of ill health to renew correspondence with her.[39] On a later summer season sojourn in London, the servants noticed the Prince of Wales visiting Harriett regularly when Sir Charles was unavailable.[40] This compromising situation was compounded by Harriet's instruction to admit nobody to the drawing room whilst the Prince was visiting. By now, Sir Charles Mordaunt knew about the Prince's visits and he warned his wife about his tarnished reputation.[41] What must have bothered Sir Charles still more was that Harriett would simply not heed his warnings and, eventually, this was brought home to him in spectacular fashion. He arrived home early one day suffering from a headache and went upstairs to lie down. A servant rose him to inform him that the Prince of Wales had arrived and was in the drawing room. Upon coming downstairs the Prince made a hasty undignified exit. This particular notorious episode was even cited by the republican newspaper the *National Reformer* as indicative of the malevolent monarchy invading the property of its citizens to sully their women folk.[42] Harriett calmed Sir Charles and, amazingly, successfully reassured him that all had been proper and above board. However, this had alerted Harriett to her need to be more circumspect in her activities and more careful in managing her communications alongside the risks involved in what contemporaries would have labelled as her own 'bad' behaviour. This was important since she had now come to realize and indeed experience, the ambivalence of servant behaviour and duty.[43]

Despite these warning signs, Sir Charles Mordaunt still maintained considerable periods of absence from Harriett for some time to come.[44] Perhaps she even saw this as an incentive for her behaviour, or a form of quiet assent to her independent actions. However, this came to an abrupt and explosive end. Sir Charles arrived home unexpectedly from an extended fishing trip in Norway to discover his wife driving a pony carriage pulled by two white ponies gifted to Harriett from the stables of the Prince of Wales. Watching approvingly from the front entrance to Walton Hall was the figure of the Prince of Wales himself. Something snapped inside Sir Charles Mordaunt who confronted the Prince, forcing the latter to again make a hasty retreat. Sir Charles was seemingly provoked into a considerably vindictive act. After the Prince had departed he asked a groom to bring the two ponies into the view of Harriett who was in the conservatory at the time. Sir Charles then ensured that both animals were summarily shot within the full view of his wife and the carriage burned.[45] This episode was evidently a shock to Harriett's system, since she set about trying to reconcile herself with her husband who considered that he had in fact been neglecting her, as he then began to contemplate withdrawing from political life.[46] This might suggest Harriett's persuasive nature in certain contexts.

Certainly this period was happier than most for Sir Charles and Harriett as they seemed to almost relaunch their marriage, with the exciting news that Harriett was at last pregnant.[47] Sir Charles obviously presumed that Harriet's condition would restrict her activities but, ironically, whilst feeling sorry for her enduring unexpected quietness, he allowed two long-time admirers (Captain Farquhar and Sir Frederic Johnstone) to visit her for long periods, much to the dismay of Sir Charles' now vigilant brothers who had long observed Harriet's activities.[48] Harriett was particularly infatuated with Johnstone and she went as far as to ask her husband why such a handsome and titled man had remained unmarried for so long. Sir Charles replied that Sir Frederic suffered from an ailment that meant marriage would have been hazardous for him and his future wife. This revelation was to have a monumental impact upon Harriett and her future.[49]

Harriett began to show signs of nervousness about her condition and immanent confinement and soon began to evidence an enhanced piety, keenly partaking of the sacrament on a regular basis.[50] This is the first sign that Harriett had lost control of her behaviour and its consequences, and was arguably the date from which contemporaries began to judge her 'mad' rather than 'bad'. When Harriett Mordaunt's baby eventually arrived, the midwife was taken aback when Harriett initially asked if the child was diseased, referring specifically to symptoms of congenital syphilis.[51] Sir Charles had persuaded himself that his new daughter, christened Violet, had been born very prematurely. However, the midwife informed Harriett that the child had been born at eight months, since it had fingernails.[52] Harriett had counted on explaining this to be a seven-month-old baby, since the distinction was utterly crucial for her continued peace of mind, for a growing number of unfortunate reasons. A short period of time after Violet's birth, Harriett evidently spent a lot of time with the midwife.[53] Later, this woman, Mrs Hancox, expressed surprise at Harriett's extensive knowledge about the nature of venereal disease and how it might manifest itself in the new-born.[54] This detail itself offers an intriguing possibility. Was this the product of Harriet's tea table discussions with her female contemporaries? If these did occur, had they revealed that other aristocratic women had reaped the unfortunate fruits of their extra-marital dalliance with diseased men? Alternatively, did this display the horror and depth of the worst possible outcomes of the gender double standard? Was this a window onto a world where a significant number of aristocratic men had, almost routinely, brought the evils of congenital venereal disease back to their households and their wives, with Harriett potentially shouldering a double burden of blame as adulteress and vector?

Soon after the birth, Violet developed an eye condition which was quickly diagnosed as opthalmia, but this detail was kept from Harriett in case she became agitated by the news.[55] Unsurprisingly, when Harriett discovered this, she reflected upon the stereotype that would have labelled her behaviour as 'bad', yet she also encouraged this by seeking to hide her actions.[56] She became fraught and involved her maidservant Jesse Clarke in creating a narrative about precisely who the baby resembled, pouring out her fears that Violet would go blind.[57] Some of Harriett's feelings would regularly become expressed as fears about her own imminent mortality.[58] This alternated with frivolous discussion of Violet as 'a silly little thing' that she had given up nursing.[59] These mood swings were unwittingly sowing the seeds of how the ensuing drama's whole cast would view Harriett Mordaunt's behaviour through a 'mad' versus 'bad' dichotomy. A desire for silence on the matter did not last and, the next day, Harriett urgently asked to see Sir Charles.[60] Upon entering the room, Harriett told Sir Charles that he was not the father of her child. Harriett revealed that Lord Cole was the father of the child and that she had also committed adultery with Sir Frederic Johnstone and the Prince of Wales.[61]

We might here pause to consider the implication of Harriett's actions at this moment. We might legitimately think she was distraught and guilt-ridden, and certainly Charles assumed she had been overcome with some mental aberration, since she contemplated her own death and once asked for poison.[62] The physician attending her, Dr Frederick Orford, was of the opinion that at this stage she was of sound mind. However, stepping back from this, we must consider how potentially foolhardy Harriett's confession might have been. Given the circles Harriett moved in, it was quite conceivable that she knew of other women who had 'covered up' inconvenient truths about their offspring.[63] Even then, why was it necessary to confess to more than one episode of adultery? Given assumptions about extra-marital affairs being monogamous, many might have considered Harriett to have been 'mad' for her serial indulgence, even more for being 'mad' enough to confess something she could have covered up. However, a focus upon Harriet herself serves to make us think differently. Was she hoping for some species of mercy from Sir Charles? Was she assuaging her conscience in facing up to her apparent 'badness' she might have perceived in the eyes of others?

Having divulged her news, Harriett Mordaunt's mental condition deteriorated into extreme listlessness and her interest in the child's welfare dwindled.[64] The doctors described her condition as 'cataleptic hysteria'.[65] Some tried to justify her behaviour and the view of the midwife, Mrs Hancox, was that Harriet's cataleptic state was aimed at gaining sympathy from Sir Charles after her unfortunate revelations. However, Mrs Hancox also thought that this tactic had backfired, as Charles believed her to be mad rather than pitiful. Mrs Hancox later observed that notable demonstrations of poor behaviour from Harriett seemed reserved for Sir Charles.[66] Harriett demonstrated regret for her extra-marital affair with Frederic Johnstone, but at this stage purely because of the opprobrium and consequences his medical condition attracted. She also suggested to Hancox that she would have indulged in an extra-marital affair anyway, since infidelity was commonplace and unremarkable in her social circles.[67] Again a strange revelation to a servant.

For a short time, Sir Charles was convinced about the genuine nature of Harriet's poor mental state, hoping that she would retract her confession. However, these hopes were deeply dashed when Harriett vehemently stuck to her story.[68] Harriett began to episodically break out of her melancholy and displayed defiance to a number of individuals, again justifying herself by citing the story of commonplace promiscuity within the highest London social circles. Observers might well have been ambivalent in their judgements upon Harriet at this moment since such wilful behaviour attracted a description of both 'mad' and 'bad'. At this time Harriett also approached Sir Charles, suggesting her reprehensible actions should not affect the continuity of their married life, still further complicating how observers would respond.[69]

What becomes interesting at this point is what the Moncrieffs variously construed as the symptoms of Harriett Mordaunt's insanity. Harriett's married sister, Helen Forbes, believed Harriett bestowing her favours upon the heir to the throne quite understandable, but the frequent assignations with other questionable men were significant aberrations that called her judgement into question.[70] This was likely the first foray into the family constructing a narrative of Harriett's insanity which came to prove vital in their campaign of damage limitation. Helen Forbes instructed Sir Charles and his brother to limit her access to men.[71] Meanwhile, Harriett's mother (Lady Louisa Moncrieff) hinted at a potential state of moral insanity, with the suggestion: 'A woman who has been as wicked as she has cannot have any conscience left.'[72] In a later, more pragmatic moment, she instead saw the mark of insanity in Harriet's decision to tell the whole truth to Sir Charles, and not to take the opportunity to recant when available.[73]

Different explanations also came forward from sources beyond the Moncrieffs. Certainly, at times her closest servant, Jesse Clarke, linked these current events to Harriett's 'reputation' for being somewhat highly strung.[74] Again Harriett did not help matters with her constant insistence that extra-marital sex in the highest London circles was a source of simple amusement.[75] The local clergyman's wife Alice Cadogan, who had befriended Harriett when she arrived at Walton Hall, believed Harriett had gone into a decline as a symptom of guilt and regret.

The medical practitioners themselves were also complicit in this act in focusing upon the precise nature of what was 'wrong' with Harriett Mordaunt. The consensus came to be 'puerperal insanity', this multi-symptomatic ailment was something of a proprietorial term; meaning that the medical profession had power over its definition and characteristics, frequently outlining that it also had an excellent prognosis. Medical professionals were also at this time using the diagnosis to emphasize a growing awareness of mental health explanations for behaviour and, importantly, their expertise in it (via the courtroom). Equally, it became the physiological explanation for the challenging behaviour of 'bad' women or women society did not want to have to deal with. This is important since it meant that Victorians either found diagnoses to explain 'mad' or 'bad' behaviour or, instead, they turned away from deviant women.

Since the revelations of Harriett's behaviour had emerged, the Moncrieff and Mordaunt families had formed themselves into two armed camps. Very quickly the Mordaunt family were keen to demonstrate that Harriett Mordaunt was clearly not insane. They took the line that she was 'faking it' either for her own ends (to delay, or potentially stop, divorce proceedings) or out of desperation, or to appease her family and its interests.[76] However, when Sir Charles Mordaunt gained access (in the presence of his two brothers) to Lady Mordaunt's private papers without her knowledge, the die was cast.[77] What Sir Charles uncovered was both revealing and shocking. Material from past lovers before they were married was revealed, although it is difficult to know what to make of this. Did Sir Charles really imagine Harriett had no prehistory? Of more obvious and immediate concern was the discovery of a number of letters and keepsakes from the Prince of Wales, which dated from before the period identified by Harriett as when she had initially received letters from him.[78] This was evidence to Sir Charles that the correspondence had been conducted in an obviously clandestine manner with an already married woman. Sir Charles began gathering a case against the idea that Harriett was insane and the physician in his employment Dr Frederick Orford encouraged this judgement.[79] He examined Lady Mordaunt for signs of venereal disease and accused her of contracting this on two separate occasions with both Captain Farquhar and Sir Frederic Johnstone. Orford later testified that she did not deny the accusation.[80]

Sir Charles Mordaunt evidently wanted to cast Harriett as 'bad' rather than 'mad'. He clearly brooded on the true meaning of the 'pre-nuptial agreement', but must equally have been irritated by Harriett's neglect of her duties as the wife of a country aristocrat. Moreover, a legal solution to her 'bad' behaviour would most likely have brought the matter to a rapid conclusion. The situation now became a still deeper pitched battle between the Moncrieffs and the Mordaunts. After legal advice, Harriet's family insisted that they were under no obligation to take her back since she was still a married woman in the charge of her husband.[81] It also seems clear that the diagnosis of insanity would prevent the Moncrieffs facing the consequences of what had happened. They also apparently plotted to enable Harriett to regain Charles's affection through a contrived reconciliation, although this never materialized.[82] There had also been earlier suggestions about confining and hiding Violet, all intent on ensuring Harriett could somehow be made to stay with her husband.[83] This may have persuaded Sir Charles that divorce was the only possible solution to his difficulties.

A parade of medical met Harriett Mordaunt, each of them primed with an agenda that suited the Mordaunts or the Moncrieffs. Her original physician Dr Frederick Orford, for instance, believed that Harriett was not suffering from delusions since her condition was not constant.[84] This cut across Dr Richard Jones' assertion that she was in a state of cataleptic hysteria.[85] The leading expert in the field, Dr Thomas Harrington Tuke, was summoned from London, but was primed by one of Harriet's sisters that Harriett complained of 'dead bodies' surrounding her and a belief that she was being poisoned. The arranged lunch passed without incident, but at the end, Harriett had a hysterical fit. Tuke then questioned her about the 'dead bodies' which Harriett affirmed that she had seen with her own eyes.[86] Jesse Clarke noted that, during this interrogation, her mistress became agitated and deeply angry, presuming the presence of Tuke was to blame. Tuke reported to Sir James Simpson, an eminent Edinburgh obstetrician enlisted by the Moncrieffs. This led to a diagnosis of 'puerperal mania' which was greatly disputed by the local physicians more likely to support the Mordaunts.[87]

The diagnosis of a puerperal illness would have been entirely plausible given the symptoms that Harriett Mordaunt displayed intermittently.[88] The medical profession's contemporary description of this, accumulated during the period when Harriett Mordaunt was a concern, was well summarized by M. D. MacLeod of the East Riding Asylum who described it in the following terms:

> The premonitory symptoms are usually a listless depression, a sense of being ill at ease, a restless irritability and impatience of control. The patient neither eats nor sleeps well, she is unconcerned about her child, or actively hostile to it, and she is suspicious about her husband and relatives; her skin is clammy and pale...an intense excitement supervenes—an excitement characterised by great restlessness, loud and rapid talking fleeting delusions, and vivid hallucinations.[89]

MacLeod argued that such behaviour and symptoms could be accompanied by denunciations of loved ones alongside obscene 'ravings' and regular engagement in 'salacious conversation'.[90] In truth, this analysis paints puerperal insanity as a catch-all term for a range of physiological and psychological disturbances attendant upon child birth and any associated trauma. Indeed insanity itself was an equally broad term.[91] With its already mentioned notoriety for having a long-term optimistic prognosis, a diagnosis of puerperal insanity was something that might have suited both families if the episodic nature of Harriett's condition and its potential 'duration' was finite.[92]

The Mordaunts and the Moncrieffs then each sought to outflank the other as they dealt with medical opinion, servants, and other witnesses. Eventually Sir Charles Mordaunt concluded that Harriett was addicted to the admiration that she cultivated from successive men, chiefly on the grounds that she flitted between them and never wanted to dissolve their marriage to pursue any of them.[93] This clearly indicated that her behaviour was 'bad' and that the case should go to court. Sir Charles' lingering distaste for the men involved was to be heightened by the appearance of them in the witness box, and many already knew (and some relished) what this would likely entail.

When Sir Charles petitioned for divorce, the Moncrieff lawyers counter-petitioned for a delay until Lady Mordaunt was of sound mind; a suggestion which some found odd, since her subsequent behaviour could often be restrained and normal.[94] Yet there were glances of an alternative persona. On one occasion, her closest servant Jesse Clarke discovered that Harriett had thrown a towel unaccountably upon the fire.[95] Of course, then as now, it is difficult to tell whether this was a psychological disturbance, or a realization that the servants would now report her every action. Eventually, everyone advanced an opinion as to the sanity or otherwise of Harriett Mordaunt. The Mordaunt side, in the guise of Sir Charles' clergyman brother Osbert, let Harriett know that all believed she was shamming to deceive her own relatives.[96] Osbert would later reverse this accusation to indict Harriet's family as the instigators of this when he wanted to stir sympathy within her.[97]

Harriet's father engineered a move for Harriett from Walton Hall to London, seemingly as a form of both surveillance and restraint, where unfortunately she became prey to the agendas of others. In London, Harriett was accessible to people who wanted to prove their own truth about the Mordaunt affair. One of these was the Royal Physician Sir William Gull and another physician who had been involved in examining Harriett earlier on, Dr Priestley. Both concluded that Harriet's physical condition was a cause for concern and her inability to answer their questions meant she was clearly of unsound mind. They thus concluded she should be removed to an institution to receive attentive care.[98] It is unclear precisely whether Sir William Gull was engaged upon doing the Prince of Wales' bidding here, but certainly confining the woman at the centre of an enormous aristocratic and royal scandal could be seen as a legitimate end in itself by some of those involved.

Sir Charles Mordaunt became deeply concerned that the combined efforts of Harriett and her family could threaten his divorce. Thus, the Mordaunts battled to prevent Harriett attaining her goal of establishing obstacles to the actions against her. Harriett, under the oversight of Tuke and Gull, was sent away to an establishment in Worthing where her behaviour deteriorated still further, with noted episodes of her disposing of clothes in the water closet or refusing to wear those chosen for her in public.[99] Although possible indicators of a troubled mental state, they could equally be construed as measured protests.

The Mordaunts had by now prepared seventeen affidavits which they believed would convince the judge that Harriett and the Moncrieffs were using her alleged insanity to prevent the divorce. These preparations were unseated, however, by the judge's seemingly independent decision to allow Gull, Tuke, and a third physician to visit Harriett in Worthing.[100] The seventeen affidavits were answered by counter ones from the doctors organized by the Moncrieffs, detailing a diagnosis of puerperal insanity. More incidents were mentioned alongside news that Harriet's manners and decorum had entirely collapsed. The conflicting affidavits eventually meant that the judge concluded that the matter should be settled in court where a jury would decide the outcome.[101]

Much has been written about the court case in detail and there are verbatim reports which give a blow-by-blow account; these do not really concern us here since these ostensibly summarize the efforts already described for public consumption.[102] The appearance of the Prince of Wales in the witness box was a notable event, yet this concession enabled him to escape being named as a possible father of Lady Mordaunt's child. Another highlight occurred when, under cross-examination, Sir Charles Mordaunt was led into uttering the immortal phrase 'When a man cries, it is called crying; when a woman cries it is called hysterics.'[103] The judge's summing up accepted the account that Lady Mordaunt was insane and incapable of instructing her counsel.[104] Most importantly it noted that Harriet had not retracted her confession when opportunities arose and had refused to ask forgiveness retorting 'she would humble herself to no man'.[105] In the context of the nineteenth century, a woman asserting this level of defiance went manifestly against rationality, since the economic and social consequences were so obviously catastrophic. Thus, the twisted logic of a sane person shamming in full knowledge that it would lead to her being labelled as an adulterous and scandalous woman, seemed very hard to accept. The jury steadfastly agreed with this verdict and pronounced Harriett insane.[106] Importantly the judge also decided that the court was considering a criminal charge and therefore the respondent was not fit to plead until they regained their sanity. This was something the newspapers attacked as a consequence of the poorly constructed Matrimonial Causes Act of 1857.[107]

Sir Charles' appeal against this verdict was itself later overruled. This created the stalemate that the Moncrieffs wanted, but which left neither Sir Charles nor Harriett Mordaunt satisfied. This outcome did spawn an enduring human interest and legal story for the press, which argued at length that the law should not be left in this form of limbo. Most of these lengthy discussions blandly assumed the truth of Harriett Mordaunt's insanity.

Harriett was afterwards confined in a number of institutions and lodgings under professional care. Whilst she is still visible to the historian, reports noted none of the extremes of behaviour that she had displayed before the court case.[108] The Mordaunt family believed the Moncrieffs continued to make Harriett perform the 'fabricated' role of the insane woman. Dr Tyler-Smith for instance, upon visiting Harriet, stated that he was convinced that she would drop the pretence of insanity if she could be assured of resuming her marriage and former life, something that prolonged the painful stalemate.[109]

Eventually, in 1874, Sir Charles Mordaunt realized that his wife's insanity was, in fact, an asset and Sir Charles pushed forward an appeal to the House of

Lords.[110] The hurdle of his wife's mental condition became an intense subject of debate and sections of the press asked openly whether a husband should be shackled to such a wife.[111] The Lords decided by a majority of three to two that his own proceedings for divorce should proceed.[112] A year later, in the divorce proceedings only Lord Lowry Cole was cited as a co-respondent, leaving the Prince of Wales out of the case. Charles was granted his *decree nisi* and eventually his *decree absolute,* freeing him to marry again, which he eventually did in 1878. However, it left the issue of maintaining Harriett, and separately, her daughter. Wrangling between the Mordaunts and the Moncrieffs was eventually settled in 1877.[113] Remaining confined to an asylum, Harriett Mordaunt eventually died in 1906.[114] This final act prompted Harriett Mordaunt's most comprehensive biographer Elizabeth Hamilton to conclude:

> It was, of course, the women who fared worst. There was all too often a price to pay in the dismal aftermath of shame, rejection and unwanted pregnancy. 'We bear all the ignominy' Harriett had so rightly observed.[115]

## Harriett Mordaunt: An Archaeology of Reputation

One thing that steadfastly emerges from our examination of this case is the crucial role that servants played in both Victorian marriage and marriage breakdown. Servants provided help and service to their employers, but incidents like the Mordaunt case highlight that their loyalties could be remarkably ambivalent. For members of the female aristocracy, servants could be barely acknowledged drudges, but equally, they could be confidantes and even friends.[116] However, this latter relationship could be episodic and conditional upon the lifestyle and decisions of the aristocratic woman involved. From confidantes, servants could suddenly change their role to be observer and informer. If they were slighted, cast aside, or simply overworked, the relationship between servant and master/mistress could alter dangerously. There were even frequent instances of servants casting themselves into a dual role, acting as confidantes in life, but recording the details in private personal diaries. These diaries became an active subculture and bargaining chip, which could make rapid fortunes for discharged servants. For Harriett Mordaunt, this was arguably where, at least for her, the archaeology of reputation began.[117] Certainly Harriett Mordaunt's predicament exemplified high-profile sexual impropriety, and was thus an important vehicle in interesting the public at large in the proceedings of the relatively recently established divorce court and its aristocratic clients.[118]

This last aspect however shaped what the newspapers would think of Harriett Mordaunt. In their rush to consider the legal implications of the case, the truth of Harriett's situation was easily lost. By highlighting the legal anomaly that a suit could not proceed against someone unfit to plead, this cemented the impression that Harriett was simply insane. The only dissenters from this view added something of a human gloss to the otherwise cursory judgement of their peers. *The Times* expressed the wish that the suit had simply not been instigated and asked why it was so necessary for dirty linen to be washed in public. It was incredulous that no private investigation about the sexual allegations and Harriett's alleged insanity had been conducted.[119] Yet of course *The Times* was not privy to the exhaustive investigation undertaken by family and doctors. The publication *John Bull* went still further. In a perceptive comment, it saw that Harriett's reputation had been made to suffer at the whim of the judge. The paper thought Harriett's confession gave her sufficient motive to feign madness and the case should have stuck firmly to proving this. The discussion of prurient detail effectively meant that Harriett suffered a sort of trial by popular culture, giving the impression that 'they were trying the criminality of Lady Mordaunt, and those supposed to be implicated by her confessions'.[120]

Later researchers who have investigated Harriett's story have often viewed it only superficially through other agendas. The historian of royalty Stanley Weintraub was equivocal in his judgement of Harriett Mordaunt. His biographical focus on the Prince of Wales meant his treatment of Harriett Mordaunt was cursory. He noted that her confession of adultery followed a terror-stricken suspicion that her daughter's eye infection was a providential symptom of syphilis. Weintraub suspected 'post-partum depression' and described in relatively graphic detail the circumstances of her confinement for insanity. Whilst arguing that Harriett could claim to be an abused wife, Weintraub remained uncertain, concluding that she 'acted indiscreetly before succumbing to madness, or to feigning it'.[121] Harriett was similarly dismissed in passing as insane in the account offered by the popular writer (and eventual Lord Chancellor) Michael Havers, Edward Grayson, and Peter Shankland. Their trade book was obviously more interested in the Prince's involvement in the Tranby Croft gambling scandal.[122]

Elizabeth Hamilton produced certainly the most exhaustive account of the Mordaunt divorce case and has done the most to investigate the character and motivations of Lady Harriett Mordaunt.[123] Hamilton's access to a previously unseen private archive makes her volume arguably the definitive factual account of the story. Although Hamilton has a measured sympathy for all involved in the Mordaunt case, she does reiterate the narrative of aristocratic women as frivolous and trapped, describing long periods when there was little to do except eat large meals and change clothes for the evening.[124] In surveying the choices open to these aristocratic young women, she characterizes their young male escorts variously as 'cousins' who used familial ties as an excuse for familiarity, 'drones' or 'retrievers' who would 'follow dog like' after young women at social occasions, and 'handsome guardsmen' who could obtain tickets for sought-after social events.[125] All were viable as escorts, but Hamilton tells us sobriety would arrive with the need for a well-researched marriage to 'older men with titles, large rent rolls and houses in both the town and in the country'.[126]

Hamilton is unsure about Harriett Mordaunt's early behaviour in this saga. On the one hand, she is obviously both sympathetic to and candid about Harriet's own nature and her attraction to a series of men. Yet Hamilton also accepts a darker side to this story, in which Harriett was the next candidate in a multi-layered game where influential men exerted power over young women. In short, Harriett was drawn into a situation where she began to receive the attentions of the Prince of Wales before her marriage to Sir Charles, something which must have been welcomed as an indicator of favour and belonging. According to Hamilton, Harriett would not have heeded cautious advice had it been available to her.[127] Around the time that her marriage to Sir Charles Mordaunt was mooted, Harriett does emerge from Hamilton's account as utterly determined to sidestep the restrictions that would have been expected of a woman of her status. Certainly, Hamilton suggests that Harriett was well aware that she was in an advantageous bargaining position and that her prospective husband might assent to her wishes.

Whatever else it does, this episode from the Hamilton account takes us some distance from the other attempts to discuss Harriett Mordaunt and her historical reputation. No longer does she appear as a supporting character in the wider biography of the British aristocracy, the British monarchy, the development of medicine, or a Victorian scandal. Instead, she emerges more obviously as an active and engaged protagonist in the events that would subsequently unfold. Indeed, we might consider whether the true innocent led into misadventure in the drama of the Mordaunt divorce case was in fact Sir Charles Mordaunt and not his erstwhile wife.

Hamilton persuades us that the accumulation of evidence, fuelled by the proximity of servants, provided something of a comprehensive account of the Mordaunt affair. As an accumulation of facts, this does tell its own story, but it also means that the voice of Harriett and her feelings remain somewhat absent from this account. In some ways, the knowledge of servants became a species of evidence in court, especially when we consider the obvious intimacy her closest female servants had with Harriet. However, servants themselves found their reactions to these events were ambivalent. They did exercise their own opinion on moral propriety on occasions, as indeed Jesse Clarke did when narrating that she was convinced that Harriett had committed adultery.[128] Yet also, these servants must have been sometimes riddled with doubt and conflicting loyalties. Either way, their knowledge of their employer's routines and actions created content and detail for others to construct an archaeology of reputation.

Perhaps unwittingly, Hamilton even has Sir Charles Mordaunt rob Harriett of any agency in the actions she was involved in, at least at the outset. For long periods, he is described as infatuated by her and unwilling to believe any of the stories told about Harriet, even when so many of them came from her own lips.

After this stage, all his subsequent anger is directed towards the men involved in cuckolding him. Hamilton envisages him musing over the trouble and expense he incurred to discover that his hospitality had been abused and his young wife defiled in cavalier fashion.[129] This narrative must also have been persuasive to him since this was the logic of the law of 'Criminal Conversation' which Hamilton suggests Sir Charles pursued, resulting in the close interviewing of the servants involved. 'Criminal Conversation' saw the husband wronged by other men and amounted to a gendered construction.[130] This emerges as a further way culpability could be taken away from Harriet. One awful realization that came later than it should have done was that Harriett was a willing accomplice and even instigator, when hitherto Charles had been led by convention and the law to consider her an innocent misled by wily and libidinous men.[131] Hamilton's final verdict is that Harriett allowed the performance of insanity to take her over so that at some point it became the reality of her mental condition. In the end, this is one answer to the ambivalence that is detectable within the case. From all Hamilton uncovered, the reasons to fake were numerous and tempting, yet the sheer weight of testimony and evidence made Hamilton feel that there was inevitably some truth to the countless stories of Harriett Mordaunt's poor mental state.

When we look elsewhere, we also find other academics who have used Harriett Mordaunt in unhelpful ways that serve to confirm her status as a passive victim. Hilary Marland's study of puerperal insanity notes how the disease was socially constructed by cultural factors dominant in the nineteenth century. The chief of these is the threat it posed to 'the sanctity of the bourgeois home'.[132] It fed this fear by producing both shared anxiety and a capacity to destabilize relationships. These turned such women against children, husbands, and servants as well as presenting symptoms of self-neglect and a lethargic attitude to domestic duty. Such women were also considered to become more sexually predatory.[133]

Marland, who was primarily interested in the socio-medical history of puerperal mania/insanity, starts her investigation from the question of whether or not Harriett Mordaunt was shamming. She notes that the *Medical Times & Gazette* believed this to be the case, but this was largely because this judgement was formed from reading Sir Charles' correspondence.[134] Marland notes Sir James Simpson argued that Harriett was suffering from puerperal melancholia because she had 'a dislike of the child', a desire to poison herself and the infant, as well as an apathy towards her husband. All supposedly described puerperal melancholia, and it was stressed that it was this, rather than mania, that she was suffering from. Sir William Gull meanwhile similarly diagnosed puerperal insanity.[135]

Marland suggests Harriett's 'condition' continued, where other contemporary judgements are more confused on the matter. Yet strangely, this does not fit with the idea of 'shamming'. Marland merely concludes that Harriett paid a high price for what happened to her, whatever the cause. In this, Harriett Mordaunt became one of Marland's highest placed victims of possible puerperal insanity. Just as

Harriett has been a colourful member of the history of monarchy's supporting cast, consideration of her mental state has made her a similar supporting player in the history of puerperal insanity. But ultimately this account, like those previously mentioned, effectively restricts full investigation, thereby both limiting her and enslaving her behaviour to the demands of other agendas.

The archaeology of Harriett Mordaunt's reputation has scarcely stopped at biographical and academic examination. The rise of the internet has ensured there are other opinions available on Harriett Mordaunt, the meaning of her story, and its place in history. These are worth investigating because they very often betray the 'leakage' of academic conclusions about stereotypes and perpetuate these. They also constitute an increasingly important way in which history is communicated, especially around issues related to monarchy and the aristocracy. Harriet's narrative is at the confluence of a great number of streams which make the Mordaunt divorce scandal still as 'appealing' as it ever was. It is short, self-contained, the narrative is reasonably well known, and its cast of characters reaches into every corner of mid-Victorian society. But it also leaves things tantalisingly unsaid. The level of culpability of the Prince of Wales and the royal family in general is one driver of this interest. This spills over into another staple fare of internet entertainment—the idea of a cover up and/or conspiracy theory. However, these agendas still significantly rob Harriett Mordaunt of choice and agency to this day.

Anne Pettigrew's brief account of the case runs in a number of directions.[136] She notes the usual speculation about why we are so interested in the Mordaunt divorce case, citing the idea of the perennial fascination in salacious gossip and a desire to see the mighty humbled. The possibility of external pressure being exerted on the divorce court judge Lord Penzance is mentioned, as is the allusion within Princess Alexandra's diary to the Prime Minister being involved at some point.[137] Beyond this, there are some other interesting speculations. The questions about the precise nature of Harriett Mordaunt's insanity contains the fleeting suggestion that her condition might have been as a result of venereal disease, or actually brought on by her detention after the court case.[138] Pettigrew sees Harriett as a passive victim, arguing that her insanity was wholly the idea of her family and that she conceivably had no part in its creation and performance.

From there, Pettigrew embodies this passivity with the comment that Harriett was 'airbrushed' out of society. She also quotes Rosa Lewis, the 'Duchess of Duke Street', who arguably knew a thing or two about such situations, striking a pose of incredulity at the behaviour of Sir Charles Mordaunt in seeking to publicize his wife's adultery when others turned a blind eye.[139] Pettigrew concludes by noting how our sensibilities have altered from the Victorian sense of propriety.[140] For the Victorians, a diagnosis of insanity was far preferable to a messy divorce involving multiple co-respondents. Whilst the twenty-first-century world finds adultery paraded, acknowledged, and preferable to actively and perhaps conspiratorially, incarcerating a vulnerable individual on the grounds of insanity. This in itself provides an oblique insight on the Victorian conception of the 'mad' or 'bad' woman.

Rupert Taylor's online publication 'A Right Royal Scandal' rehearses the traditional biographical approaches which centre on the great men of the Mordaunt divorce case, but particularly the Prince of Wales.[141] In a novel attempt at biography, the prolific hedonistic shortcomings of the heir to the throne appear in graphic detail. The fact that the paths of the Prince and Harriet crossed reflects the law of averages, with neither capable of showing much in the way of restraint. In the main, Harriett is largely just passing through in this account and the Prince is painted as escaping unscathed from this particular intrigue. Nevertheless, Harriett is labelled as an unfortunate victim of her lapse into insanity, a condition that had obviously been carefully rehearsed. In this account, the element of calculation places Harriett, in the category of 'bad' feigning 'mad'.

Tonya Mitchell's blog makes women and mental illness central to her account of the Harriett Mordaunt affair, but spoils the tone of this investigation by describing the case frivolously as 'a doozy'.[142] This blog does highlight that the diagnosis of Harriett Mordaunt as insane may have been fabricated by the people around her and certainly proved all too convenient for most of them.[143] Nonetheless, Mitchell notes that Harriet's social position meant that she was better off than many women labelled insane. She was able to afford private and relatively genteel asylum care, ensuring an infinitely better experience than other unfortunates shoehorned into public asylum institutions in the Victorian era.[144]

The blog 'The Harriett Mordaunt Scandal' by Jackie Jackson which featured in the online magazine *JAQUO* examines the pact between Sir Charles Mordaunt and Harriet, one which was only compromised when Harriett had broken its rules.[145] This lends credence to speculation about the idea of a pre-nuptial agreement and makes a point of outlining that Sir Charles himself had a number of mistresses and that this was somehow 'traditional'.[146] Much is also made of the Victorian obsession with inheritance, echoing that Harriet's most significant blunder was entering into extra-marital affairs before she had supplied Sir Charles with a son and heir.[147] Put this way, the blog forgets Harriet's own nature and her track record of forming close attachments to a succession of men. This suggestion of a deliberate and calculated series of actions where Harriett should have been circumspect and discreet ignores the widely known agreement, quoted by the blog, between Sir Charles and Harriet. This account concludes with a host of possible conspiracy elements that spill outwards in many directions. The Moncrieff family are indicted for protecting their other daughters and for persuading Harriett to sacrifice herself in their interests. The Prince of Wales is accused of perhaps misleading Harriett into believing he would protect her and potentially persuading Lord Cole to eventually accept the paternity of Harriet's child.[148] All of this sees Harriett as passive, at the mercy of the powerful, and perhaps not even allowed the luxury of a judgement of whether her actions were 'bad' or 'mad'.

If we accept that Harriett Mordaunt was either insane at some point, or was driven insane, we must also consider the archaeology of Harriett Mordaunt's reputation written by proxy. This comes in the shape of the collective biography of insane women and their exposition in nineteenth-century culture. Elaine Showalter notes that the Victorian period identified madness as a female malady and, in women, this was strongly linked to their sexuality and could be triggered by childbirth. Victorian psychiatry was also a system of surveillance and control stewarded by men, as indeed was Harriett's experience.[149] Showalter, additionally, catalogues a countrywide dramatic increase in the number of individuals confined to asylums at precisely the same time as the onset of Harriett Mordaunt's insanity.[150]

Yet some stereotypes unravel in the story of Harriet's insanity. Showalter notes that the 1880s were characterized by cases of husbands wrongfully imprisoning their wives in lunatic asylums.[151] Harriet's husband, before his eventual change of strategy, was the one person who forcefully wanted to avoid Harriet's slide into insanity, faked or otherwise! If Harriett had faked her condition, this was to actively escape circumstances that unfolded around her. The diagnosis of puerperal insanity would also have embraced and explained some of Harriet's behaviour that was labelled indelicate, since the collapse of decorum and coarseness of language were cited as a symptom.[152] Women of the highest social class were also thought by Victorian physicians to slide into moral insanity as result of their enforced idleness.[153] Hysteria was also a possible diagnosis of Harriet's condition since it described the neglect of traditional female roles, the craving for independence, and pathological attention seeking—something often linked to radical women seeking change.[154]

Showalter also notes that some women felt they had been driven insane by the myriad social and cultural restrictions upon their hopes and activities. Certainly, this would very likely open up yet another avenue of explanation for Harriet's behaviour and choices.[155] Other ways to judge Harriet's approach to life and relationships emerge from examining the text of *Lady Audley's Secret*, a novel of 1861, which describes an aristocratic woman who becomes insane after the birth of her child. Showalter makes a telling point about what Lady Audley's secret might be. In a parting shot that equally describes Harriett Mordaunt, Showalter asks 'is the secret that "insanity" is simply the label society attaches to female assertion, ambition, self-interest and outrage?'[156]

## Conclusion

So what was Harriett Mordaunt's fatal flaw? What was the point at which she very evidently lost control of her life and the opportunities open to her? It is too easily said that, if she had been content with an aristocratic ideal of marriage and its rites of passage from one stage of life to another, her experiences would have been markedly less destructive. But equally, we might argue that the pre-nuptial agreement between her and Sir Charles Mordaunt might even have worked for the entire span of their marriage.

Is it possible to argue that Harriett Mordaunt simply had too many dalliances with too many men so that the law of averages caught up with her? Maybe. Yet perhaps the most obvious point at which things began to go wrong for Harriet was her dalliance with the Prince of Wales. With considerable hindsight this really does look to be the most obviously fatal mistake. The Prince of Wales was not like the other dashing young men whose company Harriett seemed to crave, so her choice at this point seems slightly odd. Whatever else the relationship was, it was certainly a profoundly dangerous one and Harriet's involvement with the Prince becomes difficult to explain and even invites recourse to consideration of 'bad' versus 'mad'. The chance of discovery and gossip surrounding a woman involved in an extra-marital affair with the heir to the throne was extremely likely. The potential for publicity and, as we have discovered, the judgement of history was considerable. We might speculate that Harriett Mordaunt's reputation could have been preserved in some form if she had remained more obviously in the shadows. However, we should also ponder whether it is right to ask such a question at all. The idea of Harriet's 'mistake' presumes she should have settled for some life other than the one she was determined to pursue—the life she so forthrightly asked her husband for. She seemed to have had enough intimations that other women had negotiated a life that at least partly resembled the one she was pursuing.

So was Harriett Mordaunt insane and, if so, precisely at which particular points in the proceedings? Did she fall into a spiral of anxiety as she became aware of the dangerous affliction potentially visited upon her unborn child? Was it her reaction to her own child which to many exhibited the classic symptoms of 'puerperal mania'? Was Harriett not actually insane at all, but instead was this diagnosis manufactured by other people? Alternatively, Harriett herself might have realized that giving very public displays of insanity would maintain her position and help stall for time. Perhaps she genuinely believed that she could retard, or even prevent, the matter going to court and the divorce from proceeding. If this was the case, did Harriett believe that faked behaviour was protecting herself, her family (the Moncrieffs), and even the reputation of her numerous paramours?

At a simpler level was the 'madness' a part of her often remarked upon playful personality and simply to keep individuals guessing, something which was perhaps one of the few amusements left to her, once she had been confined and unable to benefit from the type of attention she craved? Of deeper significance is the fact that at crucial points in the story Harriett Mordaunt's insanity gave her a species of power. To be sane for long periods and interspersed with fleeting moments of obvious insanity perplexed individuals. Or perhaps it kept them guessing about everything from the nature of her condition, the truth of her confessions, or the opinions other people had formed of her. Insanity did hold up proceedings against Harriett and the temptation to persist with this must have been considerable. Harriett may even have seen the tactic as a way of igniting sympathy within the heart of Sir Charles Mordaunt as, after all, she had successfully persuaded him to think differently and more favourably of her in the past.

Or was Harriet's 'insanity' largely a Moncrieff creation? Harriet's family had been keen for her to contract the marriage as an advantageous one. They seemed genteel and respectable, but financially more precarious than initially appeared. Moreover, they feared the cost of Harriet's upkeep as a divorced and disgraced woman. This also jeopardized their ability to assemble dowries for their other daughters; that is, if they could conclude marriage contracts after such a scandal in the family. It is obvious that the Moncrieff family had much to lose from the Mordaunt divorce scandal, with damage limitation viewed as an absolute necessity. Certainly, they believed Harriet's freedom and personal reputation, along with the welfare of her child, was a price worth paying.

It becomes tempting here to consider that Harriet's misbehaviour and the alleged reasons for her insanity became a blank canvas on which individuals emblazoned their own experiences, hopes, and fears. Some of them perhaps revisited the 'close calls' they had experienced within their families or wider circles, others possibly reached for apocryphal narratives of what usually happened in such circumstances. As we have heard, individual accounts from many close to the events tease out specific follies and specific inferences that can be drawn. Occasionally this could be painted on a still wider canvas as an object lesson to the impressionable aristocratic young women of the next generation. Or indeed, to society as a whole, as *Reynolds's Newspaper* did, letting its readers know about the detestable aristocratic practice of 'living in a state of advanced Mormonism'.[157]

In the final analysis, the various surveys of Harriett Mordaunt's life and the actions she took before and during her marriage to Sir Charles Mordaunt do not illuminate nor explain as much as we might have hoped. But we should note what these accounts achieve, and where they are perhaps actively damaging to our historical understanding. In some, Harriett is the footnote to the lives of great men and an irritating impediment to their final conclusively unsullied reputation. She emerges also as a hedonist in narratives that see uncovering scandal as their main *raison d'être*. Elsewhere she becomes the victim of her decision to feign madness, eventually becoming enslaved by her need to craft a convincing performance of insanity so that the act eventually begat the reality. This supposedly was a real insanity from which she was never to wholly recover, resulting in her being labelled for the rest of her life. Conspiracy theory narratives about the case illuminate the injustice of Victorian double standards about the behaviour of the two genders. Such theories also have been used to reinforce the idea of multi-layered scandal and its power in contemporary nineteenth-century society to shock and to entertain—something perhaps even enhanced where the result is catastrophic. This approach also functions as a precursor and touchstone of what society might think about subsequent royal scandals much closer to our own time. Conspiracy theories (which in this case always have exclusively male agents and executors) also reiterate important points about thc place of women and their lack of room for manoeuvre when things went wrong. But equally, this interpretation serves to rob women, and Harriett Mordaunt in particular, of choice, intelligence, and agency. Her reputation has been revisited many times and Harriet's character, in labelling her 'bad', 'mad', or powerless, has too often lost out as a result.

There were certain points in the story where Harriett Mordaunt did have power and it remains important to remember this. What is almost never discussed is that Harriett Mordaunt clearly had considerable influence over the men she encountered. Although some might have flown in fear from her presence, the fact remains that a considerable number were nonetheless clearly compulsively drawn to her and her company. Harriett had the power to organize and plan assignations, even if control over servants and their reactions was beyond her capability. She had the power to negotiate with Charles before their marriage and, at certain junctures, her brokering could yet have saved the day. We must ask how many other aristocratic women were in this position and eventually manoeuvred more effectively to reach a tolerable resolution with their husbands? As we have speculated, we should seriously consider just how representative Harriett and Charles were of aristocratic men and women striking pragmatic bargains. We should also consider how long the agreement may actually have worked in practice. After all, one reading of Charles Mordaunt's behaviour is to observe that he actively turned a blind eye to the reality of what had happened as long as was humanly possible. Bizarre though it might seem, Harriett also had power when she was in the early stages of the insanity she convinced some people she was suffering from. For a brief time, she could have some control over her surroundings. Whilst people observed and pondered the precise nature of her condition, her fate was not yet sealed.

For the purposes of the wider intentions of this volume, Harriett Mordaunt's confounding of the stereotypes of female behaviour to become a deviant woman is more complicated and goes somewhat beyond this basic dichotomy. Harriett was born and brought up into a role in which her youthful vivaciousness and good looks were required to bring her success in the high stakes aristocratic society marriage market. Her choices from thereon in significantly did not reflect the prevailing views of safe companionate marriage, motherhood, and moral exemplar explored at the start of this chapter. Likewise, she did not fit emerging knowledge about the female body either. Such a science as gynaecology quite obviously also had trouble accommodating what it came to know of Harriet Mordaunt and her narrative. She seems very obviously to have been capable of elements of choice which this construction of woman, as morally grounded slave to physiology, quite obviously argued against. Harriet Mordaunt certainly desired men but quite obviously not for marriage—an institution and state she had conveniently hived off to a different compartment of her life. This was ostensibly to the 'care' of a man significantly older than her and outside of her sexual desires. She, as the young fertile wife, became the great moral danger rendering society's stereotype of the no longer fertile immoral woman caricature redundant in her story. The 'life' that Harriet had given birth to, in the shape of Violet, was scarcely a longed-for child over which Harriet, as she grew up, would lavish care and exert the requisite 'benign and humanising influence'. Sadly for Harriet, eventually the one stereotype she found herself conforming to was the assertion that insane women excelled over men in sexual depravity and the supposed foulness of their language.[158]

Harriet Mordaunt's deviance at the onset of her marriage was not to step away completely from norms and expectations, but instead to refuse to move from the ones she had been brought up to, namely the fast social life in search of the male attention which she had become accustomed to. At times and places she would contemplate how this choice had also been quietly adopted amongst other aristocratic women—so why should she be the victim of mistakes and the personal failures of so many others?

Harriett moved from this form of deviance to that of the public, albeit domesticized lunatic which persisted for a period. What happened was a deeply unfortunate collapse into the last stereotype which ironically was a descent into silent, suffering compliance—a condition Harriett Mordaunt had scarcely prepared herself for. Her eventual confinement in private asylums as a lunatic, someone who eventually was reclassified as feeble-minded, silenced her forever. She ended her days as Gubar's often cited cultural zeitgeist of the insane woman: someone suppressed and unspeakable who Victorian society had safely thrust away from the centre of human life. So without her voice and agency, Harriett Mordaunt became a veritable image of confinement, allowing Victorians to 'shelve' further consideration of her behaviour and to hide her from view. This decline took her away from the role of the empowered 'mad' woman which peopled Showalter's image of the Victorian feminine. In being removed from this narrative, she now found herself limited and confined in the world outlined by Gubar as the controlled and hidden 'madwoman in the attic'. Harriett Mordaunt, or 'HSM' as the process eventually officially reduced her to in the 1891 census, was a trope of the unacceptable and served as a warning to aristocratic and wider society. She was now actively conforming, without her consent, to a gender stereotype of the most difficult and demanding kind for Harriett herself, but one which comforted wider society and enabled it to explain away the actions of a once disreputable woman.

Yet examination of what contemporary society and subsequent historians have said about women's behaviour and misbehaviour is problematized by the Mordaunt case. If we strip away the gossip and its trappings, Harriet's behaviour only sometimes erratically followed known culturally determined patterns such as aristocratic youth, aristocratic marriage, aristocratic infidelity, the wronged woman, the domestically insane woman, and the 'mad woman in the attic', whilst dissenting from others. This seems to have happened as and when this suited her. Often these patterns also overlapped, providing a multilayered experience that cannot always be reduced to stereotype or established narrative. This is especially true of the assignment of behavioural characteristics to criminal and deviant women. This is because Harriett both followed her passions *and* was a calculating individual as *all* people are and, like many men and women, was prepared to work in order to achieve her goals. More research around the margins of experience and stereotypical narratives will likely lead to a much more nuanced appreciation of women in the past entering into deviant behaviour as willing and wholly aware protagonists, whatever their class or situation.

## Notes

1. See e.g. P. Jalland (1986) *Women, Marriage and Politics, 1860–1914* (Oxford: Clarendon Press); M. Curtin (1987) *Propriety and Position: A Study of Victorian Manners* (New York: Garland Publishing); and M. Morgan (1994) *Manners, Morals and Class in England 1774–1858* (New York: St Martin's Press).
2. See L. Davidoff (1995) *World's Between: Historical Perspectives on Gender and Class.* (Cambridge: Cambridge University Press), pp. 25–34. See also M. Hartman (1977) *Victorian Murderesses: A True History of Thirteen Respectable French and English Women Accused of Unspeakable Crimes* (London: Robson Books), pp. 236–7, for discussion of 'servant betrayal' as a specifically late nineteenth-century phenomenon.
3. For a discussion of the 1860s as a period of sexual licence and the appearance of 'fastness' see M. Mason (1995) *The Making of Victorian Sexuality* (Oxford: Oxford University Press).
4. The concept of 'Archaeology of Reputation' was first used in our volume A.-M. Kilday and D. S. Nash (2017) *Shame and Modernity in Britain 1890 to the Present* (London: Palgrave Macmillan) in chapter 4. This describes the ongoing investigation of individual lives and personalities by a number of subsequent generations, each leaving their judgement on the individual. This is also evidently constructed from the respective concerns and preoccupations of each successive generation of writers.
5. Hartman, *Victorian Murderesses*, p. 133. Hartman suggests a society-wide change in sensibility was responsible for an upsurge in adultery that became public knowledge for one reason or another.
6. O. Moscucci (1990) *The Science of Woman: Gynaecology and Gender in England, 1800–1929* (Cambridge: Cambridge University Press), p. 103. For wider and longer term perspectives see R. Porter (1989) *Mind Forg'd Manacles: A History of Madness in England from the Restoration to the Regency* (Harmondsworth: Penguin) and R. Porter (1995) *Disease, Medicine and Society in England 1550–1860* (Cambridge: Cambridge University Press).

7. Moscucci, *Science of Woman*, pp. 104–5. See also V. Bates (2016) *Sexual Forensics in Victorian and Edwardian England: Age Crime and Consent in the Courts* (Basingstoke: Palgrave), pp. 141–2, and L. Hide (2014) *Gender and Class in Victorian Asylums 1890–1914* (Basingstoke: Palgrave).
8. Moscucci, *Science of Woman*, p. 31.
9. Ibid., p. 34.
10. Ibid., p. 35.
11. Ibid., p. 36.
12. Bates, *Sexual Forensics*, pp. 25–7, 31–3, and 36.
13. Ibid., pp. 28–9.
14. This was the leading motif that emerged from the first attempts to create a viable feminist literary criticism centring on the nineteenth century. This saw women effectively reacting to various species of 'confinement' by exploring the juxtaposition between the idealized angelic selves craved by Victorian society and the destabilized mad and monstrous which haunted the imaginations of women writers in particular. This dichotomy has had something of a lasting influence upon portrayals of Victorian women's mental states. See S. Gilbert and S. Gubar (1979) *The Madwoman in the Attic: The Woman Writer and the Nineteenth-Century Literary Imagination* (New Haven: Yale University Press). For an analysis of the wider history of insanity which argues this could be a creative part of female identity see E. Showalter (1987) *The Female Malady: Women Madness and English Culture, 1830–1980* (London: Virago).
15. L. Davidoff (1973) *The Best Circles: Society, Etiquette and the Season* (London: Croom Helm).
16. A. Mitson (1998) 'An Exchange of Letters: Estate Management and Lady Yarborough', *Women's History Review*, 7, 4, pp. 547–66 at pp. 548–9.
17. A. Owens (2001) 'Property, Gender and the Life Course: Inheritance and Family Welfare Provision in Early Nineteenth-Century England', *Social History*, 26, 3, pp. 97–315.
18. See J. Phegley (2012) *Courtship and Marriage in Victorian England* (Santa Barbara, CA: Praeger), pp. 20–1. This suggests the 1860s saw the rise of a genre of sensation novels that drew inspiration from the stories emanating from the civil divorce court established by the 1857 Matrimonial Causes Act. These were, in her words, 'driven by issues related to marriage law, property, law, custody, and inheritance'.
19. J. C. Kelsey (2016) *Changing the Rules: Women and Victorian Marriage* (Kibworth Beauchamp, Wilmslow: Matador), p. 19.
20. Elizabeth Hamilton's husband inherited Walton Hall and a vast archive of letters and other material which remain in her possession. Research in this archive enabled her to write E. Hamilton (1999) *The Warwickshire Scandal* (Norwich: Michael Russell). In many places, this work reports conversations in quotation marks so it seems very likely that many letters and reports exist, although Hamilton has not always quoted these directly. This chapter therefore, where possible, refers to Hamilton's use of the material in her text. Where more details of the precise source are given these are included and referred to as the Walton Hall Collection (hereafter WHC).
21. For some fairly obvious reasons, much scholarship has focused upon formal and legal attempts to change the nature of Victorian marriage, rather than impromptu attempts

to negotiate its nature within individual cases. See e.g. M. L. Shanley (1989) *Feminism, Marriage and the Law in Victorian England 1850–1895* (London: Bloomsbury Publishing). Kelsey, *Changing the Rules*, similarly investigates problem marriages in which the husband is (respectively) an authoritarian, sexual, and economic tyrant. Kelsey also writes about the indelicacy of the Victorian marriage service (still extant from the 1662 Prayer Book) indicating how the imminent onset of sexual relations provoked images of 'ordeal', 'disgust', 'obscenity', and the 'bestial' (see pp. 202–5). See also K. Gleadle (2001) *British Women in the Nineteenth Century* (Basingstoke: Palgrave), p.179, which again notes feminist reform relied upon an unquestionable narrative of chastity. All these forms of analysis scarcely fit the Mordaunt case, although pathologizing female sexual interest as 'nymphomania' is briefly mentioned by Kelsey. Female adultery does appear in the scholarly literature, but the narrative is of a woman driven to it only eventually by a loveless marriage. For this see E. Olafson Hellerstein, l. Parker Hulme, and K. M. Offen (1981) *Victorian Women: A Documentary Account of Women's Lives in Nineteenth Century England, France, and the United States* (Brighton: Harvester), pp. 172–4, and also L. Hamburger and J. Hamburger (1994) *Contemplating Adultery: The Secret Life of a Victorian Woman* (London: Macmillan).

22. Hamilton, *The Warwickshire Scandal*, p. 22. For more on the aristocratic season and its inherent opportunities for matchmaking see Phegley, *Courtship and Marriage*, pp. 39–51.
23. See Jalland, *Women, Marriage and Politics*, p. 75, for the description of this process within aristocratic marriage as 'love inspired by judgment'.
24. Hamilton, *The Warwickshire Scandal*, p. 22.
25. Gleadle, *British Women*, p. 176. This discusses negotiated equality between husband and wife but solely so the wife could pursue interests in educational philanthropy.
26. We might here think about how Sir Charles Mordaunt's behaviour is at odds with the apparent 'sovereignty' which men of his position could otherwise expect. For this see D. Roberts (1978) 'The Paterfamilias of the Victorian Governing Classes', in A. S. Wohl (ed.), *The Victorian Family: Structure and Stresses* (London: Croom Helm), pp. 59–81 at p. 62. See also M. J. Peterson (1989) *Family, Love and Work in the Lives of Victorian Gentlewomen* (Bloomington, IN: Indiana University Press), pp. 78–9.
27. Gleadle, *British Women*, p. 175.
28. For a discussion of this ideal see Phegley, *Courtship and Marriage*, pp. 5–12 and 51–3.
29. J. Perkin (1989) *Women and Marriage in Nineteenth Century England* (London: Routledge), p. 93.
30. Hamilton, *The Warwickshire Scandal*, p. 24.
31. Ibid., p. 34.
32. Ibid, pp. 34–5.
33. Ibid., p. 35. Including letter from Prince Albert Edward to Lady Harriet Mordaunt, 13 January 1867 (WHC).
34. Hamilton, *The Warwickshire Scandal*, p. 38. Letter from Prince Albert Edward to Lady Harriet Mordaunt, 7 May 1867, alludes to the lady's umbrella (WHC).
35. Hamilton, *The Warwickshire Scandal*, pp. 41–2.
36. Ibid., p. 46.

37. Ibid., p. 9.
38. Arthur Farquhar to Harriet Mordaunt, 9 November 1867 (WHC).
39. Prince Albert Edward to Harriet Mordaunt, 12 March 1868, Prince Albert Edward to Harriet Mordaunt, 16 March 1868 (WHC).
40. Hamilton, *The Warwickshire Scandal*, pp. 70–1.
41. Ibid., p. 71.
42. *National Reformer*, 15, 10, 18 March 1870. See also D. S. Nash and A.-M. Kilday (2010) *Cultures of Shame: Exploring Crime and Morality in Britain, 1600–1900* (Basingstoke: Palgrave Macmillan), pp. 165–6.
43. See Davidoff, *World's Between*, pp. 25–34. This describes in detail the ambivalence of servant and master/mistress relationships. At times such servants obviously subscribed to the goals of those they served. Yet equally many incidents and attitudes would test these beyond endurance or sympathy.
44. This culminated in his trip to Norway in June 1868 which was to prove decisive in the history of his marriage to Harriet. See Charles Mordaunt to Harriett Mordaunt, 19 June 1868 (WHC).
45. Hamilton, *The Warwickshire Scandal*, pp. 82–3.
46. Ibid., p. 85.
47. Ibid.
48. Ibid., pp. 92–3.
49. Ibid., pp. 93–4.
50. Ibid., p. 99. See also Testimony of Elizabeth Cadogan reported in *Birmingham Daily Post*, 19 February 1870, p. 8.
51. Hamilton, *The Warwickshire Scandal*, pp. 102–3.
52. Ibid., p. 103.
53. Ibid., p. 105.
54. Ibid.
55. Ibid., p. 107.
56. Ibid, pp. 107–9
57. Ibid., p. 107.
58. Ibid., pp. 107–9.
59. Ibid., p. 110.
60. Ibid., p. 111.
61. Ibid. Hamilton quotes her as saying 'and with others, often and in open day', but quotes no specific source for this.
62. Ibid., p. 115. She later spoke of drowning herself, ibid., p. 119.
63. Perkin, *Women and Marriage*, p. 93.
64. Sir Charles Mordaunt to Lady Louisa Moncrieff, first week of March 1870, and Sir Charles Mordaunt to Lady Louisa Moncrieff, first week of March 1870, both quoted in Hamilton, *The Warwickshire Scandal*, pp. 115–16.
65. Ibid., p. 116.
66. Ibid., pp. 117–18.
67. Ibid., pp. 118–19.
68. Ibid., p. 121.
69. Ibid.

70. Ibid., p. 128.
71. Ibid., p. 131.
72. Ibid. Hamilton quotes her as using these words but gives no specific source for this.
73. Ibid., p. 128.
74. Ibid., p. 112.
75. Ibid., pp. 131 and 134.
76. Lady Louisa Moncrieff to Louisa Duchess of Atholl in early April 1870 and Lady Louisa Moncrieff to Louisa Duchess of Atholl in early/mid-April 1870, both quoted ibid., pp. 147–8. See also Helen Forbes to Lady Louisa Moncrieff in early/mid-April 1870, quoted ibid., p. 149.
77. Hamilton, *The Warwickshire Scandal.*, pp. 141–2.
78. Ibid., p. 142.
79. Ibid., pp. 143 and 159–61.
80. Ibid., p. 145.
81. Ibid., p. 149.
82. Ibid., pp. 156–7.
83. Ibid., pp. 131–2.
84. Ibid., p. 159.
85. Ibid., p. 160.
86. Ibid., p. 162.
87. Ibid., pp. 162–4.
88. Showalter, *Female Malady*, p. 58.
89. M. D. MacLeod (1886) 'An Address on Puerperal Insanity Delivered at the Annual Meeting of East Yorkshire and North Lincoln Branch of the British Medical Association', *British Medical Journal*, 7 August 1886, 2, 1336, p. 239.
90. Ibid.
91. S. Pegg (2009) '"Madness is a Woman": Constance Kent and the Victorian Constructions of Female Insanity', *Liverpool Law Review*, 30, pp. 207–23 at p. 208.
92. H. Marland (2012) 'Under the Shadow of Maternity: Birth, Death and Puerperal Insanity in Victorian Britain', *History of Psychiatry*, 23, 1, pp. 78–90 at pp. 79–80.
93. Hamilton, *The Warwickshire Scandal*, p. 171.
94. Ibid., pp. 198–9.
95. Ibid., p. 192.
96. Ibid., p. 196.
97. Ibid, p. 199.
98. Ibid., p. 203.
99. Ibid., p. 210.
100. Ibid., p. 221.
101. Ibid., p. 229.
102. See for instance Sir Charles Mordaunt (1924) *The Lady Mordaunt Divorce Case: Full Report of the Proceedings. Letters from the Prince of Wales; His Royal Highness in the Witness Box; Evidence of the Nurse and the Doctors* (London: Temple Publishing) and Anon. (1921) *The Authorised Edition of the Mordaunt Divorce Containing Medical and Other Evidence Suppressed by the Newspapers, Royal Letters to Lady Mordaunt, Family Pedigrees etc. etc.* (London: Frederic Farrah).

103. Hamilton, *The Warwickshire Scandal*, p. 334.
104. Ibid., p. 364.
105. Ibid., pp. 364–5.
106. Sir Charles Mordaunt, *The Lady Mordaunt Divorce Case*, pp. 30–2.
107. *London Journal*, 1 April 1870, p. 196.
108. Hamilton, *The Warwickshire Scandal*, pp. 377–9.
109. Ibid., p. 388.
110. *Manchester Guardian*, 6 March 1872, p. 6; 2 July 1873, p. 8; and 23 June 1874, p. 5.
111. *Punch* saw this as the fundamental issue, eclipsing the desire to prove Harriett insane or otherwise. See *Punch*, 4 July 1874, 67, p. 9. See also *London Journal*, 1 April 1870, p. 196; *Examiner and London Review*, 30 April 1870, p. 283; 11 June 1870, p. 370; and 27 June 1874, p. 283.
112. Hamilton, *The Warwickshire Scandal*, p. 406.
113. Ibid., p. 411.
114. Ibid., p. 425.
115. Ibid.
116. Davidoff, *World's Between*, pp. 25–34.
117. See e.g. *Examiner and London Review*, 26 February 1870, p. 141; *London Journal*, 1 April 1870, p. 196; and *Saturday Review*, 4 June 1870, p. 736.
118. G. Savage (2011) 'They Would if they Could: Class, Gender, and Popular Representation of English Divorce Litigation, 1858–1908', *Journal of Family History*, 36, 2, pp. 173–90 at p. 174.
119. *The Times*, 28 February 1870, p. 9.
120. *John Bull*, 26 February 1870, p. 152.
121. S. Weintraub (2000) *The Importance of Being Edward: King in Waiting 1841–1901* (London: John Murray), pp. 165–9.
122. M. Havers, E. Grayson, and P. Shankland (1988) *The Royal Baccarat Scandal* (London: Souvenir Press).
123. Hamilton, *The Warwickshire Scandal*, *passim*.
124. Ibid., p. 7.
125. Ibid., p. 4.
126. Ibid. See also Gleadle, *British Women*, p. 173, for the suggestion that this apparently new instrumentality in choosing marriage partners was an innovation of the 1860s equally criticized by some contemporaries.
127. Hamilton, *The Warwickshire Scandal*, pp. 15 and 21–2.
128. Ibid., p. 55.
129. Ibid., p. 130.
130. For more on criminal conversation see Phegley, *Courtship and Marriage*, pp. 19–20, and Shanley, *Feminism, Marriage and the Law*.
131. Hamilton, *The Warwickshire Scandal*, pp. 129 and 132–3.
132. H. Marland (2004) *Dangerous Motherhood, Insanity and Childbirth in Victorian Britain* (Basingstoke: Palgrave), p. 3.
133. Ibid., p. 5.
134. Ibid., p. 69.
135. Ibid.

136. See <https://annepettigrew.co.uk/wp-content/uploads/2019/01/Lady-Mordaunt-Scandal-1.pdf> (accessed 5 July 2021).
137. Ibid.
138. Ibid.
139. Ibid.
140. Ibid.
141. 'The Mordaunt Divorce Case and the Prince of Wales' <https://owlcation.com/humanities/A-Right-Royal-Victorian-Scandal> (accessed 5 July, 2021).
142. 'The Twisted Tale of Harriet Mordaunt' <www.tonyamitchellauthor.com/post/the-twisted-tale-of-harriet-mordaunt> (accessed 5 July 2021).
143. Ibid.
144. For more on this see D. Peschier (2019) *Lost Souls: Women, Religion and Mental Illness in the Victorian Asylum* (London: Bloomsbury); S. Wise (2013) *Inconvenient People: Lunacy, Liberty and the Mad Doctors in Victorian England* (London: Vintage Books) and A. Pedley '"A Deed at which Humanity Shudders": Mad Mothers, the Law and the Asylum, c.1835–1895' (PhD thesis, University of Roehampton).
145. 'The Harriet Mordaunt Scandal' <https://owlcation.com/humanities/A-Right-Royal-Victorian-Scandal> (accessed 5 July 2021).
146. Ibid.
147. Ibid.
148. Ibid.
149. Showalter, *Female Malady*, pp. 18–19 and 55–6.
150. Ibid., p. 102.
151. Ibid., p. 103.
152. Marland, *Dangerous Motherhood*, p. 38.
153. Showalter, *Female Malady*, pp. 58 and 60.
154. Ibid., pp. 132–4 and 146.
155. Ibid., pp. 64–5.
156. Ibid., p. 72. See also Hartman, *Victorian Murderesses*, p. 269.
157. *Reynolds's Newspaper*, 27 February 1870.
158. Moscucci, *Science of Woman*, p. 106.

# Epilogue

This book has attempted to present evidence that unravels, or problematizes, some of the preconceptions and constructed stereotypes that have burdened the historical understanding of women's criminal behaviour. In doing so it has presented evidence of women whose behaviour fails to fit these narratives. The experience of these women is clearly different from, and less typical of, those whose behaviour informed the stereotypes created both by contemporaries and by subsequent historiography. Within the world that was Victorian England, these stereotypes drew upon supposition, fear, and a society that was organized by gender and class to perpetuate ideals as much as stereotypes. These ideals informed everything from court decisions to press reporting and were responsible for systems of moral policing that, as we have found, were not always able to confront those who stepped away from such behavioural formulae.

Within historiography, attempts to write histories of particular offences, or the behaviour of specific genders and classes, readily reach for and discuss their typical offender as an important touchstone of historical analysis. Perhaps it is time for us to notice, in detail, the limitations that come with this approach. Whilst the display of regular characteristics and patterns has its own form of magnetism, this inevitability comes with dangers. Such forms of analysis 'essentialize' behaviour, as they also characterize and homogenize classes and genders. Analyses of this kind should now perhaps come with something of a health warning in a contemporary age of growing diversity and individuality, amidst a burgeoning history that recognizes this. Such developments potentially lead us to ask how far crime history's liking for stereotypes is valuable for wider for analysis around policing and criminal justice.

In this book we ourselves attempted to assess the validity of such descriptions by actively testing them in some instances, alongside the events and life history of our protagonists. This in itself has proved informative. In Chapter 3, for example, enlightenment women were 'moved' from being described as 'hand maidens of Prometheus' to becoming heirs of 'Hypatia'—intended to signal a transition from a state of subservience to one of independence, but such labels are cultural signifiers nonetheless. However, such descriptions, as the chapter demonstrates, can only be a motif to characterize and summarize and most definitely cannot act as an inspiration or fulsome and rounded analysis: there is almost always so much more going on to note. Likewise, our study of Harriet Mordaunt noted how some stereotypes of behaviour and identity were frequently mapped out for her, only

*Beyond Deviant Damsels: Re-evaluating Female Criminality in the Nineteenth Century.* Anne-Marie Kilday and David Nash, Oxford University Press.  DOI: 10.1093/oso/9780198830733.003.0009

for her to avoid and circumvent these wherever and whenever possible. Even her eventual fate and the cause of it has left historians guessing and sits uneasily within the stereotypes of the insane or of the 'typical' aristocratic woman.

Stereotypes also govern our conception of how reading and thinking publics responded to crimes with repugnance, or narratives that construct misbehaviour into less than ideal types for audiences to shudder over. We would do well to remind ourselves how so many of the microhistories covered in this book quite easily overturn these. What historians now need to do is to more readily look outwards and see how a collage style image might be created. This can often be done by looking at more particular and local investigations that are not seeking to incorporate findings into a sweeping overarching analysis. Some of these studies already do exist. Angela Brabin, for example, looked at a syndicate of women in Victorian Liverpool who murdered for the insurance money payable upon policies taken out upon their victims.[1] What emerges from this study is the apparently necessary, logical, and direct decisions made by the protagonists to indulge in these crimes, motivated by a combination of poverty and greed. These decisions occurred apparently, and simply, without the elaborate reasoning emanating from analyses that focus upon stereotypes. Beyond simple motivation, such murders were also conceivably prompted by ill-considered or negligent practices on the part of insurance and medical organizations. This suggests that institutional negligence, or failure of various kinds, was and is an intrinsic part of the landscape criminals of both genders can traverse. The reaction of the locality at large also displayed a resigned acceptance to the crime as a consequence of poverty and as being something that simply 'happened in such situations'.[2] Moreover, there appears to be evidence that the local community internalized this 'necessity' and turned a blind eye to events and murderous actions as they unfolded. It may well also have hidden and protected the miscreants against the attempts of the police to capture and arrest them.[3] Examples such as this challenge still further the value of some of our archetypal and stereotypical constructs around behaviour, and their ability to provide sustained analysis of crimes and criminals in the past.

Given this growing number of caveats, perhaps it is worth calling for a history of crime that takes a much fuller account of 'atypicality'; something that would enable concrete motives, actions, and real behaviour to become a more central part of the historical record. If extrapolated some distance from the area covered by this book, it would conceivably allow women to be more obviously mistresses of their own minds and behavioural choices. No longer would we so readily reach for literary constructs in which to frame women's hopes, aspirations and subsequent behaviour. Nor would we so readily see women driven to desperation by disappointed expectations. Instead, we might now be persuaded to recognize that these were conjured for them by popular cultural tropes and their interaction with what was, after all, fiction.

To see such 'plots' driving disappointment or simply being re-enacted is to produce another homogenizing analysis that removes agency and discrimination from those who are written about. Women (and people) do draw on fictional ideas to think with, but these ultimately do not govern their final choice of action, as this book tends to demonstrate—individuals are more unpredictable than this. Thus, there remains the opportunity for a more considered approach to motive with more tangible evidence of how this operates in practice.

We have heard so much from the historiography about the predominance of poisoning as a woman's method of murder. This then provokes curiosity about the greater variety of methods of women's murderous activity offered by the cultural repositories of songs and ballads as well as contemporary novels. Our second chapter did note, in a number of ballads, instances of the female murder of others through the use of poisoning that would fit into orthodox real-life scenarios where intimates and those known to the miscreant became victims. However, as we are also aware, there are instances of stabbings, arson, and physical chastisement that led to drowning, shootings by both pistol and arrows. We also know that Victorian crime fiction rarely explored the issue of poisoning as a *modus operandi* of the fictional murderess, prompting one analyst of the area to conclude this was one example of 'art *not* imitating life'.[4]

More exploration of this area is sorely needed. Why is there such a mismatch between the reality of women's crime as dealt with by the courts of Victorian England and the fictional representation of this? Was poison not a valuable or productive plot device? Did it introduce far too much calculation in fictional portrayals of women to inspire the requisite sympathy? Why is there a divergence between the almost non-appearance of poisoning in published fiction and its at least partial appearance in ballads? Is this an issue of the ballad form and its consumption not allowing the audience the time to fall out of sympathy with the female protagonist? Or is this an issue of class taste? Sympathy for middle-class women 'caught' in cultural traps prevented poisoning appearing in novels, whereas the 'need' to use poisoning was perhaps closer to the harsh realities of life further down the social scale.

We have recounted the stories of women who do not conform to stereotypes, likening their actions to species of escape from convention and expectation. Our own re-evaluation of the evidence causes us to wonder, as scholars of this area and historical period, why more women did not try this form of escape more often? Indeed we hope that our work may be valuable in persuading other scholars to investigate instances where women found the barriers to their behavioural choices dissolve when confronted. If this were to proceed, as we hope it should, it would allow us partly to question how powerful patriarchy actually was in reality—had it been hiding its flimsier nature as a part straw man, helped in this illusion by the historiography? Or indeed was its importance inflated by our own over-ready acceptance as scholars of norms, prescriptions, advice, and idealized narratives so often set before us.

## Notes

1. A. Brabin (2003, 2009 edition) *The Black Widows of Liverpool* (Palatine Books: Lancaster).
2. Ibid., p. 135.
3. Ibid., pp. 136–7.
4. V. Morris (1990) *Double Jeopardy: Women Who Kill in Victorian Fiction* (Lexington, KY: University Press of Kentuck), p. 34.

# Bibliography

## Primary Sources

### Unpublished Primary Sources

### Bedfordshire Galleries and Archives (Bedford)

Bedfordshire Archives, General Report of the Justices of the Peace to the Quarter Sessions, 1842–1843, QGR/3.

Bedfordshire Archives, Minute Book of Visiting Justices 1843, QGR/5, pp. 466–7.

The Higgins Art Gallery and Museum, Bedford (1843) *The Execution of Sarah Dazley* (Bedford: J. S. & W. Merry), Special Collections BEDFM 2011.16.

### British Library (London)

Anon. (1843) *Sorrowful Lamentations of Sarah Dazley, for the Murder of Her Two Husband's and Infant Son By Poison at Bedford* (London: Paul Painter), British Library, General Reference Collection, 74/1888.c.3 (62).

Patmore, C. (1858 edition) *The Angel in the House* (London: J. W. Parker & Son), British Library, General Reference Collection, 11650.c.3.

### National Archives (Kew, Surrey)

National Archives, Assizes: Norfolk Circuit, Gaol Books, ASSI 33/13.

National Archives, Assize Records: Home, Norfolk and South-Eastern Circuit—Depositions, ASSI 36/4/29.

National Archives, Assize Records: Norfolk and Home Circuits—Indictment Files, 1689–1850, Bedfordshire Calendar of Prisoners, ASSI 94/2388.

National Archives, Assize Records: Norfolk and Home Circuits—Indictment Files, 1689–1850, Inquisition Verdict 21 April 1843, ASSI 94/2388.

National Archives, Home Office Registered Papers, HO 144/108/A23081, 19 December 1882.

### National Library of Scotland (Edinburgh)

(1853) *Lament of MacFarlane, Blackwood and Young I and II*, Special Collections, L.C. Fol. 73 (124).

(1853) *The Lamentations of McFarlane, Blackwood and Young* (Glasgow: n.p.), Special Collections, L.C. Fol. 73 (125).

(1853) *Widow MacFarlane's Lamentation For Her Son*, Special Collections, L.C. Fol. 178 A.2. (096).

Swan, J. (1854/1855) *Plan of Glasgow and Suburbs: Engraved Expressly for the Post Office Directory*, Map Collection, Reference ID 117744183.

### National Library of Wales (Aberystwyth)

Records of the Court of Great Sessions, 4/72/5A, 4/74/5A, 4/197/6, 4/200/9, 4/283/1, 4/394/2, 4/398/8, 4/631/6, 4/753/4, 4/759/1, 4/830/4

National Records of Scotland (Edinburgh)
Census Records for 1881, 168/2/19/6
Census Records for 1891, 387/37/9
Census Records for 1901, 168/1/46/25
Census Records for 1911, 168/2/57/1
Justiciary Court Records, Books of Adjournal, JC4/4
Justiciary Court Records, Minute Book, JC8/5, JC8/61, JC11/110/99, JC11/113
Justiciary Court Records, Precognition Papers, AD14/53/448/2, AD14/83/260/1, AD14/90/14/1
Justiciary Court Records, Process Papers, JC26/1808/27, JC/1840/292D, JC26/1853/525/1–5, JC26/1853/526/6, JC26/1883/25, JC26/1890/222
Statutory Death Registers for 1934, 168/2/161
Statutory Death Registers for 1954, 168/1/668

## Published Primary Sources

Official Documents and Publications (in chronological order)
*Hansard: House of Commons Debates*, 26 March 1823, vol. 8, cols 709–34
*Parliamentary Papers*, 43 Geo III, c. 58 (1803)
*Parliamentary Papers*, 49 Geo III, c. 14 (1809)
*Parliamentary Papers*, 6 & 7 Will IV, c. 14 (1836)
*Parliamentary Papers*, 14 & 15 Vict, c. 13 (1851)

Newspapers and Periodicals
*Aberdeen Weekly Journal*, 13 January 1808, 26 July 1871, 29 September 1877, 12 April 1883, 27 June 1883, 13 November 1889, 22 January 1890, 11 February 1890, 12 February 1890
*Bedfordshire Mercury and Huntingdon Express*, 1 April 1843
*Berrow's Worcester Journal*, 10 August 1843, 30 July 1853
*Birmingham Daily Post*, 19 February 1870
*Daily News*, 23 July 1853, 8 August 1853, 12 August 1853
*Examiner and London Review*, 26 February 1870, 30 April 1870, 11 June 1870, 27 June 1874
*Freeman's Journal and Daily Commercial Advertiser*, 28 March 1843, 24 April 1843; 9 August 1843, 26 July 1853
*Hampshire Advertiser & Salisbury Guardian*, 12 August 1843
*Jackson's Oxford Journal*, 25 March 1843, 20 August 1853
*John Bull*, 21 January 1821, 30 July 1821, 18 November 1821, 26 February 1870
*Lloyd's Weekly London Newspaper*, 26 March 1843, 13 August 1843
*London Journal*, 1 April 1870
*Manchester Guardian*, 6 March 1872, 2 July 1873, 23 June 1874
*National Reformer*, 18 March 1870
*Punch*, 4 July 1874
*Reynolds' Newspaper*, 21 August 1853, 27 February 1870
*Saturday Review*, 4 June 1870
*The Aberdeen Journal*, 27 July 1853, 17 August 1853
*The Belfast News-Letter*, 18 August 1843
*The Bradford Observer*, 10 August 1843, 18 August 1853
*The Bristol Mercury*, 29 July 1843, 30 July 1853

*The Bury and Norwich Post and East Anglian*, 13 January 1808, 24 February 1808, 26 July 1843, 9 August 1843
*The Bury and Norwich Post and Suffolk Herald*, 17 August 1853
*The Caledonian Mercury*, 7 January 1808, 6 September 1838, 14 August 1843, 1 May 1862, 20 September 1862
*The Derby Mercury*, 27 July 1853
*The Dundee Courier and Argus*, 15 June 1853, 27 July 1853, 10 August 1853, 17 August 1853, 21 June 1870, 6 May 1872, 6 January 1873, 8 February 1878, 26 September 1879, 12 November 1880, 12 April 1883, 15 November 1889, 6 January 1890, 22 January 1890, 2 December 1892, 7 November 1896, 23 September 1897
*The Edinburgh Evening Courant*, 25 January 1844
*The Era*, 19 June 1853, 14 August 1853
*The Examiner*, 17 January 1808
*The Girl's Own Paper*, 8 July 1882
*The Glasgow Herald*, 22 July 1853, 12 August 1853, 11 March 1857, 4 December 1861, 10 September 1862, 13 July 1866, 2 January 1868, 15 September 1874, 13 November 1888, 20 December 1893
*The Guardian*, 11 February 2017
*The Hampshire Telegraph and Sussex* Chronicle, 13 August 1853
*The Hull Packet and East Riding Times*, 11 August 1843
*The Ipswich Journal*, 16 January 1808, 27 February 1808, 29 April 1843, 29 July 1843, 18 June 1853, 30 July 1853
*The Lancaster Gazette and General Advertiser*, 26 December 1807, 16 January 1808, 30 July 1853
*The Leeds Mercury*, 29 July 1843
*The Leicester Chronicle*, 8 April 1843
*The Liverpool Mercury*, 26 July 1853
*The Manchester Times*, 17 August 1853
*The Morning Chronicle*, 27 March 1843, 22 April 1843, 23 July 1853
*The Morning Post*, 11 January 1808, 22 April 1843, 25 July 1843, 7 August 1843, 17 June 1853, 25 July 1853, 8 August 1853, 13 August 1853
*The Movement and Anti-Persecution Gazette*, 8 June 1844
*The Newcastle Courant*, 12 August 1843, 17 June 1853, 29 July 1853
*The New Statesman* (UK edition), 27 July 2017
*The Northern Star and Leeds General Advertiser*, 29 July 1843
*The Preston Guardian*, 18 June 1853, 20 August 1853
*The Standard*, 27 March 1843, 24 July 1843, 7 August 1843, 23 July 1853
*The Times*, 22 November 1822, 24 March 1843, 27 March 1843, 15 April 1843, 22 April 1843, 8 August 1843, 24 September 1843, 22 September 1848, 15 June 1853, 23 July 1853, 19 April 1886
*The Woman's Signal*, 15 February 1894
*The York Herald*, 18 June 1853, 30 July 1853
*The Times*, 28 February 1870

## Online Sources

*The Proceedings of the Old Bailey Online*: https://www.oldbaileyonline.org/

## Other Works

Anderson, A. M. (1904 edition) *Criminal Law of Scotland* (Edinburgh: Bell & Bradfute).
Anderson, R. (1815) *Ballads in the Cumbrian Dialect* (Wigton: E. Rook).

Anon. (1808) *An Account of the Crime, Trial and Behaviour of Barbara Malcolm Who was Executed at Edinburgh on Wednesday last, February 10, 1808* (Gateshead: Marshall Printer). [John Johnson Collection, Allegro ID 20080125/16:54$kg.]

Anon. (1808) *The Scots Magazine and Edinburgh Literary Miscellany: Being a General Repository of Literature, History and Politics for 1808—Volume LXX* (Edinburgh: Archibald Constable & Co.).

Anon. (1810) *The Edinburgh Annual Register for 1808—Volume I*, Part II (Edinburgh: James Ballantyne & Co.).

Anon. (1821) *Suppressed Defence: The Defence of Mary Anne Carlile to the Vice Society's Indictment against the Appendix to the Theological Works of Thomas Paine* (London: Richard Carlile).

Anon. (1825) *Report of the Trial of Mrs Carlile on the Attorney General's Ex-Officio Information for the Protection of Tyrants* (London: Richard Carlile).

Anon. (1844) *The Trial of Thomas Paterson for Blasphemy, Before the High Court of Justiciary, Edinburgh, With the Whole of his Bold and Effective Defence. Also, The Trials of Thomas Finlay and Miss Matilda Roalfe (For Blasphemy), In the Sheriff's Court* (London: H. Hetherington).

Anon. (1864) *Memoirs of Jane Cameron, Female Convict, By a Prison Matron* (London: Hurst & Blackett).

Anon. (1878) *Five Years Penal Servitude: By One Who Has Endured It* (London: Richard Bentley & Son).

Anon. (1921) *The Authorised Edition of the Mordaunt Divorce Containing Medical and Other Evidence Suppressed by the Newspapers, Royal Letters to Lady Mordaunt, Family Pedigrees etc. etc.* (London: Frederic Farrah).

Anon. (2017 edition) *Concise Scots Dictionary* (Edinburgh: Edinburgh University Press).

Baring-Gould, S. (1895) *English Minstrelsie: A National Monument of English Song* (Felinfach: Llanerch).

Baring-Gould, S., and H. Fleetwood Sheppard (1895) *A Garland of Country Song: English folk Songs with their Traditional Melodies* (London: Methuen).

Baring-Gould, S., and H. Fleetwood Sheppard (1892) *Songs of the West: Traditional Ballads and Songs of the West of England: A Collection Made from the Mouths of the People* (London: Methuen).

Baring-Gould, S., and C. Sharp (1910) *English Folk-Songs for Schools* (London: Curwen & Sons).

Broadwood, L., and J. A. Fuller Maitland (1892) (eds) *English County Songs* (London: Cramer).

Broadwood, L. E., and A. G. Gilchrist (1923) 'Songs of Crime and Prison Life', *Journal of the Folk Song Society*, 7, 27, pp. 41–9.

Burke Ryan, W. (1862) *Infanticide: Its Law, Prevalence, Prevention, and History* (London: T. Richards) [Bodleian Library, (OC) 151 c/345]

Burnett, J. (1811) *Treatise on Various Branches of the Criminal Law of Scotland* (Edinburgh: George Ramsay & Co.).

Carlile, R. (1822) *Report of the Trial of Mrs Susannah Wright for Publishing, in his Shop, the Writings and Correspondence of R. Carlile; before Chief Justice Abbott, and a Special Jury in the Court of King's Bench, Guildhall, London, on Monday, July 8, 1822: Indictment at the instance of the Society for the Suppression of Vice* (London: Richard Carlile).

Carlile, R. (1822) *Speech of Mrs Susannah Wright before the Court of King's Bench on the 14th November 1822* (London).

Child, F. J. (1904) *The English and Scottish Popular Ballads* (5 vols) (London: Houghton & Mifflin).

Christison, R. (1829) *A Treatise on Poisons, in Relations to Medical Jurisprudence, Physiology, and the Practice of Physic* (Edinburgh: Adam Black).

Cosmopolite (1843) *The Bible an Improper Book for Youth and Dangerous to the Easily Excited Brain; with Immoral and Contradictory Passages from Holy Writ* (Edinburgh: Henry Robinson).

Dickens, C. (1851) 'Household Crime', *Household Words—Volume IV* [December] (New York: Angell, Engel & Hewitt Printers).

Doremus, R. O. (1893) 'Can Chemical Analysis Convict Poisoners?', *The Forum,* 16, pp. 229–39.

Evans, Revd J. (1813) *The Topographical Description of North Wales by Rev Mr Evans for the Beauties of England and Wales: Delineations, Topographical, Historical and Descriptive*, vol. 17 (London: Thomas Maiden).

Farquar-Graham, G. (1884 edition) *The Popular Songs of Scotland* (Glasgow: J. Muir Wood).

Gillington, A. G. (1907) *Eight Hampshire Folk Songs: Taken from the Mouths of the Peasantry* (London: Curwen).

Halliwell, J. O. (1851) *The Yorkshire Anthology: A Collection of Ancient and Modern Ballads, Poems and Songs Relating to the County of Yorkshire*(London: n.p.).

Halliwell, J. O. (1852) *The Norfolk Anthology: A Collection of Poems, Ballads and Rare Tracts Relating to the County of Norfolk* (London: n.p.).

Harland, J. (1875) *Ballads and Songs of Lancashire*, corrected, revised, and enlarged by T. T. Wilkinson (London: George Routledge & Sons).

Harland, J. (ed.) (1866) *Lancashire Lyrics: Modern Songs and Ballads of the County Palatine* (London: Whittaker).

Hedley, G. D. (1843) 'Cases of Death in Childbed and Deaths from Poisoning', *The Lancet*, 2, pp. 845–7.

Hume, Baron D. (1797) *Commentaries on the Laws of Scotland Respecting the Description and Punishment of Crimes—Volume I* (Edinburgh: Bell & Bradfute).

Kay, J. (1850) *The Social Condition and Education of the People in England and Europe—Volume I* (London: Longman, Brown & Green), p. 447. [Bodleian Library Ref. 247126 e.207.]

MacLeod, M. D. (1886) 'An Address on Puerperal Insanity Delivered at the Annual Meeting of East Yorkshire and North Lincoln Branch of the British Medical Association', *British Medical Journal,* 7 August, 2, 1336, p. 239.

Mayhew, H. (1968 edition) *London Labour and the London Poor—Volume IV* (New York: Dover).

Miller, J. (1859) *Prostitution Considered in Relation to its Cause and Cure* (Edinburgh: Sutherland & Knox).

Mordaunt, Sir C. (1924) *The Lady Mordaunt Divorce Case: Full Report of the Proceedings. Letters from the Prince of Wales; His Royal Highness in the Witness Box; Evidence of the Nurse and the Doctors* (London: Temple Publishing).

Sharp, C. (1907) *English Folk-Song: Some Conclusions* (London: Simpkin & Co.).

Sharp, C., and L. Broadwood (1916) 'Narrative and Historical Ballads and Songs', *Journal of the Folk-Song Society*, 5, 20, pp. 253–67.

Smith, J. G. (1824 edition) *The Principles of Forensic Medicine, Systematically Arranged, and Applied to British Practice* (London: Thomas and George Underwood).

Tod, T. M. (1938) *The Scots Black Kalendar: A Record of Criminal Trials and Executions in Scotland 1800–1910* (Perth: Munro & Scott Ltd).

Tyler Smith, W. (1867) 'An Address on Infanticide and Excessive Infant Mortality', *British Medical Journal*, 12 January, pp. 21–5.

Waugh, E. (1857) *Poems and Lancashire Songs* (London: Whittaker).

## Secondary Sources

### Monographs and Key Edited Collections


Abelson, E. S. (1989) *When Ladies Go A-Thieving: Middle-Class Shoplifters in the Victorian Department Store* (New York and Oxford: Oxford University Press).

Ager, A. W. (2014) *Crime and Poverty in Nineteenth-Century England: The Economy of Makeshifts* (London: Bloomsbury).

Altink, R. D. (1970) *Victorian Studies in Scarlet: Murders and Manners in the Age of Victoria* (New York: W. W. Norton & Co.).

Archibald, M. (2012) *A Sink of Atrocity: Crime in Nineteenth Century Dundee* (Edinburgh: Black and White Publishing).

Archibald, M. (2014) *Bloody Scotland: Crime in Nineteenth Century Scotland* (Edinburgh: Black and White Publishing).

Archibald, M. (2014 edition) *Glasgow: The Real Mean City—True Crime and Punishment in the Second City of the Empire* (Edinburgh: Black and White Publishing).

Arnup, K., A. Lévesque, and R. R. Pierson (eds) (1990) *Delivering Motherhood: Maternal Ideologies and Practices in the Nineteenth and Twentieth Centuries* (London: Routledge).

Badinter, E. (1981 edition) *The Myth of Motherhood: An Historical View of the Maternal Instinct* (London: Souvenir Press).

Ballinger, A. (2000) *Dead Woman Walking: Executed Women in England and Wales 1900–1955* (Aldershot: Ashgate).

Bamfield, J. A. N. (2012) *Shopping and Crime* (Basingstoke: Palgrave).

Barker, H., and E. Chalus (eds) (2014) *Gender in Eighteenth-Century England: Roles, Representations and Responsibilities* (London: Longman).

Bates, V. (2016) *Sexual Forensics in Victorian and Edwardian England: Age Crime and Consent in the Courts* (Basingstoke: Palgrave).

Beattie, J. M. (1986) *Crime and the Courts in England 1660–1800* (Oxford: Princeton University Press).

Berg, M. (2005) *Luxury and Pleasure in Eighteenth-Century Britain* (Oxford: Oxford University Press).

Boyd, K., and R. McWilliam (eds) (2007) *The Victorian Studies Reader* (London: Routledge).

Brabin, A. (2009 edition) *The Black Widows of Liverpool* (Lancaster: Palatine Books).

Branca, P. (1975) *Silent Sisterhood: Middle Class Women in the Victorian Home* (London: Croom Helm).

Brandon, D. (2001) *Stand and Deliver: A History of Highway Robbery* (London: Sutton Publishing).

Brownstein, R. (1982) *Becoming a Heroine: Reading about Women in Novels* (New York, Viking Press).

Burney, I. A. (2012 edition) *Poison, Detection and the Victorian Imagination* (Manchester: Manchester University Press).

Cabantous, A. (2002) *Blasphemy: Impious Speech in the West from the Seventeenth to the Nineteenth Century* (New York: Columbia University Press).

Calder, J. (1977) *The Victorian Home* (London: Batsford).

Cameron, J. (1983) *Prisons and Punishment in Scotland* (Edinburgh: Canongate).

Cannadine, D. (2019) *Victorious Century: The United Kingdom, 1800–1906* (London: Penguin).

Carter Wood, J. (2004) *Violence and Crime in Nineteenth Century England: The Shadow of our Refinement* (London: Routledge).

Chamberlain, M. (2010) *Old Wives' Tales: The History of Remedies, Charms and Spells* (London: History Press).
Chesney, K. (1970) *The Victorian Underworld* (Trowbridge: Readers Union).
Chinn, C. (1995) *Poverty amidst Prosperity: The Urban Poor in England 1834–1914* (Manchester: Manchester University Press).
Chinn, C. (1988) *They Worked All their Lives: Women of the Urban Poor in England, 1880–1939* (Manchester and New York: Manchester University Press).
Clark, A. (1993) *The Struggle for the Breeches* (London: University of California Press).
Clark, R. (2007) *Women and the Noose: A History of Female Execution* (Stroud: Tempus).
Cohen, D. (2006) *Household Gods: The British and their Possessions* (New Haven: Yale University Press).
Conklin, J. E. (1972) *Robbery and the Criminal Justice System* (Philadelphia: J. B. Lippincott Co.).
Conley, C. A. (2007) *Certain Other Countries: Homicide, Gender, and National Identity in Late Nineteenth-Century England, Ireland, Scotland, and Wales* (Columbus, OH: Ohio State University Press).
Conley, C. (2020) *Debauched, Desperate, Deranged; Women Who Killed, London 1674–1913* (Oxford: Oxford University Press).
Croall, H. (1998) *Crime and Society in Britain* (London and New York: Longman).
Curtin, M. (1987) *Propriety and Position: A Study of Victorian Manners* (New York: Garland Publishing).
Dally, A. (1983) *Inventing Motherhood: The Consequences of an Ideal* (London: Schocken Books).
Darnton, R. (1999 edition) *The Great Cat Massacre* (New York: Basic Books).
Davidoff, L. (1973) *The Best Circles—Society, Etiquette and the Season* (London: Croom Helm).
Davidoff, L. (1995) *Worlds Between: Historical Perspectives on Gender and Class* (London: Polity Press).
Davidoff, L., and C. Hall (2002 edition) *Family Fortunes: Men and Women of the English Middle Class, 1780–1850* (London: Routledge).
Davies, J. (2007 edition) *A History of Wales* (London: Penguin).
D'Cruze, S. (1998) *Crimes of Outrage: Sex, Violence and Victorian Working Women* (London: Routledge).
D'Cruze, S., S. Walklate, and S. Pegg (2006) *Murder: Social and Historical Approaches to Understanding Murder and Murderers* (Cullumpton: Willan).
D'Cruze, S., and L. Jackson (2009) *Women, Crime and Justice in England since 1660.* (Basingstoke: Palgrave)
Dugaw, D. (1989) *Warrior Women and Popular Balladry, 1650–1850* (Cambridge: Cambridge University Press).
Duke, T. (2014) *Rogues of the Road: Highwaymen and Highway Robbery in Eighteenth Century England* (Union Bay, BC: Duke Publications).
Eigen, J. (2004) *Unconscious Crime: Mental Absence and Criminal Responsibility in Victorian London* (Baltimore: Johns Hopkins University Press).
Elias, N. (2000) *The Civilizing* Process, tr. E. Jephcott (Oxford: Wiley Blackwell).
Emsley, C. (2005 edition) *Crime and Society in England, 1750–1900* (Harlow: Pearson).
Emsley, J. (2005) *Elements of Murder* (Oxford: Oxford University Press).
Fildes, V. (1988) *Wet Nursing: A History from Antiquity to the Present* (Oxford: Basil Blackwell).
Flanders, J. (2007 edition) *Consuming Passions: Leisure and Pleasure in Victorian Britain* (London: Harper Perennial).

Flanders, J. (2011) *The Invention of Murder: How the Victorians Revelled in Death and Detection and Created Modern Crime* (London: Harper Collins).
Fletcher, A. (1995) *Gender, Sex and Subordination in England 1500–1800* (New Haven: Yale University Press).
Fumerton, P. (2021) *The Broadside Ballad in Early Modern England: Moving Media, Tactical Publics* (Philadelphia: University of Pennsylvania Press).
Fumerton, P., and A. Guerrini (2010) (eds) *Ballads and Broadsides in Britain, 1500–1800* (Farnham: Ashgate).
Forbes, T. R. (1985) *Surgeons at the Bailey: English Forensic Medicine to 1878* (New Haven and London: Yale University Press).
Gatrell, V. A. C., B. Lenman, and G. Parker (eds) (1980) *Crime and the Law: The Social History of Crime in Western Europe since 1500* (London: Europa Publications).
Gilbert, S., and S. Gubar (1979) *The Madwoman in the Attic: The Woman Writer and the Nineteenth-Century Literary Imagination* (New Haven: Yale University Press).
Gleadle, K. (2001) *British Women in the Nineteenth Century* (Basingstoke: Palgrave).
Godfrey, E. (2012) *Femininity, Crime and Self-Defence in Victorian Literature and Society. From Dagger-Fans to Suffragettes* (Basingstoke: Palgrave Macmillan).
Goold, I., and C. Kelly (eds) (2009) *Lawyers' Medicine: The Legislature, the Courts and Medical Practice, 1760–2000* (London: Hart Publishing).
Gorham, D. (1982) *The Victorian Girl and the Feminine Ideal* (London: Croom Helm).
Graham, K. (2008) *'Gone to the Shops': Shopping in Victorian England* (Westport, CT: Praeger).
Gray, D. G. (2016) *Crime, Policing and Punishment in England, 1660–1914* (London: Bloomsbury).
Gregory, E. D. (2006) *Victorian Songhunters: The Recovery and Editing of English Vernacular Ballads and Folk Lyrics 1820–1883* (Oxford: Scarecrow Press).
Gurney, P. (2019 edition) *The Making of Consumer Culture in Modern Britain* (London: Bloomsbury), pp. 95–7.
Hamburger, L., and J. Hamburger (1994) *Contemplating Adultery: The Secret Life of a Victorian Woman* (London: Macmillan).
Hamilton, E. (1999) *The Warwickshire Scandal* (Norwich: Michael Russell).
Harris, J. (1994 edition) *Private Lives, Public Spirit: Britain 1870–1914* (London: Penguin).
Harrison, P. (1993) *Hertfordshire and Bedfordshire Murders* (Newbury: Countryside Books).
Hartman, M. (1977) *Victorian Murderesses: A True History of Thirteen Respectable French and English Women Accused of Unspeakable Crimes* (London: Robson Books).
Havers, M., E. Grayson, and P. Shankland (1988) *The Royal Baccarat Scandal* (London: Souvenir Press).
Heslop, P. (2009) *Murderous Women: From Sarah Dazley to Ruth Ellis* (London: History Press).
Hide, L. (2014) *Gender and Class in Victorian Asylums 1890–1914* (Basingstoke: Palgrave).
Hitchcock, T., and H. Shore (2003) (eds) *The Streets of London: From the Great Fire to the Great Stink* (London: Rivers Oram Press).
Hobsbawm, E. (2000) *Bandits* (London: Abacus).
Howard, S. (2008) *Law and Disorder in Early Modern Wales: Crime and Authority in the Denbighshire Courts, c.1660–1730* (Cardiff: University of Wales Press).
Howell, D. W. (2016 edition) *Land and People in Nineteenth-Century Wales* (London: Routledge).
Howell, D. W. (2000) *The Rural Poor in Eighteenth-Century Wales* (Cardiff: University of Wales Press).

Hughes, M., and R. Stradling (2001 edition) *The English Musical Renaissance 1840–1940: Constructing a National Music* (Manchester: Manchester University Press).
Ireland, R. W. (2015) *Land of White Gloves? A History of Crime and Punishment in Wales* (Abingdon: Routledge).
Jalland, P. (1986) *Women, Marriage and Politics, 1860–1914* (Oxford: Clarendon Press).
Johnston, H. (2015) *Crime in England 1815–1880: Experiencing the Criminal Justice System* (London and New York: Routledge).
Jones, D. J. V. (1992) *Crime in Nineteenth-Century Wales* (Cardiff: University of Wales Press).
Jones, R. (2018) *Crime, Courts and Community in Mid-Victorian Wales: Montgomeryshire, People and Places* (Cardiff: University of Wales Press).
Kellie, J. (2018) *Hanged until Dead: Men and Women Hanged in Nineteenth-Century Scotland* (Cumnock: Carn Publishing).
Kent, S. K. (2006) *Gender and Power in Britain, 1640–1990* (London: Routledge).
Kelsey, J. C. (2016) *Changing the Rules: Women and Victorian Marriage* (Kibworth Beauchamp: Matador).
Kilday, A.-M. (2013) *A History of Infanticide in Britain, c.1660 to the Present* (Basingstoke: Palgrave).
Kilday, A.-M. (2018) *Crime in Scotland 1660–1960: The Violent North* (London: Routledge).
Kilday, A.-M. (2007) *Women and Violent Crime in Enlightenment Scotland* (Woodbridge: Boydell & Brewer).
Kilday, A.-M., and D. S. Nash (eds) (2010) *Histories of Crime: Britain 1600–2000* (Basingstoke: Palgrave Macmillan).
Kilday, A.-M., and D. S. Nash (2017) *Shame and Modernity in Britain 1890 to the Present* (London: Palgrave Macmillan).
King, P. (2006) *Crime and Law in England, 1750–1840* (Cambridge: Cambridge University Press).
King, S., and A. Tomkins (eds) (2003) *The Poor in England 1700–1850: An Economy of Makeshifts* (Manchester: Manchester University Press).
Knelman, J. (1998) *Twisting in the Wind: The Murderess and the English Press* (Toronto: University of Toronto Press).
Kowaleski-Wallace, E. (1997) *Consuming Subjects: Women, Shopping and Business in the Eighteenth Century* (New York: Columbia University Press).
Lane, B. (1992) *The Encyclopaedia of Forensic Science* (London and New York: Headline Book Publishing).
Langland, E. (1995) *Nobody's Angels: Middle-Class Women and Domestic Ideology in Victorian Culture* (Ithaca, NY, and London: Cornell University Press).
Lawton, D. (1993) *Blasphemy* (London: Harvester Wheatsheaf).
Lee, A. J. (1979) *The Origins of the Popular Press, 1855–1914* (London: Rowman & Littlefield).
Leslie, D. (2017) *Launched into Eternity: Crime and Punishment, Hitmen and Hangmen* (Edinburgh: Black and White Publishing).
Lewis, J. (ed.) (1986) *Labour and Love: Women's Experience of Home and Family 1850–1940* (Oxford: Basil Blackwell).
Lewis, J. (1984) *Women in England 1870–1950: Sexual Divisions and Social Change* (Sussex: Wheatsheaf Books).
Loeb, L. A. (1994) *Consuming Angels: Advertising and Victorian Women* (New York: Oxford University Press).
Loetz, F. (2016) *Dealings with God: From Blasphemers in Early Modern Zurich to a Cultural History of Religiousness* (Abingdon: Routledge).

Lysack, K. (2008) *Come Buy, Come Buy: Shopping and the Culture of Consumption* (Athens, OH: Ohio University Press).
McDonald, F. (2012) *Gentlemen Rogues and Wicked Ladies: A Guide to British Highwaymen and Highwaywomen* (Stroud: History Press).
McLynn, F. (1991) *Crime and Punishment in Eighteenth-Century England* (Oxford: Oxford University Press).
Mahood, L. (2013 edition) *The Magdalenes: Prostitution in the Nineteenth Century* (London: Routledge).
Mangham, A. (2007) *Violent Women and Sensation Fiction: Crime, Medicine and Victorian Popular Culture* (Basingstoke: Palgrave Macmillan).
Marland, H. (2004) *Dangerous Motherhood: Insanity and Childbirth in Victorian Britain* (Basingstoke: Palgrave).
Mason, M. (1995) *The Making of Victorian Sexuality* (Oxford: Oxford University Press).
Moore, E., and C. O. Moore (1966) *Ballads and Folk Songs of the Southwest: More than 600 Titles, Melodies, and Texts Collected in Oklahoma* (Oklahoma: University of Oklahoma Press).
Morgan, M. (1994) *Manners, Morals and Class in England 1774–1858* (New York: St Martin's Press).
Morgan, G., and P. Rushton (1998) *Rogues, Thieves and the Rule of Law* (London: Routledge).
Morris, V. (1990) *Double Jeopardy: Women Who Kill in Victorian Fiction* (Lexington, KY: University Press of Kentucky).
Moscucci, O. (1990) *The Science of Woman: Gynaecology and Gender in England, 1800–1929* (Cambridge: Cambridge University Press).
Murphy, D. J. I. (1986) *Customers and Thieves: An Ethnography of Shoplifting* (Aldershot: Gower).
Nagy, V. M. (2015) *Nineteenth-Century Female Poisoners: Three English Women Who Used Arsenic to Kill* (Basingstoke: Palgrave Macmillan).
Nash, D. S. (1999) *Blasphemy in Modern Britain 1789–Present* (Aldershot: Ashgate).
Nash, D. S. (2007) *Blasphemy in the Christian World: A History* (Oxford: Oxford University Press).
Nash, D. S., and A.-M. Kilday (2010) *Cultures of Shame: Exploring Crime and Morality in Britain, 1600–1900* (Basingstoke: Palgrave Macmillan).
Nash, D. S., and A.-M. Kilday (eds) (2016) *Law, Crime and Deviance since 1700: Micro-Studies in the History of Crime* (London: Bloomsbury).
Nelson, C. (2007) *Family Ties in Victorian England* (Westport, CT: Praeger).
Nelson, C., and A. S. Holmes (eds) (1997) *Maternal Instincts: Visions of Motherhood and Sexuality in Britain, 1875–1925* (Basingstoke: Palgrave).
Newark, P. (1979) *The Crimson Book of Highwaymen* (London: Juniper Books).
Olafson Hellerstein, E., L. Parker Hulme, and K. M. Offen (1981) *Victorian Women: A Documentary Account of Women's Lives in Nineteenth Century England, France, and the United States* (Brighton: Harvester).
Parascandola, J. (2012) *King of Poisons: A History of Arsenic* (Washington, DC: Potomac Books).
Parolin, C. (2010) *Radical Spaces: Venues of Popular Politics in London, 1790–c.1845* (Canberra: Australian National University E Press).
Perrini, S. (2012) *Women Serial Killers of the 19th Century: The Golden Age of Poisons* (London: CreateSpace Publishing).
Peschier, D. (2019) *Lost Souls: Women, Religion and Mental Illness in the Victorian Asylum* (London: Bloomsbury).

Peterson, M. J. (1989) *Family, Love and Work in the Lives of Victorian Gentlewomen* (Bloomington, IN: Indiana University Press).
Phegley, J. (2012) *Courtship and Marriage in Victorian England* (Santa Barbara, CA: Praeger).
Philips, D. (1977) *Crime and Authority in Victorian England: The Black Country 1835–1860* (London: Croom Helm).
Place, F. (1972) *The Autobiography of Francis Place, 1771–1854* [edited by Mary Thale], (Cambridge: Cambridge University Press).
Porter, R. (1995) *Disease, Medicine and Society in England 1550–1860* (Cambridge: Cambridge University Press).
Porter, R. (1989) *Mind Forg'd Manacles: A History of Madness in England from the Restoration to the Regency* (Harmondsworth: Penguin).
Rendall, J. (1990) *Women in an Industrializing Society: England 1750–1880* (Oxford: Basil Blackwell).
Roberts, E. (1984) *A Woman's Place: An Oral History of Working Class Women 1890–1914* (Oxford and New York: John Wiley).
Roberts, E. (1988) *Women's Work 1840–1940* (Basingstoke: Macmillan Education).
Rogers, H. (2000) *Women and the People Authority: Authorship and the Radical Tradition in Nineteenth Century England* (Aldershot: Ashgate).
Rose, L. (1986) *The Massacre of the Innocents: Infanticide in Britain 1800–1939* (London: Routledge & Kegan Paul).
Ross, E. (1993) *Love and Toil: Motherhood in Outcast London, 1870–1018* (New York and Oxford: Oxford University Press).
Roud, S. (2017) *Folksong in England* (London: Faber & Faber).
Schwarz, L. (2013) *Infidel Feminism: Secularism, Religion and Women's Emancipation, England 1830–1940* (Manchester: Manchester University Press).
Schwarzkopf, J. (1991) *Women in the Chartist Movement* (Basingstoke: Macmillan).
Segrave, K. (2001) *Shoplifting: A Social History* (Jefferson, NC: McFarland & Co.).
Shanley, M. L. (1989) *Feminism, Marriage and the Law in Victorian England 1850–1895* (London: Bloomsbury Publishing).
Sharpe, J. A. (1999 edition) *Crime in Early Modern England 1550–1750* (Harlow: Longman).
Shoemaker, R. B. (1998) *Gender in English Society 1650–1850* (Harlow: Pearson).
Shoemaker, R., and M. Vincent (eds) (1998) *Gender and History in Western Europe* (London: Arnold).
Showalter, E. (1987) *The Female Malady: Women Madness and English Culture, 1830–1980* (London: Virago).
Sindall, R. (1990) *Street Violence in the Nineteenth Century: Media Panic or Real Danger?* (Leicester: Leicester University Press).
Skelton, D. (2003) *Deadlier than the Male: Scotland's Most Wicked Women* (Edinburgh: Black and White Publishing).
Skelton, D. (2009) *Glasgow's Black Heart: A City's Life of Crime* (Edinburgh and London: Mainstream Publishing).
Smart, C. (ed.) (1993 edition) *Regulating Womanhood: Historical Essays on Marriage, Motherhood and Sexuality* (London: Routledge).
Spraggs, G. (2001) *Outlaws and Highwaymen: The Cult of the Robber in England from the Middle Ages to the Nineteenth Century* (London: Pimlico).
Staiger, J. (2005) *Media Reception Studies* (London: New York University Press).
Steinbach, S. L. (2012) *Understanding the Victorians: Politics, Culture and Society in Nineteenth-Century Britain* (London and New York: Routledge).

Stratmann, L. (2016) *The Secret Poisoner: A Century of Murder* (New Haven: Yale University Press).
Taylor, B. (1983) *Eve and the New Jerusalem: Socialism and Feminism in the Nineteenth Century* (London: Virago).
Thompson, F. M. L. (1988) *The Rise of Respectable Society: A Social History of Victorian Britain 1830–1900* (London: Fontan Press).
Thurer, S. L. (1994) *The Myths of Motherhood: How Culture Reinvents the Good Mother* (London: Penguin).
Tickell, S. (2018) *Shoplifting in Eighteenth-Century England* (Woodbridge: Boydell).
Vaughan-Thomas, W. (1985) *Wales: A History* (London: Michael Joseph).
Vicinus, M. (ed.) (1977) *A Widening Sphere: Changing Roles of Victorian Women* (London: Methuen & Co.).
Vickery, A. (2009) *Behind Closed Doors* (London: Yale University Press).
Villa-Flores, J. (2006) *Dangerous Speech: A Social History of Blasphemy in Colonial Mexico* (Phoeniz, AZ: University of Arizona Press).
Walker, G. (2003) *Crime, Gender and Social Order in Early Modern England* (Cambridge: Cambridge University Press).
Walker, N., and S. McCabe (1984) *The Historical Perspective; Crime and Insanity in England* (Edinburgh: Edinburgh University Press).
Walliss, J. (2018) *The Bloody Code in England and Wales, 1760–1830* (Basingstoke: Palgrave).
Ward, R. M. (2014) *Print Culture, Crime and Justice in Eighteenth-Century London* (London: Bloomsbury).
Watson, K. (2004) *Poisoned Lives: English Poisoners and their Victims* (London: Hambledon).
Weintraub, S. (2000) *The Importance of Being Edward: King in Waiting 1841–1901* (London: John Murray).
Whitlock, T. C. (2005) *Crime, Gender and Consumer Culture in Nineteenth-Century England* (Aldershot: Ashgate).
Wiener, M. J. (2004) *Men of Blood: Violence, Manliness and Criminal Justice in Victorian England* (Cambridge: Cambridge University Press).
Williams, L. (2016) *Wayward Women: Female Offending in Victorian England* (Barnsley: Pen and Sword History).
Wilson, P. (1971) *Murderess: A Study of Women Executed in Britain since 1843* (London: Michael Joseph).
Wise, S. (2013) *Inconvenient People: Lunacy, Liberty and the Mad Doctors in Victorian England* (London: Vintage Books).
Wohl, A. S. (ed.) (1978) *The Victorian Family: Structure and Stresses* (London: Croom Helm).
Wolfstein, M., and N. Leites (1977 edition) *Movies: A Psychological Study* (New York: Atheneum Press).
Wood, M. (1994) *Radical Satire and Print Culture, 1790–1822* (Oxford: Clarendon Press).
Worsley, L. (2013) *A Very British Murder: The Story of a National Obsession* (London: BBC Books).
Zedner, L. (1991) *Women, Crime and Custody in Victorian England* (Oxford: Clarendon Press).

## Journal Articles

Abelson, E. S. (1989) 'The Invention of Kleptomania', *Signs*, 15, 1, pp. 123–43.

Arnot, M. L. (1994) 'Infant Death, Child Care and the State: The Baby-Farming Scandal and the First Infant Life Protection Legislation of 1872', *Continuity and Change*, 9, 2, pp. 271–311.

Bartrip, P. (1992) 'A "Pennurth of Arsenic for Rat Poison": The Arsenic Act, 1851 and the Prevention of Secret Poisoning', *Medical History*, 36, pp. 53–69.

Bates, K. (2014) 'Empathy and Entertainment? The Form and Function of Violent Crime Narratives in Early-Nineteenth Century Broadsides', *Law Crime and* History, 4, 2, pp. 1–27.

Baylen, J. O. (1972) 'The New Journalism in Late Victorian Britain', *Australian Journal of Politics and History*, 18, 3, pp. 367–85.

Bearman, C. J. (1997) 'Resources in the Vaughan Williams Memorial Library: The Lucy Broadwood Collection: An Interim Report', *Folk Music Journal*, 7, 3, pp. 357–65.

Beattie, J. M. (1975) 'The Criminality of Women in Eighteenth-Century England', *Journal of Social History*, 8, pp. 80–116.

Behlmer, G. K. (1979) 'Deadly Motherhood: Infanticide and Medical Opinion in Mid-Victorian England', *Journal of the History of* Medicine, 34, 4, pp. 403–27.

Bell, M. J. (1988) '"No Borders to the Ballad Maker's Art": Francis James Child and the Politics of the People', *Western Folklore*, 47, 4, pp. 285–307.

Burney, I. A. (1999) 'A Poisoning of No Substance: The Trials of Medico-Legal Proof in Mid-Victorian England', *Journal of British Studies*, 38, 1, pp. 59–92.

Burney, I. A. (2002) 'Testing Testimony: Toxicology and the Law of Evidence in Early Nineteenth-Century England', *Studies in History and Philosophy of* Science, 33, pp. 289–314.

Coar, L. (2012) 'Sugar and Spice and All Things Nice: The Victorian Woman's All-Consuming Predicament', *Victorian Network*, 4, 1, pp. 48–72.

Clow, A., and N. L. Clow (1945) 'Vitriol in the Industrial Revolution', *Economic History Review*, 15, 1–2, pp. 44–55.

Davies, A. (1999) '"These Viragoes are No Less Cruel than the Lads": Young Women, Gangs and Violence in Late Victorian Manchester and Salford', *British Journal of Criminology*, 39, 1, pp. 72–89.

Digby, A. (1992) 'Victorian Values and Women in Public and Private', *Proceedings of the British* Academy, 78, pp. 195–215.

Diski, J. (2011) 'The Secret Shopper', *The New Yorker*, 87, 29, pp. 115–20.

Emmerichs, M. B. W. (1993) 'Trials of Women for Homicide in Nineteenth-Century England', *Women and Criminal Justice*, 5, 1, pp. 99–109.

Feeley, M., and D. Little (1991) 'The Vanishing Female: The Decline of Women in the Criminal Process 1687–1912', *Law and Society Review*, 25, pp. 719–57.

Finn, M. (1996) 'Women, Consumption and Coverture in England, 1760–1860', *istorical Journal*, 39, 3, pp. 703–22.

Finn, M. (2000) 'Men's Things: Masculine Possession in the Consumer Revolution', *Social History*, 25, 2, pp. 133–55.

Flynn, M. (1995) 'Blasphemy and the Play of Anger in Sixteenth Century Spain', *Past and Present*, 149, 1, pp. 29–56.

Fox, A. (2011) 'The Emergence of the Scottish Broadside Ballad in the Late Seventeenth and Early Eighteenth Centuries', *Journal of Scottish Historical Studies*, 31, 2, pp. 169–94.

Frost, G. (2003) '"The Black Lamb of the Black Sheep": Illegitimacy in the English Working Class, 1850–1939', *Journal of Social History*, 37, 2, pp. 293–322.

Fullerton, R. A., and G. N. Punj (2004) 'Shoplifting as Moral Insanity: Historical Perspectives on Kleptomania', *Journal of Macromarketing*, 24, 1, pp. 8–16.

Griffin, E. (2018) 'The Emotions of Motherhood: Love, Culture, and Poverty in Victorian Britain', *American Historical Review*, 123, 1, pp. 60–85.

Griffiths, C. C. (2014) 'The Prisoners' Counsel Act 1836: Doctrine, Advocacy and the Criminal Trial', *Law, Crime and History*, 2, pp. 28–47.

Hager, T. (2008) 'Compassion and Indifference: The Attitude of the English Legal System towards Ellen Harper and Selina Wadge, Who Killed their Offspring in the 1870s', *Journal of Family History*, 33, 2, pp. 173–94.

Harker, D. (1981) 'Francis James Child and the "Ballad Consensus"', *Folk Music Journal*, 4, 2, pp. 146–64.

Higginbotham, A. R. (1989) '"Sin of the Age": Infanticide and Illegitimacy in Victorian London', *Victorian Studies*, 32, 3, pp. 319–37.

Holligan, C. (2018) 'Life in a Forgotten Scottish Gulag: Punishment and Social Regulation in HM Peterhead Prison', *Journal of Historical Sociology*, 31, pp. 165–81.

Homrighaus, R. E. (2001) 'Wolves in Women's Clothing: Baby-Farming and the British Medical Journal, 1860–1872', *Journal of Family History*, 26, 3, pp. 350–72.

Hunt, A. (2006) 'Calculations and Concealments: Infanticide in Mid-Nineteenth Century Britain', *Victorian Literature and Culture*, 34, 1, pp. 71–94.

Johnston, H. (2018) 'Imprisoned Mothers in Victorian England, 1853–1900: Motherhood, Identity and the Convict Prison' *Criminology and Criminal Justice*, 18, 6, pp. 1–17.

Kilday, A.-M. (2013) 'Hell-Raising and Hair-Razing: Violent Robbery in Nineteenth Century Scotland', *Scottish Historical Review*, 92, 235, pp. 255–74.

Kilday, A.-M. (2014) '"Criminally Poor?" Investigating the Link between Crime and Poverty in Eighteenth Century England', *Cultural and Social History*, 11, 4, pp. 507–26.

King, P. (1996) 'Female Offenders, Work and Life-Cycle Change in Late-Eighteenth-Century London', *Continuity and Change*, 11, 1, pp. 61–90.

Knepper, P., and A. Johansen (eds) (2016) *The Oxford Handbook of the History of Crime and Criminal Justice* (Oxford: Oxford University Press).

Krueger, C. L. (1997) 'Literary Defenses and Medical Prosecutions: Representing Infanticide in Nineteenth Century Britain', *Victorian Studies*, 40, 2, pp. 271–94.

Lemire, B. (1990) 'The Theft of Clothes and Popular Consumerism in Early Modern England', *Journal of Social History*, 24, 2, pp. 255–76.

McCalman, I. (1980) 'Females, Feminism and Free Love in an Early Nineteenth Century Radical Movement', *Labour History*, 38, pp. 1–25.

Manheimer, J. (1979) 'Murderous Mothers: The Problem of Parenting in the Victorian Novel', *Feminist Studies*, 5, 3, pp. 530–46.

Marland, H. (2012) 'Under the Shadow of Maternity: Birth, Death and Puerperal Insanity in Victorian Britain', *History of Psychiatry*, 23, 1, pp. 78–90.

Mitson, A. (1998) 'An Exchange of Letters: Estate Management and Lady Yarborough', *Women's History Review*, 7, 4, pp. 547–66.

O'Brien, P. (1983) 'The Kleptomania Diagnosis: Bourgeois Women and Theft in Late Nineteenth-Century France', *Journal of Social History*, 17, 1, pp. 65–77.

Owens, A. (2001) 'Property, Gender and the Life Course: Inheritance and Family Welfare Provision in Early Nineteenth-Century England', *Social History*, 26, 3, pp. 97–315.

Pegg, S. (2009) '"Madness is a Woman": Constance Kent and the Victorian Constructions of Female Insanity', *Liverpool Law Review*, 30, pp. 207–23.

Reid, A., R. Davies, E. Garrett, and A. Blaikie (2006) 'Vulnerability among Illegitimate Children in Nineteenth Century Scotland', *Annales de Démographie Historique*, 1, 111, pp. 89–113.

Robb, G. (1997) 'Circe in Crinoline: Domestic Poisonings in Victorian England', *Journal of Family History*, 22, 2, pp. 176–90.

Roberts, D. E. (1993) 'Motherhood and Crime', *Iowa Law Review*, 79, pp. 95–141.
Ross, E. (1982) 'Fierce Questions and Taunts: Married Life in Working-Class London, 1870–1915', *Feminist Studies*, 8, 3, pp. 575–602.
Savage, G. (2011) 'They Would if they Could: Class, Gender, and Popular Representation of English Divorce Litigation, 1858–1908', *Journal of Family History*, 36, 2, pp. 173–90.
Selimić, I. (2016) 'Female Criminality, Class, and Deviance during the Rise of the Twentieth Century Department Store', *LSE Law Review*, 1, pp. 1–30.
Sharpe, J. A. (1985) '"Last Dying Speeches": Religion, Ideology and Public Execution in Seventeenth-Century England', *Past and Present*, 107, pp. 144–67.
Shoemaker, R. (2006) 'The Street Robber and the Gentleman Highwayman: Changing Representations and Perceptions of Robbery in London 1600–1800', *Cultural and Social History*, 3, 4, pp. 381–405.
Sindall, R. (1987) 'The London Garotting Panics of 1856 and 1862', *Social History*, 12, 3, pp. 351–9.
Walkowitz, J. D. (1998) 'Going Public: Shopping, Street Harassment, and Streetwalking in Late Victorian London', *Representations*, 62, pp. 1–30.
Watson, K. D. (2006) 'Medical and Chemical Expertise in English Trials for Criminal Poisoning, 1750–1914', *Medical History*, 50, 3, pp. 373–90.
Watson, K. D. (2013) 'Women, Violent Crime and Justice in Georgian Wales', *Continuity and Change*, 28, 2, pp. 245–72.
Wharton, J. C. (2010) *The Arsenic Century: How Britain was Poisoned at Home, Work and Play* (Oxford: Oxford University Press).
Whitlock, T. C. (1999) 'Gender, Medicine and Consumer Culture in Victorian England: Creating the Kleptomaniac', *Albion*, 31, 3, pp. 413–37.
Wiener, M. (2001) 'Alice Arden to Bill Sikes: Changing Nightmares of Intimate Violence in England, 1558–1869', *Journal of British Studies*, 40, 2, pp. 184–212.
Woodward, N. (2008) 'Burglary in Wales, 1730–1830: Evidence from the Great Sessions', *Welsh History Review*, 24, pp. 60–91.
Woodward, N. (2008) 'Seasonality and Sheep-Stealing: Wales, 1730–1830', *Agricultural History Review*, 56, 1, pp. 24–47.
Woodward, N. (2009) 'Horse-Stealing in Wales, 1730–1830', *Agricultural History Review*, 57, I, pp. 70–108.
Zedner, L. (1991) 'Women, Crime and Penal Responses: A Historical Account', *Crime and Justice*, 14, pp. 307–62.

## Chapters from Edited Collections

Bentley, D. (2005) 'She-Butchers: Baby-Droppers, Baby-Sweaters, and Baby-Farmers', in J. Rowbotham and K. Stevenson (eds), *Criminal Conversations: Victorian Crimes, Social Panic, and Moral Outrage* (Columbus, OH: Ohio State University Press), pp. 198–214.
Christ, C. (1977) 'Victorian Masculinity and the Angel in the House', in M. Vicinus (ed.), *A Widening Sphere: Changing Roles of Victorian Women* (London: Methuen & Co.), pp. 146–62.
Davidoff, L., and C. Hall (2007) 'Separate Spheres', in K. Boyd and R. McWilliam (eds), *The Victorian Studies Reader* (London: Routledge), pp. 307–17.
Davis, J. (1980) 'The London Garotting Panic of 1862: A Moral Panic and the Creation of a Criminal Class in Mid-Victorian England', in V. A. C. Gatrell, B. Lenman, and G. Parker (eds), *Crime and the Law: The Social History of Crime in Western Europe since 1500* (London: Europa Publications), pp. 190–213.

Hall, C. (1998) 'The Early Formation of Victorian Domestic Ideology', in R. Shoemaker and M. Vincent (eds), *Gender and History in Western Europe* (London: Arnold), pp. 182–96.

Holmes, A. S. (1997) '"Fallen Mothers": Maternal Adultery and Child Custody in England, 1886–1925', in C. Nelson and A. S. Holmes (eds), *Maternal Instincts: Visions of Motherhood and Sexuality in Britain, 1875–1925* (Basingstoke: Palgrave), pp. 37–57.

Holmes, A. S., and C. Nelson (1997) 'Introduction', in C. Nelson and A. S. Holmes (eds), *Maternal Instincts: Visions of Motherhood and Sexuality in Britain, 1875–1925* (Basingstoke: Palgrave), pp. 1–12.

Horrell, S., J. Humphries, and K. Sneath (2013) 'Cupidity and Crime: Consumption as Revealed by Insights from the Old Bailey Records of Thefts in the Eighteenth and Nineteenth Centuries', in M. Casson and N. Hashimzade (eds), *Large Databases in Economic History: Research Methods and Case Studies* (London: Routledge), pp. 246–67.

Hussey, D. (2008) 'Guns, Horses and Stylish Waistcoats? Male Consumer Activity and Domestic Shopping in Late-Eighteenth and Early-Nineteenth-Century England', in D. Hussey and M. Ponsonby (eds), *Buying for the Home: Shopping for the Domestic from the Seventeenth Century to the Present* (Aldershot: Ashgate), pp. 47–69.

Jamieson, L. (1986) 'Limited Resources and Limiting Conventions: Working-Class Mothers and Daughters in Urban Scotland c. 1890–1925', in J. Lewis (ed.), *Labour and Love: Women's Experience of Home and Family 1850–1940* (Oxford: Basil Blackwell), pp. 55–62.

Kilday, A.-M. (2013) 'Outrageous Acts and Everyday Rebellions: Criminal Women in Eighteenth Century Scotland', in K. Barclay and D. Simonton (eds), *Women in Eighteenth Century Scotland: Intimate, Intellectual and Public Lives* (London: Ashgate), pp. 253–70.

Kilday, A.-M. (2013) '"That Women are But Men's Shadows": Examining Gender, Violence and Criminality in Early Modern Britain', in M. G. Muravyeva and R. M. Toivo (eds), *Gender in Late Medieval and Early Modern Europe* (London: Routledge), pp. 53–72.

Kilday, A.-M. (2014) 'Angels with Dirty Faces? Violent Women in Early Modern Scotland', in P. Blanc and R. Hillman (eds), *Female Transgression in Early Modern Britain* [published in French and English] (London: Routledge), pp. 141–62.

Kilday, A.-M. (2016) 'Constructing the Cult of the Criminal: Kate Webster—Victorian Murderess and Media Sensation', in A.-M. Kilday and D. S. Nash (eds), *Law, Crime and Deviance since 1700: Micro-Studies in the History of Crime* (London: Bloomsbury), pp. 125–48.

Nash, D. S. (2013) 'Blasphemy and Witchcraft: A Gendered Mirror Image?', in K. Reyes and M. Muravyeva (eds), *Why Gender? The Concept of Gender Relations in the Medieval and Early Modern World* (Abingdon: Routledge), pp. 153–71.

Nash, D. S. (2020) '"Police Fiasco", "The Black Army", "Devil Dodgers" and "Humbug": The Apparent Inevitability of Unfair Blasphemy Trials up to 1922', in D. S. Nash and A-M. Kilday (eds), *Fair and Unfair Trials in Nineteenth Century England* (London: Bloomsbury), pp. 175–94.

Palk, D. (2003) 'Private Crime and Public and Private Places: Pickpockets and Shoplifters in London, 1780–1823', in T. Hitchcock and H. Shore (eds), *The Streets of London: From the Great Fire to the Great Stink* (London: Rivers Oram Press), pp. 135–50.

Pierson, R. R., A. Lévesque, and K. Arnup (1990) 'Introduction', in K. Arnup, A. Lévesque, and R. R. Pierson (eds), *Delivering Motherhood: Maternal Ideologies and Practices in the Nineteenth and Twentieth Centuries* (London: Routledge), pp. xii–xxiv.

Roberts, D. (1978) 'The Paterfamilias of the Victorian Governing Classes', in A. S. Wohl (ed.), *The Victorian Family: Structure and Stresses* (London: Croom Helm), pp. 59–81.

Shore, H. (2010) 'Criminality, Deviance and the Underworld since 1750', in A.-M. Kilday and D. S. Nash (eds), *Histories of Crime: Britain 1600–2000* (Basingstoke: Palgrave Macmillan), pp. 120–40.

Sloboda, S. (2009) 'Porcelain Bodies: Gender, Acquisitiveness, and Taste in Eighteenth-Century England', in A. Myzelev and J. Potvin (eds), *Material Cultures, 1740–1920: The Meanings and Pleasures of Collecting* (Burlington, VT: Ashgate), pp. 19–36.

Smart, C. (1993 edition) 'Disruptive Bodies and Unruly Sex: The Regulation of Reproduction and Sexuality in the Nineteenth Century', in C. Smart (ed.), *Regulating Womanhood: Historical Essays on Marriage, Motherhood and Sexuality* (London: Routledge), pp. 7–32.

Styles, J. (2003) 'Custom or Consumption? Plebeian Fashion in Eighteenth-Century England', in M. Berg and E. Eger (eds), *Luxury in the Eighteenth Century: Debates, Desires and Delectable Goods* (Basingstoke: Palgrave), pp. 103–15.

Van Der Heijden, M. (2016) 'Women and Crime, 1750–2000', in P. Knepper and A. Johansen (eds), *The Oxford Handbook of the History of Crime and Criminal Justice* (Oxford: Oxford University Press), pp. 250–67.

Vicinus, M. (1977) 'Introduction: New Trends in the Study of Victorian Women', in M. Vicinus (ed.), *A Widening Sphere: Changing Roles of Victorian Women* (London: Methuen & Co.), pp. ix–xix.

Vickery, A. (1998) 'Golden Age to Separate Spheres? A Review of the Categories and Chronology of English Women's History', in R. Shoemaker and M. Vincent (eds), *Gender and History in Western Europe* (London: Arnold), pp. 197–225.

Walker, G. (1994) 'Women, Theft and the World of Stolen Goods', in J. Kermode and G. Walker (eds), *Women, Crime and the Courts in Early Modern England* (Chapel Hill, NC, and London: University of North Carolina Press), pp. 81–105.

Walkowitz, J. (1977) 'The Making of an Outcast Group: Prostitutes and Working Women in Nineteenth-Century Plymouth and Southampton', in M. Vicinus (ed.), *A Widening Sphere: Changing Roles of Victorian Women* (London: Methuen & Co.), pp. 72–93.

Walsh, C. (2008) 'Shopping at First Hand? Mistresses, Servants and Shopping for the Household in Early-Modern England', in D. Hussey and M. Ponsonby (eds), *Buying for the Home: Shopping for the Domestic from the Seventeenth Century to the Present* (Aldershot: Ashgate), pp. 13–26.

Ward, T. (2005) 'A Mania for Suspicion: Poisoning, Science and the Law', in J. Rowbotham and K. Stevenson (eds), *Criminal Conversations: Victorian Crimes, Social Panic and Moral Outrage* (Columbus, OH: Ohio State University Press), pp. 140–56.

Watson, K. (2006) 'Criminal Poisoning in England and the Origins of the Marsh Test for Arsenic', in J. R. Bertomeu-Sánchez and A. Nieto-Galan (eds), *Chemistry, Medicine, and Crime: Mateu J. B. Orfilia (1787–1853) and his Times* (Sagamore Beach, MA: Science History Publications), pp. 183–206.

Watson, K. D. (2009) 'Is a Burn a Wound? Vitriol-Throwing in Medico-Legal Context, 1800–1900', in I. Goold and C. Kelly (eds), *Lawyers' Medicine: The Legislature, the Courts and Medical Practice, 1760–2000* (London: Hart Publishing), pp. 61–78.

Watson, K. D. (2016) 'Love, Vengeance and Vitriol: An Edwardian True-Crime Drama', in D. S. Nash and A-M. Kilday (eds), *Law, Crime and Deviance since 1700: Micro-Studies in the History of Crime* London: Bloomsbury), pp. 107–24.

Whitlock, T. (2016) 'Forms of Crime: Crime and Retail Theft', in P. Knepper and A. Johansen (eds), *The Oxford Handbook of the History of Crime and Criminal Justice* (Oxford: Oxford University Press), pp. 155–69.

## Unpublished Theses and Dissertations

Cage, R. A. (1974) 'The Scottish Poor Law, 1745–1845' (PhD Thesis, University of Glasgow).
Hopps, R. S. (2017) 'Narratives of Crime and Disorder: Representations of Robbery and Burglary in the London Press, 1780–1830' (PhD Thesis, The Open University).
Monholland, C. S. (1989) 'Infanticide in Victorian England, 1856–876: Thirty Legal Cases' (MA Dissertation, Rice University).
Pearman, J. (2017) 'Bastards, Baby Farmers and Social Control in Victorian Britain' (PhD Thesis, University of Kent).
Pedley, A. (2020) '"A Deed at which Humanity Shudders": Mad Mothers, the Law and the Asylum, c. 1835–1895' (PhD Thesis, University of Roehampton).

## Online Publications

Mitchell, T. (2 April 2020) 'The Twisted Tale of Harriet Mordaunt', https://www.tonyamitchellauthor.com/post/the-twisted-tale-of-harriet-mordaunt (accessed 5 July 2021).
Pettigrew, A. (7 December 2018) 'The Lady Mordaunt Scandal', https://annepettigrew.co.uk/wp-content/uploads/2019/01/Lady-Mordaunt-Scandal-1.pdf (accessed 5 July 2021).
Taylor, R. (20 February 2020) 'A Right Royal Victorian Scandal', Owlcation, https://owlcation.com/humanities/A-Right-Royal-Victorian-Scandal (accessed 5 July 2021).
Watson, K. D. (25 March 2017) 'Doom for Demembring: Assault in Scots Law',https://legalhistorymiscellany.com (accessed 26 December 2018).
Watson, K. D. (13 September 2017) 'Acid Attacks in Nineteenth-Century Britain', https://legalhistorymiscellany.com (accessed 26 December 2018).

## Key Websites

http://ballads.bodleian.ox.ac.uk/
https://crimeandpunishment.library.wales/
https://www.oldbaileyonline.org/
www.ancestry.com
www.workhouses.org.uk/Scotland

# Index

For the benefit of digital users, indexed terms that span two pages (e.g., 52–53) may, on occasion, appear on only one of those pages.